BIOLOGY

Longman Science 11–14

General Editor: John L Lewis O B E

Also in the series:

Physics	**0 582 29419 3**
Chemistry	**0 582 29418 5**
Biology Teachers Guide	**0 582 09373 2**
Chemistry Teachers Guide	**0 582 09372 4**
Physics Teachers Guide	**0 582 09374 0**

Addison Wesley Longman Limited
Edinburgh Gate, Burnt Mill, Harlow, Essex, CM20 2JE, England
and Associated Companies throughout the World.

First published 1983
Second edition 1991
Sixth impression 1995
Third Edition 1996
Third impression 1998
ISBN 0 582 294207

Set in 11/12pt Univers Light Linotron 202
Printed in Singapore (COS)
NPC/06

The Publisher's policy is to use paper manufactured from sustainable forests.

BIOLOGY

Peter Mawby M A
Headmaster Lancaster Royal Grammar School
Formerly Head of Science, Cheltenham College

Michael Roberts M A Ph D
Formerly Head of Biology, Marlborough College
and Cheltenham College

 LONGMAN

Acknowledgements

We are grateful to the following for permission to reproduce copyright material:
Jonathan Cape Limited for an extract from *The Human Zoo* by Desmond Morris; the
author's agent for a simplified extract from *Across the Russias* by John Massey
Stewart; The Observer Limited for an extract from 'The Body Report, Part 4' by
A. Prentice from *The Observer Magazine*; Oxfam and UNICEF for an adapted
extract from *Together for Children* 1979; Thames and Hudson for an adapted extract
from *The Doomsday Book* by Gordon Rattray Taylor; Times Newspapers Limited for
extracts from articles 'Miner and his defiant meadow take top prize' by Michael
McCarthy in *The Times* 14.3.89 and 'Merger to life quality of UK beef production'
by John Young in *The Times* 26.8.89. both © Times Newspapers Limited 1989.
We have unfortunately been unable to trace the copyright holder of *Alexander
Fleming and Penicillin* by W. Howard Hughes and would appreciate any information
which would enable us to do so.

We are grateful to the following for permission to reproduce photographs and other
copyright material: Aquila Photographics, fig 1.4 (c) (photographer C.R. Varndell); ARC
Aggregates, 11.13 and 11.14; Ardea, 9.17 pea pod (Jean-Paul Ferrero), 10.10, 11.12
(Ian Beames), 13.3 (a) panda, 14.1 fruit bat (P. Morris) and 17.3 hedgehog (Liz
Bomford); Biofotos/Heather Angel, 1.4 (a), 2.8 (a), 3.13, 7.2, 7.6, 7.9, 7.11, 7.12, 12.2,
14.1 child and 20.9; Biophoto Associates, 3.14, 4.7, 4.11, 4.12 (b) and (c), 4.18, 8.9,
8.14, 9.10, 9.13, 11.16, 16.12, 17.9, 19.3 and 19.9; J. Allan Cash Photolibrary, 15.5;
Churchill Livingstone, 17.14 (from *Textbook of physiology* by D. Emslie-Smith *et al*):
Bruce Coleman, 7.4, 7.13 (Kim Taylor), 9.17 dandelion, 9.17 sycamore (Jane Burton),
11.1 (Norman Myers), 17.3 mongoose (Norman Myers) and 17.3 dog; Lupe Cunha,
18.10; Vivien Fifield, 16.19; Geoscience Features, 10.4; Sally and Richard Greenhill,
18.11; J.E. Gregory, 12.6; Health Education Authority, 20.3; Holt Studios, 6.8 Hereford,
9.2 and 9.15 (all Nigel Cattlin); Eric and David Hosking, 2.8 (b), 9.14, 12.5, 12.7, 14.1
lion and 20.10; Hutchison Library, 6.5 (Juliet Hughet); ICCE Photolibrary, 14.1
hippopotamus, 14.1 dog, 17.3 butterfly, 20.7 and 20.12 (all Mark Boulton); Camilla
Jessel, 18.6 and 18.7; Frank Lane Picture Agency, 1.4 (b) (M.J. Thomas), 1.7 (c)
(T. and P. Gardner), 6.1 beetle (B. Borell), 7.3 (R. Van Nostrand), 7.14 (R. Wilmshurst),
11.5 (a) (Roger Wilmshurst), 12.9 (Mark Newmann), 13.3 (a) lizard (W. Rohdich), 13.7
Anthony Wharton), 14.1 chimpanzee (Mark Newmann), 17.3 thrush (Roger Wilmshurst)
and 19.5; Macmillan, L.J.F. Brimble, *Intermediate Botany*, 8.17 (Dr G. Bond); National
Medical Slidebank, 19.6; Natural History Photographic Agency, 1.4 (d) (C.J. Cambridge),
1.7 (b) (John Shaw), 6.8 ancestor (Patrick Fagot), 6.8 Friesian (G.I. Bernard), 11.5. (c)
(Peter Johnson), 12.4 (David Woodfall), 13.3 (b) fly (N.A. Callow), 14.1 dolphin (Henry
Ausloos) and 19.1 (M.I. Walker); Natural Science Photos, 8.15 (Jeremy Burgess);
Oxford Scientific Films, 4.15 (Carolina Biological Supply Co.), 6.11 (a) (Robin Redfern),
6.11 (b) (David Tipling), 7.1 (Nick Bergkessel), 7.5 (John Gerlach), 7.10 (Niall Benvie),
13.3 (a) cheetah (Frank Schneidermeuer), 13.3 (a) rhinocerous (Stan Osolinski), 13.3 (b)
wild boar (David Houghton), 14.2 (G.I. Bernard), 19.2 (Tim Shepherd), 19.8 (Breck P.
Kent) and 20.11 (b) (Stan Osolinski); Photo Researchers Inc. 12.10 and 12.11; Planet
Earth Pictures/Seaphot, 1.7 (a) (John Lythgoe), 6.1 tree frogs (Ken Lucas), gannets
(Richard Matthews), lions (Jonathan Scott), 6.2 (J. Bracegirdle), 8.3 (John Lythgoe),
9.17 goose grass (Andrew Mounter), 11.3 (Mark Mattock, 11.5 (b) (Jonathan Scott),
11.15 (John Lythgoe), 12.8 (Hans Christian Heap), 12.10 (Linda Pitkin), 13.3 (a) stag
(Sue Earle), bear (David McChesney) and 20.8 (Hans Christian Heap); Plant Breeding
International, Cambridge, 6.8 wheat; Science Photo Library, 4.12 (a) (Sinclair Stammers),
4.12 (d) (Eric Grant), 8.2 (Dr Jeremy Burgess), 9.5, 9.7 (both Jeremy Burgess), 10.2
(Adam Hart Davis), 15.4 (Biophoto Associates), 15.6 (Martin Dohrn) and 19.10
(St. Mary's Hospital Medical School); Survival Anglia Photo Library, 1.7 (d) (T.D. Timms);
The Times, 18.10 and 18.11 (Andrew Bourne); C. James Webb, 4.17, 6.6, 16.16, 19.4,
20.2 and 20.4; Wildfowl and Wetlands Trust, 20.11 (a) (Joe B. Blossom); Wildlife
Matters, 11.8. Figures 15.1, 15.2, 15.3 and 16.17 by Longman Photographic Unit.

Cover photograph of red-eyed tree frogs by Oxford Scientific Films/Zig Leszczynski.

Contents

Good laboratory practice

 **Danger**

 **Biohazard**

 **Flammable**

 **Corrosive**

 **Harmful or Irritant**

 **Toxic**

 **Wear eye protection**

These are the safety symbols used in these books. You should get to know these so that you can recognise hazards that you might come across during your science lessons.

To avoid accidents you should:

- take special care when you see one of these symbols.
- always read through **all** the instructions given before you start doing your experiments.
- check with your teacher if you are not sure about any of the instructions.
- always check with your teacher before beginning any experiment that you have designed yourself.
- always wear eye protection when you see the eye protection symbol or when your teacher tells you.
- always wash your hands thoroughly with soap and water after handling pond water, soil, microbes, plants and animals.
- always stand when you are handling liquids so that you can move out of the way quickly if you spill anything.
- if you do spill anything on the bench wipe it up with a damp cloth, being careful not to get it on your hands.
- if you spill anything on your skin wash it off immediately and thoroughly with water. If you spill anything on your clothes tell your teacher.
- if you get anything in your eyes tell your teacher immediately.

Preface

To the teacher

This book is an introduction to biology for those working to Key Stage 3 of the National Curriculum in Science and for students preparing for the Common Entrance Examination to Independent Schools. It is designed to be a two-year course, and the sequence of topics is intended to fit in with the seasons. This is explained in more detail in the Teacher's Guide.

Exploration and discovery are pervading themes in the National Curriculum, and these are certainly important components of this book. People discover things about themselves and their surroundings by question and investigation. For this reason we have included numerous questions and investigation in this book. The investigations are of a type that can easily be carried out with the minimum of equipment. The questions are of two main kinds: some are intended to be a basis for class discussion; others are more suitable for homework and private study.

Overall, there is more in the book than could be covered in the time but we hope that teachers will pick and choose the parts they want to use.

Most of the investigations are accompanied by clear step by step instructions. However, real science is not like that. Pasteur wasn't given instructions telling him how to show that there are micro-organisms in the air, and Fleming wasn't told how to discover penicillin! To give a feel of what real science is, we have included twenty six 'explorations' in which students plan and devise their own investigations.

Plainly students cannot discover everything for themselves; much knowledge comes from reading or listening to the teacher. This method of acquiring knowledge is very valuable, particularly if it prompts further questions and opens the way to discovery. We certainly hope that the information provided in this book fulfils this aim. Because we attach considerable importance to reading, we have included selected passages of background reading at the ends of most of the chapters.

Producing a book which is suitable for a wide range of abilities at this level is no easy matter. If we have succeeded it is largely because of the help we have received from many friends and colleagues. We would particularly like to thank Richard Balding, Mary Cullen, Alec Porch, Robert Powell and Grace Monger, all of whom have read the manuscript and made many valuable suggestions. We are also grateful to members of the CLEAPSS and ASE organisations for ensuring that the text meets with current safety recommendations.

Finally we owe grateful thanks to John Lewis for his advice on the manuscript and his never failing support and encouragement.

Peter Mawby
Michael Roberts
Lancaster and Chillington, 1996

Chapter 1   Where animals and plants live

What is biology?

Biology is about living things and a person that studies living things is called a **biologist**. Most of the living things that you will study are either plants or animals. One of the first questions a biologist asks about an animal or plant is, 'where does it live?' The place in which an animal or plant lives is called its **habitat**.

This chapter is about habitats, but we shall also look at the surroundings of living things. An animal or plant's surroundings make up its **environment**. Every habitat must provide the animals and plants which live there with the right environment, and to survive the animals and plants must be suited, or **adapted**, to the environment.

What is your environment now?

At this moment you are probably sitting in a classroom or laboratory. For the time being this is your habitat, and it provides you with a suitable environment in which to live and work: light to read by, air to breathe, a hard surface to support your weight, and perhaps a heater to keep you warm. We call these the **physical features** of your environment.

However, you are also affected by other people, and also by other forms of life round about you, such as bacteria in the air. These make up the **biological features** of your environment.

Experiment 1.1
Measuring the physical features of your environment

Two of the most important physical features of your environment are light and temperature. Can you suggest a way of measuring these two features in the room in which you are working?

Measure the temperature in different parts of the room and work out the average. (To do this, add up the temperatures and divide by the total number of readings.) If the necessary equipment is available, also measure the light in different parts of the room.

Questions for class discussion

1 Make a list of other physical features of your environment besides the ones you have measured. Which ones are essential for life? Which might be changed by your presence in the room?

2 A student measured the temperature of six different rooms at home and obtained the following readings: 13 °C, 17 °C, 18 °C, 21 °C, 15 °C, 12 °C.
   a By how many degrees did the temperature vary?
   b What was the average temperature?
   c Suggest reasons for such variable readings.

3 Four different students measured the temperature of their classroom at three different times of the day and got these results:
   9 a.m. 13.2°C   12 noon 17.5°C   3 p.m. 16.9°C
Andrew recorded the average as 16 °C, Gill as 15.9 °C, Peter as 15.866 °C and Diane as 15 °C.
Whose answer is best, and why? What is wrong with the others?

Artificial habitats

One of the best ways of learning about habitats is to make an artificial one. For example, you could set up a large bottle containing various animals that live on the ground: we call this a **terrarium**. Or you could make a **wormery** out of two plates of glass with soil in between, or an ants' nest out of plaster of Paris. Your teacher will tell you how to set up such habitats.

One of the simplest habitats to make and maintain is a fresh water **aquarium**, and it has the advantage that you can look at it at frequent intervals and make measurements easily.

Experiment 1.2
Setting up an aquarium

You will need a container: a bowl, deep tray or tank will do, but it is best if it is wide and fairly shallow. Wash it thoroughly, then add a few centimetres of sand or gravel. Carefully pour in some stream or pond mud and spread a few large stones round the bottom. Finally add water, preferably river or pond water, pouring it over one of the stones to reduce disturbance of the mud. *The depth of the water should not be greater than half the width of the open surface of the container.*

If the aquarium is to be left outside, cover it with perforated zinc or fine-mesh chicken wire to keep out dead leaves. If it is to be kept indoors, cover it with a sheet of glass or wire-reinforced plastic and make sure it is well lit: a fluorescent strip is best if there is insufficient daylight.

When the mud has settled, make a rough sketch-map of your aquarium as seen from above. You can make your map more

Safety note

Wash your hands carefully with soap and water after collecting animals and plants.

accurate if you attach strings 10 cm apart across the top of the aquarium dividing it into squares of equal size (a **grid**) as shown in Fig 1.1.

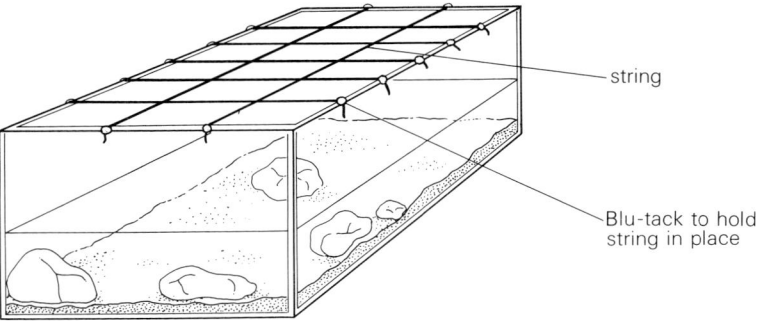

string

Blu-tack to hold string in place

Fig 1.1 An aquarium with grid.

Questions for class discussion

1 Why do you think the water in your aquarium must not be too deep?

2 What are the advantages of covering an indoor aquarium with glass or plastic?

3 Why is it necessary to light the aquarium well, and why is a fluorescent strip a good source of light?

4 As your aquarium settles down, various changes take place. What do you think will happen to it:
   a in the first 24 hours
   b if it is left untouched for several months?

Life in an aquarium

We refer to living things, both animals and plants, as **organisms**. Many small organisms found in fresh water can be kept in an aquarium, and your next job will be to find some. But first, think about the number and types of organisms which you want. Apart from size, what should you consider? Where will you get them from? What sort of equipment will you need? Your teacher will help you to answer these questions.

Experiment 1.3
Stocking up your aquarium

Fig 1.2 shows some of the organisms which you might put into your aquarium as a start. They are common in ponds and streams.

Take a net, a bucket and any other equipment you think you may need, and go out to a nearby pond, lake, river, stream, ditch – even a gutter or water butt might do – and find as many

Safety note

Wash your hands carefully with soap and water after collecting animals and plants.

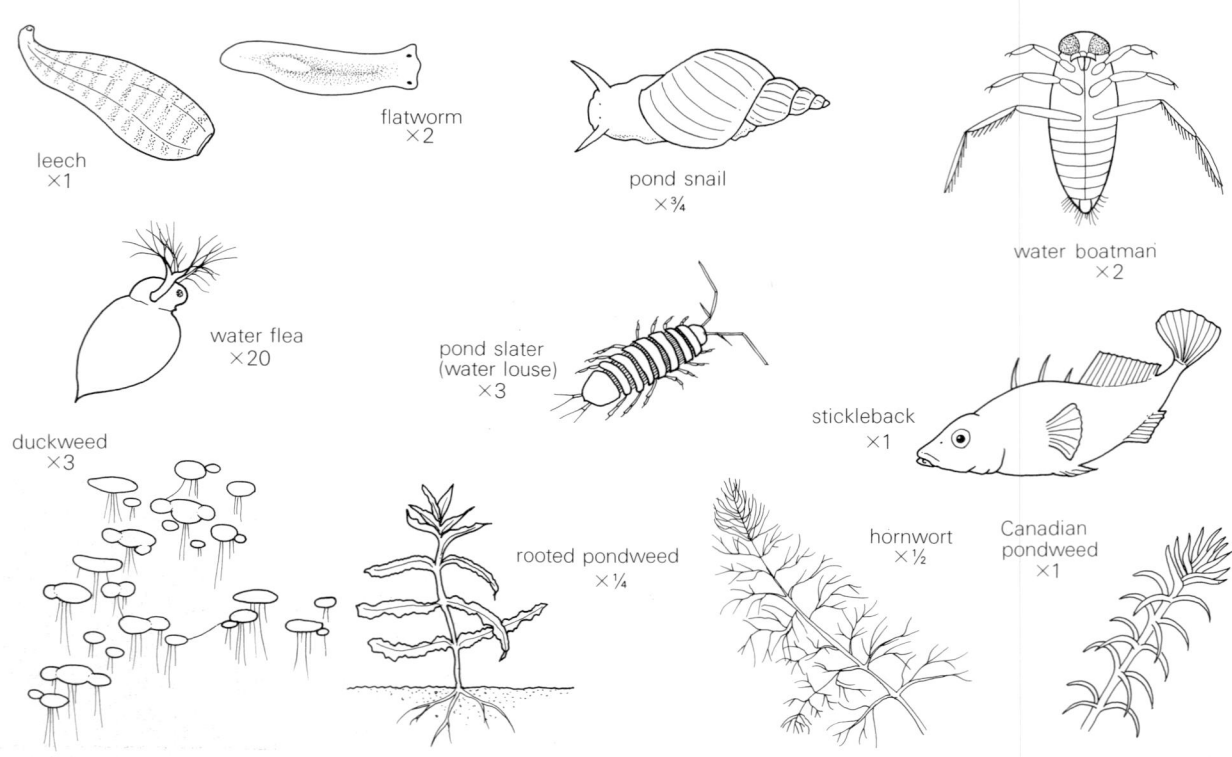

Fig 1.2 Some organisms that you might put in an aquarium.

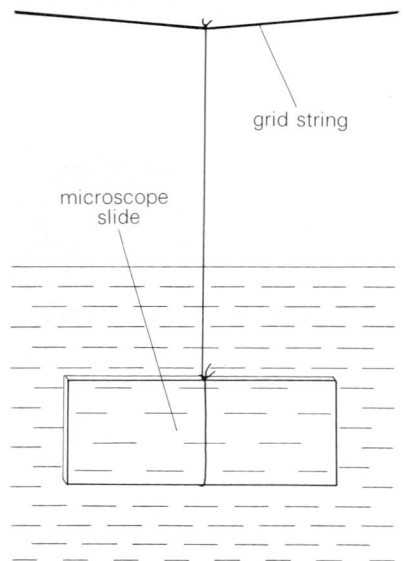

Fig 1.3 A method of collecting microscopic organisms in an aquarium.

of the organisms as you can. Bring them back to the laboratory.

Before you put any organisms into your aquarium, bear in mind the following important points:

1 Try not to disturb the mud when you put in the organisms. Plants with roots should be weighted down with stones and carefully lowered into the mud.
2 Many small organisms are better than a few large ones, and the more different kinds the better. Why?
3 Make sure you put in plenty of plants and *not* too many animals. Why do you think this is important? More animals can be added if extra air is provided by an aerator.

Make a list of the animals and plants which you put into your aquarium and note how many there are of each type. Indicate on your map (Experiment 1.2) the positions of the plants and other organisms.

Finally hang some microscope slides from the grid strings as shown in Fig 1.3: with luck, some small organisms will become attached to the slides and grow on them.

Questions for class discussion

1 If your aquarium is kept indoors, the water level will gradually fall. Why does this happen? Which of the following should you add to keep the conditions inside constant: tap water, rain water or pond water?

2 A cold water aquarium does not need much attention, but it is advisable to check it from time to time and remove any dead animals or plants. Why should this be necessary in an aquarium when it does not happen in a pond or river?

Natural habitats

There are all sorts of natural habitats. Some of them are shown in Fig 1.4. Examine them carefully and write down one feature which distinguishes each habitat from all the others.

Fig 1.4 Four natural habitats.

(a) A wood.

(b) Moorland.

(c) A meadow.

(d) A sand dune.

The name given to all the different kinds of living organisms in a habitat is a **community**. One of the most familiar examples of a community is a lawn. Although it consists mainly of grass, even some of the best-kept lawns contain 'weeds' such as the ones illustrated in Fig. 1.5. The positions of the various organisms in a community are called their **distribution**.

Experiment 1.4
Mapping a plant community

Visit a lawn or playing field near your school and make a map of part of the plant community as follows:

1 Work in groups of three or four.

2 Choose an area to map – not more than about ten paces across.

3 Measure and mark out the outline of the area and make a rough sketch map noting any main features such as trees, walls etc (see Fig 1.6a).

4 Transfer the information to a piece of squared paper to make a scale map e.g. 1 cm to 1 pace.

5 Outline the areas occupied by each type of plant. Do not show individual plants unless they are large and isolated from others of the same kind (Fig 1.6b).

When you get back to the classroom, you could put all the maps together to make a **habitat map** of the whole area.

Fig 1.5 Some weeds found in a lawn.

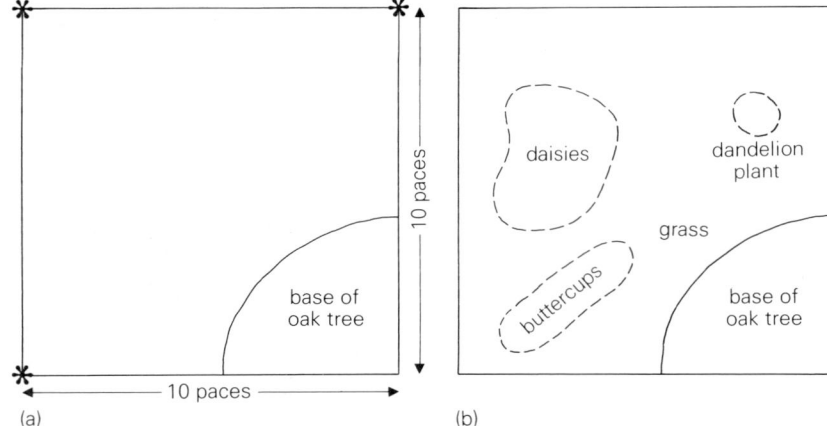

Fig 1.6 Mapping a plant community.

Questions for class discussion

1 Your map shows only the plant communities in the lawn. What animals might live in the habitat or might visit it occasionally? How might these animals affect the plants?

2 Are certain plants more common in some areas than in others?

If so, suggest possible reasons. Two questions might help:

a Are there any hollows in the lawn? Does a particular plant occur more frequently in the hollows than elsewhere? If so, which plant is it? What advantages might there be to living in a hollow?

b A lawn is a comparatively simple habitat to map. Why?

Changes in natural habitats

Do you think the lawn you mapped in Experiment 1.4 will be the same tomorrow, next month, next year? In fact the changes in the plant communities of a lawn are not very great.

One habitat which changes considerably from hour to hour each day is the seashore. If you can visit a rocky shore or examine a rock pool you will be able to watch the changes taking place. These **daily changes** are mainly caused by the movements of the tide but other environmental factors such as light and temperature may play a part as well. Even if you live in the centre of a city, there are plenty of habitats with interesting animals and plants for you to examine: roofs, gutters, walls and loose stones for example. You will find that there is daily variation in these habitats too.

If you visit a wood at different times of year you would find that many changes take place: these are called **seasonal changes**. Here are three reasons why the animals and plants found in a wood in Britain change between the summer and winter seasons:

1 **Hibernation**. Some animals that find it difficult to feed and keep warm through the winter become less active in the autumn and may go to sleep. An example is the dormouse.

2 **Migration**. Many birds, and some other animals, travel long distances in the autumn to warmer places. They do this in order to avoid the harsh conditions of winter. Can you name some of them? Where do they go?

3 **Leaf fall**. In temperate countries many trees shed their leaves in the autumn. This allows more light to reach the ground. It also cuts off the food supply for animals that feed on living leaves, but increases the food supply for organisms that feed on dead leaves.

Questions for class discussion

1 Make a list of the main changes that occur in a wood in the spring.

2 Habitats and communites abroad, for example a desert or a tropical rain forest, will differ considerably from those found in Britain. What special features might these habitats provide, and why are they particularly suitable for the organisms that live there? To what extent do they change with the seasons?

Table 1.1

Date	Depth
1 December	16 cm
15 December	13 cm
1 January	10 cm
15 January	9 cm
1 February	9 cm
15 February	9 cm
1 March	6 cm
15 March	5 cm
1 April	5 cm
15 April	3 cm

3 Return to your aquarium. What changes can you see? Try to explain why the distribution of some organisms has changed while that of others has stayed the same.

Homework assignments

1 Some students carried out a project to find out what happens to fallen leaves in an oak wood. They cordoned off an area of four square metres with chicken wire, and they measured the depth of the dead leaves at regular intervals. Their results are shown in Table 1.1.

   a Suggest reasons why the depth of dead leaves gets less.

   b Why do you think the depth remains unchanged between the middle of January and the middle of February?

2 Carefully examine the animals and plants shown in Figure 1.7. Describe the sort of environment in which you would expect to find each one, giving reasons for your choice.

3 You are asked to find out as much as possible about a local pond and its plant and animal life. How would you set about the task of making a map of the pond and its immediate surroundings?

Fig 1.7 In what sort of environment would you expect to find these animals and plants?

(a) Cactus.

(b) Polar Bear.

(c) Sea Lion.

(d) Hawthorn.

4 Suppose you visited a woodland habitat in late summer. Describe *three* differences you would expect to observe when revisiting the same habitat in the middle of winter.

5 You are supplied with a glass-sided aquarium about 30 cm × 15 cm × 15 cm high, some sand and small stones, Canadian pondweed and some duckweed. Describe the stages by which you would make the aquarium ready to receive pond animals.

Background Reading

The animal life of Siberia

Polar bears and camels, walruses, tigers and Japanese cranes ... and birds and mammals only recently thought to be extinct. Greater Siberia has an extraordinary range of *fauna* in its five million square miles, fifty-three times the size of the United Kingdom. Across it stretch three belts of vegetation: *tundra, taiga* (or coniferous forest) and *steppe* (see Fig 1.8).

The tundra *zone* is now shrinking fast as a result of the increase of far northern temperatures over the past fifty years. Forests have advanced north into the tundra at the rate of almost half a mile every year. In the summer of the midnight sun the tundra comes to life. The Arctic fox, snowy owl and its favourite prey, the *lemming*, are joined by animals migrating north – brown bear for instance, blue fox, reindeer and wolf, all escaping from the so-called 'scourge of the taiga', the blood-sucking mosquitoes, midges, gnats and horse-flies which accompany the summer's warmth and can drive both man and animals demented.

The taiga, by far the largest vegetational belt of Greater Siberia, supports a far richer fauna than the tundra: about 150 *species* of mammals and more than 200 species of birds. The taiga's

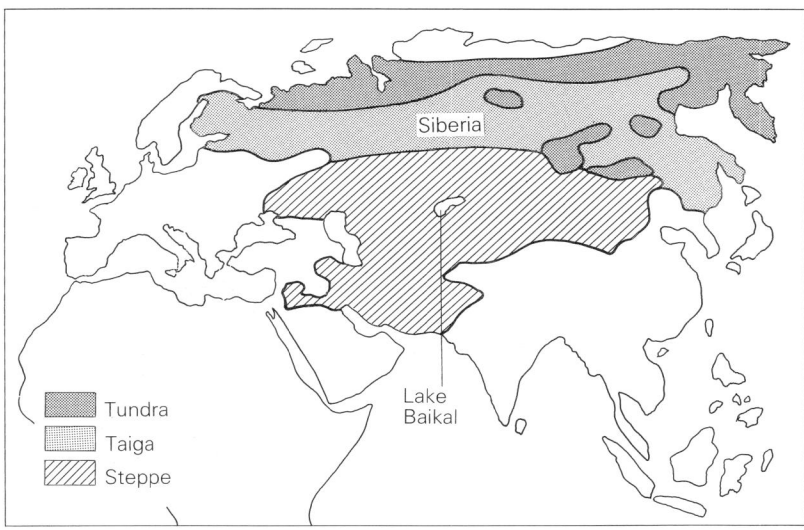

Fig 1.8 Map to show Siberia.

mammals incorporate the elk, reindeer, roebuck and the beautiful (protected) maral deer, the wolf, fox, glutton (or wolverine), lynx and the master of the taiga, the seven to eight foot brown bear.

South of the taiga most of the original steppe vegetation has been ploughed up. But in its last vestiges, hosts of butterflies flutter among the flowers and scorched grasses, and birds abound. Abundant too are the rodents and burrowing animals but Przhevalsky's horse is no more and man has killed off the *aurochs*.

Certainly the most remarkable *aquatic* habitat is Lake Baikal, the world's oldest and deepest lake and the greatest body of fresh water on Earth. Its water is by nature exceptionally pure thanks to a tiny underwater creature, the dotted cymatoa, which lives on the micro-organisms normally responsible for 'water bloom'. It filters the lake water through its tendrils, cleaning the entire surface layer several times a year, so that the water flowing out of the lake is actually much cleaner than that flowing in. Largest of all the lake's fauna is the freshwater seal, which numbers about 35 000 and lives in winter beneath the ice, breathing through ice-holes and bearing its young in lairs on the ice surface.

The most famous of all Siberia's fauna, however, has been *extinct* for just over 10 000 years: the mammoth. But that, as they say, is another story.
(From *Across the Russias* by John Massey Stewart, published by Harvil.)

Questions
1 Using a dictionary if necessary, give the meaning of each word in italics in the passage.

2 To what seasonal changes does the author refer?

3 Why do you think the taiga has a richer fauna than the tundra?

4 Why is the water that flows out of Lake Baikal cleaner than the water flowing in?

5 What kind of animal was a mammoth?

Summary

1 A **habitat** is a place in which organisms live, and it provides the organisms with a set of conditions which together make up the environment.

2 The **environment** is composed of physical and biological features, and organisms are **adapted** to the environment.

3 The organisms which live in a habitat make up a **community** and their positions are called their **distribution**.

4 Habitats and communities are always changing, for example, with the seasons. Some change more than others.

5 Seasonal changes bring about leaf fall, hibernation and migration.

Chapter 2

Observing and measuring living things

Similarities and differences

How *different* are you from the other members of your class? Which would you say are the main features by which your teachers and school friends recognise you?

How *similar* are you to the rest of the class? How many likenesses can you think of? If you list the similarities and differences, which list is longer?

Now consider the similarities more carefully. How many of the features are exactly the same (*identical*)? Perhaps you have included age in your list. Are any of your class *exactly* the same age as you? Your list may have included some characteristics of the human body: two eyes, one nose – but the eyes will be of different colours and the noses will differ in length and shape.

Only identical twins have identical features. This chapter deals with the differences between individuals, starting with you.

Experiment 2.1
Measuring differences in human height

Height is not difficult to measure, but you must follow the instructions carefully to obtain an accurate measurement.

1 Work in groups of three or four.

2 Fix a pair of metre rules end to end to a wall or door, making sure that the centimetre scale on each rule runs from 0 at the bottom to 100 at the top.

3 Decide who will be the first person in the group to be measured (the subject). The subjects remove their shoes and stand with their backs to the rules with their feet together (Fig 2.1).

4 The measurer places a ruler at right angles to the metre rule across the top of the subject's head.

5 A third member of the group checks that the subject is standing correctly (heels on ground, shoulders back) and ensures that the ruler is level.

6 The subject walks away and the measurer keeps the ruler in position. The height opposite the ruler's lower edge is read to the nearest millimetre, the smallest division on a metre rule.

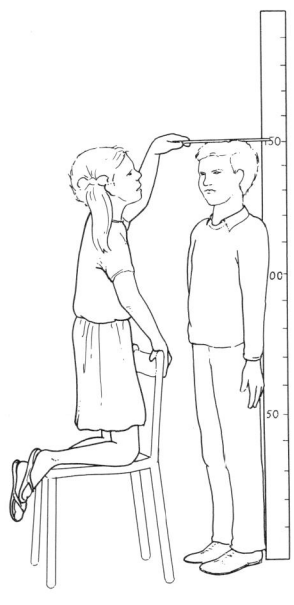

Fig 2.1 Measuring height.

Table 2.1

Name	Height (in centimetres)
John Smith	121.3
Susan Jones	153.1
Pat Brown	130.5

7 Write down the subject's height in centimetres. Do not forget to add 100 to the reading to allow for the lower rule.

8 Now take it in turn to measure the other members of your group.

9 Make a list of the names of the people in your class and write down their heights in a column beside their names. You have now expressed your results in a **table**. Do not forget to write down the units you have used: in this case centimetres. Part of your table might look like Table 2.1.

10 Underline the height of
  a the tallest person in the class
  b the shortest person in the class.
    Subtract **b** from **a** to obtain the **height range**.

11 Add together the heights of all the people and divide by the number measured to obtain the **average height**. Write down the range and the average beside your table. Together they give useful information about the differences in height of the people in your class.

12 Finally, it is important to record the accuracy of your measurement. If you followed the instructions carefully, and if you were able to read the rule to the nearest millimetre, then your measurements should have been within half a millimetre of the 'correct' height. Write this beside the table in the following way:

Accuracy = ±0.5 mm.

Drawing a histogram

Measurements such as the ones you have taken are usually shown in the form of a **histogram**. It is more convenient than a table of results, especially if a large number of measurements has been obtained. It also makes it easier to compare the measurements at a glance.

1 You have already found the height range for your class in Experiment 2.1, part 10. Divide the range into 5 to 8 equal parts. For example, if the smallest person is 121.3 cm and the tallest is 153.1 cm, the height groups could be 120–125 cm, 125–130 cm, 130–135 cm, 135–140 cm, 140–145 cm, 145–150 cm and 150–155 cm.

2 Make a table with the height groups listed on the left-hand side.

3 Put a tick beside the height group for each person's measurement. The person whose height was 153.1 cm would go in the class 150–155 cm. A height which is between two height groups such as 130.0 cm should be placed in the upper group 130–135 cm.

4 Add up the number of people whose heights fall within each height group, and write the total for each height group in the right-hand column of your table. Your table should look like Table 2.2.

Table 2.2

Height group (cm)	People in each height group	Total in height group
120–125	✓	1
125–130	✓ ✓	2
130–135	✓ ✓ ✓	3
135–140	✓ ✓ ✓ ✓ ✓ ✓	6
140–145	✓ ✓ ✓	3
145–150	✓ ✓	2
150–155	✓	1
	Total number of pupils	18

5 Take a piece of graph or squared paper and draw a horizontal line about 3 cm from the lower edge. This is the **horizontal axis** and will represent the height groups. Now draw a vertical line about 3 cm from the left-hand margin of your paper. This is the **vertical axis** and will represent the number of people in each height group.

6 How many height groups did you have? Our example had seven height groups. Divide the horizontal axis into sections of equal size, for example 2 cm each. Label each section with its range.

7 What was the largest number of people in a single height group? In our example there were six people in the 135–140 cm group. Divide the vertical axis into equal-sized sections to take the largest number of measurements in the right-hand column of your table. The axes for your histogram should now look like Fig 2.2.

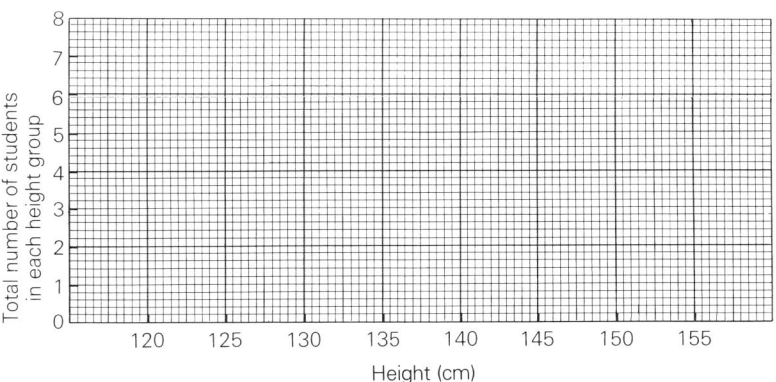

Fig 2.2 Drawing the axes for a histogram.

8 Now draw a series of columns, one in each height group. The columns should represent the figures in the final column of your table. If the total in height group 120–125 cm is 1, then the column will go up to the 1 on the vertical axis.

What does a histogram tell us?

How many people did you measure and include in your histogram? The number of people measured is called the **sample**. If the sample is large enough, we expect the highest point to be approximately half way along the height range – quite close to the average height. This is called a **normal distribution**. You can see an example in Fig 2.3.

The differences that you observe between members of your class are referred to as **variation**. If your histogram of variation in height does not look like a normal distribution you should try to suggest reasons. The questions that follow may help you.

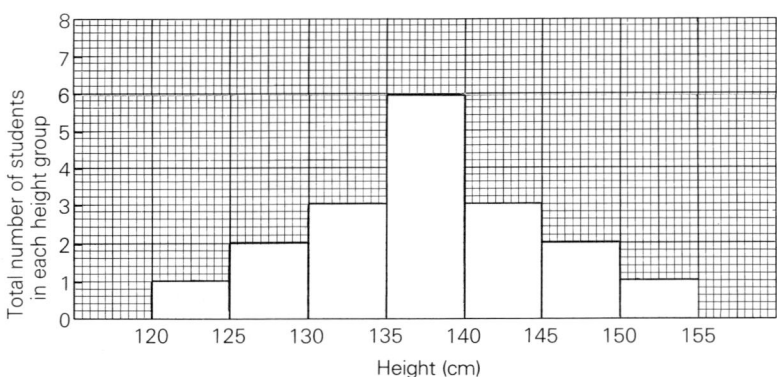

Fig 2.3 A histogram based on the measurements in Table 2.2.

Questions for class discussion

1 Find and mark the point on your histogram corresponding to:
   a the mid-point of the height range
   b the average height
   c the highest point (**peak**) of your histogram.

2 If the heights of the people in your class give a normal distribution, then **a**, **b** and **c** in Question 1 will be roughly the same. How close are they?

3 Suppose you were able to measure twice as many people of your age. What difference would you expect it to make to your histogram?

4 What would be the effect on your histogram of including *all* the students in your school?

5 If your measurements had been made on a group of boys or a group of girls only, would there have been any differences?

6 Suppose the measurements had been taken less accurately (say ±1 cm). How would the histogram be affected?

7 Which of these can be found from your histogram *alone*:
   a the range of heights
   b the average height
   c the size of your sample
   d the height of an individual person in your class
   e the age of an individual if you know his or her height?

Experiment 2.2
Finding some other differences

Here are some other differences which you might study. You may be able to think of some more. Record your own details in your notebook, then collect together the class results.

Body mass

A pair of bathroom scales is suitable, although you may have to convert the mass from stones and pounds into kilograms. Your teacher will explain how this can be done. Proceed as follows:

1 Adjust the scales to zero.

2 Remove your shoes and jacket.

3 Stand in the centre of the step.

Arm span

Any smooth vertical surface will do to measure your arm span; alternatively a laboratory bench could be used.

1 Stand against the blackboard or wall, or lean over the bench.

2 Stretch out both arms as widely as possible (Fig 2.4).

Fig 2.4 Measuring arm span.

3 Mark the positions of the fingertips with chalk.

4 Measure the span with a rule or tape.

Finger prints

Your finger print pattern can be seen with a hand lens, but it is made clearer if the finger is inked on a stamp pad, and pressed against a sheet of paper (Fig 2.5).

1 Place a drop of ink on the pad and allow it to soak in. (Some pads do not need to be inked.)

2 Roll your finger lightly on the pad. Then roll it on a piece of white paper.

3 Repeat on another part of the paper, without re-inking your finger, until the ink runs out.

4 Select the clearest print. Examine it carefully under a hand lens and compare it with the prints of the rest of your class.

Fig 2.5 Finger prints.

Questions for class discussion

1 Finger prints are often used in evidence when a person is suspected of having committed a crime.
  a List as many differences as you can between the finger prints of your class. Are any the same?
  b Finger prints would be difficult to measure, but they can be divided into groups. Suggest how this might be done and estimate how many members of your class would be included in each group.
2 Look carefully at the height, mass and arm span measurements of the members of your class. Has the tallest student got the largest arm span? Is the smallest also the lightest? Can you see any other connections?

Homework assignments

1 A school friend knows nothing about histograms. Try to explain very simply what is meant by a normal distribution, using the words *sample*, *average* and *range* in your explanation.

2 The height of each 11-year-old student in a London school was measured. The results are shown in Table 2.3.

Table 2.3

Height (cm)	Number of students in each height group
120–125	1
125–130	10
130–135	18
135–140	17
140–145	9
145–150	1

a Show these measurements on a histogram.

b Show on your histogram:
  (i) the *average* height (134.0 cm)
  (ii) the middle of the height *range*
  (iii) the height group containing most students.

3 Compare the results given in Question 2 with the results which you obtained in Experiment 2.1. List the differences and try to suggest some reasons for them.

Experiment 2.3
Using a hand lens

Suppose you want to distinguish between the individuals in a group of small animals. If they are too small to see clearly or if you have to examine them in detail, a **hand lens** is very useful.

These lenses usually make an object look five to ten times as large as their life size. We say that their **magnification** is 'times five' or 'times ten' and we write this as ×5 or ×10. This is called the **scale**. Practise using a hand lens by looking at a coin, stamp or piece of microfilm.

1 Hold the object in one hand under a good light.

2 Hold the lens in your other hand *close to your eye*.

3 Move the object slowly up towards the lens, starting about 30 cm away, until it just becomes clear and sharp (Fig 2.6).

4 Look at the details on the stamp or coin (for example, the decorations on the crown).

5 Work out the approximate magnification using the perforations on the edge of the stamp, or the number of letters visible on the microfilm.

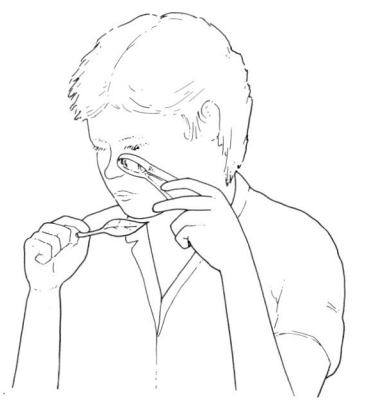

Fig 2.6 Using a hand lens correctly.

Experiment 2.4
Recording what you see

Recording your observations by means of sketches or drawings is a very useful skill. You do not have to be a good artist, but you do have to train yourself to observe carefully.

You need a small animal such as a woodlouse, a hand lens, a ruler, a soft rubber, a sharp HB pencil and a sheet of plain paper. Proceed as follows:

1 Measure your paper and decide how large your drawing is to be when completed. Make the drawing as large as you can, but allow space for a heading and some labels.

2 Measure the length and the breadth of the specimen and decide how many times larger your drawing will be.

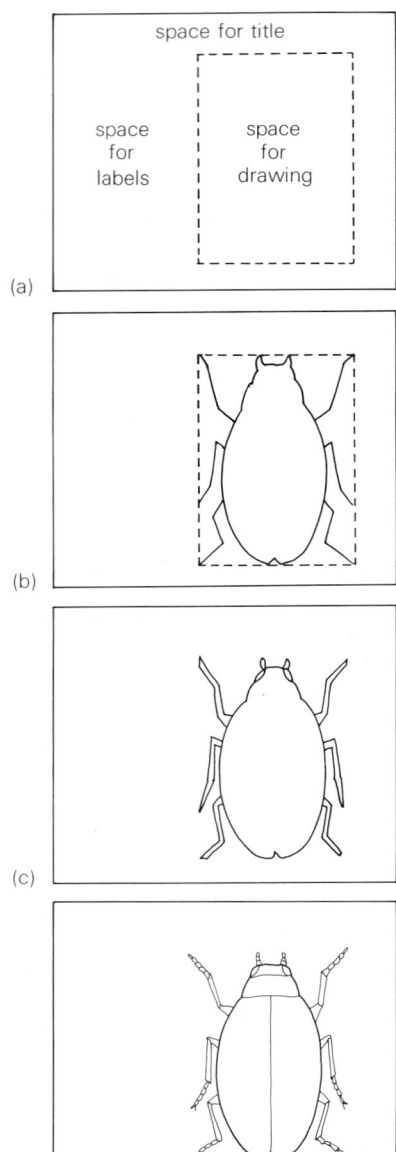

Fig 2.7 Recording observations by drawing.

3 Now use the ruler to indicate, with very faint pencil lines on your paper, the vertical and horizontal edges of your drawing (Fig 2.7a).

4 Now sketch the *outline* of the specimen, very softly. Make corrections if necessary until you are satisfied with the outline (Fig 2.7b).

5 Sharpen your pencil again if necessary and go over the final sketched outline to give a firm, clear, single outline. Avoid the common mistake of giving the specimen a fuzzy outline; try to go right round corners with a single movement of the pencil. Rub out all the sketch lines once the outline is complete (Fig 2.7c).

6 Fill in the details, if necessary using the hand lens to get them accurate in shape and position (Fig 2.7d).

7 Write the names of the main parts of the specimen (for example, head, feelers, legs) alongside the drawing and use a ruler to join the name to the drawing. This is called **labelling** your drawing.

8 Do not forget to add:
   a the name of the specimen
   b the place where it was found
   c the magnification of your drawing. This can be written as ×10 (refer back to **2**) or by giving an indication of the natural size such as 'length = 7 mm'.

Questions for class discussion or homework

1 The photographs in Fig 2.8 all show common objects reduced in size. Use a hand lens to identify the objects. Make sure the lens is close to your eye and the book is in a good light.

 (a)    (b)    (c)

Fig 2.8 What are these common objects?

2 The magnification or scale is often used to describe the actual size of an object from a drawing, map or plan. Can you answer the following questions about scale?
   a An architect's drawing shows my house 20 cm wide. What is the actual width if the drawing's scale is 1:10?
   b The famous cannon in Edinburgh Castle called Mons Meg is 4 metres long. How many centimetres long would a 1:40 kit model be? (1 metre = 100 cm).

c The Ordnance Survey produces maps of the whole of Britain based on a 1:50 000 scale. How long would the largest bridge span in Britain, the Humber Estuary Bridge, appear on the map? Its actual length is 1.4 km. Give your answer in centimetres (1 km = 1000 metres).

3 The lens I normally use is marked ×10. When I use it to look at a ladybird 3 mm long, how large does the ladybird appear to be? My drawing of the ladybird is five times as large as it appears under my lens. Will it fit a piece of paper the size of this page?

4 The graph in Fig 2.9 compares the average heights of boys in the United Kingdom aged between 10 and 19 in 1878 and 1958. Examine it carefully before attempting the questions.
   a What is the average difference in height between 1878 boys and 1958 boys?
   b At what age is there the greatest difference in height between 1878 boys and 1958 boys?
   c In which year of the boys' life was growth most rapid:
      (i) in 1878 (ii) in 1958?
   d What reasons can you think of to explain the greater height and earlier growth of 1958 boys? Do you think the changes are likely to continue?

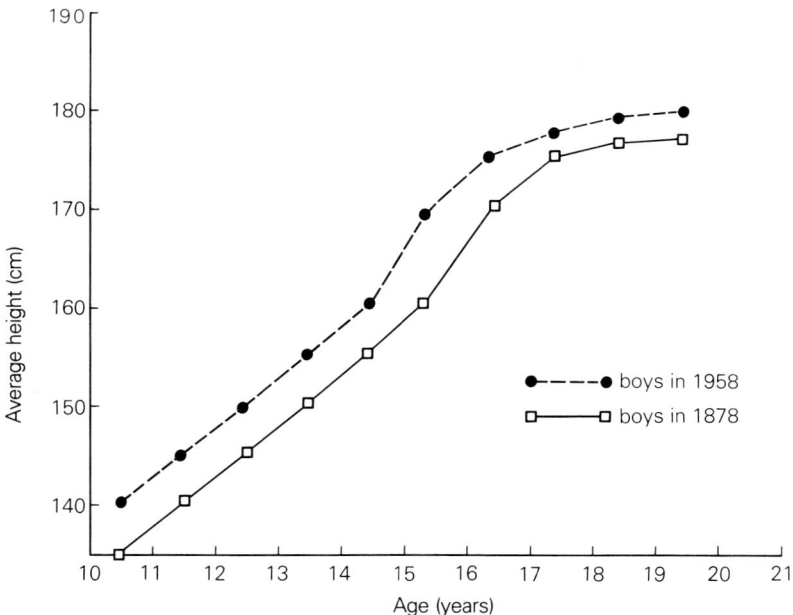

Fig 2.9 Average heights of boys in the UK.

5 Refer to the picture in Fig 3.5 on page 24.
   a Which drawing is less than life size?
   b Which is the largest animal shown?
   c What is the length of the water beetle?

6 A student studying variation in size within a single species of snail, collected a large number of snails from a railway embankment and arranged them into groups according to their length (Table 2.4).

Table 2.4

Length (mm)	Number of snails in each length group
0– 2.5	0
2.5– 5.0	35
5.0– 7.5	175
7.5–10.0	185
10.0–12.5	190
12.5–15.0	55
15.0–17.5	5
17.5–20.0	0

a Make a histogram showing these results.
b What type of distribution does the histogram show?
c What is the most common length group?
d Why is it not possible to work out the average snail length from the information given?
e Suggest a reason for the absence of snails in the range 0–2.5 mm and a reason for the absence of snails longer than 17.5 mm.

Summary

1 Organisms of a single type show differences from each other; careful measurement and observation is needed to detect this **variation**.

2 Measurements can be analysed by calculation of the **average** and **range**.

3 The measurements can also be shown as a **histogram**. If the sample is large enough, a **normal distribution** is frequently obtained.

4 Small differences can be observed and measured using a **hand lens**. The observations are recorded by making a careful drawing. The **magnification** or **scale** of the drawing is always noted.

Chapter 3

Sorting and naming living things

Sorting living things

If you have a collection of any kind, you will know how difficult it can be to sort out the items. In this chapter you will learn how living things are arranged in groups or sets. Biologists call this process **classification**.

Experiment 3.1
Putting things into groups

Your teacher will give you six items to classify. Suitable things might include coins, laboratory glassware (beakers, flasks, test-tubes etc.) or ironmongery (nails, screws, bolts etc.)

1 Make sketches in your notebook. Give each item a letter or name so that you can refer to it easily (Fig 3.1).

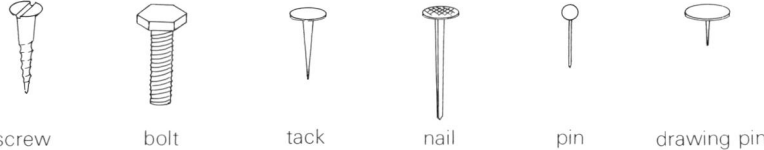

| screw | bolt | tack | nail | pin | drawing pin |

Fig 3.1 A collection of ironmongery.

2 Look for one feature that some of the items possess but the rest do not. Separate the items into two piles on your desk and record the feature you used in your book (Fig 3.2).

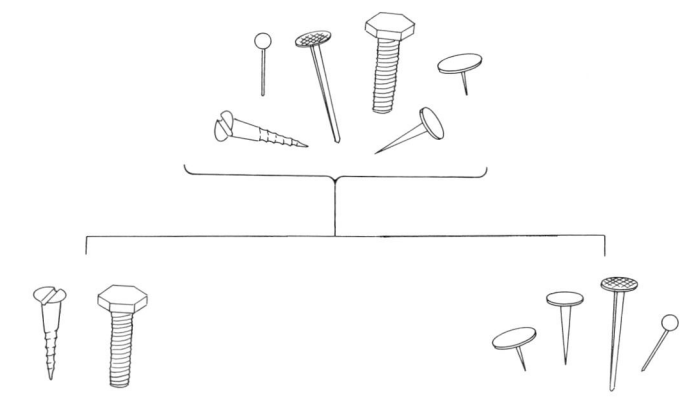

items with a screw thread   items without a screw thread

Fig 3.2 Separating the collection into two groups.

3 Now choose a feature that separates the items in *one* of the piles. Move them apart and continue until each item is on its own.

4 Do the same with the other piles and record what you have done. The record in your book should look like Fig 3.3.

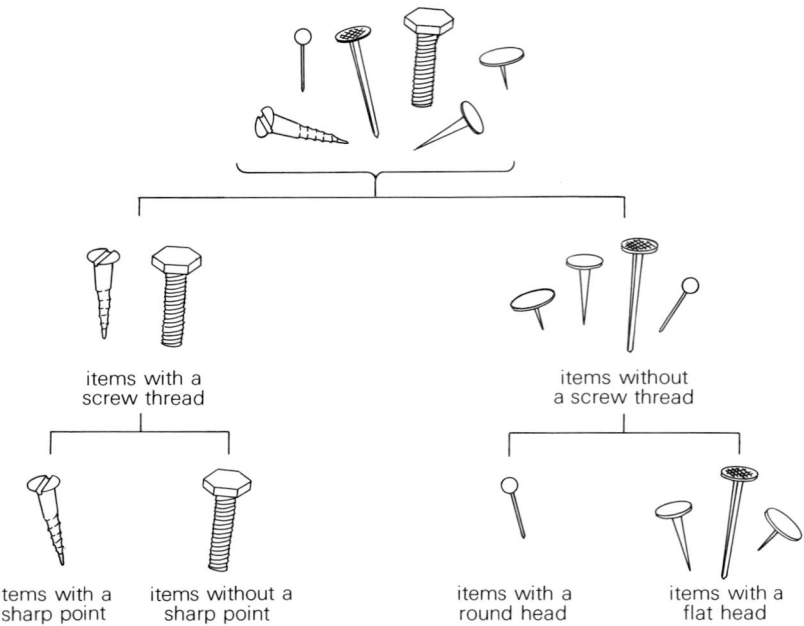

Fig 3.3 Separating the collection into four groups.

items with a screw thread

items without a screw thread

items with a sharp point

items without a sharp point

items with a round head

items with a flat head

Questions for class discussion

1 Look at Fig 3.3 and find which items have not been separated. What feature could you use to separate these items?

2 The ironmongery items in Fig 3.3 differ in size but they have not been separated according to their size. Why not?

3 Most stamp collections are arranged by country. What other methods could be used to classify collections of stamps? Suggest one advantage and one disadvantage of grouping a stamp collection by colour.

Homework assignments

1 The six shapes in Fig 3.4 have been partly separated into groups for you. Copy down the scheme, writing in the features that were used to separate them, and then complete the classification.

2 Use the method described in Experiment 3.1 to separate the following items into groups:
   a knife, fork, teaspoon, dessertspoon, tablespoon
   b cow, sheep, pig, horse, hen
   c bicycle, car, bus, train, aeroplane.

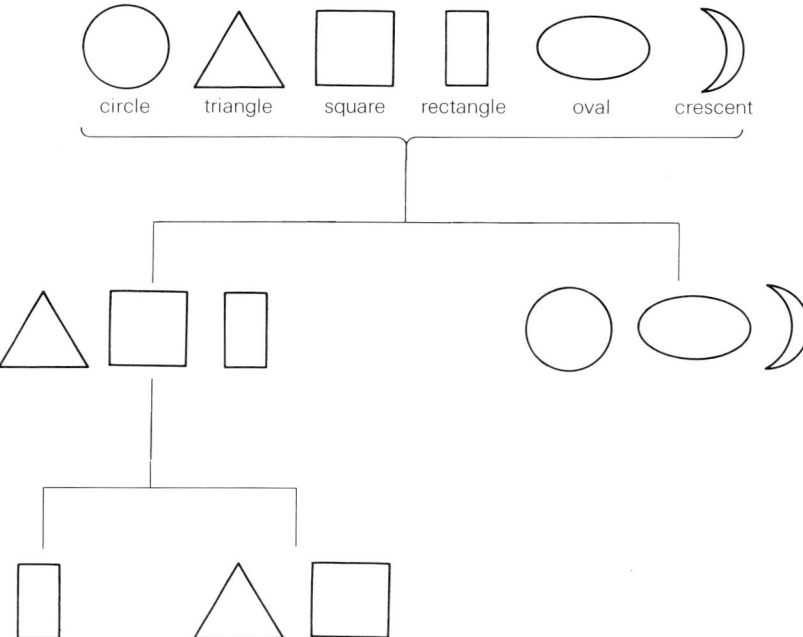

Fig 3.4 Which features have been used to separate these shapes into groups?

Experiment 3.2
Classifying living things

There are almost a million different kinds of animals and a third of a million different kinds of plants known and named. You will be given, or asked to collect, specimens of 6–10 living things, for example, twigs, fruits or leaves from different kinds of trees, or shells of different animals.

1 Sketch each organism and give it a name or letter for identification.

2 Use the method described in Experiment 3.1 to separate them into two groups, then divide each group until each organism is on its own.

3 Record what you have done, as in Fig 3.3.

Questions for class discussion

1 Exchange your classification and collection of specimens with your neighbour's. Compare different methods of classification. Are some methods better than others? If so, can you decide why?

2 How useful would your classification be:
   a in a year's time
   b at a different time of year
   c with other kinds of specimens?

Homework assignment

Fig 3.5 shows some animals which you might find in your aquarium.

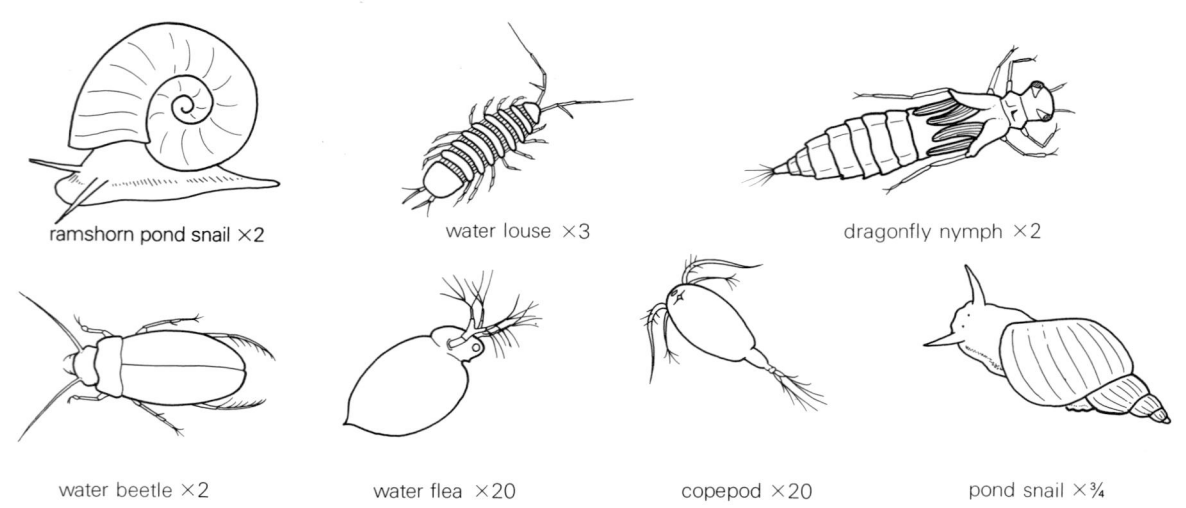

ramshorn pond snail ×2   water louse ×3   dragonfly nymph ×2

water beetle ×2   water flea ×20   copepod ×20   pond snail ×¾

Fig 3.5 Some aquarium animals.

1 Sort the animals into three pairs according to obvious external features. Which is the odd one out?

2 Make a classification of them, similar to the classification in Fig 3.3.

Naming living things

Each particular kind of animal has its own common name. You will be familiar with many of them, for example, robin, snail and human. What do you call the little animals which are drawn in Fig 3.6?

The most common name is probably 'woodlouse' or 'slater' but you may be surprised to learn that in Devon alone there are over thirty-four different names for these animals. To make things even more complicated, the word 'woodlouse' is used to refer to at least thirty-eight different kinds of animal. Three kinds are shown in Fig 3.6.

Each different kind of animal and plant is called a **species** and scientists have given each species a different scientific name; no other species has the same name. The names of each of the three species of woodlice are written below the drawings in Fig 3.6. You will notice two things about these names.

First, they are in Latin. All the scientific names given to living organisms are in Latin because this was the international language of scholars in the 18th century when the system of naming we use today was begun.

Second, each organism has two names. The first name tells you the group of organisms, or **genus**, to which it belongs and the second name identifies the species. As biologists collect organisms more widely and study them more closely, new species are being discovered and named each year. Each new discovery has to be examined and compared with species which already have names. The biologist looks for similarities and differences so that the specimen can be placed in the right group and given an appropriate name.

Questions for class discussion

1 Your scientific name is *Homo sapiens*. Which part of your name refers to your genus and which part to your species? Do you know what each of the Latin names means in English?

2 Archaeologists have discovered some fossils which are about half a million years old. They have called them *Homo habilis* and *Homo erectus*. What do these names suggest about these creatures?

3 Scientific names can tell us about the relationships between organisms. Fill in the blanks in the sentences that follow.
   a The blackbird (*Turdus merula*) and song thrush (*Turdus philomelus*) belong in the same _____.
   b The two kinds of woodlice found most frequently in this country are *Armadillidium vulgare* and *Oniscus asellus*. They are not in the same _____ or _____.
   c All varieties of domestic dogs from the Great Dane to the Chihuahua are named *Canis canis* so they all _____.

4 Examine the three kinds of woodlouse shown in Fig 3.6.
   a Write down *three* differences between *Armadillidium vulgare* and *Oniscus asellus* and *three* differences between *Oniscus asellus* and *Porcellio scaber*.
   b Write down three ways in which all three kinds of woodlouse are similar.
   c Complete the following sentence which refers to the classification of the woodlice shown in Fig 3.6. In spite of the similarities between the three kinds of woodlouse, all three belong to a different _____ and a different _____.

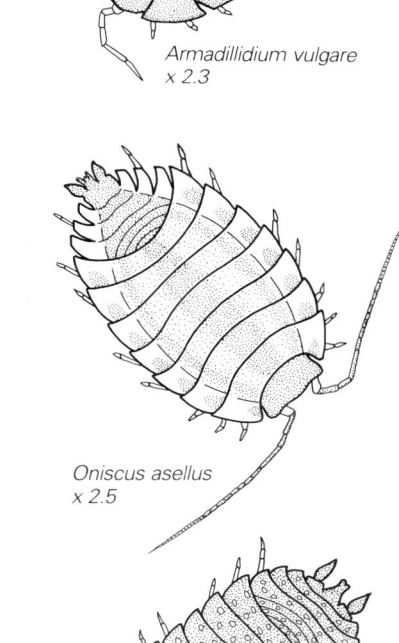

Armadillidium vulgare
x 2.3

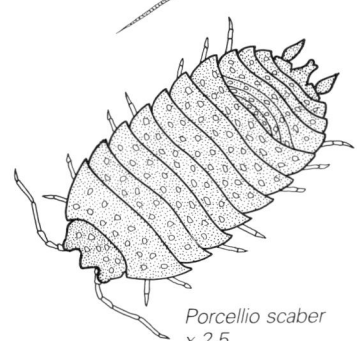

Oniscus asellus
x 2.5

Porcellio scaber
x 2.5

Fig 3.6 What is the common name for these animals?

Finding the name of an organism

Have you used a book to find the name of an animal or plant? It can be quite difficult, even if the book has detailed pictures.

Most identification books contain some sort of **key** to help you find your way quickly to the correct picture or description.

The simplest type of identification key is called a **spider key** and it is suitable for identifying the major groups to which organisms belong. It gets its name from its shape – an example is shown in Fig 3.7 overleaf.

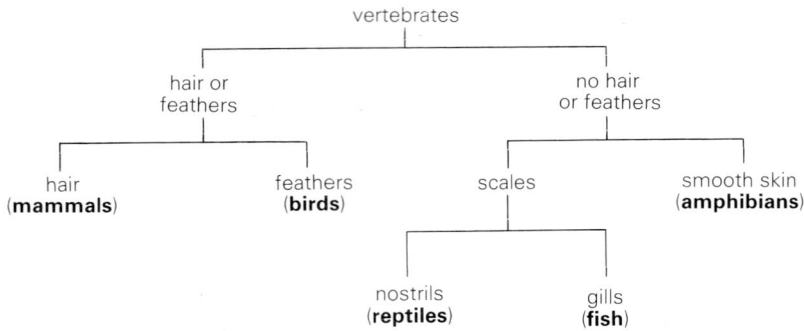

Fig 3.7 Spider key to identify the groups of vertebrates (animals with backbones).

Individual species are usually identified using a **numbered key**. There are several examples in the Appendix. They consist of a series of clues, each of which has two alternative answers. The answers lead to a further clue or to the name of the species.

Using a numbered key

Fig 3.8 Put these vertebrates into groups using the key.

With practice, you should be able to use the large keys in flower and animal books, but here is a simple key to start with. Use it to place the vertebrates in Fig 3.8 into their correct groups.

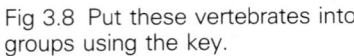

Key to vertebrates in Fig 3.8

Clue **1** Vertebrates with hair or feathers .... Go to Clue **2**

Vertebrates without hair or feathers .... Go to Clue **3**

Clue **2** Hair or whiskers on face and body .... **mammals**

Feathers cover most of the body .... **birds**

Clue **3** Body covered in scales .... Go to Clue **4**

Body without scales; wet, smooth skin . **amphibians**

Clue **4** Nostrils and lungs; lay eggs on land ...... **reptiles**

Gills and fins; live in water .... **fish**

1 Examine picture (a) carefully.

2 Decide which of the alternatives in Clue **1** of the key fits this animal. You will see that it has no hair or feathers, so you should go on to Clue **3**.

3 Go through all the clues until you come to the name of the group to which the animal belongs. Of course it is a crocodile and it is a reptile.

4 Write down the number of each clue you have used and the name of the group like this:

Animal (a) Clues **1** → **3** → **4**: Group **reptile**

5 Do the same for animals (b) to (h).

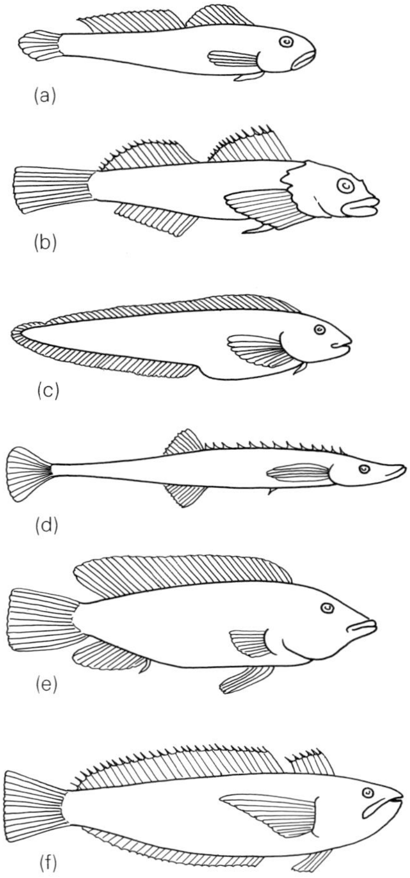

Homework assignment

1 The key below identifies eight fish. Six of them are drawn in Fig 3.9. Which scientific name refers to which fish?

1 The fins or body have spines along the top (dorsal) surface **2**

No obvious dorsal spines **3**

2 Spines on the fins **4**

Separate spines on the body but not on the fins **5**

3 Single dorsal fin **6**

Two dorsal fins .... **Gobius**

4 Dorsal fins similar in size .... **Cottus**

The front dorsal fin much smaller than the rear one .... **Trachinus**

5 Snout upturned, body slender .... **Spinachia**

Snout not upturned, body not slender .... **Gasterosteus**

6 Distinct tail fin **7**

Dorsal fin merged with the tail fin .... **Zoarces**

7 Elongated body; tail fin with central notch ...... **Ammodytes**

Body not noticeably elongated; tail fin smooth .... **Labrus**

(a)

(b)

(c)

(d)

(e)

(f)

Fig 3.9 Identify these fish.

2 Here is a key for grouping animals. Study it carefully and then answer the questions that follow it.

1 External nostrils present **2**
No external nostrils **6**

2 Air-breathing **3**
Breathes in water using gills .... **fish**

3 Fur or hair absent **4**
Fur or hair present .... **mammal**

4 Feathers present .... **bird**
No feathers **5**

5 Scales present .... **reptile**
Has smooth skin and no scales .... **amphibian**

6 External skeleton present **7**
Has no external skeleton **11**

7 Body segmented (arranged in rings) **8**
Body not segmented **10**

8 Body divided into 3 parts, with 3 pairs of
legs .... **insect**
Body divided into 2 parts **9**

9 Four pairs of jointed legs .... **spider**
Five or more pairs of jointed legs .... **crustacean**

10 Outer shell .... **mollusc**
Spiny-skinned .... **echinoderm**

11 Body segmented (arranged in rings) .... **worm**
Body not segmented .... **other
invertebrates**

a To which animal group does the following refer: It has *no* external nostrils; it has an external skeleton to which seven pairs of jointed legs are attached; its segmented body is divided into two parts?
b Name *two* types of animal (from the key) that have no external nostrils, but have external skeletons that are not segmented.
c Use the key to find *two* items of information that apply to *both* reptiles and mammals.

3 Use the key in the Appendix to identify these animals in an aquarium tank:
a A red, worm-like creature sticking out of the mud.
b An animal with no limbs in a single flat shell stuck to the side of the tank.
c A round-bodied animal with a tough outer covering, just visible to the naked eye, propelled by numerous jointed limbs.

The kingdoms

Most modern classifications divide all living organisms into several separate **kingdoms**. The two main kingdoms are the **animal kingdom** (see below) and the **plant kingdom** (see page 30). There are other important groups of organisms including micro-organisms which are discribed in Chapter 19.

The animal kingdom

The vertebrates shown in Fig 3.8 belong to one of the main groups (or **phyla**) in the animal kingdom. All vertebrates have a backbone running down their bodies. The other animal groups are all **invertebrates** (without a backbone). They can be recognised by the features shown in Fig 3.10.

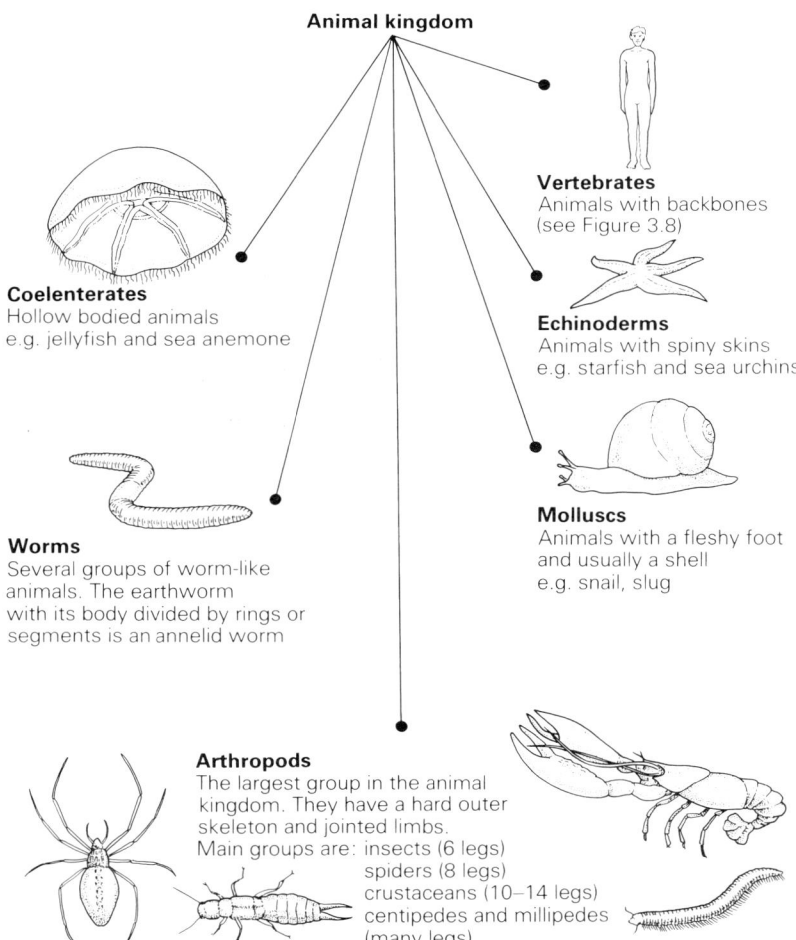

Animal kingdom

Vertebrates
Animals with backbones
(see Figure 3.8)

Echinoderms
Animals with spiny skins
e.g. starfish and sea urchins

Coelenterates
Hollow bodied animals
e.g. jellyfish and sea anemone

Molluscs
Animals with a fleshy foot
and usually a shell
e.g. snail, slug

Worms
Several groups of worm-like
animals. The earthworm
with its body divided by rings or
segments is an annelid worm

Arthropods
The largest group in the animal
kingdom. They have a hard outer
skeleton and jointed limbs.
Main groups are: insects (6 legs)
spiders (8 legs)
crustaceans (10–14 legs)
centipedes and millipedes
(many legs)

Fig 3.10 The main groups in the animal kingdom.

The plant kingdom

The plants most familiar to us are those which bear cones (the conifers) or flowers (the flowering plants). However there are other important groups of plants shown in Fig 3.11.

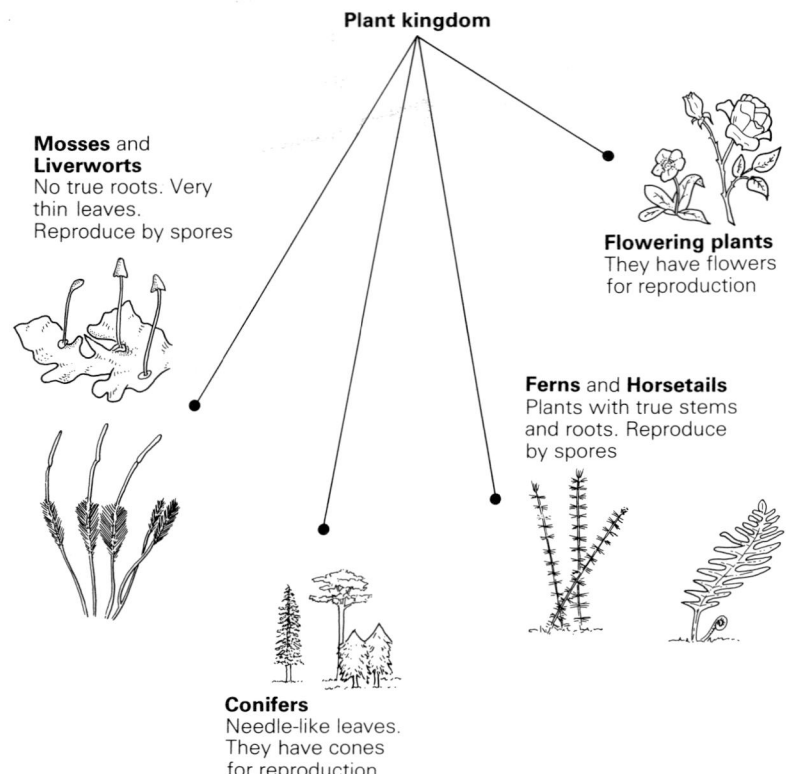

Plant kingdom

Mosses and **Liverworts**
No true roots. Very thin leaves. Reproduce by spores

Flowering plants
They have flowers for reproduction

Ferns and **Horsetails**
Plants with true stems and roots. Reproduce by spores

Conifers
Needle-like leaves. They have cones for reproduction

Fig 3.11 The main groups in the plant kingdom.

Experiment 3.3
Making a collection

Making a collection of living organisms is fun. It does not have to be large and you need not go far afield. You might simply set some pitfall traps (see page 139) or use a butterfly net or collect fungi in the autumn. However there are a few rules which you should observe when collecting.

1 Take notes, drawings or photographs where possible. Never take more specimens than you need.

2 Remember that some wild plants are poisonous, therefore do not taste or eat any. Do not handle any dead animals you may find.

3 Leave flowers for others to enjoy, and birds' eggs to hatch and develop.

4 Consider other people's property. Always ask permission if in doubt. It will usually be granted readily.

Safety note

Wash your hands carefully with soap and water after collecting animals and plants.

5 Do not disturb animals or plants if you can help it. Even visiting a bird's nest may lead to the parents deserting it, so take care.

There are many books which give helpful advice about collecting, identifying and mounting specimens. Do not worry if you cannot give a name to everything you find; just identify it as far as you can. Present your collection in an attractive and informative way so that the rest of the class can enjoy looking at it.

Homework assignments

1 Complete the following sentences by selecting the best word or phrase. You may need to use the index.

    a Man is classified as a mammal because . . .
        he has hair on his body
        he is warm blooded
        he has a backbone

    b The molluscs include . . .
        jellyfish
        snails
        earthworms

    c Mosses and ferns reproduce by . . .
        spores
        seeds
        larvae

2 Look carefully at the drawings of the seven invertebrates shown in Fig 3.12. Copy down the numbered key shown below, filling in each of the blanks where indicated.

    1 Body in five parts, covered in spines .... **starfish**
       Body not arranged in five parts or covered in
       spines **2**

    2 Three pairs of legs or limbs **3**
       No legs or limbs; body mainly smooth **4**

    3 _____ .... **housefly**
       _____ .... **cockroach**

    4 No antennae or feelers visible **5**
       Antennae or feelers on top of head **6**

    5 _____ .... **leech**
       _____ .... **earthworm**

    6 _____ .... **slug**
       _____ .... **garden snail**

3 Suppose a spacecraft returns from a mission to a newly discovered moon of Saturn with several specimens of living organisms. Describe how you would go about the task of classifying and naming them.

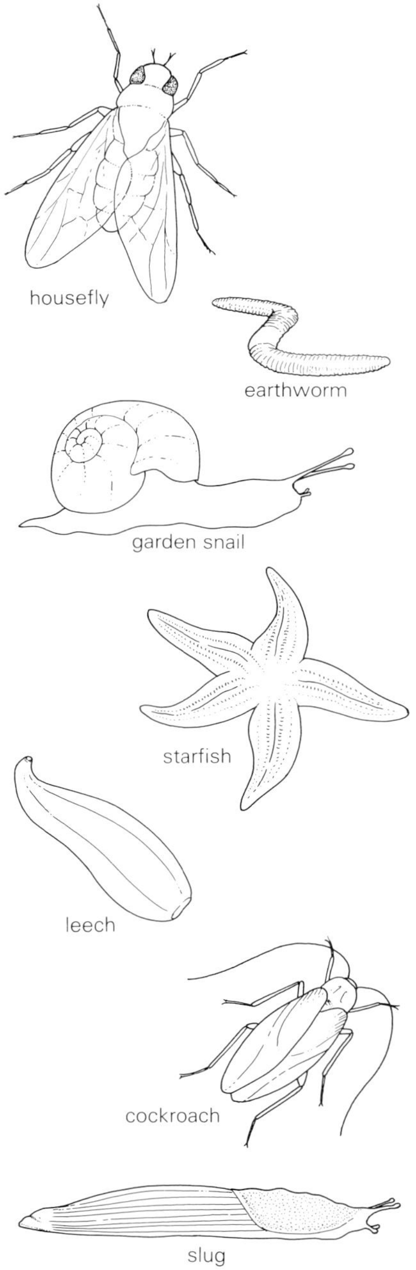

housefly

earthworm

garden snail

starfish

leech

cockroach

slug

Fig 3.12 Put these invertebrates into groups using the key.

4 Duckweed is a common plant of canals, lakes and ponds. Using the 'Key to plants and micro-organisms in aquarium tanks' (page 287) find the answers to the following questions:

a are duckweeds microscopic organisms?

b are duckweeds free-floating or rooted in the mud?

c what are the two main differences between common and ivy-leaved duckweeds *which are referred to in the key*?

d the scientific name for common duckweed is *Lemna minor* and, for ivy-leaved duckweed, *Lemna trisulca*. Does this tell you that common duckweed and ivy-leaved duckweed belong to the same (i) genus or (ii) species?

e a third kind of duckweed is quite common in the South and East of England. It is called *Lemna polyrhiza*. Using the pictures in the appendix and a dictionary, describe or sketch the possible appearance of this third species.

5 Make your own key to the animal or plant kingdom. Do this by obtaining suitable pictures from newspapers or magazines and using them to make a diagram similar to Fig 3.10 or Fig 3.11. If you have a camera, you could use photographs as illustrations.

Life in the past

Geologists believe that the planet Earth was formed about 4 600 million years ago. The first living organisms may have appeared about three thousand million years ago but the human race first walked the Earth only about one hundred thousand years ago. It may help you to understand these figures if you think of the history of the Earth in terms of a single year. On 1st January, the planet was formed and on 1st April the first primitive living organisms appeared. At 11.50 p.m. on 31st December, *Homo sapiens* emerged.

Our information about living organisms in the past comes mainly from the study of **fossils** – the remains of living organisms found

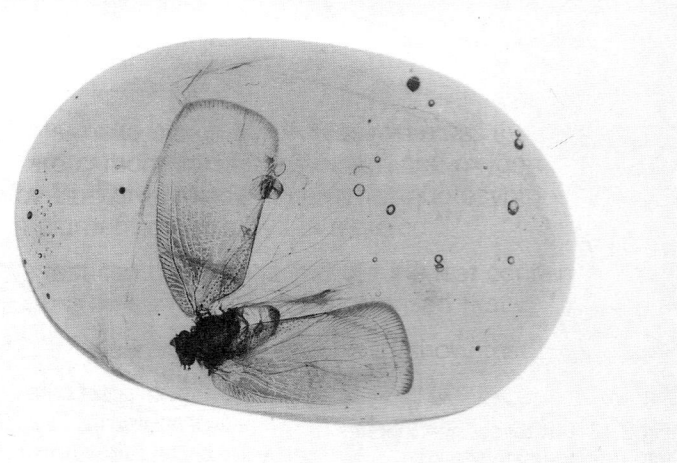

Fig 3.13 An insect trapped in amber.

in the rocks. The Background Reading which follows this section tells you how most fossils are formed. Animals and plants can also be preserved in other ways. Extinct mammoths have been discovered buried in the ice in Siberia and huge dragonflies have been found caught in the solidified sap (amber) of prehistoric tree (Fig 3.13).

Most scientists now agree that living organisms are constantly changing. This process, called **evolution**, means that the animals and plants which are around us today are very different from those which existed in the past.

Background Reading

Fossils

Fig 3.14 A fossil ammonite; this was once a water-living animal.

The vast majority of living things leave no trace of their existence after their passing. Their flesh *decays*, their shells and bones become scattered and turn to powder. Very occasionally, one or two individuals out of a *population* of many thousands have a different fate. A reptile becomes stuck in a swamp and dies. Its body rots but its bones settle in the mud. Dead vegetation drifts to the bottom and covers them. As the centuries pass and more vegetation accumulates, the deposit turns to peat. Changes in sea level may cause the swamp to be flooded and layers of sand to be deposited on top of the peat. Over great periods of time, the peat is compressed and turns to coal. The reptile's bones still remain within it. The great pressure of the overlying sediments and the mineral-rich solutions that circulate through them cause chemical changes in the calcium phosphate of the bones. Eventually they are turned to stone.

The most suitable places for fossilisation are in seas and lakes where *sedimentary* deposits such as sandstones and limestones are slowly accumulating. On land, where for the most part rocks are not built up by *deposition* but broken down by *erosion*, deposits, such as sand dunes, are only very rarely created and preserved. In consequence, the only land-living creatures likely to be fossilised are those that happen to fall into water. Since this is an exceptional fate for most of them, we are never likely to know from fossil evidence anything approaching the complete range of land creatures that has existed in the past. Water-living animals such as fish, molluscs, sea urchins and corals, are much more promising candidates for preservation. Even so, very few of these perished in the exact physical and chemical conditions necessary for fossilisation. Of those that did, only a tiny proportion happen to lie in the rocks that outcrop on the surface of the ground today; and of these few, most will be eroded away and destroyed before they are discovered by fossil hunters. The astonishment is that, in the face of these adverse odds, the fossils that have been collected are so numerous and the record they provide so detailed and coherent.

(From *Life on Earth* by David Attenborough, published by Collins/BBC.)

Questions

1 What is the meaning of the words in italics in the text?

2 What prevents the bones of the reptile from decaying?

3 Explain in your own words why water-dwelling animals are more frequently found in the fossil record than land animals.

4 Suggest one other way in which animals or plants can be preserved apart from fossilisation.

5 Find out, and report on, one of the following:
   a what fossils tell us about the first land animals
   b the coelacanth, a 'fossil' fish
   c the fossil record
   d the rise and fall of the dinosaurs.

Summary

1 Dividing things into groups is a process called **classification**.

2 The **kingdoms** are divided into main groups called **phyla**.

3 Each phylum is divided into sub-groups containing many **genera**.

4 Within each **genus** there are one or more individual **species**.

5 Each species is identified by two Latin names. The **first** refers to its **genus** and the **second** refers to the **species** itself.

6 **Keys** are used to find the names of species or the group to which they belong.

7 There are about 950 000 named species in the animal kingdom and about 340 000 named species in the plant kingdom.

Chapter 4   Microscopes and cells

To find out about the detailed structure of an animal or plant, we have to look at small pieces of its body under the **microscope**.

In this chapter we shall start by learning about the microscope, and then we shall use it to study the structure of some animals and plants.

Preparing specimens for viewing under the microscope

Usually a specimen that is to be viewed under the microscope is first placed in a drop of fluid on a rectangular piece of glass called a **slide**. It is then covered with another, much thinner, piece of glass called a **coverslip** (Fig 4.1). The coverslip flattens the specimen and prevents the fluid evaporating from underneath. When a specimen is prepared in this way, it is said to have been **mounted**.

The fluid in which the specimen is mounted may be pure water, or it may be some kind of stain. Transparent specimens are mounted in a stain because it helps them to show up. The disadvantage of using a stain is that it usually kills the specimen.

Sometimes the specimen is mounted in a transparent cement which sets hard. Specimens mounted in this way are called **permanent preparations**, and can be examined under the microscope years later.

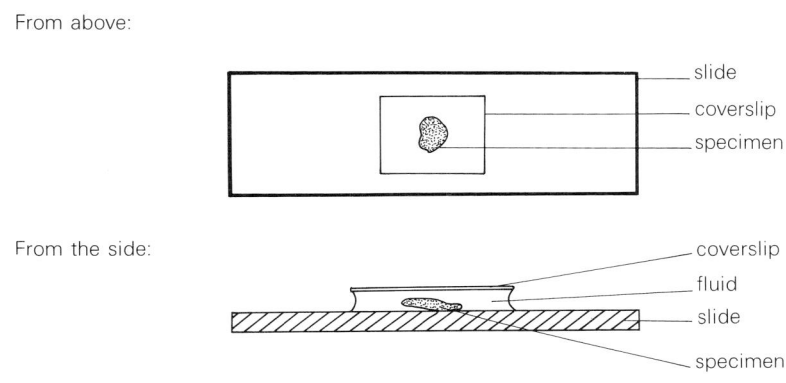

From above:

— slide
— coverslip
— specimen

From the side:

— coverslip
— fluid
— slide
— specimen

Fig 4.1 A specimen mounted on a slide ready for viewing under the microscope.

The microscope

A microscope can magnify objects much more than a simple hand lens can. It has two lenses, one above the other, and it has special devices for lighting and focusing the specimen.

A typical school microscope is shown in Fig 4.2. Not all microscopes are like this one. For example, some models have a built-in light under the stage.

Fig 4.2 A microscope of the kind that you may have in your school laboratory.

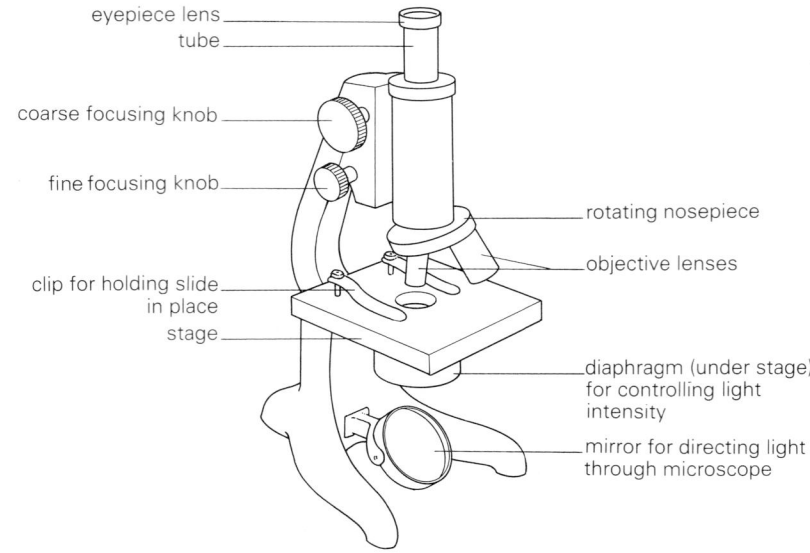

eyepiece lens
tube
coarse focusing knob
fine focusing knob
rotating nosepiece
objective lenses
clip for holding slide in place
stage
diaphragm (under stage) for controlling light intensity
mirror for directing light through microscope

Fig 4.3 Setting up a microscope.

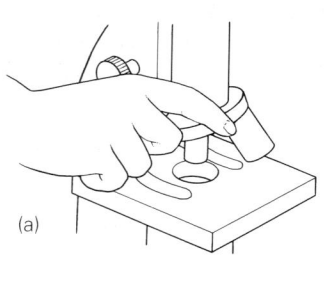

(a)

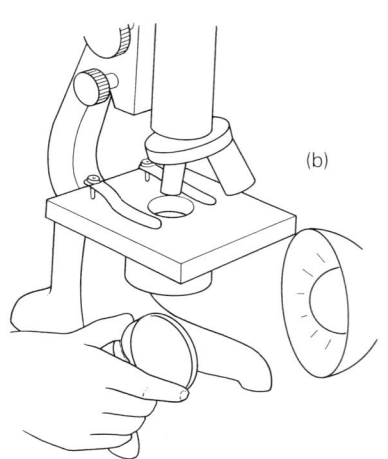

(b)

Experiment 4.1
Learning to use the microscope

Study your microscope carefully and find its various parts. Use Fig 4.2 to help you. Make sure you know the name of each part, and understand what it is for, before you start using the microscope.

Your teacher will give you a specimen which has been mounted on a slide. To set it up under the microscope, do this:

1 Rotate the nosepiece of your microscope so that the *small* objective lens is immediately above the centre of the stage: the nosepiece should click into position (Fig 4.3a).

2 Place a lamp in front of the microscope, and set the angle of the mirror so that the light is directed up through the microscope (Fig 4.3b).

⚠ If you are near a window, you may use daylight as a source of light but do not reflect sunlight through the microscope as this can damage your eyes.

3 Look down the microscope through the eyepiece. The round, bright area is called the **field of view**. Adjust the diaphragm so that the field of view is not too bright (Fig 4.3c).

Fig 4.3 Setting up a microscope (continued).

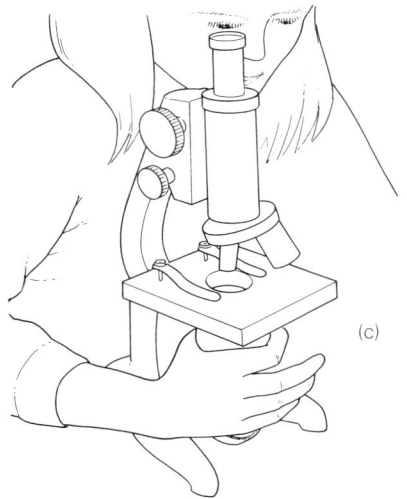

(c)

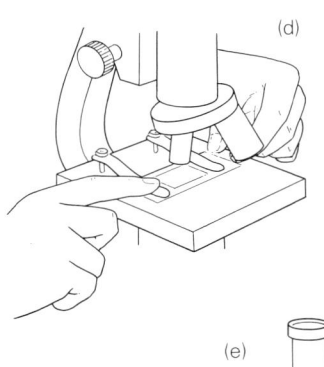

(d)

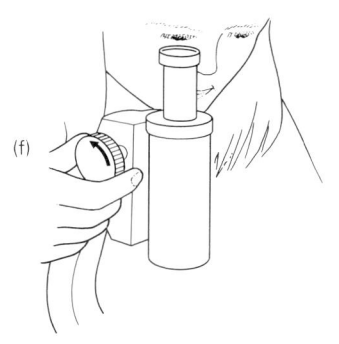

(e)

(f)

4 Place the slide on the stage. Arrange it so that the specimen is in the centre of the hole in the stage. When you have positioned the slide, fix it in place with the clips (Fig 4.3d).

5 *Look at the microscope from the side.* Turn the coarse focusing knob in the direction of the arrow in Fig 4.3e. We call this 'racking down': it moves the tube downwards. Continue turning the knob until the tip of the objective lens is about 10 mm from the coverslip.

6 Now look down the microscope again. Slowly turn the coarse focusing knob in the other direction. We call this 'racking up': it moves the tube upwards (Fig 4.3f). The specimen on the slide should soon come into view. Now use the fine focusing knob to focus the specimen as sharply as possible.

7 If necessary, re-adjust the diaphragm and the angle of the mirror so that the specimen is correctly lit. *You will get a much clearer picture if you do not have too much light coming through the microscope.*

You are now looking at the specimen under **low power**, i.e. at a low magnification. To look at it under **high power**, i.e. at a greater magnification, do this:

8 Rotate the nosepiece so that the *large* objective lens is immediately above the specimen (Fig 4.3g). The nosepiece should click into position as before. You will find that the lens is very close to the coverslip.

9 Look down the microscope. The specimen should be in focus, if it is not a very slight movement of the fine adjustment knob should bring it into focus (Fig 4.3h). If, having done this, you still cannot see the specimen, ask your teacher to help you.

10 If necessary, increase the lighting by opening the diaphragm or altering the angle of the mirror.

You are now looking at the specimen under high power. You will find that it appears much larger than under low power.

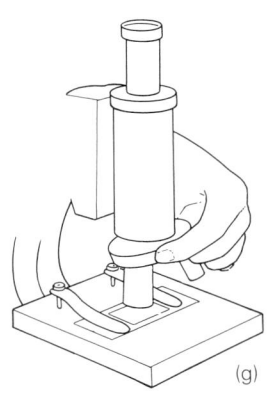

(g)

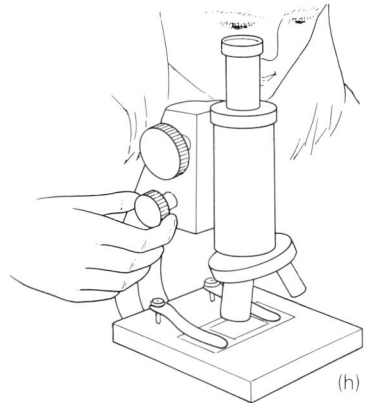

(h)

Important rules for using the microscope

1 Always treat the microscope with great care: it is an expensive instrument.

2 Carry it with *both* hands as shown in Fig 4.4, and put it down *gently* on the laboratory bench.

3 Cover the microscope when you are not using it.

4 Make sure the lenses never get scratched or damaged. Clean them with lens tissue only, *never* with a handkerchief.

5 Never rack downwards with the coarse adjustment knob while you are looking down the microscope.

6 When changing slides, make sure that the tip of the objective lens is well clear of the coverslip.

7 If you use daylight as a light source, *never* align the mirror with the Sun. It can harm your eye.

Questions for class discussion

1 When mounting a specimen, it is important not to put too much fluid on the slide. What would happen if you did, and what might the consequences be?

2 Why should you never rack downwards with the coarse focusing knob while you are looking down the microscope?

3 Suggest two reasons why it is a bad idea to have too much light coming through your microscope.

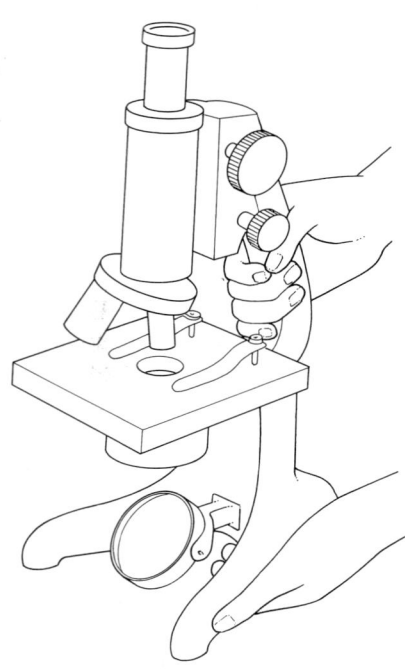

Fig 4.4 The right way to carry a microscope.

The magnifying power of the microscope

The magnification which can be achieved by your microscope is the magnifying power of the eyepiece multiplied by the magnifying power of the objective lens. The magnifying powers of the eyepiece and objectives are usually engraved on them. Find these and work out the magnification of your microscope on low and high powers.

Copy Table 4.1 and fill in the first three columns.

Table 4.1

	Magnifying power		Total magnification	Diameter of field of view
	Eyepiece lens	Objective lens		
Low power				
High power				

Experiment 4.2
Estimating the size of an object under the microscope

1 Place a transparent ruler, or graduated slide with a millimetre scale, on the stage of your microscope. Using the low-power objective lens, focus on to the lines on the scale.

2 Count how many millimetre divisions fit across the low-power field of view. What is the diameter of the low-power field of view in millimetres?

3 Now rotate the nosepiece so that the high-power objective lens is immediately above the scale. What is the approximate diameter of the high-power field of view to the nearest tenth of a millimetre?

4 Fill in the fourth column of your table of magnifications.

5 Remove a hair from your head, place it on a slide and look at it under low power. Estimate its width in millimetres.

Homework assignments

1 a If the magnifying power of the eyepiece of a microscope is ×10, and that of the high-power objective is ×40, what will be the total magnification which this microscope can achieve?
  b Suppose that a microscope has two objective lenses (×10 and ×40) and two alternative eyepieces (×6 and ×10). Write down the four different magnifications which this microscope can achieve. In each case show how you arrive at your answer.

2 A student tries to work out the diameter of the field of view of her microscope using a transparent ruler with a millimetre scale. Fig 4.5a shows what she sees when she looks at the ruler under the microscope. She then looks at a little animal under the microscope at the same magnification, and its appearance is shown in Fig 4.5b. Work out as accurately as possible:
  a the diameter of the field of view
  b the actual length of the animal.

3 Another student attempts to look at a specimen under the microscope, but he cannot see anything at all. Make a list of as many reasons as you can think of for his lack of success.

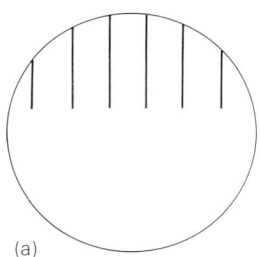
(a)

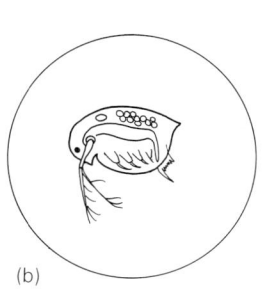
(b)

Fig 4.5 Measuring the size of an object under the microscope.

Cells

A house is made of bricks. In the same way, the bodies of animals and plants are made of **cells**. A cell is really more like a little box than a brick, and it contains some important structures which we will look at presently.

A fully grown human is made of about one hundred million million cells. If the body is made of so many cells, each individual cell must be very small. In fact they can only be seen with a microscope.

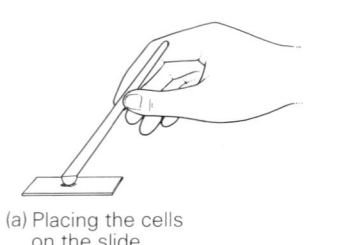

(a) Placing the cells
    on the slide

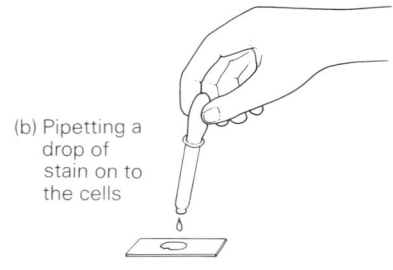

(b) Pipetting a
    drop of
    stain on to
    the cells

(c) Putting on
    the coverslip

Fig 4.6 The procedure for looking at
skin cells under the microscope.

Experiment 4.3
Looking at animal cells

1 Your teacher will tell you how to obtain some of your own skin
  cells. Alternatively you will be given some cells from the surface
  of an animal's skin. These cells are constantly flaking off the
  surface, so they are quite easy to obtain.

2 Place the cells on a clean microscope slide, as close to the
  centre as possible (Fig 4.6a).

3 With a pipette, add a drop of 0.5 per cent methylene blue
  solution to the cells on the slide (Fig 4.6b). This will stain the
  cells and help to show them up.

4 Carefully cover the cells with a coverslip. Support one side of
  the coverslip with a finger, and lower the other side with a
  needle (Fig 4.6c). If you lower the coverslip gently, you will not
  get any air bubbles underneath.

5 Examine your slide under the low power of the microscope.
  Can you see lots of semi-transparent objects each with a blob
  inside? Each semi-transparent object is a cell. The blob is oval in
  shape, rather like a rugby football.

6 Now look at one of the cells under high power. Make a careful
  drawing of it in pencil. Do not use colour and do not label it for
  the moment. If you cannot see the cells very well, then look at
  the skin cells in Fig 4.7.

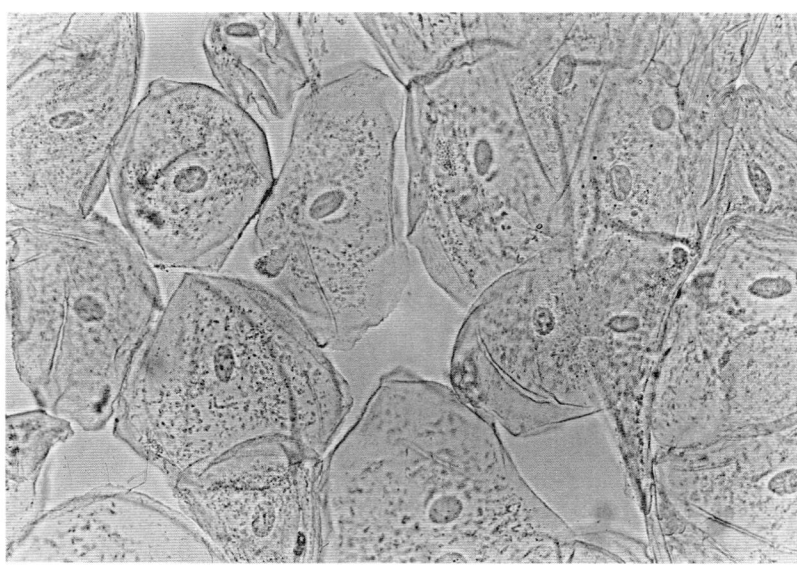

Fig 4.7 Skin cells as they appear
under the microscope, high power.

Questions for class discussion

1 Some of the cells which you have been looking at may appear
  crumpled. What does this tell us about them?

2 Your teacher may have taken some cells from the surface of an animal's skin to do this experiment. Do you think this would harm a living animal? If not, why not?

The structure of a typical animal cell

The cells you have just looked at are typical animal cells. The main parts of a typical animal cell are shown in Fig 4.8.

The **cell membrane** (also known as the **cell surface membrane**) forms a very thin covering to the cell. It controls what enters and leaves the cell: it allows oxygen and dissolved food substances to get in and waste substances to get out.

The **cytoplasm** makes up most of the inside of the cell. In the cytoplasm, many important chemical reactions take place. Some of these reactions transfer energy which helps to keep the cell alive. If you look at the cytoplasm carefully under the microscope, you will see that it contains numerous tiny dots. We call these **granules**: some of them consist of stored food.

The **nucleus** is the dark blob in the centre of the cell. It is the control centre of the cell, regulating everything that goes on inside it. The nucleus contains structures called **chromosomes**; they are made up of **genes** which are passed from parents to offspring. The genes determine the person's features such as the colour of his or her eyes.

Now that you know the parts of a typical animal cell, label your drawing of the skin cell.

Experiment 4.4
Estimating the size of a cell

To do this experiment you will need to know the width (that is, the diameter) of the high-power field of view of your microscope. This is explained in Experiment 4.2 (page 39). You can use your slide from Experiment 4.3 for this experiment, or your teacher may give you a prepared slide.

1 Locate a cell which has a regular shape, and look at it under high power.

2 As accurately as possible, estimate how many cells of this size would fit side-by-side across the diameter of the field of view.

3 Knowing the diameter of the field of view, work out the width in millimetres of the cell.

4 Look back at your drawing of a skin cell and with a ruler measure its width in millimetres. How many times wider is your drawing than the actual cell? This figure is the magnification of your drawing. Write the figure underneath your drawing with a times sign (×) in front of it. You have now given your drawing a scale.

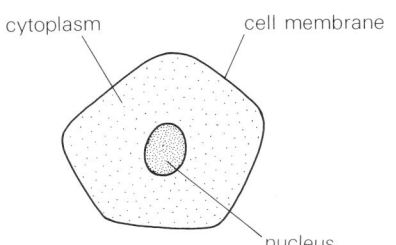
cytoplasm   cell membrane

nucleus

Fig 4.8 A typical animal cell.

Expressing the size of a cell

A typical animal cell is approximately one fiftieth of a millimetre wide. It is awkward to express such a short distance as a fraction of a millimetre, and so a smaller unit is used. This is called a **micrometre**. A micrometre is one millionth of a metre; since there are a thousand millimetres in a metre, it is one thousandth of a millimetre. If a cell is one fiftieth of a millimetre wide, what is its width in micrometres? The answer, of course, is 20 micrometres. The abbreviation for a millimetre is mm, and for a micrometre is μm.

A typical cell is $\frac{1}{50}$ mm wide, which is 20 μm.

Look again at your drawing of the skin cell. What is the width of the actual cell in millimetres? Convert this to micrometres and write it under your drawing.

Experiment 4.5
Looking at moss cells

You will need a piece of moss which has been carefully pulled away from a path or wall.

1 Take off one of the little leaves. Place the leaf on a slide and add a drop of water to it. Cover it with a coverslip.

2 Look at the leaf under the low power of the microscope. Can you see that it is composed of numerous cells which are arranged rather like bricks in a wall?

3 Examine one cell under high power. Make a drawing of it in pencil. Do not label it yet.

4 Estimate the scale of your drawing, and write this under the drawing.

5 Work out the length of the actual cell in micrometres, and write it under the drawing.

6 With the fine adjustment knob, rack up half a turn and then down half a turn. How does the appearance of the cell change as you rack up and down? What does this tell you about the three-dimensional shape of the cell?

Questions for class discussion

1 Compare your drawings of the skin cell and the moss cell.
  a Which one is larger?
  b How do they differ in shape?
  c What structures could you see in the moss cell which were not visible in the skin cell?

2 You were probably unable to see a nucleus in the moss cell. Suggest reasons for this.

The structure of a typical plant cell

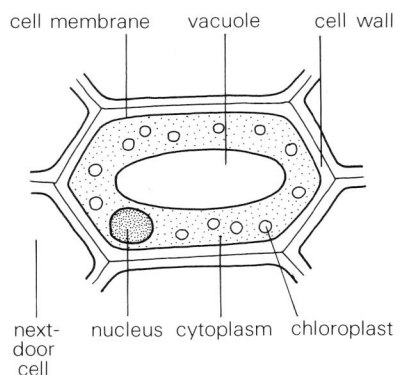

Fig 4.9 A typical plant cell.

A typical plant cell has the cell membrane, cytoplasm and nucleus typical of animal cells. However, it has three extra structures which are found *only* in plant cells. These are chloroplasts, a vacuole and a cell wall (Fig 4.9).

The **chloroplasts** contain a green substance called **chlorophyll**. This is what makes leaves and stems look green. Chlorophyll is needed for the process by which plants make food. We call this process **photosynthesis**.

The **vacuole** is a large space in the centre of the cell. It is filled with a watery fluid containing sugar and salts.

The **cell wall** is situated outside the cell membrane. It is much thicker and tougher than the cell membrane and is made of a substance called **cellulose**. Cellulose is important to us because paper and various other products are made from it.

Now that you know the structure of a typical plant cell, label your drawing of the moss cell.

Question for class discussion

Although chloroplasts are found in many plant cells, they are not always present. Suggest two places in a dandelion plant where you would *not* expect to find chloroplasts in the cells.

Homework assignments

1 Copy out Table 4.2. Put a tick in the box if the structure listed on the left is present, and a cross if it is not.

Table 4.2

	Typical animal cell, e.g., skin cell	Typical plant cell, e.g., moss leaf cell
Cell membrane Cell wall Chloroplasts Cytoplasm Nucleus Vacuole		

2 Which of the structures listed in the previous question
  a provides us with a source of paper
  b is the control centre of the cell
  c carries out photosynthesis
  d releases energy to help keep the cell alive
  e is filled with a watery fluid?

3 Fig 4.10 shows a group of cells.
  a Name the structures labelled A, B and C.
  b Are the cells from an animal or a plant?
  c Give three reasons to support your answer to **b**.

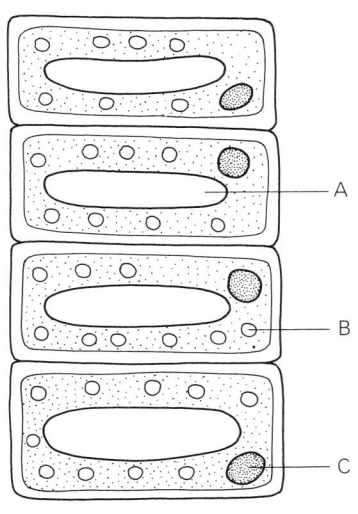

Fig 4.10

4 A student observes a cell down the microscope and estimates it to be $\frac{1}{100}$ mm wide.

a What is the cell's width in micrometres (μm)?

b Why is it better to express its width in micrometres rather than millimetres?

c The student draws the cell, and the width of the drawing is 25 mm. What is the scale of the drawing?

Different cells for different jobs

The skin cells which you looked at earlier are just one kind of cell found in an animal's body. These particular cells help to protect the various structures underneath. This is their job or **function**.

There are many other kinds of cells in the body, and each one has a particular job to do. For example, the brain contains cells which transmit electrical messages from place to place, a muscle is made up of cells which can shorten and so move the animal, and blood contains cells which carry oxygen round the body.

The same principle applies to plants. For example, most of the cells in a leaf contain chloroplasts and carry out photosynthesis: they are responsible for feeding the plant. In contrast, cells in the root do not have chloroplasts: they carry out the important job of taking up water and mineral salts from the soil.

In spite of these differences, all cells have the same basic structure. For example, all cells have cytoplasm and a cell membrane and nearly all have a nucleus.

The special features of a particular kind of cell can usually be related to its job. Or, putting it another way, the cell is adapted to carry out its functions. For example, nerve cells have thin, thread-like extensions which in some cases may be several metres long. Messages pass rapidly along these extensions (Fig 4.11).

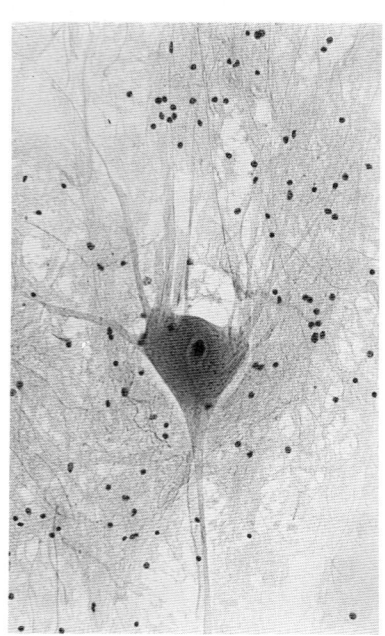

Fig 4.11 A nerve cell in the brain, as seen under the microscope. Notice the thread-like extensions projecting from the main part of the cell. Other cells also do special jobs, for example the ciliated epithelial cell (page 47), sperm cell and egg cell (page 61), leaf palisade cell (page 91) and root hair cell (page 93).

Questions for class discussion

1 In what ways is the cell in Fig 4.11 similar to, and different from, the skin cells in Fig 4.7?

2 The scale in Fig 4.11 is x180. What is the actual size of the cell?

Safety note

Wash your hands carefully with soap and water after collecting animals and plants.

Experiment 4.6
Looking at small organisms under the microscope

We have seen how the microscope can be used to study cells. It can also be used to study little organisms which are too small to be seen with the naked eye or magnifying glass.

1 Obtain a jam jar of water from the bottom of a pond or ditch: the muddier the better.

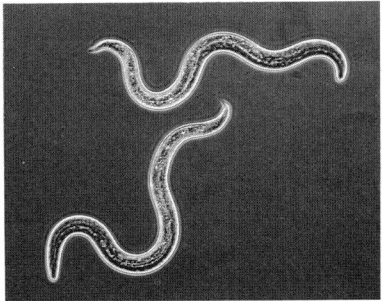

(a) Roundworm (2–5 mm)

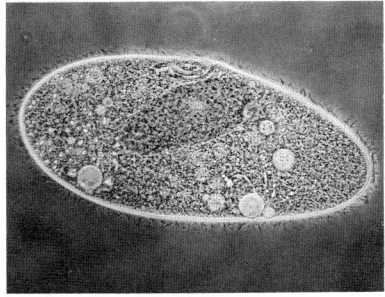

(b) *Paramecium* (250 μm)

Fig 4.12 Some small pond water organisms which you might see under your microscope. The approximate length of each organism is given after their name.

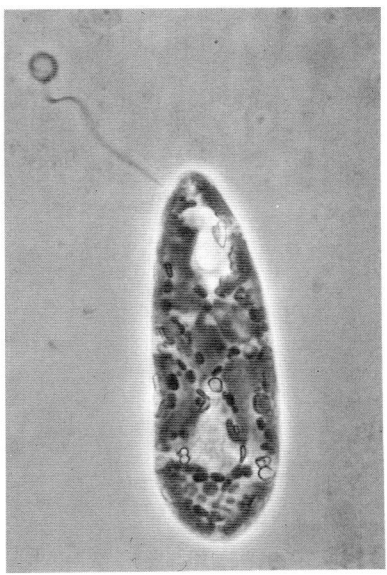

(c) *Euglena* (40 μm)

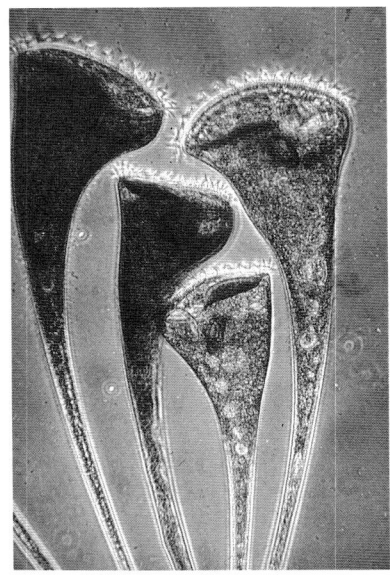

(d) *Stentor* (250 μm)

2 Place a drop of the water on a slide and cover it with a coverslip.

3 Examine it under the microscope, low power first, then high power. Can you see any small organisms swimming around? Fig 4.12 shows some of the organisms which you may see under the microscope.

Single-celled organisms

Some of the little organisms shown in Fig 4.12 consist of only one cell. There are many kinds of single-celled organisms and some of them live in ponds and ditches. Other kinds live inside the bodies of organisms: they feed on the living material inside the body and may do a great deal of harm. The disease **malaria** is caused by a single-celled organism which lives in the human bloodstream. These single-celled organisms therefore matter a lot to humans.

Another, quite different, group of single-celled organisms are **bacteria**. They have a simple kind of cell structure, without a proper nucleus. Some of them cause diseases, but others are very useful.

Perhaps the most famous single-celled organism is yeast. This is a type of fungus. Why is it famous? The answer is that it produces ethanol (alcohol).

The single-celled organisms can only be seen with a microscope. Such organisms are called **micro-organisms** or just **microbes**. They help to maintain the balance of nature and are important to humans in all sorts of ways. There is more about them in Chapter 19.

How do cells multiply?

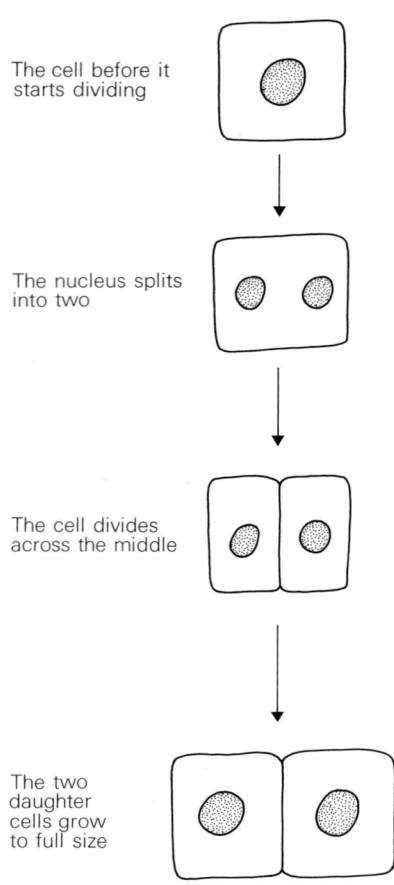

The cell before it starts dividing

The nucleus splits into two

The cell divides across the middle

The two daughter cells grow to full size

Fig 4.13 How a cell divides.

When an animal or plant grows, it gets larger. To enable the organism to increase in size, its cells divide as shown in Fig 4.13. First the nucleus splits into two and then the cell divides across the middle. This is called **cell division**. The two cells resulting from the division are called **daughter cells**. The daughter cells now grow to their full size, after which each one may divide again. The result will be a total of four cells, and if each of these then divides again there will be eight cells – and so on.

How can you tell if a cell has just divided? You can usually tell from the sizes of the daughter cells: they will be smaller than a full grown cell of the same kind. A good place to see cells that have just divided is in a simple water weed.

Experiment 4.7
Looking at divided cells in a water weed

The water weed you will look at consists of long slimy threads. It is found in ponds and slow-flowing rivers where it occurs in clumps.

1 With a pair of tweezers place a few threads of the water weed on a slide, together with a drop of water, and cover it with a coverslip.

2 Look at the threads under the microscope, low power first then high power. Notice that each thread is divided up into a series of compartments. Each compartment is a cell (Fig 4.14). The cells look green because they contain chloroplasts.

3 Compare the sizes of the cells. You may find that some are shorter than others. If you find two short cells side by side, they were probably formed by a larger cell dividing into two. This kind of cell division enables the threads to get longer; in other words, it results in growth.

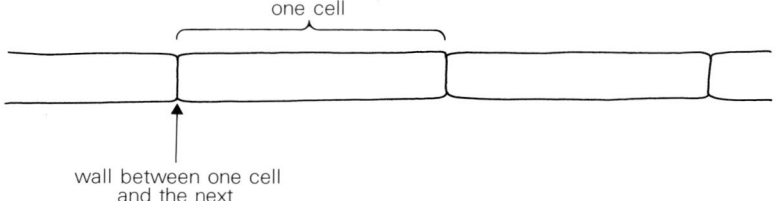

one cell

wall between one cell and the next

Fig 4.14 Part of one thread of a water weed.

Tissues

When you looked at animal cells under the microscope you may have noticed that some of the cells, instead of being on their own, fitted together like 'crazy paving'. In most organisms cells

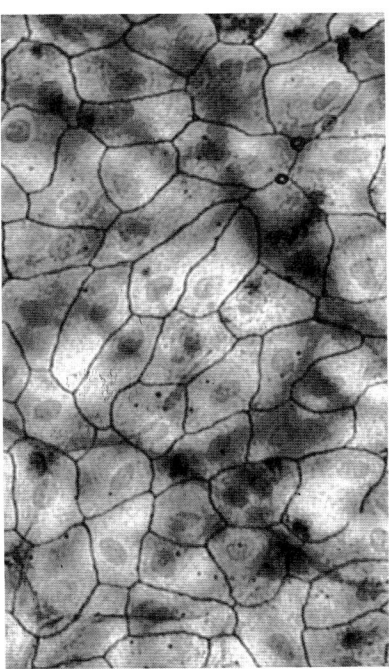

Fig 4.15 Epithelial tissue from a cat, as seen under the microscope (low power). The cells fit together like crazy paving. Notice the nucleus inside each cell.

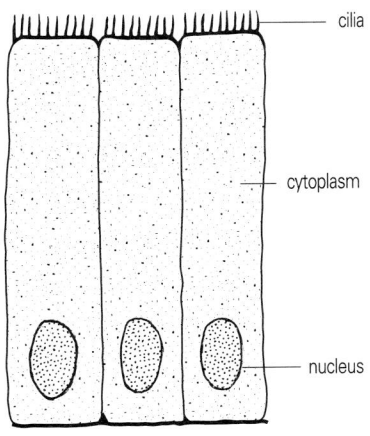

Fig 4.16 Ciliated epithelial cells.

are massed together in this kind of way. The mass of cells is called a **tissue**.

There are many different types of tissue. The function of each type depends on the kind of cells it is made of. The type of tissue at the surface of an animal's skin is called **epithelial tissue**. This kind of tissue is also found lining the various organs inside the body (Fig 4.15). In plants, a similar tissue lines the leaves, stems and other parts. It is called **epidermal tissue**.

Questions for class discussion

1 What functions do you think are carried out by the epithelial tissue in the skin of a frog or toad, and by the epidermal tissue at the surface of a holly leaf?

2 By using your imagination and/or by reading books, suggest one other type of tissue (besides epithelial tissue) which occurs in animals. What kind of cells would you expect it to be made of, and what functions would it carry out?

3 Our breathing passages are lined with a special kind of epithelial tissue called **ciliated epithelium**. The cells bear tiny, hair-like **cilia** at one end (Fig 4.16). The cilia beat by moving backwards and forwards, rather like the oars of a rowing boat. Their job is to sweep germs and dust particles away from the lungs, thereby protecting the lungs from infection and damage.
   a In what ways is a ciliated epithelial cell in one of our breathing passages adapted to carry out its function?
   b In order to move particles in one direction, i.e. away from the lungs and not towards them, how would the cilia have to beat?
   c The little organism in Fig 4.12(b) (*Paramecium*) is covered with cilia – you can see them in the photograph. It uses them for swimming through the water. How do the cilia enable the organism to swim?

What happens inside cells?

Inside cells all sorts of chemical reactions take place. Together these reactions make up **metabolism**. Some of the reactions provide energy for the organism's activities, they are called **respiration** (see page 195); others make chemical substances and structures which are needed for growth or for replacing worn-out parts of the body.

The reactions which take place inside organisms are speeded up by special substances called **enzymes**. They are rather like catalysts which you have met in chemistry. Without an enzyme, a reaction could take hours to complete. But if the right enzyme is present, it may take only seconds.

Enzymes belong to a group of chemical substances called proteins (see page 182). As proteins, they have a number of important properties. One is that they are destroyed by heating: if the temperature rises much above 40°C they stop working.

Another important property of enzymes is that they are readily affected by poisons. For example, cyanide stops the action of an enzyme which catalyses one of the reactions which transfers energy in our cells. This is why cyanide is a very dangerous poison.

Most of our enzymes are inside cells, which is where metabolism takes place. However, enzymes also occur in the gut where they play an important part in digesting food. We shall return to this in Chapter 15.

Questions for class discussion

1 How do you think human life would change if all our enzymes worked at half their normal speed?

2 Enzymes not only speed up the chemical reactions which take place inside cells, but they also control them. How do you think enzymes *control* the reactions, and why is this necessary?

Making use of enzymes

Enzymes are used in industry to make certain reactions take place. As a result, useful substances can be produced. Often the enzymes are present in micro-organisms such as bacteria and yeast.

Take yeast, for example. This organism contains enzymes which turn sugar into ethanol. Why this happens is explained on page 198. The process is called **fermentation**. The brewing industry uses yeast to produce beer and other alcoholic drinks. See *Chemistry 11–14*, page 20–21.

A by-product of alcoholic fermentation is carbon dioxide gas. This is made use of by the baking industry in making bread. The gas given off by the yeast makes the dough rise.

Another use for enzymes is in biological washing powders. These particular enzymes break down proteins. They help to remove things like soup stains and blood from people's washing (Fig 4.17).

These are examples of how enzymes can be used. It is part of **biotechnology**, one of our most rapidly expanding industries. In some cases the enzymes are extracted from living organisms, purified and then used in the manufacturing process. In other cases, the enzymes are left inside the organisms, and the organisms themselves are used. There is more about biotechnology in Chapter 19.

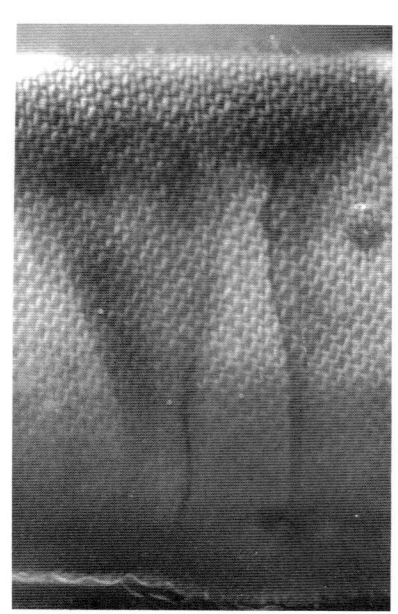

Fig 4.17 Bio-detergent digesting a blood stain.

Background Reading

How cells were discovered

Cells were discovered in the 17th century by an English scientist, Robert Hooke. In the following passage, Hooke explains how he made his discovery. Below is a reproduction of Hooke's orginal drawing of cork cells.

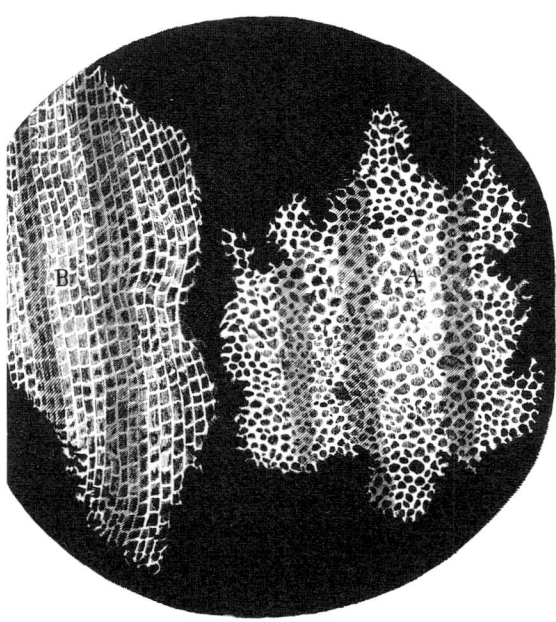

Fig 4.18 Robert Hooke's drawing of cork cells.

'I took a good clear piece of cork, and with a Penknife sharpen'd as keen as a Razor, I cut a piece of it off, and thereby left the surface of it exceedingly smooth, then examining it very diligently with a Microscope methought I could perceive it to appear a little porous: but I could not so plainly distinguish them, as to be sure that they were pores ... I with the same sharp Penknife, cut off from the former smooth surface an exceeding thin piece of it, and placing it on a black object Plate, because it was itself a white body, and casting the light on it with a deep plano-convex Glass, I could exceedingly plainly perceive it to be all perforated and porous, much like a Honeycomb, but that the pores of it were not regular ... these pores, or cells, were not very deep, but consisted of a great many little Boxes ... Nor is this kind of texture peculiar to Cork only; for upon examination with my Microscope, I have found that the pith of an Elder, or almost any other Tree, the inner pulp or pith of the Cany hollow stalks of several other Vegetables: as of Fennel, Carrets, ... Teasels, Fearn ... etc. have much such a kind of Schematisme, as I have lately shewn that of Cork.'

(From *Micrographia* by Robert Hooke, published by the Wellcome Trustees.)

Questions

1 Why do you think Hooke chose cork for examination under the microscope?

2 How do the cork cells in his drawing differ from the animal cells shown in Fig 4.7? Why do you think they are different?

3 Hooke described his cells as 'pores' and as 'boxes'. Which word is the better one, and why? (Hint: look up 'pore' in a dictionary.)

Summary

1 We use a **microscope** for looking at organisms, or parts of organisms, which are too small to be seen with the unaided eye or hand lens.

2 When observing a specimen under the microscope, it is important to know the **magnification** and to record the **scale**.

3 A typical animal cell contains **cytoplasm** and a **nucleus** and is surrounded by a **cell membrane**. It is approximately $\frac{1}{50}$ mm wide (20 μm).

4 A typical plant cell has cytoplasm, a nucleus and cell membrane, plus **chloroplasts**, a **vacuole** and **cellulose cell wall**.

5 A complex organism such as the human contains millions of cells. Different kinds of cells carry out different jobs.

6 Cells of a particular kind may be massed together to form a **tissue**.

7 Cells multiply by splitting into two (**cell division**).

8 Many organisms exist which can be seen only under a microscope. Some of these organisms consist of only one cell.

9 Many chemical reactions take place inside cells. They are speeded up by **enzymes**.

10 Enzymes are used in industry, for example in brewing and baking.

Chapter 5   **Asexual reproduction**

Reproduction is the process by which an organism produces new individuals (offspring). Cell division, which we studied in the last chapter, is the basis of reproduction.

In humans and many other organisms reproduction involves two individuals, the male and the female. We call this sexual reproduction. However, some organisms can reproduce on their own without another individual. We call this **asexual reproduction**. In this chapter, we shall look at some of the methods by which organisms reproduce asexually.

Splitting in two

Amoeba is a single-celled organism which lives in ponds and puddles (see page 251). It reproduces by splitting in two. We call this **binary fission** (*fission* means 'splitting' and *binary* means 'two'). The process is just like cell division described in the previous chapter (page 46): first the nucleus divides into two, and then the cell splits across the middle as shown in Fig 5.1. The two new amoebas then grow, and after a day or so each of them may split again.

Questions for class discussion

1 When it is warm and plenty of food is available, *Amoeba* may split once every 24 hours. Dividing at this rate, how many amoebae could be formed from a single amoeba after seven days?

2 Bacteria also multiply by cell division but they do so much faster than *Amoeba*: in good conditions division may occur once every 20 minutes. At this rate, how many cells would be formed from a single bacterial cell after 24 hours?

Budding

Yeast reproduces by **budding**. The cell sends out a small outgrowth which gets larger and eventually breaks away from the

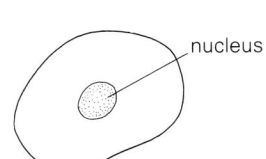
the cell rounds off

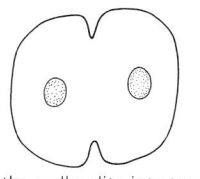
the cell splits into two

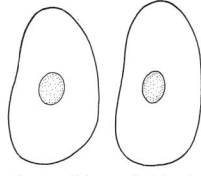
the cell has divided into two daughter cells

Fig 5.1 *Amoeba* reproduces asexually by dividing into two.

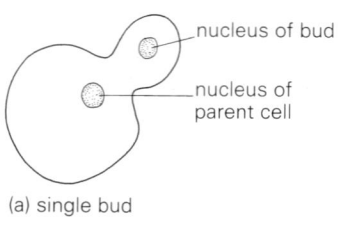

(a) single bud

(b) a chain

Fig 5.2 Yeast cells budding.

parent cell (Fig 5.2a). Meanwhile the nucleus divides into two. One of the two resulting nuclei stays in the parent cell, and the other one moves into the bud.

Sometimes the new cell starts budding before it has broken away from the parent cell, thus giving rise to a chain of cells as shown in Fig 5.2b.

Experiment 5.1
Observing yeast budding

1 Pour a ten per cent solution of glucose into a test-tube until it is three-quarters full.

2 Add a pinch of yeast to the test-tube and shake well. The cells will separate from the solid yeast and form a suspension in the glucose solution. Leave your test-tube in a warm place overnight.

3 Next day shake the test-tube, then transfer a drop of the yeast suspension on to a slide. Put on a coverslip. Examine the drop under the microscope, low power first, then high power. Can you see any yeast cells with buds? Make a drawing of a budding yeast cell.

Question for class discussion

When you put yeast cells and glucose together, the yeast cells multiply quickly. In what way is this useful to brewers?

Spores

A mushroom is also a fungus, but a very different one from yeast. Mushrooms, like many other fungi, reproduce by means of **spores**. A spore is a tiny round cell enclosed within a thick protective wall. The wall enables the spore to withstand unfavourable conditions such as frost and drought.

The spore is like a tiny speck of dust and is so light that it can float through the air. If it lands in a suitable place it breaks open and gives rise to a new fungus.

Experiment 5.2
To see the spores produced by a mushroom or toadstool

1 Your teacher will give you a fully grown mushroom or toadstool with a large flat cap. Look at the underside of the cap. Can you see a series of delicate brown membranes fanning out from the stalk, like the spokes of a bicycle wheel? The spores are formed on these membranes (Fig 5.3).

2 Cut off the stalk as high up as possible. Place the cap, lower surface downwards, on a sheet of white paper. Cover it with a dish, and leave it for two or three days.

Some mushrooms and toadstools are poisonous, so wash your hands thoroughly with soap and water after handling them.

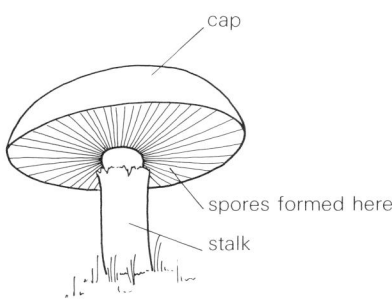

Fig 5.3 The spore-forming body of a mushroom or toadstool.

3 After two or three days remove the dish and carefully lift up the cap. Can you see any spores on the sheet of paper? Approximately how many are there? What you have produced is a **spore print**.

4 With a dry paintbrush, transfer a few spores to a slide. Add a drop of water and put on a coverslip. Examine the spores under the low power of the microscope. Make a rough estimate of the width of one of the spores (see page 39).

5 Make your spore print permanent by spraying it lightly with varnish. You can then stick it in your notebook.

Questions for class discussion

1 Spores are formed by these three main groups of organisms: fungi, mosses and ferns. As well as providing a method of reproduction, spores enable the species to spread rapidly over a wide area. How do they achieve this?

2 Some serious diseases of crop plants such as wheat are caused by fungi. Once they get into the crop they are very difficult to get rid of. Why do you think this is?

Tubers

The potato plant forms underground **tubers** which rest in the soil during the winter and produce new plants the next year.

The tuber is the familiar 'potato' which people eat. It is full of stored food which is made by the leaves of the parent plant during the summer. In the autumn, the leaves and stem of the parent plant die, but the tubers remain in the soil until the following spring. Then each one may sprout into a new potato plant.

Tubers enable potato plants to reproduce asexually. They also enable the species to survive the winter so that potato plants can grow up again year after year.

Experiment 5.3
Examining a potato tuber

1 You may have heard people talk about the 'eyes' of a potato. They are shown in Fig 5.4. Can you see any 'eyes' on your potato tuber? Each one is a very small bud which is capable of sprouting into a new potato plant.

You will also see little black specks dotted about over the skin of the potato. These are little holes called **lenticels** which allow air to get through the skin so that the tuber can breathe.

2 Cut a potato tuber in two. With a knife, scrape away a little of the white pulp and put it on a slide. Add a drop of dilute iodine solution to the pulp, and cover it with a coverslip.

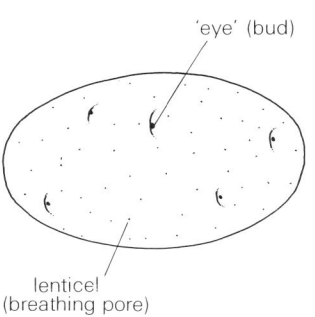

Fig 5.4 A potato tuber.

3 Look at the potato pulp under the microscope. Do you see a lot of dark blue, egg-shaped objects? These are **starch grains**.

4 Keep another potato in the window of your laboratory. You may find that eventually leafy shoots start growing out of it.

Questions for class discussion

1 Where did the starch in the potato tuber come from? What will happen to it eventually?

2 What disadvantages has the method of reproduction used by potato tubers compared with reproduction by spores?

3 As well as providing a means of reproduction, potato tubers are useful to the plant for another reason. What is this reason?

4 What is it about potatoes that makes them so suitable as a food for humans?

Experiment 5.4
Growing potatoes

You will need a 'seed' potato which is just beginning to sprout.

1 Remove all the shoots except one. Rub them off with your thumb or finger (Fig 5.5).

2 Plant the tuber in a large pot of well watered soil mixed with compost. The tuber should be covered by about 10 cm of soil, and the shoot should be pointing upwards. Put the pot in a well lit place.

3 When the young plant is about 15 cm high, spread some compost on the soil so that it covers the buds at the bottom of the stem (Fig 5.6). These buds will then produce underground branches which will swell up to form young tubers ('new potatoes').

4 Loosen the soil every now and again, and water it regularly. Add more compost every few weeks so as to keep the lowest buds well covered.

5 After about two months dig the plant up carefully and wash the soil off the roots and tubers. How many new tubers has the potato plant produced? Can you see the remains of the old tuber? What does it look like now?

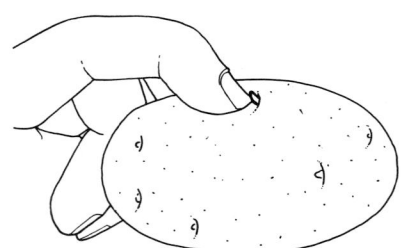

Fig 5.5 Rubbing unwanted shoots off a potato tuber.

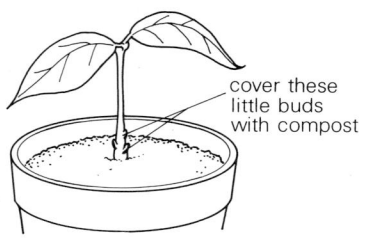

cover these little buds with compost

Fig 5.6 How to encourage a potato plant to form tubers.

Questions for class discussion

1 Why should you remove most of the shoots from the tuber before you plant it?

2 Why is it important to loosen the soil every now and again?

3 When potatoes are grown out of doors, the tubers should be planted at least 30 cm apart. Why?

Bulbs

Daffodils, onions, hyacinths and many other plants can reproduce and survive the winter as **bulbs**. A bulb is like a tuber in that it contains a store of food. However, its structure is more complicated. It can sprout into a new plant, and it can also give rise to new bulbs.

Experiment 5.5
Examining a bulb

You will need two bulbs: onions are suitable.

1 Slice one of the bulbs lengthways, and the other one crossways (Fig 5.7). How does the inside of the bulb differ from that of the potato? What part of the plant do you think the bulb is formed from?

2 In the centre of the bulb there is a small bud which will sprout into a new onion plant. Can you see the bud in your sliced bulbs?

3 A bulb is capable of producing new bulbs. If you look at a daffodil bulb you can sometimes see small 'daughter' bulbs attached to the side of the parent bulb.

4 Fill a milk bottle with water and place a daffodil bulb on top of it so that the roots dangle in the water. Put it in a warm, well lit place. Watch it at intervals during the next few weeks and describe what happens.

Question for class discussion

When you sliced your bulb in half crossways, did you notice that it consists of a series of 'rings'? These are actually leaves. In what ways do they differ from normal leaves? Explain the reasons for the differences.

Experiment 5.6
Growing daffodils from bulbs

You will need a 'prepared' bulb and a pot of good, well watered soil mixed with compost.

1 Push the bulb into the soil. The top of the bulb should be about 4 cm below the surface of the soil.

2 Place the pot in a well lit place, and observe it every day for the next few weeks. Water the soil regularly. Record what happens in your notebook.

3 After about two months dig the plant up carefully and wash the soil off the bulb. What does the bulb look like now?

Be very careful not to cut yourself when using a sharp knife.

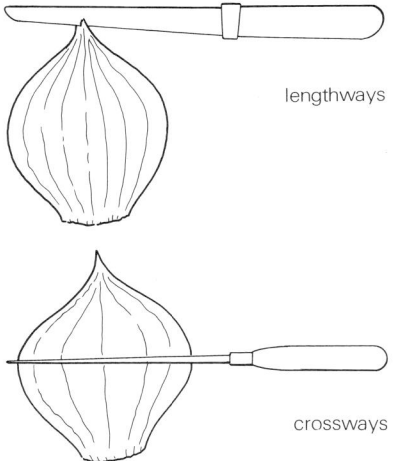

lengthways

crossways

Fig 5.7 How to slice a bulb to see its internal structure.

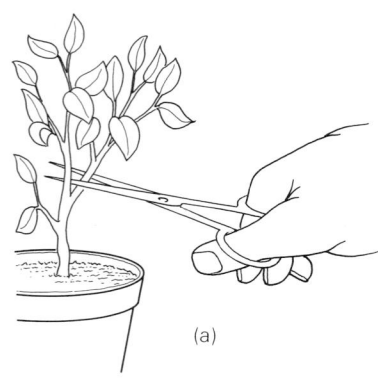

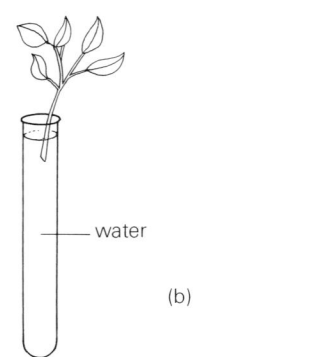

— water

(b)

Fig 5.8 How to take a cutting of a Busy Lizzie plant.

Fig 5.9 How to plant a Busy Lizzie cutting.

Questions for class discussion

1 Covering the bulb with soil when you plant it ensures that it will be in the dark. This causes roots to grow down into the soil before the shoot starts developing. Why is this desirable?

2 Many plants which flower in the spring have bulbs. Can you suggest why?

3 A bulb will generally produce a flowering shoot only if it is first subjected to a period of cold.
a Why do you think this is?
b Describe an experiment to find out how low the temperature has to be before the bulb will produce a shoot.

4 Suggest three uses that humans make of bulbs. In each case give at least one example.

Cuttings

If a side branch of a plant is cut off and stuck into some soil or compost, roots may grow out of it so that it becomes a new plant. This is called a **cutting**.

Gardeners often take cuttings of plants which they particularly like. However, not all plants will grow from cuttings.

Experiment 5.7
Taking cuttings of Busy Lizzie

Busy Lizzie is a plant from which it is particularly easy to take cuttings. You will need a test-tube in a rack, and a pair of scissors.

1 Cut off a side branch from the Busy Lizzie plant, cutting cleanly with a sharp pair of scissors. (Fig 5.8a). If possible choose a branch with no flowers on it. This is your cutting.

2 Fill the test-tube with water almost to the top, and stick your cutting into it as shown in Fig 5.8b. Put it in a warm, well lit place, and leave it for a week or two. Top up the test-tube with water when necessary.

3 Observe your cutting every day. Watch for roots growing out of it. How long does it take for the first roots to appear? What part of the cutting do the roots grow from?

4 When several roots have grown out, remove the cutting from the test-tube and plant it in a pot of moist compost: make a hole in the compost with your finger, and carefully stick the cutting into it as shown in Fig 5.9. Press the soil round the cutting, taking care not to damage the roots. Leave it in a warm, well lit place and water the soil from time to time. If the cutting roots itself successfully you will have obtained a new Busy Lizzie plant.

Questions for class discussion

1 Taking cuttings is an artificial way of reproducing plants, used by gardeners. In what circumstances might this kind of reproduction occur naturally?

2 Why is it best to take cuttings from branches which do not have any flowers on them?

3 Some gardeners take cuttings by sticking the branch straight into the soil; others put the branch in water until new roots start growing out and *then* they stick it in the soil. What are the advantages and disadvantages of each method?

Advantages and disadvantages of asexual reproduction

The most obvious advantage of asexual reproduction is that there is no need for the organism to have a partner. When asexual reproduction occurs by the formation of spores it occurs rapidly and enables the species to spread quickly over a wide area. Tubers and bulbs enable the plant to survive the winter.

The main disadvantage is that the offspring are always exactly like the parent. It is therefore impossible to produce new *kinds* of organisms by this method. In other words asexual reproduction does not give rise to variety. Variety can only be produced by sexual reproduction as we shall see in the next chapter.

Importance of asexual reproduction to humans

Suppose a gardener has a plant with a particularly good feature. How could the gardener produce a lot of plants with the same feature? Asexual reproduction produces offspring which are exactly like the parent, so it would be sensible to propagate the plant by asexual means, for example by taking cuttings.

New varieties of useful plants with good features are created by sexual reproduction and then propagated by asexual methods. This is particularly important to farmers and market gardeners who produce commercially important plants such as potatoes on a large scale.

Homework assignments

1 Four methods of asexual reproduction are listed below. In each case, write down the name of *one* organism which uses the method.
Binary fission, budding, spore formation, tuber formation.

2 Of the four methods of asexual reproduction listed in Question 1, which ones:

a enable the organism to survive the winter

b result in two or more of the offspring remaining attached to one another for a while

c produce two offspring every time reproduction occurs

d involve the formation of an underground structure containing food

e enable the species to spread quickly over a wide area?

3 The fern is a plant which has two methods of asexual reproduction: like the mushroom it can form numerous spores, and it also possesses an underground **rhizome** from which a new plant grows up each spring.

Suggest two advantages which the spores have over the rhizome as a means of reproduction.

Summary

1 Asexual reproduction is reproduction that does not involve two individuals.

2 Four of the main methods of asexual reproduction found amongst organisms are:

a **binary fission** (e.g. *Amoeba*)

b **spores** (e.g. mushroom)

c **tubers** (e.g. potato)

d **bulbs** (e.g. onion, daffodil).

3 Taking **cuttings** is an artificial method of producing new plants used by gardeners.

4 The main advantages of asexual reproduction are that:

a it does not require two individuals

b it may be rapid and result in wide dispersal

c it often enables the species to survive adverse conditions.

5 The main disadvantage of asexual reproduction is that it does not give rise to variety.

6 Asexual reproduction is useful to farmers and market gardeners who may wish to produce large numbers of identical plants with a particular feature.

Chapter 6

Sexual reproduction

In Chapter 5 you saw how new individuals can be produced by a single parent, a process called asexual reproduction. But you probably know that in most organisms *two* parents are needed to produce young and they have to be male and female. This method is called **sexual reproduction**. Each parent produces special sex cells known as **gametes** (pronounced 'gam-eets').

In animals, the gametes produced by the female are called **eggs** and those produced by the male are called **sperms**. In flowers, the male gametes are transported in the pollen grains.

Offspring only develop if a male and a female gamete meet and join together.

What happens when animals mate?

An important part of sexual reproduction in many animals is the process of **mating**. If the eggs and the sperms are released when the parents are very close together, there is a much better chance that a sperm will meet an egg. So, in many kinds of animal, the male climbs on to the female to mate with her. The photographs in Fig 6.1, overleaf, show animals mating. In each photograph a male and female can be seen.

Questions for class discussion

1 Use the keys on pages 26 and 28 to name the group to which each pair of animals in Fig 6.1 belongs.

2 Describe the positions of the two animals in each photograph. What does this suggest about their sexes?

3 Look carefully for the differences in the appearance of the two animals in each photograph. Why do you think male and female animals often look different?

Experiment 6.1
Watching animals mating

If it is spring and you have a pond near your school, you may be lucky enough to see common frogs or toads mating. Perhaps

Fig 6.1 Animals mating.

instead you may have locusts or African clawed toads in your laboratory. Under the right conditions they will mate at any time of the year.

Watch the mating animals very carefully without disturbing them. Write a clear description of mating, including details of the positions of the two animals. It may help if you make a sketch of them.

Questions for class discussion

1 Describe at least three differences in appearance between the male and the female.

2 What movements, sounds or responses did you observe before and during mating? Can you explain why they occurred?

3 What passed between the two animals while they were mating? Could you see any sign of this transfer taking place?

Fig 6.2 Male black grouse display their striking plumage at a traditional arena or **lek**.

Courtship

Before mating takes place, many animals perform a complicated series of actions referred to as **courtship**. Often the male establishes a territory to live in before finding a suitable partner to share it with. Fig 6.2 shows a typical example of courtship behaviour in birds.

Eggs and sperms

When you watched animals mating you were probably unable to see anything passing between them. This is because their bodies were very close together to make sure that the eggs and sperms met. Eggs and sperms are single cells. Eggs are rather large cells because they often contain a store of food called yolk. Sperms are very small and have a long tail which lashes from side to side, enabling them to swim to the egg. Fig 6.3 compares the eggs and the sperms of locust, hen and human.

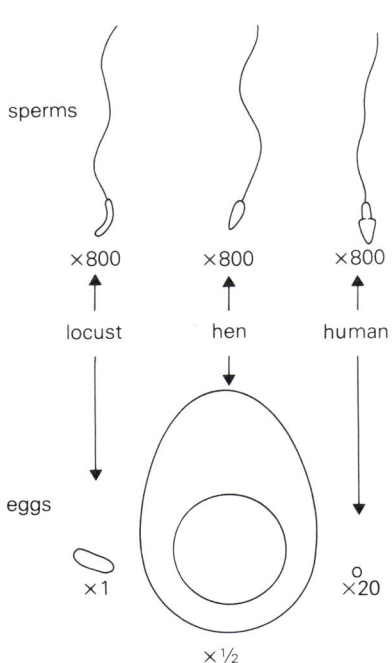

Fig 6.3 Eggs and sperms of locust, hen and human.

Questions for class discussion

1 Use the scales on the drawings in Fig 6.3 to calculate the diameters of the eggs and the lengths of the sperms in micrometres (μm). Make a table in your notebook giving the sizes, and calculate how many times larger the egg is than the sperm.

2 Suggest a reason why sperms are so much smaller than eggs.

3 Apart from size, what other differences are there in appearance between eggs and sperms? Can you suggest how these differences relate to the functions of the egg and the sperm?

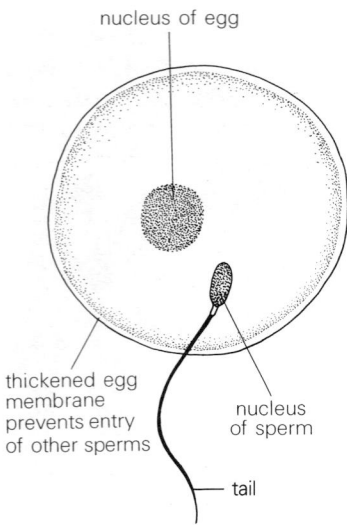

nucleus of egg

thickened egg membrane prevents entry of other sperms

nucleus of sperm

tail

Fig 6.4 Fertilisation of a rat's egg, showing detail of the egg cell and sperm cell.

Fertilisation

When the sperm and the egg meet, a process called **fertilisation** takes place. The nucleus of the sperm combines with the nucleus of the egg. The fertilised egg is called a **zygote** (pronounced zy-goat). It forms the first cell of the **offspring**. A similar process takes place in flowers to produce the zygote inside a seed.

It is much more difficult to see fertilisation taking place than it is to watch animals mating, because the sperms can only just be seen under the highest power of a microscope. However, the drawing in Fig 6.4 shows what happens.

Eggs and sperms are not produced by the male and female in equal numbers. Millions of sperms are released for each egg even though only one will be needed to fertilise it. This increases the chances of successful fertilisation.

Questions for class discussion

1 In what ways is the structure of the sperm cell in Fig 6.4 similar to, and different from, a typical animal cell such as the skin cells you looked at in Chapter 4?

2 How are egg cells and sperm cells adapted to carry out their functions (see page 44)?

Where does fertilisation take place?

At certain times of the year, fish such as herring and cod are full of 'roe'. You may be able to obtain such a fish, or a small quantity of the roe it contains. The female roe is hard and lumpy and contains the eggs, while the male roe consists of a milky liquid containing sperms.

The male and female fish gather in enormous shoals to breed, and they release their eggs and sperms into the sea. The sperms swim using their long tails until they find an egg to fertilise. Since the egg is fertilised outside the mother's body, we call this **external fertilisation**.

On land, it would be difficult for fertilisation to take place outside the body of the mother since the sperms would be unable to move over dry ground or through the air. Reptiles, birds, mammals and some invertebrates such as insects have solved this problem by releasing their sperms directly into the body of the mother. The sperms swim to the egg and the result is **internal fertilisation**.

Hermaphrodites

Not all living organisms have separate male and female sexes. An earthworm or a snail, for example, produces both eggs and sperms but the eggs produced by a single individual are seldom fertilised by sperm from the same individual. If you go outside with a torch on a warm, damp autumn evening, you may find earthworms mating on the surface of your lawn. They are exchanging small packets of sperm which will be stored inside their bodies and later used to fertilise the eggs when they are laid.

Questions for class discussion

1 List the animals shown in Fig 6.1. For each animal say whether fertilisation takes place inside or outside the mother's body.

2 An unfertilised frog's egg will start to develop into a tadpole if it is pricked with a fine needle. However, growth soon stops and the eggs never hatch. In *normal* fertilisation, what is needed to:
a start development
b continue development to the point of hatching?

Homework assignments

1 An egg is a special kind of cell. List the similarities and differences between a hen's egg and a human skin cell (see page 41).

2 How many times larger is a hen's egg (Fig 6.3) than an onion cell 0.1 mm across? Can you suggest any reasons why onion cells cannot grow to the size of hens' eggs?

3 Explain briefly, in words which a non-biologist would understand, what you mean by *gamete*, *fertilisation* and *zygote*.

4 Name an animal in which fertilisation occurs inside the body, and another which has external fertilisation. Give one advantage of each method.

Similarities and differences explained

Why do brothers and sisters in a family differ from each other if the eggs and sperms came from the same mother and father? It is often said that a child 'takes after his mother' or that a particular characteristic has 'come from his father'. You can probably think of examples in your own family or your friends. In the family in Fig 6.5 overleaf, which features in the children have been inherited from each parent?

Fig 6.5 Similarities and differences in a family.

Inherited characteristics

Asexual reproduction produces identical offspring, each one looking exactly like the others, and just like the parent. However, offspring produced by sexual reproduction differ from each other and from their parents. What causes this variation?

From Chapter 3 you will remember that each cell is controlled by a nucleus. The nucleus of each human body cell contains forty-six **chromosomes** (see Fig. 6.6). When fertilisation takes place, a set of twenty-three chromosomes from the father's sperm combines with a set of twenty-three chromosomes from the mother's egg. Each chromosome carries a very large number of instruction, called **genes**, in the form of a chemical code. We can think of the genes of the parents as resembling two separate packs of playing cards; the formation of eggs and sperms is like shuffling and dealing the cards. When fertilisation occurs the genes are put together again in a completely new combination. (Fig 6.7). The characteristics of the offspring are thus inherited randomly from both parents.

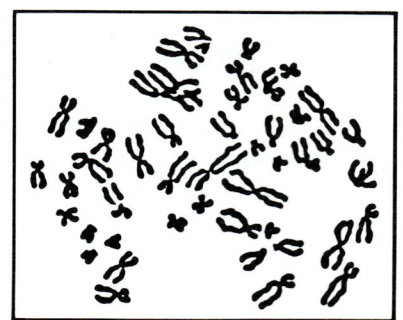

Fig 6.6 Human chromosomes.

Variation caused by the environment

Even the offspring of asexual reproduction are seldom identical in appearance. The new hedge in my garden is made from plants grown from cuttings (see page 56). Some of the plants are now two metres high but others are less than half a metre in height. These differences must have been caused by differences in the environment of the individual plants. How many such differences can you think of?

Doctors now know that our environment affects us even before we are born. For example, mothers who smoke produce babies of lower average birth weight than mothers who do not smoke. Throughout life our environment continues to affect us. By taking sensible precautions, we can often reduce the risk of ill-health and accidents (see Chapter 20).

Twins

Are there any twins in your school? If so, do they look alike (identical twins) or different (non-identical or fraternal twins)? **Identical twins** develop from two cells formed when a single fertilised egg divides inside their mother. Since each cell contains the same genes, the twins are the same sex and look very similar in appearance. Usually we can only tell them apart because of small differences in their personality or behaviour. These differences are caused by the environment. **Non-identical twins** develop from two separate fertilised eggs and so, apart from being the same age, they are no more similar than any two brothers, two sisters or brother and sister. Their differences are mainly caused by genetic variation.

Fig 6.7 How characteristics are inherited.

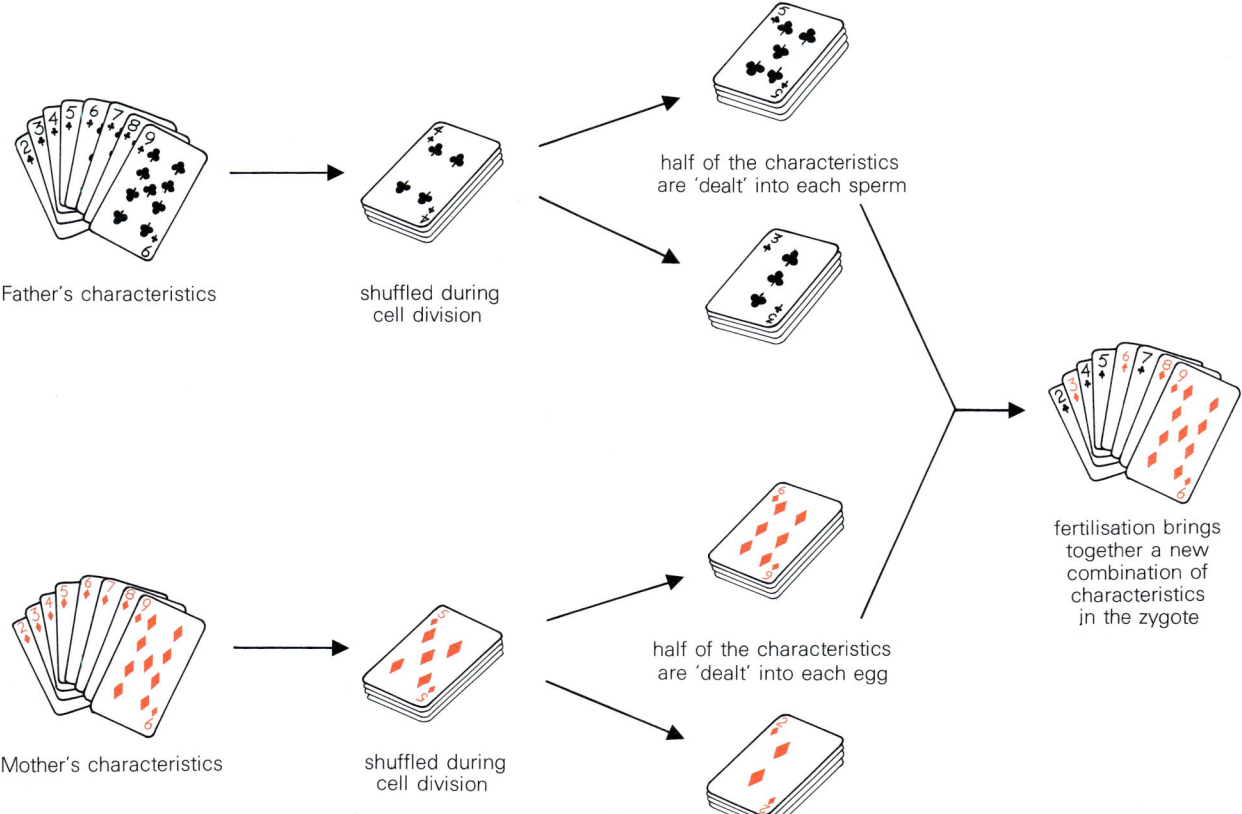

Father's characteristics

shuffled during cell division

half of the characteristics are 'dealt' into each sperm

Mother's characteristics

shuffled during cell division

half of the characteristics are 'dealt' into each egg

fertilisation brings together a new combination of characteristics in the zygote

Inherited diseases

Sometimes children are born with genetic characteristics which are not seen in either of their parents. Very occasionally these can result in diseases such as cystic fibrosis. Perhaps the best known example of an inherited disease is **haemophilia**. A sufferer from haemophilia must be very careful to avoid cutting himself because his blood does not clot properly. The disease, which mainly affects males, is caused by a gene on one of the mother's chromosomes. Since the mother has the gene but does not suffer from the disease, she is called a **carrier**. Queen Victoria was a carrier of haemophilia and she gave the gene to at least three of her nine children.

Questions for class discussion

Scientists who want to find out which human features are inherited, and which ones are affected by the environment, often study identical twins.

a Why are identical twins useful in this sort of investigation?

b Which of the following characteristics would you expect identical twins to share?

height	arm span	finger prints
body mass	eye colour	intelligence

c Identical twins separated at birth and brought up in different families show greater differences than twins brought up together. Can you suggest why this should be so?

Breeding animals and plants

How many different varieties of dogs can you name? All the different varieties which we see today have been created over hundreds of years by dog-breeders selecting certain characteristics and rejecting others. This is made possible because sexual reproduction gives rise to variation. Even if two pedigree dogs of the same breed are mated, their offspring will be different from each other and also from their parents. Breeding two 'mongrels' will give even more variety.

Suppose a farmer wishes to produce a new kind of plant or animal which is more resistant to a disease. An individual is selected which is disease-resistant and used to fertilise another individual which has all the other features which are required. The offspring are examined until one is found which seems to possess most of the characteristics required, including good resistance to disease.

A plant breeder can then propagate the new variety asexually (see Chapter 5). An animal breeder must rely on further breeding and selection to establish a group of animals, all of which have the required characteristics.

Fig 6.8

(a) A breed similar to the ancestor of domestic cattle and two modern breeds, the Friesian and the Hereford.

(b) Old and new varieties of wheat.

Most of our modern domestic animals and food crops have been produced in this way and they now look very different from their wild ancestors as you can see in Fig 6.8.

Growth

What changes take place as a newly fertilised egg (zygote) turns into a fully grown organism? The most obvious change is the increase in size (**growth**) which is necessary.

An elephant's zygote is about 0.1 millimetres across; the adult elephant is about 5000 millimetres long. How many times longer is the adult than the zygote? Assume that the elephant is also 5000 millimetres tall and broad, i.e. a cube. Calculate the volume

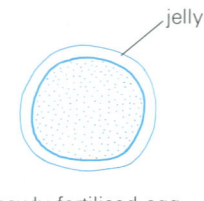

newly-fertilised egg

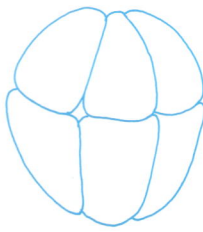

embryo: eight cells

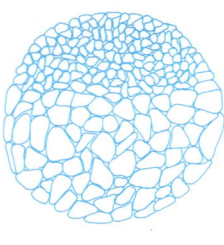

embryo: many cells

Fig 6.9 Early stages of growth in
Xenopus eggs.

of the elephant and compare it with that of the egg. Now you
have some idea of the enormous growth which takes place, and
the number of new cells which are required as the zygote becomes
an adult elephant.

The zygote divides and grows into an **embryo**. The early stages
can be seen quite easily in frogs or toads.

Experiment 6.2
Watching the zygote divide

The early stages of division of the egg are visible in frogs or
toads. A microscope or lens can be used, but a binocular
microscope will give the clearest view.

1 Place a few eggs into a watch glass or cavity slide, using a
   wide-mouthed pipette. Suck them up gently or they will be
   damaged. There is no need to add a coverslip.

2 Examine them under the lens or low power of the microscope.

3 Try to find and draw newly laid eggs, 2-cell, 4-cell and 8-cell
   embryos and one or two later stages (Fig 6.9).

Questions for class discussion

1 The upper surface of a fertilised frog's egg is dark, but the
   lower surface is light. What advantages are there in this pattern?

2 Most frog and toad spawn contains some eggs which do not
   divide and grow. How can you recognise these eggs and what
   proportion of the total number do they represent? Suggest
   reasons for the failure of these eggs to grow normally.

Development

If you watch the growth of amphibian embryos for 24–48 hours,
you will begin to see new changes which cannot be explained by
growth and an increase in the number of cells alone. The round
shape of the early embryo begins to change into the sausage shape
of the tadpole. If you look carefully you will see new features start to
appear on the surface. Inside the body, the heart and blood are
forming. These changes, which we refer to as **development**,
begin soon after the egg is fertilised.

Some organisms develop steadily towards adult shape, size
and structure. For example, a baby has most of the features of an
adult human being long before it is born. However, a tadpole looks
very different from the frog into which it will develop. We call the
tadpole a **larva**.

Caterpillars and maggots are examples of the larval stage of
insects, but they do not turn directly into adults. Instead, the
change from larva to adult takes place inside a protective case.
This stage is called the **pupa**.

If you keep your tadpoles for 2–3 months, you will probably see the tremendous change which takes place as the tadpole turns into a frog or toad. A sudden change during development is called **metamorphosis**. The larval structures are broken down and replaced by the adult structures. Different types of development in human, frog and butterfly are shown in the form of a **life cycle** in Fig 6.10.

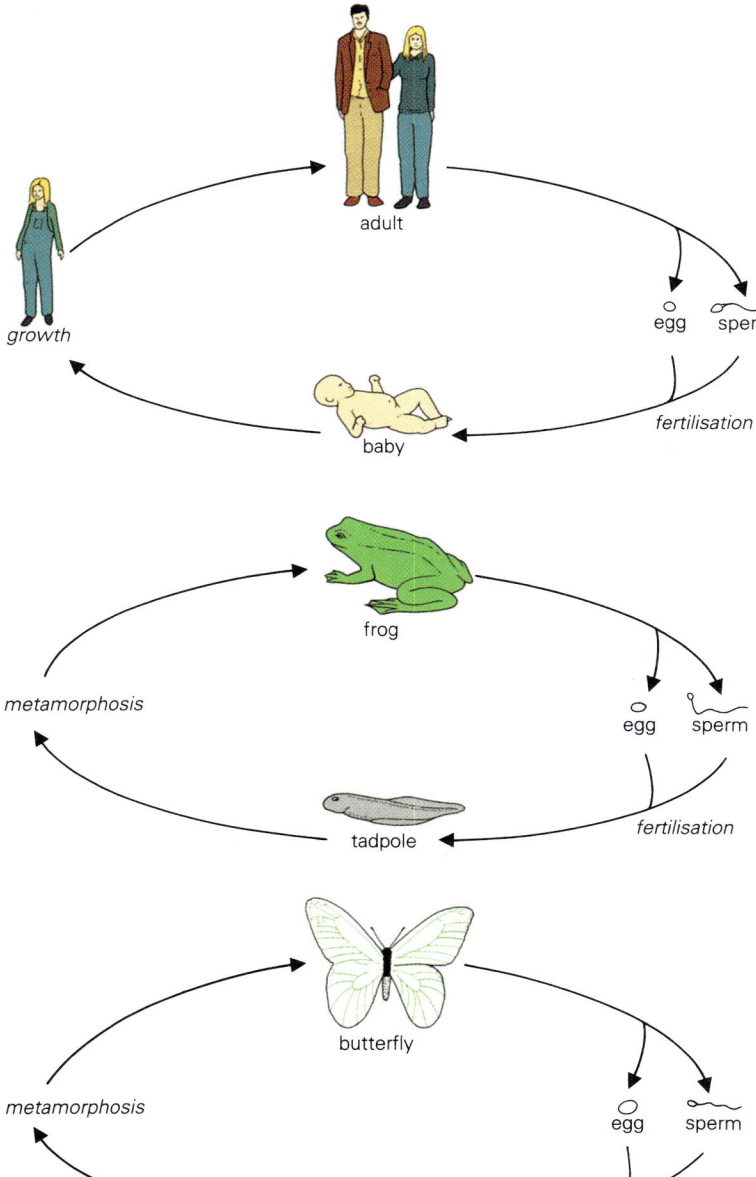

Fig 6.11 Song thrush (*Turdus philomelos*) and blackbird (*Turdus merula*)

Fig 6.10 Life cycles of human, frogs and butterflies.

How are new species formed?

We saw earlier that sexual reproduction can result in the formation of different varieties of animals and plants.

These different varieties can interbreed. This is how mongrel dogs are produced (see page 66). But different species cannot normally interbreed because the differences between them are greater than between members of the same species. Scientists believe that the huge number of species which inhabit the world today have arisen by sexual reproduction from other species that existed in past. This process is called **evolution**.

Questions for class discussion

1 Fig 6.11 shows a blackbird (*Turdus merula*) and a song thrush (*Turdus philomelos*). As you can tell from their scientific names, they both belong to the same genus but they are different species (see page 25). Make a list of the similarities and differences between them.

2 Suppose you examined a large number of blackbirds, all the same age and sex. In what sort of ways would you expect them to differ from each other?

3 The blackbird and the robin (*Erithacus rubecula*) each belong to a different genus. Would you expect the differences between them to be greater or less than the differences between the blackbird and the song thrush? Explain your answer.

Homework assignments

1 Compare sexual and asexual reproduction giving suitable examples. Explain briefly the advantages and disadvantages of each method.

2 The table below shows the changes in mass of a family of mice.

Days after birth	0	5	10	15	20	25	30	35	40
Average mass (g)	1.5	3.0	5.0	7.5	10.0	15.0	19.0	21.0	22.5

a Plot a graph to show the growth of the mice, putting days after birth along the horizontal axis.
b How long did it take the baby mice to double their mass after the first measurements?
c How long did it take them to double their mass in the period ending in the last measurement?
d What does this tell you about the rate of growth of the young mice at different stages of development?

3 Write out each of the following sentences. Choose the best word from the list to complete each sentence.

  a An egg can only develop into an adult after _____ .

  b _____ is an important part of sexual reproduction in all land animals.

  c The change from larva to adult is called _____ .

  Words: metamorphosis
  mating
  fertilisation

4 Sperms and eggs are special sex cells. What general name do we give to such cells? Describe three ways in which sperm cells and egg cells are different and one way in which they are similar.

Background Reading

Biological time-bombs

Inside our bodies, tiny biological time-bombs are ticking away. In the cells that make up our muscles, bones, and organs are genes that have gone wrong. Each of us has about a hundred thousand genes which determine our physical characteristics and attributes – but every person also has at least five or six that have become altered in a dangerous way. These are genes for genetic diseases.

Usually people are unaware they are carriers of such hereditary disorders – because their health is unaffected. But sometimes a carrier meets and marries another carrier – unaware of their mutual condition – and they produce a child that has a genetic disease. When that happens, one of these biological bombs 'explodes'. Parents can face the harrowing experience of watching a child slowly die or undergo painful treatment and surgery.

(From *The Genetic Jigsaw* by Robin McKie, published by Oxford Paperbacks.)

Questions

1 Why is a person with only *one* altered gene called a *carrier*? Suggest *two* ways in which scientists might be able to identify a carrier.

2 In most cases, people only suffer from genetic diseases if their body cells contain *two* identical genes which have been altered. Explain why marriages between related people (e.g. cousins) are more likely to result in children with hereditary disorders.

3 Birth rates for most inherited diseases are low. For example haemophilia (see page 66) affects one person in 10 000. Other genetic diseases are more common however. Cystic fibrosis, a fatal wasting disease, occurs in one in 2 000 births and muscular dystrophy, a progressive weakening of the muscles, affects one in 5 000. What do these figures tell you about the number of people who are carriers of these diseases?

4 It is now possible to test for a few genetic disorders. In some cases the effects of the harmful genes can be detected before the baby is born; in others the actual gene can be identified in affected babies. What action do *you* think should be taken if a baby is found to have a fatal genetic disease before it is born?

Summary

1 Most animals possess male and female sexes, and reproduce by **sexual reproduction**.

2 Sex cells are called **gametes**. **Sperms** are produced by the male and **eggs** are produced by the female. An egg and a sperm combine in a process called **fertilisation** to form a **zygote**.

3 The zygote **grows** by cell division to form an **embryo** which **develops** into an adult.

4 Some embryos develop steadily into an adult; others first form a larva which undergoes a sudden change or **metamorphosis** into an adult.

5 The main advantage of sexual reproduction over asexual reproduction is that the offspring differ from each other and differ from their parents.

Explorations 1

A How does an outdoor environment change?

In Chapter 1, you measured some physical features of the environment in your classroom. Choose one of these physical features, and take measurements out-of-doors as often as you can over a period of 24 hours.

1 Show your results by means of tables and graphs.

2 Explain how the daily variation in this physical feature affects the lives of animals and plants in the area where your measurements were taken.

B Observing changes through the year

Natural habitats change through the year. The changes occur because the environment changes.

Choose a habitat such as a hedgerow, fresh water pond or woodland. Keep a diary over a whole year. Each month (or more often if you like) write down the changes which have occurred in your habitat. Record changes in the environment (e.g. temperature) as well as changes in the organisms that occur there.

To what extent can you relate the changes that occur in the organisms to changes in the environment?

C Studying a habitat

Choose a small, undisturbed area of countryside, garden or park.

1 Write a short account of the area you have chosen, describing the animals and plants found there.

2 Draw a sketch map of the area, labelling the main features.

3 Each month, revisit the area and record any changes you can see.

4 At the end of the year, has the area changed in its general appearance?

This is an extended version of Exploration B and you should use the experience gained with that to study an area that is as different as possible.

D What shape should a water animal be?

To move quickly, water animals must be the right shape. Usually this means being streamlined. Can you think of some water animals that are streamlined, and some that are not?

Your teacher will give you a large measuring cylinder and some Plasticine. Use them to find how the shape of an object affects the speed at which it falls through water.

Design a 'perfect water animal' which combines high speed with good stability.

E Observing animals

Choose a species of animal and make a detailed study of it. If you live in the country, you may be able to find a badger's **sett** or a fox's **den**. An occupied nest box in a garden or a family pet would provide suitable alternatives if you live in a town or city.

F Measuring small things

Measuring very small objects can be difficult even if you have the right equipment. Sometimes the information can be obtained in another way.

1 You are provided with a telephone directory. Estimate the thickness of a page of the directory using a ruler.

2 You are provided with an electronic balance. Estimate the number of crystals of sugar in a sugar lump.

3 You are provided with a microscope, a slide and a plastic ruler. Estimate the size of the object which your teacher has given you using the apparatus provided.

G Taking cuttings

Read about how to take cuttings on page 56. How good a cut branch is at forming roots depends on a number of things. Plan, and carry out, experiments to answer these questions:

a Does it matter whereabouts you make your cut along the length of a side branch?

b Does it help roots to form if you dip the cut end of the branch in 'rooting powder'? (Rooting powder can be bought in garden shops. Try to find out what it is.)

Chapter 7

How biologists investigate

So far in your biology course you have gathered information by observing, describing and measuring. Biologists are constantly doing such things but sometimes they need to go further: they want to find out *why* and *how* things happen.

Becoming a biological detective

A good detective needs to have sharp eyes and a keen 'nose' for evidence. Many of the most important scientific discoveries have been made because someone looked more carefully or measured more accurately than anyone had done before. The discovery of penicillin by Alexander Fleming resulted from a chance observation which many scientists would have ignored (see page 261).

Now look at the pictures on the next page (Figs 7.1–7.4) and describe what you see. Use the knowledge you have obtained from the course so far to help you identify the living organisms shown in the photographs, and comment on anything you think is unusual or unexpected.

Suggesting explanations

When a detective has collected all the evidence, the next stage in the investigation is to put all the clues together and come up with an explanation which can be tested by making further enquiries.

Thinking up explanations is a very important part of the work of a scientist. A possible explanation of something is called a **hypothesis** (plural: hypotheses). Perhaps you suggested some explanations for observations you made when you looked at the photographs in the previous section.

Questions for class discussion

The swallow (Fig 7.5) nests throughout north-west Europe. In the autumn British swallows migrate south to spend the winter in South Africa (see Fig 7.6). The following spring they return, often to the same nest site.

Fig 7.1

Fig 7.2

Fig 7.3

Fig 7.4

1 Suggest as many different methods of navigation as you can think of to explain how swallows find their way back to their nests – a distance of over 14 000 km.

2 Scientists have studied bird migration for thousands of years. Indeed, the Romans used swallows to carry the results of chariot races back to their homes. Here are two discoveries which have been made about swallows:
   a Parents and young swallows do not usually travel together.
   b Swallows migrate at night as well as during the daytime.

How does this additional information affect the suggestions you made in answer to Question 1?

3 Here are two further clues:
   a If birds are transported several hundred miles to the east or west of their normal migration route and then released, they continue to migrate in the usual direction.
   b Migrant birds, observed by radar over the sea, have been shown to lose their way if they fly into cloudy weather.

Use this additional information to propose a hypothesis to explain how swallows navigate.

Designing and planning experiments

Biologists have one important advantage over detectives: they can test their explanations by doing experiments. Sometimes a very simple experiment is all that is required. (Read about William Harvey's experiment on the circulation of blood on page 213, for example.) However, it is important that the experiment is carefully designed so that it really does test the hypothesis. We call such an experiment a **fair test** (see page 85).

Experiment 7.1
Keeping warm

Look at Fig 7.7 Warm-blooded animals in a cold environment often huddle close together. You can probably suggest more than one reason for this but you are going to test the hypothesis that animals in a group lose heat energy more slowly than separate individuals. To do this we shall use **models** rather than real animals.

1 Work in a group of at least three students.

2 Prepare a table for the results with headings as shown in Table 7.1

Fig 7.5 Swallow at nest with young.

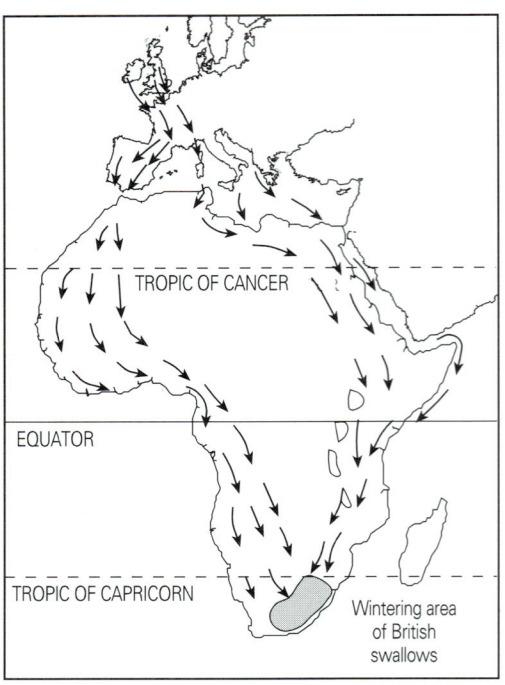

Fig 7.6 The migration route of British swallows.

Fig 7.7 Mongolian gerbils

Table 7.1

Time from start (minutes)	Temperature (°C)		
	Single tube	Two tubes	Four tubes

3 You will need a total of seven boiling tubes. Mark each tube at exactly the same point about halfway up the side so that you can pour the same quantity of water into each one.

4 Now clamp the tubes to retort stands: one tube on its own; two tubes (held together by rubber bands); and four tubes.

5 Fix a thermometer into one tube in each of the three groups so that the bulb of each thermometer is just clear of the bottom of the tube.

6 Pour hot water (just below boiling point) into all the tubes and record the time and the temperatures in your table.

7 Continue to record the temperatures in the tubes at regular intervals.

Questions for class discussion

1 What hypothesis were you testing?

2 How far do the results support the hypothesis?

3 Why was it necessary to fill all the tubes to the same level?

4 Suggest two reasons why the use of a model in this experiment is better than using living animals. Are the boiling tubes a good model?

5 Is the experiment a fair test? Suggest ways in which the experiment could be improved.

6 What further investigations can you suggest on this topic?

Looking for explanations

The way biologists investigate things is summarised in Fig 7.8. You will have a chance to follow this procedure in some of the Explorations which follow this chapter.

Questions for class discussion

Look carefully at Figs 7.9 to 7.14, and then answer the questions which follow.

1 The dormouse in Fig 7.9 hibernates during the winter. What causes it to start hibernating – the drop in temperature or the

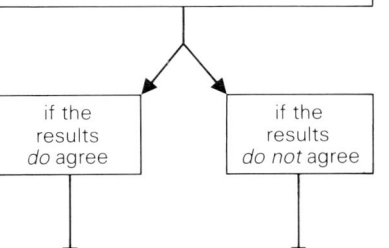

Fig 7.8 The way a biologist often works. You will have a chance to follow this process in some of the Explorations.

Examine the problem, look for clues record observations accurately

Suggest an explanation (*hypothesis*) to account for the observations

Design an experiment to test the hypothesis. Remember to include a comparison (control)

Compare the results of the experiment with the expected results

if the results *do* agree

if the results *do not* agree

Do further experiments to confirm and extend the hypothesis

Abandon the hypothesis and suggest a new one

shorter hours of light each day? Describe an experiment which would test these two possibilities.

2 The red squirrel *Sciurus vulgaris* is now rare in many parts of Britain although its relative, the grey squirrel *Sciurus carolensis*, thrives (Figs 7.10 and 7.11). The grey squirrel was introduced into Britain from North America about a hundred years ago. Suggest a reason for the red squirrel's decline. What clues might support your suggestion and what evidence would you look for?

3 The red breast is a distinctive feature of robins (Fig 7.12). What is its function? Suggest a possible hypothesis and describe how it could be tested.

4 Why is it difficult to swat a fly (Fig 7.13)? Does it sense your presence by seeing you with its large eyes or by feeling air movements? Scientists have tested these hypotheses. How do you think they did it?

5 The behaviour of birds has been studied by ornithologists in great detail. Fig 7.14 shows a young herring gull seeking food from its parent by pecking at the parent's bill. What do you think is the function of the red spot on the parent's bill? How would you investigate this?

Homework assignments

1 A woman bought some young plants from a garden centre and planted them in her garden. Unfortunately, the plants did not grow as tall as she had been led to believe they would.
   a Suggest two possible reasons why the plants did not grow well.
   b Choose one of your reasons and write down the plan of an experiment to find out if it is correct.

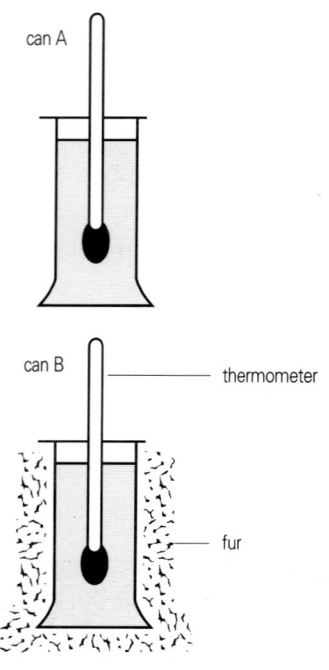

can A

can B ———— thermometer

———— fur

Fig 7.15

2 Two identical cans were filled with equal amounts of water at 80°C. They were set up as shown in Fig 7.15. The temperature of the water in each can was taken at regular intervals as it cooled.
   a What hypothesis was being tested by this experiment?
   b The results for can A are shown in the graph in Fig 7.16.
     i On a copy of the graph sketch the cooling curve that you would *expect* for can B.
     ii Explain why this curve differs from the curve for can A.

3 On a certain farm the liquid and solid waste matter from the animals is drained into a hole in the corner of a field. Large numbers of stinging nettles grow in this corner, whereas there are very few nettles in the rest of the field.
   a Suggest two possible reasons why stinging nettles thrive near the hole.
   b Choose one of your reasons and describe an experiment which you could do to find out if it is correct.

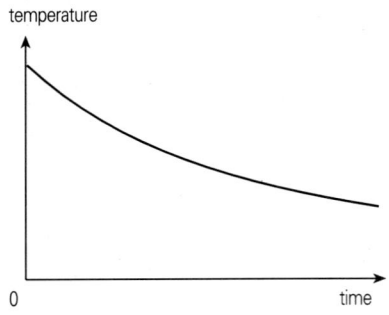

temperature

0   time

Fig 7.16

Fig 7.9 Dormouse feeding on hawthorn berry

Fig 7.10 Red squirrel

Fig 7.11 Grey squirrel

Fig 7.12 Robin

Fig 7.13 Fly

Fig 7.14 Herring gull chick pecking at the red spot on the adult's bill

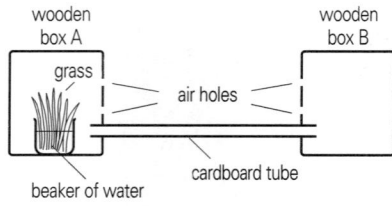

Fig 7.17

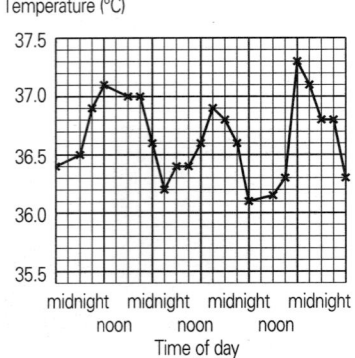

Fig 7.18

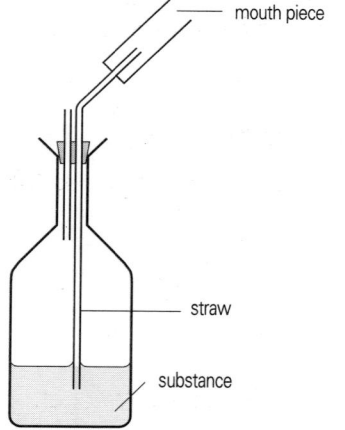

Fig 7.19

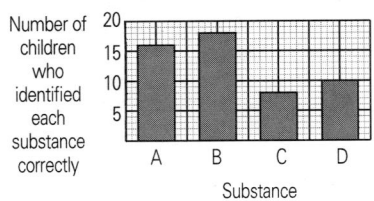

Fig 7.20

4 A student wanted to investigate how locusts sense their food, so he set up the apparatus shown in Fig 7.17. Ten locusts were placed in box B. After a few minutes six locusts moved through the cardboard tube into box A.
  a What sense was the student trying to test?
  b In what way should the locusts be treated before the experiment?
  c What should the student do to make this a *controlled* experiment?

5 The garden shrub *Buddleia* has dense clusters of small, coloured flowers. In summer large numbers of butterflies may be seen hovering round the flowers.
  a Suggest two features of the flowers which might attract butterflies.
  b Choose one of the features and describe an experiment which could be done to find out if butterflies are attracted to it.

6 To measure a person's body temperature a special type of thermometer is placed under the tongue for a few minutes. The graph in Fig 7.18 shows the body temperature of a healthy person during the course of three days.
  a In what way does the thermometer need to be 'special'?
  b **i** Describe one feature of the graph which strikes you as interesting.
    ii Suggest a possible explanation of this feature.

7 Four bottles, like the one shown in Fig 7.19, were set up. Each bottle contained a well-known, edible substance, A, B, C or D, dissolved in water. All four substances were equal in concentration. The bottles were all identical and made of dark glass. Twenty children were asked to identify the substance in each bottle. The results are shown in Fig 7.20.
  a What was the purpose of this investigation?
  b Name two features of the experiment which helped to make it a fair test.

8 Some children collected blackberries from a hedge which sloped down towards a pond. Nobody else had picked blackberries from this hedge, and there were no trees or buildings near it. The children noticed that one side of the hedge had very few ripe blackberries, but there were lots on the other side.
  a Suggest one reason why there were more ripe blackberries on one side of the hedge than the other side.
  b What clues would you look for to support your suggestion?

Chapter 8   **Plant nutrition**

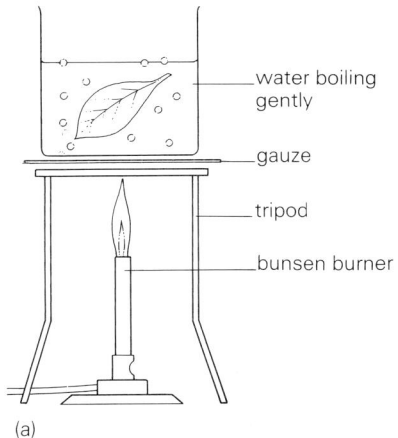

water boiling gently

gauze

tripod

bunsen burner

(a)

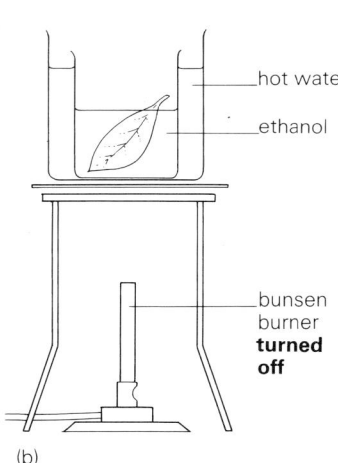

hot water

ethanol

bunsen burner **turned off**

(b)

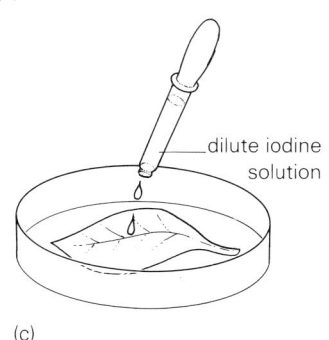

dilute iodine solution

(c)

Fig 8.1 How to test a leaf for starch.

You and I feed by taking in solid food substances. Have you ever wondered how plants feed? This chapter is all about how they feed.

Two parts of the plant are involved with feeding: the **leaves** and the **roots**. Later we shall see what the leaves and roots do. However, for the moment let us concentrate on this important fact: the leaves of plants normally contain **starch**.

We can prove that a leaf contains starch by testing the leaf with iodine solution. If starch is mixed with iodine, it turns a blue-black colour. To see this colour change in a leaf, it is necessary to remove the green substance first.

Experiment 8.1
Testing a leaf for starch

The test should be carried out on the leaf of a potted plant such as a geranium. The plant should have been kept in a well lit place for several days beforehand. Wear eye protection for this experiment.

1 *Half fill* a beaker with water and place it on a gauze on top of a tripod. Use a bunsen burner to bring the water to the boil, then adjust the flame so that it goes on simmering gently.

2 Drop the leaf into the boiling water for about a minute (Fig 8.1a). This will make it soft and easy to penetrate by fluids. Then remove the leaf with a pair of tweezers.

Safety note
The next step should not be carried out until your teacher tells you.

3 *Turn out the bunsen burner.* Pour a little ethanol (just enough to cover the leaf) into a small beaker. Carefully, place the small beaker inside the larger beaker of hot water. The ethanol will soon come to the boil.

4 Now drop the leaf into the beaker of ethanol (Fig 8.1b). After about five minutes the ethanol will remove the green pigment from the leaf, making it go a whitish colour.

5 Take the leaf out of the ethanol with tweezers, and wash it in tap water.

6 Place the leaf in a dish and pipette dilute iodine solution over it (Fig 8.1c). Watch what happens. If the leaf turns blue-black, starch is present.

Questions for class discussion

1 Did the whole of your leaf turned blue-black? If it did not, can you suggest a reason?

2 Why was it necessary to turn out the bunsen burner before putting the beaker of ethanol into the boiling water?

3 When you were boiling the leaf in ethanol, what happened to the colour of the ethanol? Explain.

4 If you were to take a green leaf off a plant and immerse it in iodine solution, it would *not* go blue-black. Why not?

Light and starch formation

Green plants grow only in places where there is **light** (Fig 8.2). What do they need light for? A possible reason is that they need light for making starch. We will now do an experiment to test this suggestion.

Fig 8.2 Plants growing in a glasshouse under artificial lighting.

Experiment 8.2
To find out if a green plant needs light to make starch

Your teacher will give you two potted geranium plants which have had all the starch removed from their leaves. The starch has been removed by placing the two plants in darkness for several days.

1 Place the two destarched plants in the window. Cover one of them with an upturned cardboard box so that it gets no light. Leave the other plant uncovered so that it gets plenty of light. Leave the plants for at least 24 hours.

2 After 24 hours, take a healthy green leaf from each plant and test it for starch with iodine solution (see Experiment 8.1 page 84). Do you find that the leaf from the uncovered plant contains starch, whereas the leaf from the covered plant does not?

Do your results support the suggestion that the plant needs light for making starch?

Questions for class discussion

1 Why did you have to use destarched plants for this experiment?

2 Why was it necessary to set up *two* plants, one in the dark and the other in the light?

3 It is important that both plants should be given exactly the same conditions except for the condition you are investigating, namely light. Were they? (Be really critical!) Why is this important?

These questions illustrate three essential features which make the experiment a *good* one. By 'good' we mean that the experiment really does test the idea that light is needed for the plant to make starch. In other words, it is a fair test (see page 77).

The illuminated plant (the one that was left in the light), provides a standard with which the plant in the dark can be compared. We call the illuminated plant the **control plant**. Without the control, we cannot be sure that it was lack of light that prevented the other plant from making starch. Having the right control is an essential part of a fair test. An experiment involving a control is called a **controlled experiment**.

Photosynthesis

We have seen that plants make starch in the light. This process is called **photosynthesis** (*photo* means 'light' and *synthesis* means 'making' or 'manufacturing'). Starch is the plant's food, and so the plant is able to *make* its own food. In order to do this, energy is required and the energy comes from sunlight.

Another thing that is needed for photosynthesis is the green pigment **chlorophyll** which is found in all green parts of the plant, particularly the leaves. You saw this pigment when you decolourised your leaf in Experiment 8.1.

Experiments show that the raw materials for photosynthesis are carbon dioxide and water, and that oxygen gas is given off as a by-product.

We can sum up photosynthesis like this:

water + carbon dioxide	sunlight and chlorophyll →	starch + oxygen
raw materials		products

The words 'sunlight and chlorophyll' are written by the arrow because they are needed for photosynthesis to take place. The function of the chlorophyll is to absorb the energy from sunlight so that it can be used by the plant for making starch.

Starch is not formed straight away. Sugar is formed first. The sugar may then be turned into starch. Light is needed for sugar formation, but not for the conversion of sugar to starch.

In plants such as sugar cane and sugar beet, the sugar which is made by photosynthesis is not turned into starch but remains as sugar. So these plants are used by us as sources of sugar (Fig 8.3).

Fig 8.3 Sugar cane: the thick stems contain sugar which has been made in the leaves by photosynthesis.

(a)

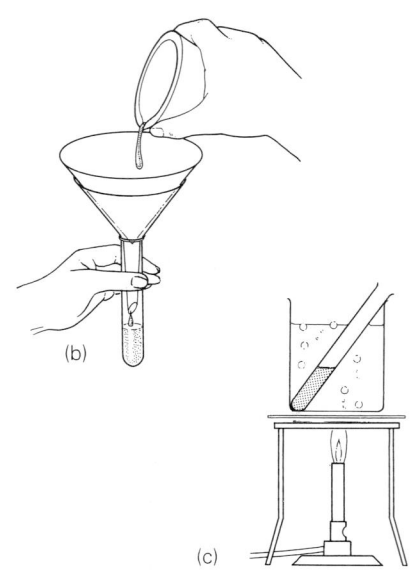

(b)

(c)

Fig 8.4 Testing a plant for sugar.

Experiment 8.3
To find out if a plant contains sugar

You can find out if a plant contains sugar by testing it with **Benedict's solution**. Try it on an onion.

1 Put a few pieces of the onion into a mortar. Add a pinch of sand and cover with water.

2 Grind up the pieces of onion with a pestle (Fig 8.4a).

3 Filter the contents of the mortar into a test-tube to a depth of about one centimetre (Fig 8.4b).

4 Pour an equal amount of Benedict's solution into the test-tube, and shake.

5 Stand the test-tube in a beaker of boiling water until the contents boil (Fig 8.4c).

6 Observe what happens to the solution in the test-tube. If it goes a cloudy green, brown or red colour, sugar is present.

Questions for class discussion

1 Why did you have to grind up the pieces of onion before carrying out this test?

2 Why did you heat the test-tube by standing it in a beaker of boiling water rather than heating it over a flame?

3 If you carried out this test on the majority of plants, you would find that there was little or no sugar present. Why?

What happens to the products of photosynthesis?

The sugar which a plant makes in its leaves is dissolved in water. In other words it is soluble and exists in liquid form. In this state it can be transported from the leaves to other parts of the plant. It may then be turned into starch and stored until it is needed.

The products of photosynthesis can be turned into other substances too. These include cellulose, fats and oils, and proteins. In fact *everything* a plant makes arises from photosynthesis.

Questions for class discussion

1 Think of some examples of plants which store large quantities of starch inside themselves. In each case say whereabouts in the plant the starch is stored, and why the store is necessary.

2 'Plants are like factories, churning out useful things that can be used by humans'. Explain this statement, giving examples to show what it means.

Experiment 8.4
To show that a green plant produces oxygen

For this experiment we will use a water plant called Canadian pondweed (*Elodea canadensis*). It is a common green plant in British ponds and lakes.

1 Place a handful of Canadian pondweed under a funnel and set it up as shown in Fig 8.5. The upturned test-tube must be full of pond water.

2 Leave the pondweed in a well lit place for about a week.

3 Set up another sample of Canadian pondweed in exactly the same way, but leave it in the dark for a week.

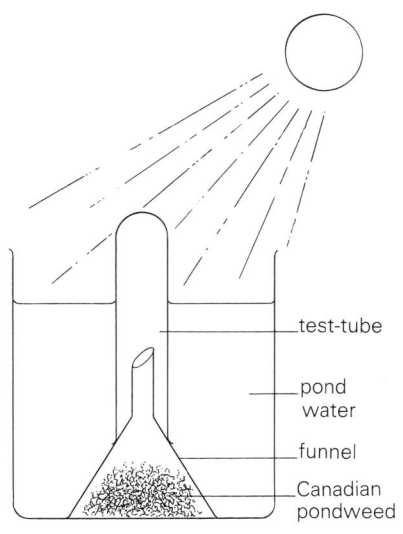

test-tube

pond water

funnel

Canadian pondweed

Fig 8.5 Experiment to find out if Canadian pondweed gives off oxygen in the light.

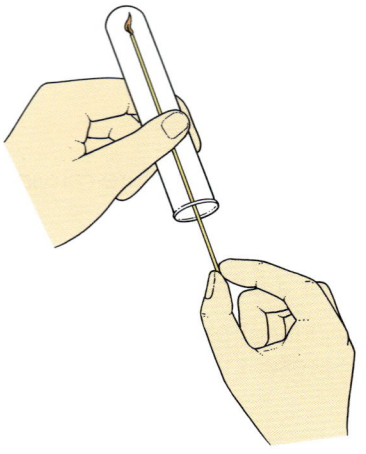

Fig 8.6 Testing the gas given off by Canadian pondweed for the presence of oxygen.

pieces of black paper attached to both surfaces of leaf

Fig 8.7 Experiment to find out if light is needed for a leaf to make starch.

4 After a week examine the two samples of pondweed. Has any gas gathered in either of the test-tubes? If so, in which one?

You should find that only the illuminated pondweed has given off any gas; in fact you may see bubbles of gas rising from it.

How could you show that this gas contains oxygen? The simplest test would be to see if it will ignite a glowing splint (Fig 8.6).

Question for class discussion

Why was it necessary to have two samples of pondweed in this experiment, one in the light and one in the dark?

Homework assignments

1 Photosynthesis is a plant's way of making food.
  a List four things which a leaf must have for photosynthesis to take place.
  b Which of these things are 'raw materials'?
  c Describe an experiment which you could do to show that a green plant cannot make starch if one of the four things which you have listed is missing.

2 One way of finding out if light is needed for a leaf to make starch is shown in Fig 8.7.
  a What should be done to the plant beforehand, and why?
  b If, after 24 hours, you test the leaf with iodine solution, what would you expect the result to look like?
  c Where is the control in this experiment?
  d Is the control satisfactory? Can you suggest a better one?

3 Your friend was away when you were shown how to test a leaf for starch. Write out some instructions, stressing the precautions to be taken.

4 Give two reasons why photosynthesis is important to humans.

5 In the 17th century a scientist called van Helmont did the following experiment. He planted a willow in a pot of soil, having weighed the willow and the soil separately beforehand. He then left the willow for five years, making sure that the soil was kept well watered. Five years later he dug up the willow and weighed it, and he also weighed the soil on its own again. His results are shown in Table 8.1.

Table 8.1

	Before planting	Five years later
mass of willow	2 kg	77 kg
mass of soil	100 kg	100 kg

How had the willow managed to increase in mass?

6 In the 18th century Joseph Priestley carried out the following experiment. He burned a candle in a sealed chamber until the flame went out. He then divided the air into two separate glass containers. In one container he placed a green plant; no plant was placed in the other container. Both containers were put in a sunny place. Ten days later he found a lighted candle would burn in the first container, but not in the second. How would you explain this?

Obtaining light for photosynthesis

The part of a plant in which photosynthesis mainly takes place is the **leaves**. The cells inside the leaf contain chlorophyll. Leaves are generally flat, and together they have a large surface area for catching as much light as possible.

Experiment 8.5
Estimating the leaf surface of a tree

The best kind of tree to use for this experiment is beech which has simple leaves all more or less the same size.

1 Detach one leaf and lay it on a sheet of squared paper. Trace the outline of the leaf with a pencil (Fig 8.8).

2 From the squares that fall inside the outline, work out the approximate surface area of the leaf in square centimetres.

3 Now estimate the approximate number of leaves on the tree. This is not an easy thing to do; if you do not know how to set about it, you may find Chapter 11 helpful (see page 125).

4 Calculate the leaf surface of the tree by multiplying the surface area of a single leaf by the total (estimated) number of leaves. Give your answer in square metres.

5 Measure the dimensions of your laboratory and work out the floor area in square metres.

Questions for class discussion

1 How does the leaf area of your tree compare with the floor area of your laboratory? Why is it useful to make this kind of comparison?

2 How could you make your estimation of the leaf area more accurate?

3 Suppose you wanted to estimate the leaf area of a plant with only twenty-five leaves. How would you do it?

4 Plants generally have a large number of small leaves rather than a small number of large leaves. Suggest reasons for this.

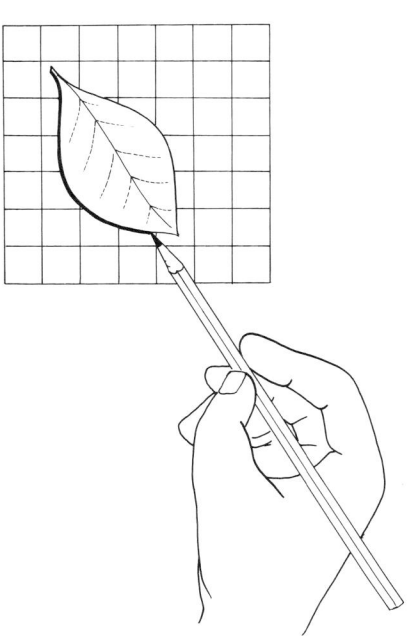

Fig 8.8 Tracing the outline of a beech leaf on squared paper.

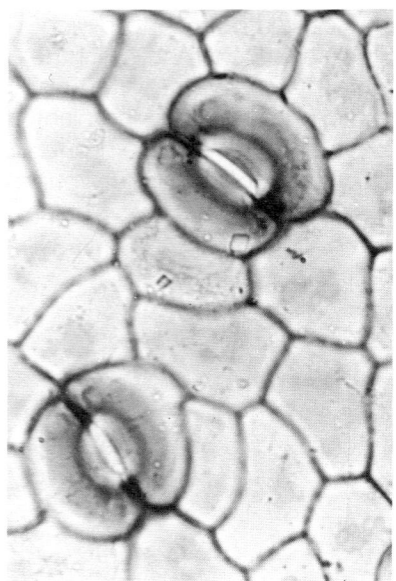

Fig 8.9 Stomata seen in surface view down a microscope × 300.

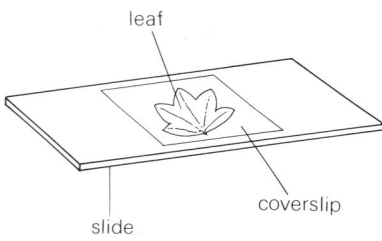

Fig 8.10 A leaf of ivy-leaved toadflax mounted on a slide.

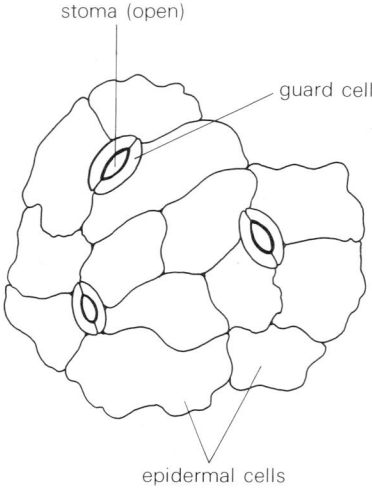

Fig 8.11 Stomata in the epidermis of a leaf of ivy-leaved toadflax.

Obtaining carbon dioxide for photosynthesis

The carbon dioxide which a plant needs for photosynthesis comes from the surrounding air.

Leaves are covered with a thin 'skin' called the **epidermis**. The epidermis has tiny holes in it called **stomata** (singular: **stoma**) (Fig 8.9). Carbon dioxide passes through the stomata to the inside of the leaf where photosynthesis takes place.

Experiment 8.6
Looking at stomata

The leaves of ivy-leaved toadflax are very good for looking at stomata because they are thin and semi-transparent. Ivy-leaved toadflax can often be found growing on old walls.

1 Remove a leaf from the plant and place it on a slide. *The lower side of the leaf should be uppermost.* Put a coverslip on top of the leaf so as to flatten it (Fig 8.10). There is no need to add any water or stain to the leaf.

2 Examine the leaf under the microscope, low power first, then high power.

3 Describe one of the stomata in detail, and make a sketch of it in your notebook.

Questions for class discussion

1 Could you see that the opening of the stoma is bounded by a pair of sausage-shaped cells? These are called **guard cells** (Fig 8.11). What do you think their function might be? Where are the guard cells in Fig 8.9?

2 What other things besides carbon dioxide might pass into, or out of, the leaf through the stomata?

3 How could you estimate the number of stomata in a square millimetre of leaf surface?

4 Most leaves have many more stomata on the lower side than on the upper side. Suggest a reason.

Experiment 8.7
Looking at the structure of a leaf

Think what a leaf has to do. It has to make sugar from carbon dioxide and water, and at least some of the sugar has to be sent to other parts of the plant. Bear this in mind as you study a leaf.

Your teacher will give you a whole leaf and a very thin cross-section of the same type of leaf mounted on a slide.

1 Examine the whole leaf and identify the parts shown in Fig 8.12a.

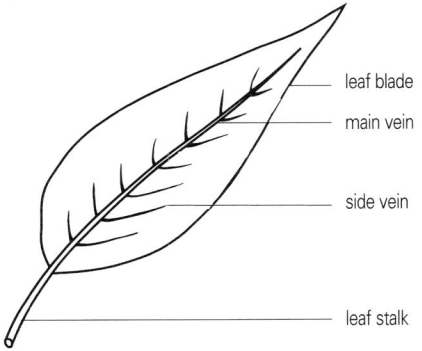

leaf blade

main vein

side vein

leaf stalk

(a) External structure

Fig 8.12 Structure of a leaf.

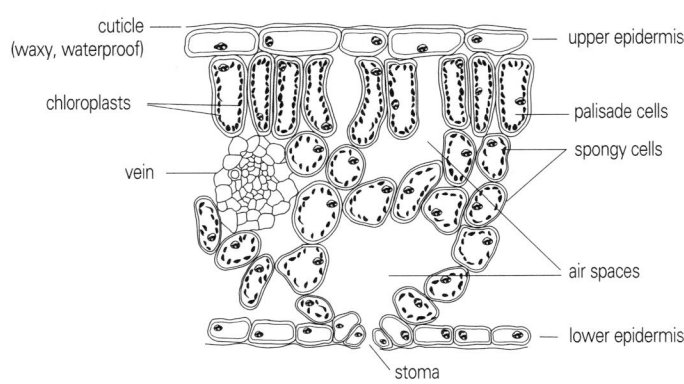

cuticle (waxy, waterproof)

chloroplasts

vein

upper epidermis

palisade cells

spongy cells

air spaces

lower epidermis

stoma

(b) Internal structure

2 Examine the thin section under the microscope, using low power. Try to find the parts shown in Fig 8.12b.

Notice two things in particular:

1 The **palisade cells** and **spongy cells**. They contain chloroplasts and this is where photosynthesis takes place. Most of the chloroplasts are in the palisade cells, so most photosynthesis occurs here.

2 The **veins**. They contain tube-like cells which transport water and mineral salts from the roots to the leaves, and soluble sugar and other products of photosynthesis from the leaves to other parts of the plant.

Questions for class discussion

1 Leaves are often a paler green on the lower side than on the upper side. Suggest a reason.

2 What makes the palisade cells so suitable for photosynthesis?

3 What are the air spaces for?

4 The air spaces contain carbon dioxide at night but not during the day. Why?

5 Suppose the leaf belongs to a growing potato plant (see page 53). Suggest two parts of the potato plant to which sugar will be transported from the leaves. What do these parts of the plant do with the sugar?

6 As well as transporting substances, the veins strengthen the leaves and help to hold them out flat. Why is this important?

Obtaining water

The plant obtains its water from the soil: it is absorbed by the roots and taken up the stem to the leaves. Only a fraction of this water is used in photosynthesis. Most of it evaporates from the leaves through the stomata.

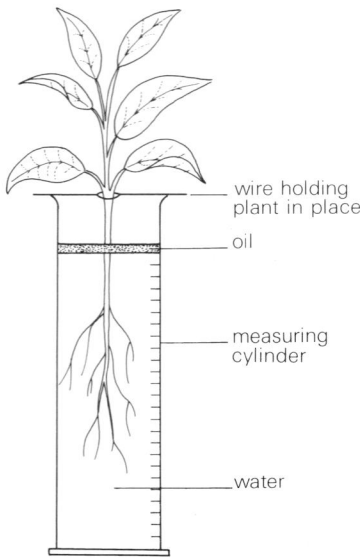

Fig 8.13 Apparatus for measuring the volume of water taken up by a leafy plant.

Experiment 8.8
Measuring the volume of water taken up by a plant

You will need a measuring cylinder with a capacity of 25 cm^3.

1 Find a small plant growing near the laboratory. Your teacher will help you. The above-ground part of the plant should have well developed leaves and should be about 10 cm high.

2 With a trowel, dig up the plant very carefully so as not to damage the roots.

3 Take the plant into the laboratory and *gently* wash the soil off the roots with cold tap water.

4 Place the roots of your plant in the measuring cylinder. Then fill the measuring cylinder with water exactly to the 25 cm^3 mark.

5 Carefully pour a little olive oil into the measuring cylinder, so that it forms a thin layer on the surface of the water. This should stop any water evaporating from the measuring cylinder (Fig 8.13).

6 Fill a second measuring cylinder with water up to the 25 cm^3 mark, and pour a little olive oil on to the surface as before. This will be your control.

7 After a week, record the level of the surface of the water in both measuring cylinders.

Questions for class discussion

1 In which measuring cylinder has the water level fallen most, and why?

2 Water does not always travel through a plant at the same speed; sometimes it travels very slowly but at other times it may travel much faster. The speed depends on how quickly water evaporates from the leaves. What conditions in the plant's environment are likely to speed up the rate at which water evaporates from the leaves?

3 If a plant does not get enough water, it may droop (Fig 8.14). This is called **wilting**. It happens if water evaporates from the leaves faster than it is absorbed by the roots.
   a When is this most likely to happen to garden plants?
   b What does it tell you about *one* function of water in plants?
   c In very dry weather the stomata close. The guard cells move together rather like a pair of doors. Why is this useful to the plant?
   d The surfaces of leaves are covered by a waterproof **cuticle** (see Fig 8.12 on the previous page).
      i Why is the cuticle useful?
      ii The cuticle is usually thicker on the upper surface of a leaf than on the lower surface? Suggest a reason.

Fig 8.14 On the left is a *Coleus* which was not watered by its absent-minded owner. On the right is the same plant shortly after watering.

Fig 8.15 The root of a young seeding showing the root hairs.

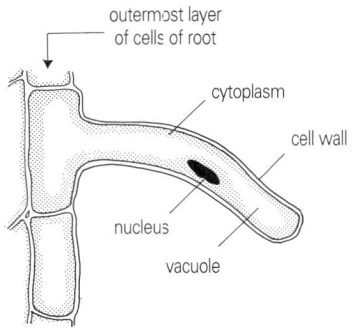

Fig 8.16 A root hair cell.

Fig 8.17 Barley plants grown in (left to right) complete nutrient solution: and solutions lacking potassium, nitrogen and phosphorus respectively.

4 A short way back from the tip, each root has a covering of very fine outgrowths called **root hairs** (Fig 8.15).
   a In what way might these root hairs help the plant to absorb water?
   b What other functions might be carried out by the root hairs?

5 Each root hair is a single cell. A **root hair cell** is shown in Fig 8.16. It has a long extension which lies between the soil particles. It absorbs water and mineral salts from the soil.
   a In what ways is a root hair cell different from, and similar to, a palisade cell in a leaf?
   b In what ways is a root hair cell adapted to carry out its functions?

Obtaining mineral salts

Mineral salts such as nitrates and phosphates are dissolved in the soil water. They come from the dead remains of animals and plants that have rotted (decayed) in the soil. **Manure** or **fertilisers** are added to the soil to enrich it in mineral salts.

Mineral salts are compounds of chemical elements such as nitrogen, phosphorus and potassium (N, P and K). The plant absorbs them, through the roots. If it is deprived of any of the elements that it needs, it will show poor growth and may die, as is shown by the following experiment.

A series of plants is grown in the laboratory. One of the plants, the control, is given all the elements required for good growth. Each of the other plants is given all the elements minus one. The growth and other features of each plant are then compared with the control.

The results of one such experiment are shown in Fig 8.17. Notice the poor growth shown by the three right hand plants. Potassium, nitrogen and phosphorus are the three main elements in fertilisers. Nitrogen is particularly important: it is needed to convert the sugars made by photosynthesis into protein.

Energy from respiration is needed to absorb mineral salts. This means that the roots need a supply of oxygen. Oxygen comes from air spaces between the soil particles. Plants grow much better if the soil is well aerated and well drained. Soil which is full of water (**waterlogged**) lacks air spaces and has a low oxygen content. Plants in waterlogged soil cannot absorb mineral salts efficiently, so they show poor growth.

Questions for class discussion

1 The pots in which potted plants are grown have a small hole in the bottom. Why? What advice would you give to people about watering their potted plants?

2 Look carefully at Fig 8.17. How do the barley plants that were deprived of nitrogen differ from the normal barley plants? Suggest a reason for the differences.

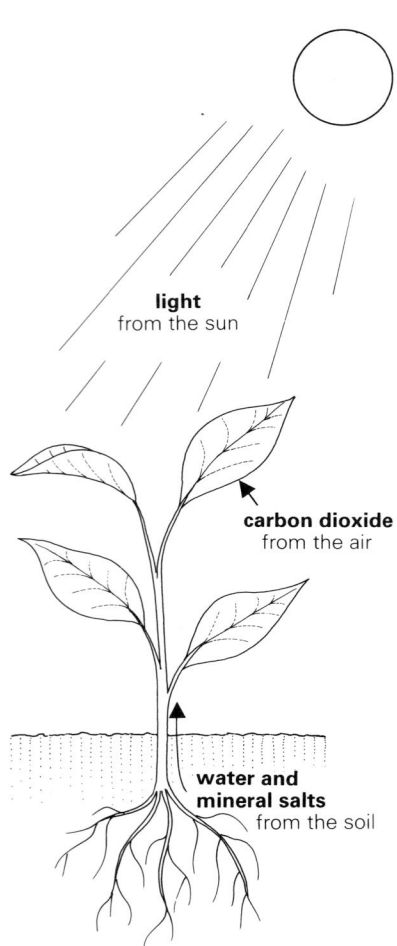

Fig 8.18 How a plant gets the things it needs for photosynthesis.

Summary of a plant's requirements

Fig 8.18 summarises the various things which a plant needs for photosynthesis and growth, and where it gets them.

Gaseous exchange in a plant

Plants undergo two quite distinct processes, both involving an exchange of gases between the leaves and the surrounding air.

Photosynthesis: the plant's method of making food. In this process the plant takes in carbon dioxide and gives out oxygen. Photosynthesis requires light, and so it will only take place during the day. It stops at night.

Respiration: the plant's method of obtaining energy. In this process the plant takes in oxygen and gives out carbon dioxide. Respiration occurs all the time, at night as well as during the day.

How do plants affect the atmosphere?

During the day, when it is light, green plants take in more carbon dioxide for photosynthesis than they give out in respiration. The result is that they remove carbon dioxide from the air around them. This is particularly so around midday when the light is at its brightest.

At night, when it is dark, photosynthesis stops but the plants continue to respire. The result is that they now add carbon dioxide to the air around them.

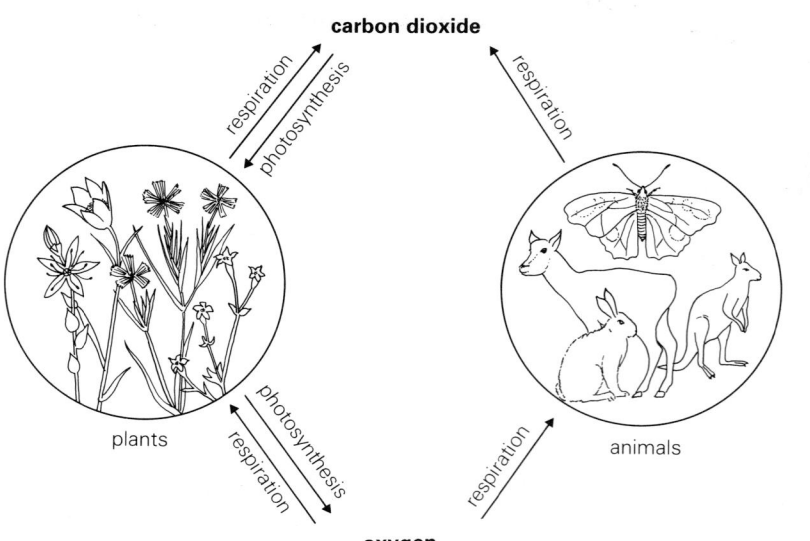

Fig 8.19 How animals and plants affect the atmosphere. Their combined activities keep the amount of carbon dioxide in the atmosphere more or less constant.

Animals, of course, respire all the time, so they constantly add carbon dioxide to the surrounding air.

Fig 8.19 sums up how animals and plants affect the atmosphere. The diagram includes oxygen as well as carbon dioxide.

The carbon cycle

Thanks to photosynthesis, carbon and its compounds can be used over and over again in nature. In other words, it circulates in the environment. This is called the **carbon cycle** (see Fig 8.20).

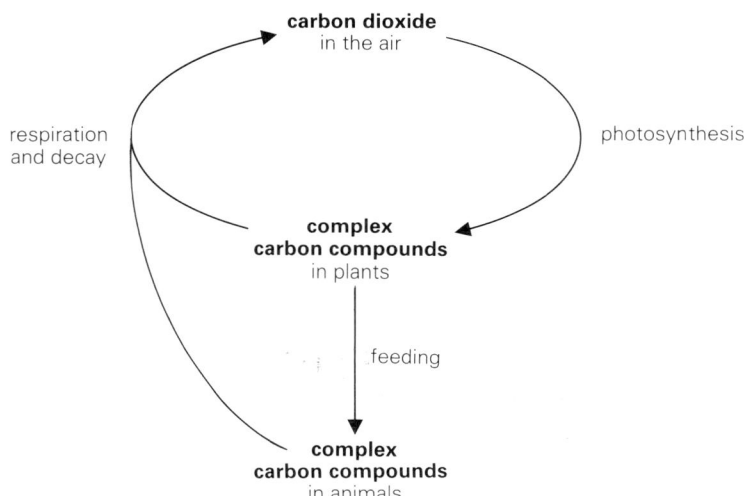

Fig 8.20 The carbon cycle.

Carbon dioxide in the air is used by plants to make starch and other complex carbon compounds. These may then be eaten by animals, including ourselves. Carbon dioxide is returned to the air when the animals and plants respire, and also when they decay after dying. Decay is brought about by microbes, and their respiration puts carbon dioxide back into the air (see page 162).

The carbon cycle brings home to us a very important thing: we, and all other animals, are completely dependent on plants. Plants, through their photosynthesis, give us two things that we cannot do without: food and oxygen. Without plants, life as we know it could not exist.

Questions for class discussion

1 In America there are car stickers which say '*Have you thanked a green plant today?*' What do we have to thank green plants for? Think of as many things as you can, not just the ones mentioned in this chapter.

2 There could be carbon atoms in your body which were in Henry VIII's body. What makes this possible?

3 In the world as a whole, the concentration of carbon dioxide in the air is kept at a steady level by a balance between respiration and photosynthesis. However, in the last one hundred years or so, the concentration of carbon dioxide in the air has increased.
   a) Suggest possible causes of the increase.
   b) What might its consequences be?

Homework assignments

1 Gardeners and farmers often add fertilisers to their soil. These fertilisers contain, amongst other things, the element nitrogen. Why do plants need this element?

2 Scientists have found that, in an area with dense vegetation such as a wood, the amount of carbon dioxide in the air varies slightly.
   a At what time of day would you expect it to be at its highest?
   b At what time of day would you expect it to be at its lowest?
   Explain your answers.

3 At one time nurses used to take all the plants out of a hospital ward at night.
   a Why do you think this was done?
   b Suggest a reason why it is no longer thought to be necessary.

4 Scientists have made accurate measurements of the average amount of carbon dioxide in the air at different times of the year. They found that in the early spring the carbon dioxide content was very slightly greater than in the late summer. Explain the difference.

5 It is possible to grow plants such as mosses and small ferns in a stoppered jar that will not let in any fresh air. The plants will not grow much but they can last for years. How do they survive, and why do they not grow much?

Summary

1 Green plants make starch by **photosynthesis**: the raw materials are carbon dioxide and water, and oxygen is a by-product. Sunlight provides energy for photosynthesis, and the green pigment **chlorophyll** is required.

2 The iodine test can be used to find out if a leaf contains starch. The leaf must be softened and decolourised first.

3 A controlled experiment can be done to show that light is needed for a green plant to make starch.

4 Another experiment can be done to show that Canadian pondweed will produce oxygen gas when illuminated.

5 In photosynthesis sugar is formed first, and this may then be turned into starch. Other substances arising from photosynthesis include cellulose, fats and oil, and proteins.

6 Photosynthesis takes place mainly in the **leaves**. Green plants have a large leaf area for obtaining as much light as possible.

7 Water is absorbed from the soil by the **roots**. It then passes up the **stem** to the leaves from which it evaporates.

8 The roots also absorb mineral salts from the soil. These are needed for healthy plant growth.

9 Experiments can be carried out to show the effects of depriving plants of particular mineral elements.

10 The gaseous exchanges which take place in green plants can affect the amount of carbon dioxide in the surrounding air.

11 The **carbon cycle** describes how carbon circulates in nature.

Chapter 9

Sexual reproduction in flowering plants

Sexual reproduction in animals involves two individuals, a male and a female. The male produces sperms and the female produces an egg. A sperm combines with the egg in the process that we call fertilisation. In flowering plants the same kind of thing takes place, though the details are different.

The flower

The reproductive structures are found in the **flowers**, which are formed towards the top of the plant (Fig 9.1). There are many different kinds of flowers, but they all have certain features in common. We shall start by looking at a well known flower.

Experiment 9.1
Looking at a geranium flower

Geraniums can be grown out of doors in the summer, and in pots indoors. You will need a plant that is in flower.

1 Detach a fully opened flower from the plant.

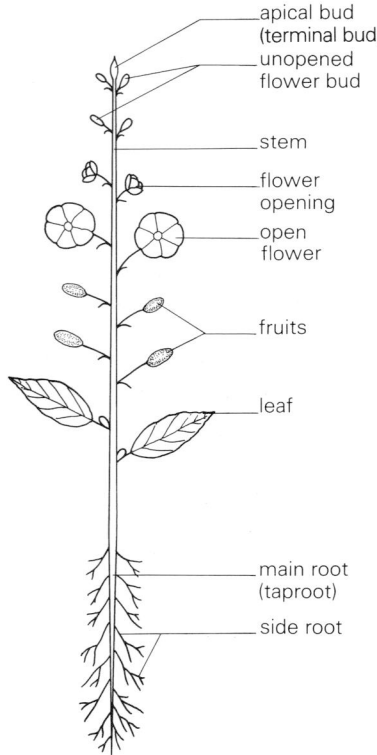

apical bud
(terminal bud)
unopened
flower bud

stem

flower
opening

open
flower

fruits

leaf

main root
(taproot)

side root

Fig 9.1 The main parts of a typical plant.

Fig 9.2 A flower showing the reproductive structures.

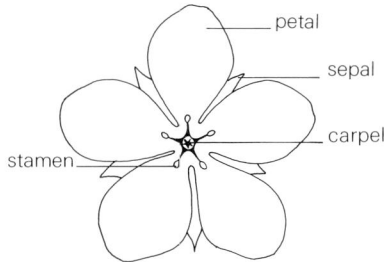

(a) The whole flower looking from above

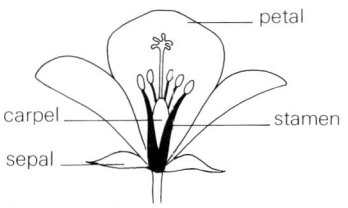

(b) Looking from the side with two sepals and two petals removed

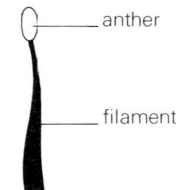

(c) A stamen, the male part of the flower

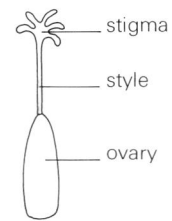

(d) A carpel, the female part of the flower

Fig 9.3 The structure of a geranium flower.

2 Observe the flower without pulling it to pieces.

You will see that it consists of a series of rings of structures (Fig 9.3a). From the outside inwards these structures are:

Sepals: five small green leaves round the outside of the flower.
Petals: five usually brightly coloured structures, larger than the sepals.
Stamens: five in all, each consisting of a stalk with a yellow knob at the end.
Carpel: a tall, column-like structure in the centre of the flower with a swollen base and five short branches at the top.

3 Remove one of the sepals and examine it carefully under a hand lens. How does it differ from an ordinary leaf?

Look at an unopened flower bud on the geranium. Does this tell you anything about the function of the sepals?

4 Carefully remove two of the petals on one side of the flower. This will enable you to see the inside of the flower more easily (Fig 9.3b).

5 Examine a stamen in detail (Fig 9.3c). The yellow knob is called the **anther**, and the stalk is called the **filament**. Squeeze one of the anthers with a pair of tweezers. Can you see any small yellow specks? These are **pollen grains**. The stamens are the male part of the flower, and the pollen grains carry the male gametes which are equivalent to an animal's sperm.

6 Observe a carpel in detail (Fig 9.3d). It consists of three parts: the **stigma** at the top, **style** in the middle, and **ovary** at the base. The ovary contains five little ball-like **ovules**, each of which contains a microscopic **egg cell**. The carpel is therefore the female part of the flower.

7 With a scalpel or razor blade, slice open the ovary lengthways. Can you see any ovules inside the ovary?

Safety note

Hold the carpel in such a way that your fingers are well clear of the cutting edge of the blade.

Questions for class discussion

1 Are the other flowers on the geranium plant identical with the one that you have studied? If not, how do they vary?

2 Not all plants have flowers similar to geranium flowers. From your memory of flowers which you have seen in your school grounds, or perhaps in your garden at home, how do the flowers of other plants differ from the geranium flower?

Experiment 9.2
Observing different kinds of flowers

Your teacher will give you the flowers of three different species of plant.

1 Examine each flower carefully and compare it with the others.

2 Write out Table 9.1 in your notebook.

Table 9.1

name of plant	Flower A	Flower B	Flower C
number of sepals number of petals number of stamens number of carpels colour of petals shape of the flower time of flowering (give months)			

3 Complete this table for your three flowers. Fill in as many of the spaces as possible from your own observations. Where necessary, look up the answer in a book.

Question for class discussion

List those features of the three flowers which are similar, and those features which vary from one species to another.

Homework assignments

1 The picture in Fig 9.4 shows a flower viewed from above.
  a Name the structures A, B and C.
  b Suppose you sliced through this flower along the dotted line; draw the probable appearance of the cut surface.

2 What part of a flower:
  a protects the flower bud before it opens
  b contains an egg
  c is equivalent to an animal's testis
  d contains the male gametes?

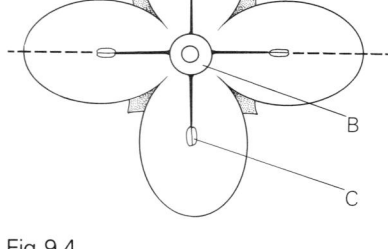

Fig 9.4

Pollination

For a flowering plant to reproduce sexually, the pollen grains must be transferred from an anther to a stigma. We call this process **pollination**.

Fig 9.5 A bee visiting a chamomile flower. Note the pollen on its leg.

In many plants, including the chamomile and the geranium, the pollen grains are transferred by insects such as bees, butterflies and moths (Fig 9.5).

When the insect visits a flower, it brushes against the anthers, and some of the ripe pollen grains stick to its hairy body. The pollen grains of some plants have little spikes projecting from them which make them 'sticky' and so help them cling to the insect. The insect then visits another flower, and some of the pollen grains fall off its body and stick to a stigma (Fig 9.6).

Why does the insect visit the flower in the first place? It does so in order to obtain **nectar**, a sugary fluid produced at the base of the petals. Insects feed on nectar. The honey which bees make and store in their hive is concentrated nectar.

The flowers of many plants have special features which attract insects. For example, the petals may be large and brightly coloured, and their smell may be pleasant. Scientists have done experiments which show that insects are attracted by the colours and scents of flowers. What features of the geranium flower may attract insects?

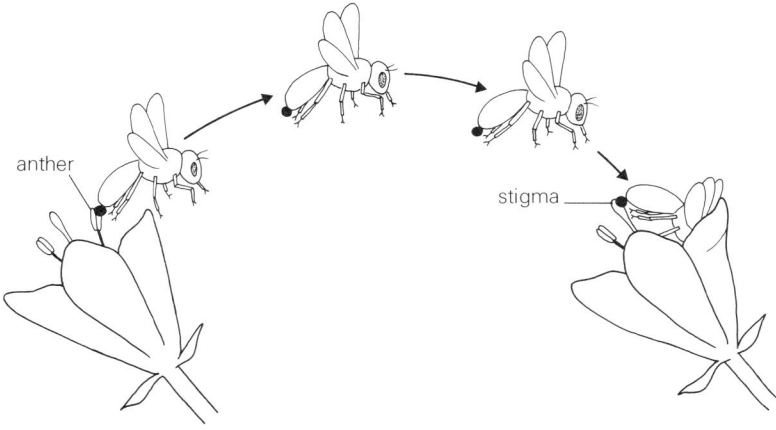

Fig 9.6 These diagrams show how a bee carries pollen from one flower to another.

Experiment 9.3
Watching insects visiting flowers

When you get a chance, watch insects visiting flowers. Record the name of the plant, and make a list of the insects which visit it.

Try to answer these questions as accurately as you can:

1 What part of the flower does the insect land on?

2 What does the insect do after it has landed?

3 How long does the insect spend visiting the flower?

4 Which features of the flower might attract the insect?

5 What features of the insect might help it to pick up pollen grains?

Pollination by wind

Pollen is not always transferred by insects. In some plants it is blown from one flower to another by wind.

An example of a wind-pollinated plant is hazel. The flowers are small and massed together into a catkin (Fig 9.7). The catkins hang down, and the pollen is readily scattered when they are shaken.

Experiment 9.4
Looking at pollen grains

You will need mature flowers from several different plants. The anthers should have split open to release their pollen grains.

With a paintbrush pick up a few pollen grains from an anther and place them on a microscope slide. Examine the pollen grains under the microscope.

Questions for class discussion

1 How could you estimate the approximate size of a pollen grain?

2 Does the appearance of the pollen grain suggest how it may be transferred from one flower to another?

3 Usually pollen grains are carried from the flowers of one plant to the flowers of a different plant of the same kind. We call this **cross-pollination**. However, on occasions a pollen grain may land on a stigma of the *same* flower. We call this **self-pollination**. Which do you think is better, cross-pollination or self-pollination? Explain your answer.

Fig 9.7 Hazel catkins. Note the pollen falling from the flowers.

4 The pollen grains of wind-pollinated plants are usually smaller than those of insect-pollinated plants. Why?

5 The pollen grains of wind-pollinated plants are usually more numerous than those of insect-pollinated plants. Why?

Fertilisation

What happens when a pollen grain lands on a stigma? The pollen grain sends out a tube which grows into the stigma and down the style to the ovary. Eventually it reaches the egg cell. Then a male nucleus in the tip of the pollen tube combines with the egg nucleus (Fig 9.8). This is **fertilisation**. Do not confuse fertilisation with pollination. **Pollination** is simply the transfer of the pollen grains from the stamen to the stigma.

Experiment 9.5
Watching the growth of pollen tubes

1 Put a drop of sugar solution (10 per cent sucrose) onto the centre of a slide.

2 Obtain a flower with opened anthers. With a paintbrush pick up a few pollen grains from an anther and place them in the sugar solution. Cover with a coverslip.

3 Set up a second slide, but this time put the pollen grains in a drop of water rather than sugar solution.

4 Place your two slides in a closed petri dish and leave them in a warm, dark place for at least 30 minutes. Then look at the pollen grains under the microscope (low power). Have they changed in their appearance? Describe what has happened.

Questions for class discussion

1 Why did you have to put the two slides in a petri dish in this experiment?

2 Did all the pollen grains send out pollen tubes, or only some of them? If only some did, can you suggest a reason?

3 There might be a substance in the stigma which makes the pollen grain send out a pollen tube. Does this experiment help you to guess what this substance might be? What could you do to confirm your guess?

4 Describe an experiment which you could do to find
  a) the best temperature
  b) the best sugar concentration
  for the development of pollen tubes by the pollen grain of a given species of plant.

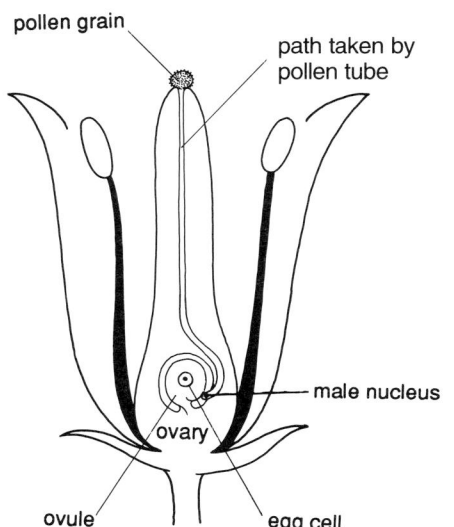

Fig 9.8 Fertilisation in a flower. The male nucleus is about to combine with the egg nucleus.

pollen grain

path taken by pollen tube

male nucleus

ovary

ovule

egg cell

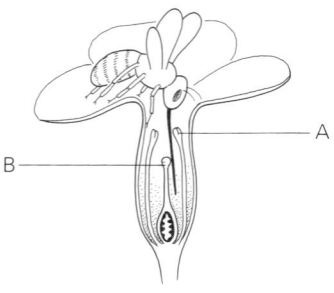

Fig 9.9 A flower being visited by a bee.

5 How do the male gametes of a flowering plant differ from the male gametes of a mammal such as the human?

Homework assignments

1 Study Fig 9.9, then answer the questions below.
  a Name a substance which the bee obtains when it visits the flower.
  b How is the structure of the bee suited for obtaining this substance?
  c What does the bee use this substance for?
  d Name structures A and B.
  e What does the plant gain from being visited by bees? Explain your answer fully.
  f Bees are insects. Write down one feature of the bee, visible in the picture, that tells you it must be an insect.

2 Carefully explain the difference between:
  a self-pollination and cross-pollination
  b pollination and fertilisation.

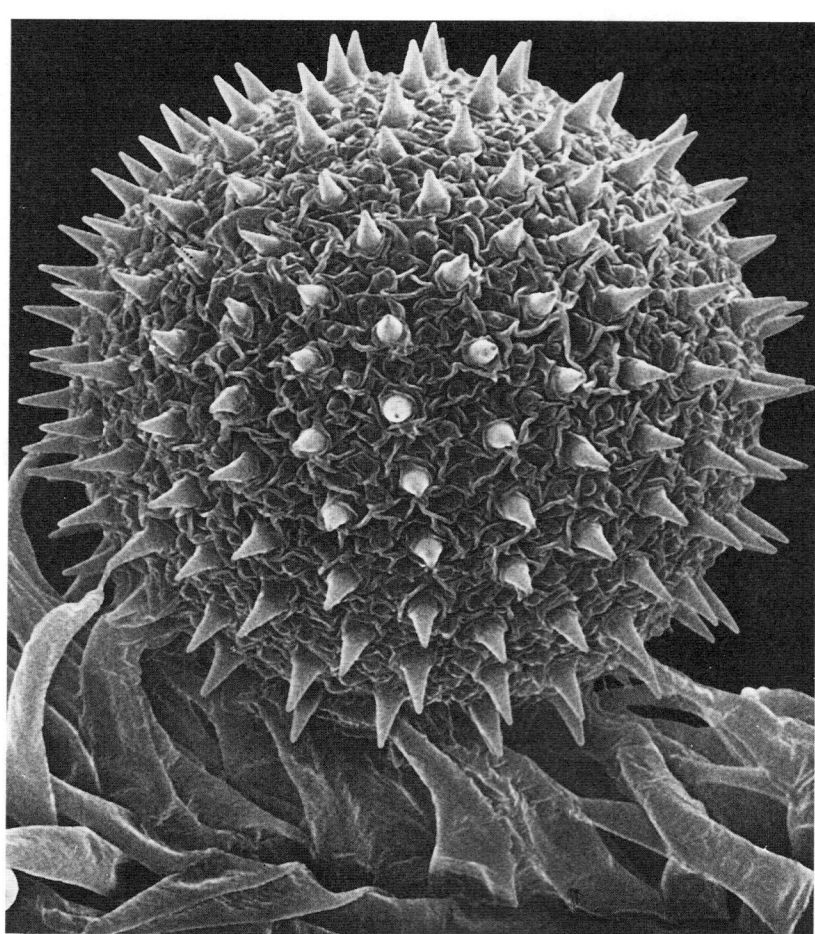

Fig 9.10 A pollen grain magnified a thousand times.

(a) External view

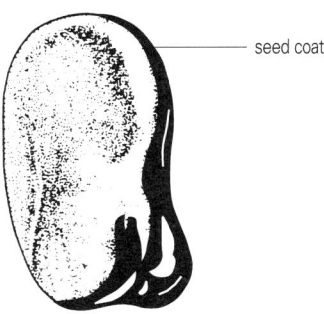

seed coat

(b) Seed coat removed to show embryo

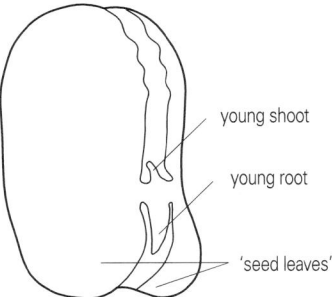

young shoot

young root

'seed leaves'

Fig 9.11 Structure of a broad bean seed.

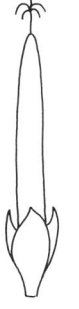

Fig 9.12 The fruit of a geranium is known as the 'crane's bill' because of its shape.

3 Fig 9.10 shows the pollen grain of a species of plant, greatly magnified. From the appearance of the pollen grain, how do you think the plant is pollinated?

After fertilisation

When the egg has been fertilised, the fertilised egg (zygote) divides repeatedly and develops into an **embryo**. The embryo becomes surrounded by a hard wall. This hard wall with the embryo inside, is known as the **seed**.

The seed contains a store of food, usually starch. This will nourish the embryo later when it develops into a new plant.

The final stage in the formation of a seed is that it gets extremely dry, and in this state the embryo becomes **dormant** – it goes to sleep, rather like an animal hibernating. However, it is still alive and capable of developing into a new plant. It may remain in this state for months or even years.

Experiment 9.6
Looking inside a seed

Before you look inside a seed, bear in mind that it has to contain everything necessary to make a new, self-supporting plant.

Your teacher will give you a broad bean seed which has been soaked in water to make it soft.

1 Look at the outside of the broad bean seed and observe the **seed coat** (Fig 9.11a).

2 Carefully remove the seed coat. You are now looking at the embryo. Can you see the parts shown in Fig 9.11b?

3 Put the embryo in a dish and cover it with dilute iodine solution. Which parts of the embryo turn blue-black?

Questions for class discussion

1 The blue-black colour shows that starch is present. Which part or parts of the embryo contain starch?

2 What is the function of the starch?

3 Seeds are used as a source of food for humans. Give examples of such seeds, apart from the broad bean, and say what sort of food we get from them. Why are seeds such a good source of food?

Fruits

The part of the flower surrounding the seed, or seeds, develops into the **fruit**. In most plants the fruit is formed from the ovary which, after fertilisation, may swell up considerably (Fig 9.12).

Fig 9.13 A female blackbird about to eat a berry.

Fig 9.14 Burdock fruits.

Fig 9.15 Dandelion fruits.

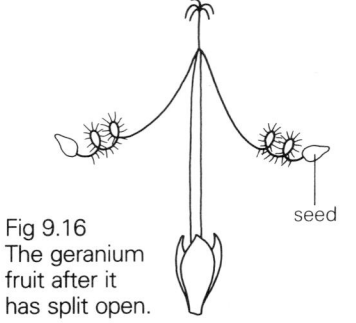

Fig 9.16
The geranium
fruit after it
has split open.

seed

Experiment 9.7
Watching fruits forming

Some biological experiments take a long time, and this is one of them. Be patient!

1 Select a flower of a potted geranium plant which has been pollinated. Observe the flower every time you come into the laboratory. Make notes and sketches to show any changes which take place in its appearance.
   What happens to the sepals, petals, stamens and carpels?
   Which part of the flower develops into the fruit?

2 Examine a fully formed fruit, and make a drawing of it in your notebook.

3 Carry out similar observations on other flowers as instructed by your teacher.

Dispersal of seeds

The job of the fruit is to help to carry the seeds as far as possible from the parent plant. We call this process **dispersal**. Why is it important for the seeds to be dispersed as widely as possible?
   Fruits help to disperse their seeds in four main ways.
   Some fruits are eaten by animals such as birds. The seeds are not digested but pass out with the bird's droppings, often a long way from where the bird ate them. An example is cherry: the stone contains the seed.
   Fleshy fruits often look and taste nice, so animals are attracted to them (Fig 9.13).
   Some fruits disperse their seeds by splitting open. This may occur with such force that the seeds are scattered quite a long way from the parent plant. The bean family have fruits of this sort: the 'pod' is the fruit and the 'beans' are the seeds.
   Some fruits are covered with little hooks. The hooks enable the fruit to cling to the fur of animals, thus aiding the dispersal of the seeds. A well known example is the fruit of burdock which clings to your clothes (Fig 9.14).
   Some fruits have wings or hairs. These slow their fall allowing them to be carried away by the wind. Sycamore trees have winged fruits, and dandelions have hairy parachutes (Fig 9.15).

Experiment 9.8
Fruits and dispersal

You will need a fully formed fruit from a geranium plant.

1 Lay the fruit on a *warm* hotplate, or place it in a desiccator, to dry out. Watch carefully. Does it split open? If not look at one which has already split open. Note its appearance (Fig 9.16). How does this fruit release and disperse its seeds?

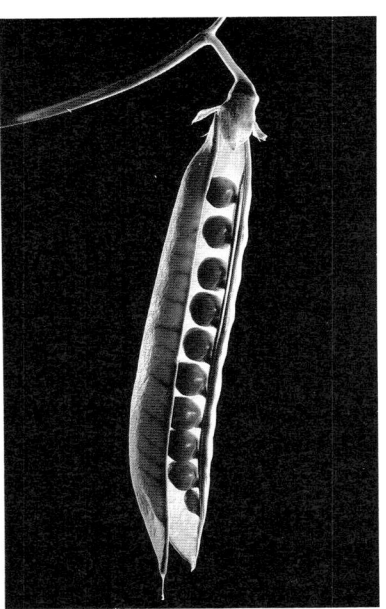

Fig 9.17 The fruits of four well known plants, dandelion, sycamore, goosegrass and pea.

2 Your teacher will give you the fruits of other kinds of flowers. Examine them carefully. In each case cut the fruit open and look for the seeds. How do you think the seeds are dispersed?

Questions for class discussion

1 The following are well known features of hedgerows in Britain: hips, haws, sloes, and old man's beard. What are they?

2 What tree do conkers come from, and what is the conker?

3 Fig 9.17 shows the fruits of four well known plants. If possible, look at real specimens of each one. Explain how each fruit aids in the dispersal of its seeds.

4 A fruit contains seeds but it does not provide them with nourishment. Yet many fruits are packed full of food substances. That is why we eat them. Give examples of such fruits and explain what use the food substances are to the plant.

Homework assignments

1 a Why do most flowers come out in the spring and summer?
b Why do most fruits appear in the autumn?

2 What happens to
a the petals
b the ovule
c the ovary
d the stamens
after the eggs inside a flower have been fertilised?

3 A biologist wished to show that geranium flowers cannot make fruits unless they have been pollinated. An unopened flower was shut in a polythene bag, and looked at carefully every day. A week later the biologist was surprised to find that a fruit had appeared.

a How might the flower have been pollinated?

b What should the biologist have done to prevent pollination?

c What should the control have been in this experiment?

4 Give the name of a flowering plant which you have studied.

a In what sort of habitat is it normally found?

b At what time of year does it flower?

c How is its pollen transferred?

d What features of the flower suit this method?

e How does it disperse its seeds?

Summary

1 The part of a plant responsible for sexual reproduction is the **flower**.

2 The flower consists of **sepals**, **petals**, **stamens** and one or more **carpels**.

3 In the process of **pollination**, pollen grains are transferred from the anthers of one flower to the stigmas of another flower. Pollination may be brought about by insects or by wind.

4 **Fertilisation** involves the growth of a pollen tube into the carpel. A male nucleus in the pollen tube combines with the egg cell nucleus in the ovary.

5 After fertilisation the zygote develops into an **embryo**, the ovule into the **seed**, and the ovary into the **fruit**.

6 The seed has a protective coat and inside there is a store of food as well as the embryo.

7 Fruits have special features which help to disperse the seeds.

Chapter 10

Growth and development of flowering plants

In the last chapter we saw how sexual reproduction in flowering plants results in the formation of seeds. In this chapter we shall see what happens to the seeds.

Germination of seeds

After being dispersed, the seeds may remain in the soil through the winter. In the following spring or summer, each seed bursts open and a new plant starts growing out of it. We call this process **germination**.

Why is it important that germination should be delayed until the spring or summer? What do you think prevents germination taking place in the middle of winter?

What do seeds need to germinate?

What sorts of things do you think a seed *might* need in order to germinate? Make a list of them in your notebook. Think of an experiment which could be done to test each of your suggestions.

One of your suggestions is probably water. We will now do an experiment to find out if water is needed for germination.

Experiment 10.1
To find out if water is needed for germination

For this experiment use the seeds of mustard or cress.

1 Set up two petri dishes side by side. Place moist blotting paper in one of them, and dry blotting paper in the other.

2 Sprinkle the seeds on to the blotting paper in each dish (Fig 10.1). Cover the dishes, and place them in a warm, well lit place.

3 Observe the seeds at intervals during the next few days.

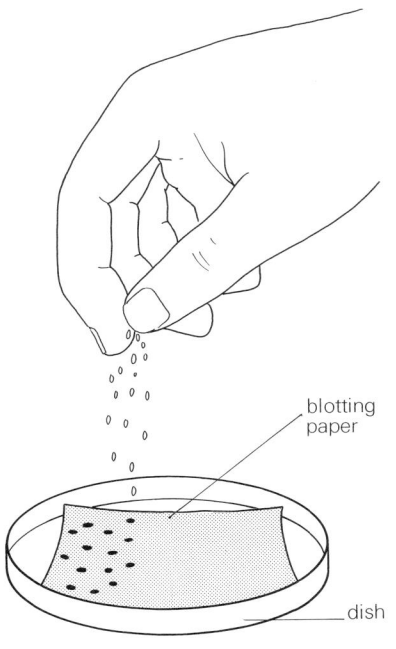

blotting paper

dish

Fig 10.1 Sowing seeds of mustard or cress on blotting paper.

Questions for class discussion

1 Do your results support the suggestion that water is needed for seeds to germinate?

2 Why was it necessary to set up a dish with dry blotting paper as well as one with moist blotting paper?

3 In fact the following conditions have been found to be needed for the germination of seeds in temperate parts of the world such as Britain: water (moisture), oxygen and a temperature of between about 10 °C and 30 °C.

Why do most seeds germinate in the spring or summer?

Homework assignments

1 A single plant may produce as many as one million seeds. However, only a small percentage of these germinate. Write down some reasons why the rest do not germinate.

2 Cress seeds were sown on moist blotting paper in three petri dishes and then placed as follows:

A in an incubator at 50 °C;
B on a warm windowsill;
C in a refrigerator at 4 °C.

Which dish of seeds would you expect to germinate first? Give two reasons for your choice.

Experiment 10.2
The absorption of water by a seed

You will need a dry broad bean seed for this experiment.

1 Weigh the dry seed, and write down its mass in grams.

2 Put the seed in a jar of water and leave it for about 24 hours.

3 Take the soaked seed out of the water and blot it gently. Then weigh it, and write down its mass.

4 Subtract the dry mass from the wet mass. This gives the increase in mass.

5 Express the increase in mass as a percentage of the original mass. We call this the **percentage increase**.

$$\text{Percentage increase in mass} = \frac{\text{increase in mass}}{\text{original mass}} \times 100$$

Questions for class discussion

1 Why was it necessary to blot the soaked seed before weighing it? Why did you have to blot it *gently*?

2 Why is it useful to express the increase in mass as a percentage of the original mass?

Fig 10.2(a) A wheat seed germinating. The root is growing out of the seed but the shoot has not yet appeared.

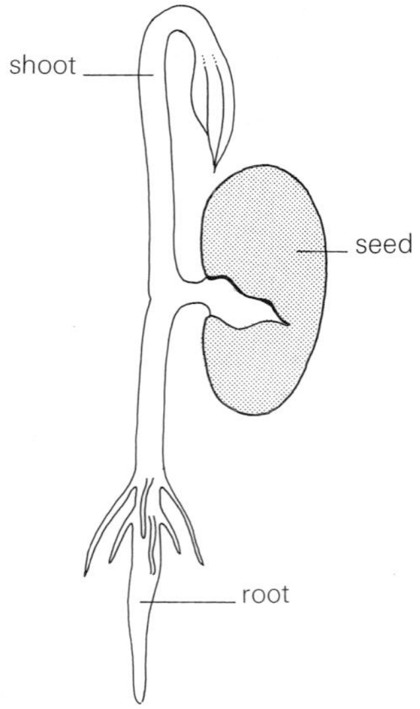

shoot

seed

root

Fig 10.2(b) A young broad bean seedling.

3 How do you think the seed takes up water?

4 Why does the seed need to take up water before it can germinate?

The seedling

The young plant which grows out of the seed is called a **seedling** (Fig 10.2). The seedling has two main parts: the **root** which grows down into the soil, and the **shoot** which grows up into the air. In time the shoot develops green leaves.

Experiment 10.3
Observing the development of a broad bean seedling

You will need a broad bean which has been soaked for 24 hours. The one from Experiment 10.2 will do.

1 Pour water into a glass jar to a depth of about 3 cm.

2 Roll up a sheet of blotting paper and place it in the jar as in Fig 10.3a. The blotting paper should soak up the water and stick to the side of the jar.

3 Push the broad bean seed between the blotting paper and the side of the jar (Fig 10.3b).

4 Observe the jar at intervals during the next two weeks. Describe the changes which take place and record them in your notebook.

Questions for class discussion

1 When the seed germinated, did you notice that the root appeared before the shoot? Why should the root appear first?

2 How many days after the experiment was set up did your seedling look like the one in Fig 10.2b?

3 As the root grew, did you notice that it was covered with fine hairs a short way behind the tip? What are these hairs for?

4 When the shoot grew out of the seed did you notice that the tip was bent back as in Fig 10.2b? Suggest a reason for this.

5 The tip of the root is covered by a slimy covering of cells called the **root cap**. What do you think this is for?

How is the seedling nourished?

At first the young seedling gets all the food it needs from starch stored inside the seed. How could you show that a broad bean contains starch?

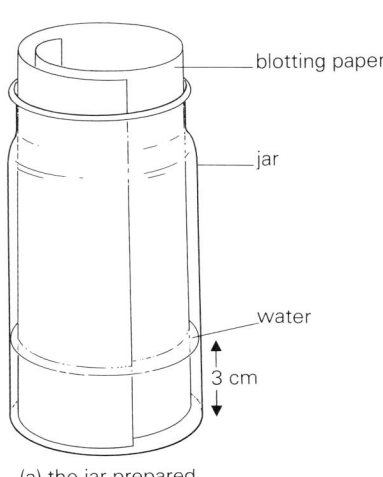

blotting paper

jar

water

3 cm

(a) the jar prepared

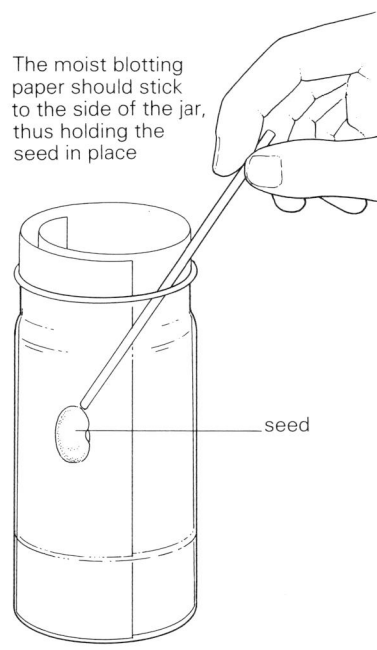

The moist blotting paper should stick to the side of the jar, thus holding the seed in place

seed

(b) pushing the seed into position

Fig 10.3 Procedure for observing a broad bean seed germinating.

Later on, the shoot develops green leaves, and the seedling starts making its own food by photosynthesis. How many days after germination did you observe green leaves on your seedling? The green colour is caused by the presence of a certain pigment in the leaf cells. What is this pigment called?

Homework assignments

A technician allowed a soaked broad bean seed to germinate in moist sand. The seedling was weighed every day between the third and twentieth days after germination. The measurements are shown in Table 10.1

Table 10.1

Days after germination	Mass (grams)
3	4·9
4	5·1
5	5·2
6	5·4
7	5·6
8	5·9
9	6·1
10	6·2
11	5·7
12	6·2
13	7·1
14	7·6
15	8·4
16	9·0
17	9·6
18	10·7
19	11·0
20	11·5

1 Plot these results on graph paper, putting days on the horizontal axis and mass on the vertical axis.

2 Explain the reason for:
   a the increase in mass between the third and tenth days
   b the loss of mass between the tenth and eleventh days
   c the increase in mass between the eleventh and twentieth days.

The importance of light to the developing seedling

When a seed germinates in the soil, the shoot grows up and breaks through the surface of the soil. Once the shoot has broken through, light falls on it. Is light important for the further growth and development of the seedling? We can find out by growing seedlings in the dark.

Experiment 10.4
Investigating the effect of darkness on the development of seedlings

1 Sprinkle mustard or cress seeds in two dishes containing moist blotting paper.

2 Put one dish in a well lit place, and put the other dish under a cardboard box.

3 Observe the two dishes of seedlings at intervals during the next week and notice any differences in their appearance.

4 Make a careful drawing of a seedling from the well lit dish, and one from the darkened dish.

5 Make a list of the ways in which the seedlings grown in the dark differ from the well lit ones.

Questions for class discussion

1 A seedling which is grown in the dark differs from a well lit one in three main ways:
a the stem is taller and thinner
b the leaves are yellow instead of green
c the leaves are smaller.
   A plant with this appearance is described as **etiolated**. What can you say about the functions of light in the development of a seedling?

2 What other things, besides light, are necessary for seedlings to grow and develop properly? Make a list of as many as you can think of.

Homework assignments

1 A student took some dwarf pea seeds and planted them in two trays of soil. One (a) was left in a well lit place; the other (b) was placed in a dark cupboard. After two weeks the student examined them and found that they looked like the photograph (Fig 10.4). As well as the differences that can be seen in the photograph, the plants in (b) were yellow whereas the plants in (a) were green.
a Write down two differences, other than colour, between the two lots of plants.
b Apart from the amount of light, name two other factors which might have produced the differences between the plants.
c Explain how you could carry out an experiment with dwarf pea seedlings to try to find out if it is only light that is producing the differences.

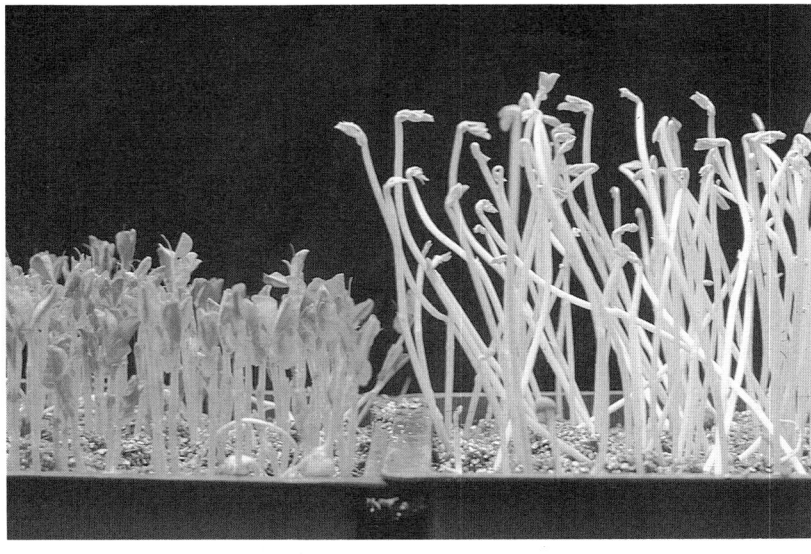

Fig 10.4 Experiment to find out what happens to a plant left to grow in a dark place.

(a)   (b)

2 a Name a plant that you have studied. Describe briefly how you would measure the rate of growth of the plant.

b Describe how you would carry out an experiment to discover whether this plant grows better when alone or in large groups.

Growth of the seedling into a new plant

It is fun to plant seeds and watch the young seedlings grow up into mature plants. At the same time you can do experiments to find out what sort of conditions give the best results. To do this you need to be able to measure the amount of growth which takes place in a given period of time.

Experiment 10.5
Measuring the growth of seedlings

1 Your teacher will give you a shallow box of soil containing young seedlings of barley, wheat or maize.

2 With a ruler measure the height in millimetres of each seedling (Fig 10.5), and work out the average height.

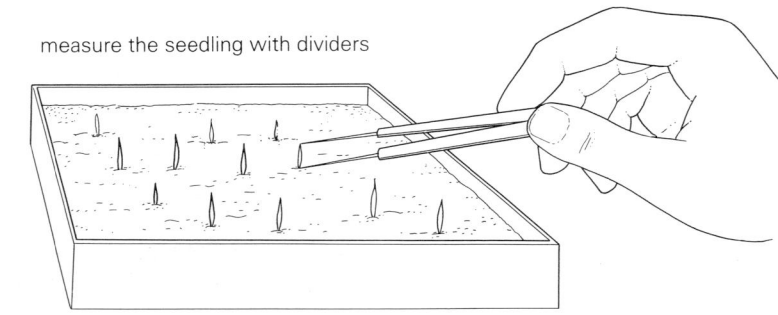
measure the seedling with dividers

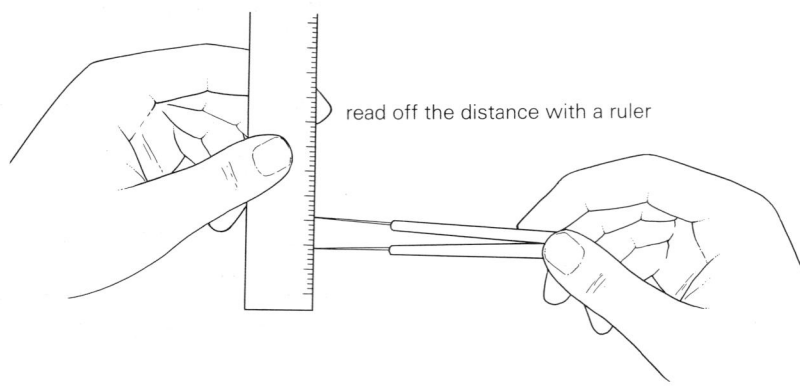
read off the distance with a ruler

Fig 10.5 Measuring the height of a seedling.

3 Repeat this at regular intervals for the next two weeks. The seedlings should be kept in a warm, well lit place and the soil should be kept moist by watering it regularly.

4 Plot your results on a sheet of graph paper: put the average heights on the vertical axis, and time in days on the horizontal axis.

Questions for class discussion

1 At the end of the two week period what is the height of
a the tallest
b the shortest plant?

2 How would you describe the shape of the curve on your graph? Explain the reason for the shape.

3 What is the height range in your sample (see page 12)? Suggest possible reasons why some seedlings grow taller than others.

Experiment 10.6
Growing radishes from seed

If it is summer you can grow radishes out of doors. Alternatively, fill a shallow box with moist soil almost to the top.

1 Make a channel in the soil about 2 cm deep. If you plant more than one row, the rows should not be too close together.

2 Open a packet of radish seeds at the corner. Let the seeds trickle out into the channel in the soil (Fig 10.6).

3 Cover the seeds with a thin layer of soil. Pat the soil gently to make it firm. If you are using a soil box, leave the box in a warm, well lit place.

4 Examine the soil whenever you can. If necessary water it occasionally. How long does it take for the first shoots to appear?

5 Observe the plants over the next three weeks. Gently pull up one of the plants every two or three days and examine its roots; then throw it away.

Questions for class discussion

1 How long does it take for the roots to start swelling up into radishes?

2 The swellings are called **root tubers** and they are filled with stored food: this is why they are good to eat. What use are these tubers to the radish plant? Where does the stored food come from, and how does it get into the tubers? (Chapter 5 may help you to answer these questions.)

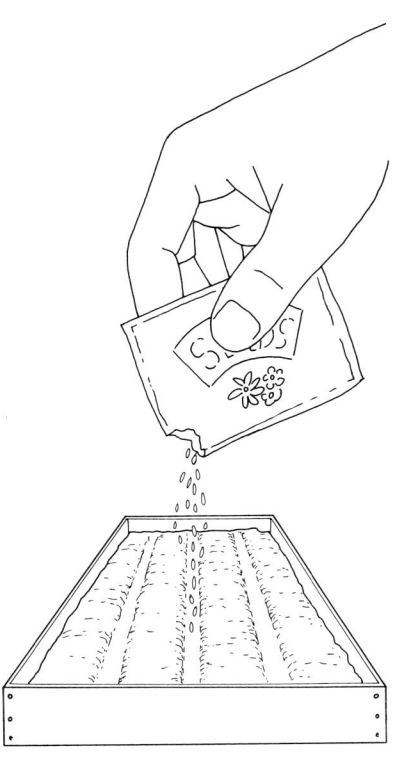

Fig 10.6 Sowing radish seeds in soil.

Homework assignments

1 A scientist planted a seed and as soon as the shoot appeared its height was measured. Measurements were made every day for three weeks. Conditions such as temperature and light were kept constant throughout this period. The measurements are shown in the graph in Fig 10.7.

Fig 10.7 Graph to show the growth rate of a shoot.

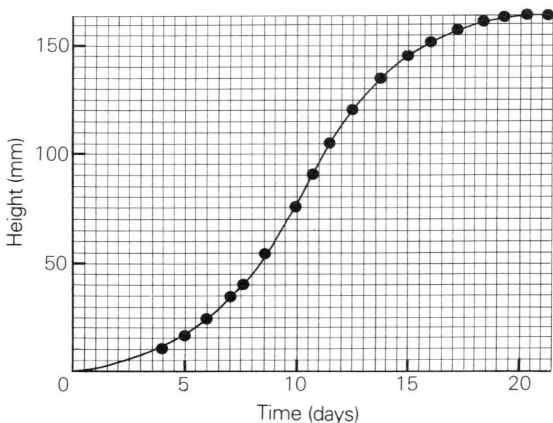

a During which days was growth
  (i) fastest
  (ii) slowest?
b Suggest possible reasons for the changes in the rate of growth which took place.

2 Two next-door neighbours, A and B, shared a packet of onion seeds which they sowed in their back gardens. A's onion plants grew to be large and healthy, but B's were small and unhealthy.
  a Suggest reasons why A's plants were better than B's.
  b Choose one of your suggestions and describe an experiment which you could do to find out if it is correct.

The life cycle of flowering plants

The last two chapters have dealt with sexual reproduction and the growth and development of flowering plants. Together these processes make up the **life cycle** (Fig 10.8).

Some flowering plants grow to full size, produce seed and die within one year. We call these **annual plants**. Other plants go on growing year after year, producing seeds each summer. We call these **perennial plants**.

Some examples of perennial plants are trees. Many trees shed their leaves in the autumn. They are known as **deciduous trees**: examples are horse chestnut ('conker' tree) and beech. Other trees bear leaves all the year round. They are known as **evergreens**: examples are holly and yew.

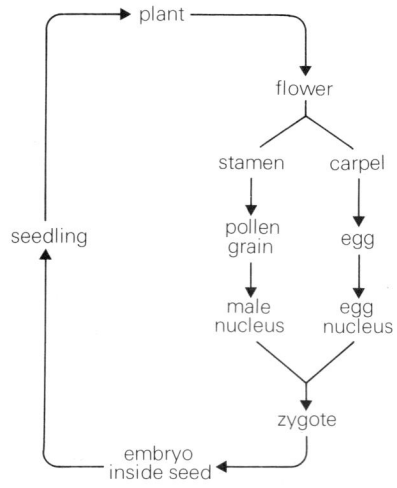

Fig 10.8 The life cycle of a flowering plant.

Question for class discussion

Compare the life cycle of a flowering plant with that of the human (see page 69). Do this by drawing, side by side, the life cycle of the human and the life cycle of a flowering plant. Put the equivalent stages of both life cycles in the same relative positions.

What are the *main* similarities and the *main* differences between the two life cycles? How would you explain the differences?

Experiment 10.7
What happens to the buds of a tree?

1 Cut off a winter twig of a horse chestnut tree about 20 cm from the end. Identify the parts of the twig shown in Fig 10.9.

2 Put the cut end of the twig in a jar of water, and place the jar in a warm, well lit part of the laboratory.

3 Observe the twig over the next few weeks. Pay particular attention to what happens to the bud at the end of the twig. List any changes in its appearance.

Questions for class discussion

1 Bringing a horse chestnut twig indoors causes the bud to open before it would have done out of doors. Suggest reasons why the bud opens more rapidly indoors.

2 What effect does the opening of the bud have on the length of the twig? How would this affect the overall size of the tree?

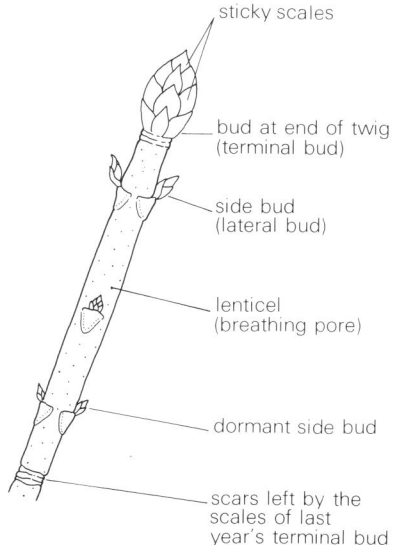

sticky scales

bud at end of twig
(terminal bud)

side bud
(lateral bud)

lenticel
(breathing pore)

dormant side bud

scars left by the
scales of last
year's terminal bud

Fig 10.9 A winter twig of a horse chestnut tree.

How do trees grow?

In Experiment 10.7 you saw how the winter buds on a tree produce new shoots in the spring. This has the effect of lengthening the branches.

At the same time the trunk gets thicker. If you look at the trunk of a felled tree you can see a series of rings (Fig 10.10). These are called **annual rings**, and they are new layers of **wood** which are produced each year. The outermost ring is the most recent layer of wood, and the innermost ring is the oldest. You can work out the age of a tree by counting its annual rings. How old do you think the tree in Fig 10.10 was when it was felled?

When is the new ring of wood formed each year? It happens when conditions are best for growth, which of course is mainly in the spring and summer. In the winter, when it is cold, very little growth takes place.

Fig 10.10 End-on view of the trunk of a felled tree showing the annual rings.

Table 10.2

Ring number	Year of formation	Thickness
1	1977	5.0 mm
2	1976	1.0 mm
3	1975	8.0 mm
4	1974	5.0 mm
5	1973	1.5 mm
6	1972	4.5 mm
7	1971	5.5 mm
8	1970	4.0 mm

Homework assignments

A student measured the thickness of the annual rings in the outer region of the trunk of a felled tree, and obtained the results shown in Table 10.2

1 Plot these results as a bar chart.

2 In 1975 the ring was thicker than usual.
  a What does that suggest about the growth of the tree?
  b What does it suggest about the weather conditions in 1975?

3 a In which two years was growth slight?
  b Suggest *four* possible reasons for this slight growth.

Questions for class discussion

1 Think of as many uses as you can for wood. In each case suggest what it is about the wood that makes it so suitable for the use which you mention.

2 In 1988, an area of the Amazon forest the size of Holland was felled and cleared. Much of the wood was burned. What effects might such mass destruction of the world's natural forests have on the environment? What do you think should be done about it?

Dormancy

Plants do not develop continuously. At certain times of the year – usually the winter – the plant (or part of it) stops developing and goes into a prolonged sleep, rather like an animal hibernating. As explained in the last chapter, this is known as **dormancy**.

You have met two plant structures which become dormant in winter: seeds and buds. Dormancy is important because it enables the plant to survive an unfavourable period such as winter; it resumes its development when conditions become suitable.

The story of a wheat field
A farmer explains how he grows wheat

First of all I choose the variety of wheat that I want to grow. There are lots of different varieties. This year I chose a high-quality variety which is suitable for bread-making. It's a winter wheat: the seeds are sown in the autumn, and the shoots come up before the winter sets in. Growth stops during the winter, and then starts up again next spring.

In September I prepared the soil. I ploughed it, and added lime to it. I'm lucky with my soil. It's heavy and fairly fertile, so nature's on my side.

I like my field to produce as much wheat as possible, so I sowed the seeds quite close together. I used a machine on the back of my tractor. It's called a seed drill. It places the seeds in the soil at just the right depth, about three centimetres deep. I aim to have about 250 plants per square metre.

After I'd sown the seeds, Joe, my assistant, spread a fertiliser over the soil. It feels a bit like sand and is a mixture of phosphorus and potassium (P and K). I hoped it would rain within a day or two so as to dissolve it and wash the nutrients into the soil. It would help the seeds to germinate successfully and give nice strong seedlings.

I didn't want to have lots of weeds in my wheat field. So I put a weedkiller (herbicide) onto the soil before the first wheat shoots appeared. I hoped this would kill all those grasses and broad-leaved weeds which were such a nuisance last year.

Last year my wheat got infected with a virus. My agricultural adviser told me that it's carried from one plant to another by a particular type of aphid. So this year I sprayed my crop with an insecticide to kill any aphids that might be present. This was at the end of October when the shoots had three or four leaves. After that there was nothing more for me to do till spring.

When the spring came, I put another weedkiller onto the field. It is supposed to kill the weeds which escaped being killed in the autumn. It's a *selective* weedkiller which kills the weeds but doesn't harm the wheat.

I don't need to kill *all* the weeds, just the large ones that would compete with the wheat for sunshine and nutrients. The smaller ones are kept down by the wheat itself. A botanist who works at the local university told me that by letting some weeds grow in my wheat field I am helping with conservation.

There are other pests which must be got rid of. Fungi are a particular nuisance. There's one called 'take-all'. It's a good name for it because it robs the wheat of its goodness and causes it to die in patches. Unfortunately there's no chemical way of controlling this fungus. However, my adviser told me how to grow my wheat so as to reduce the chance of getting the disease. He also suggested which chemicals I should use to protect my crop against other diseases.

I next applied a nitrogen fertiliser to my crop. I used ammonium nitrate, though urea from animal waste would do just as well. This fertiliser helps my wheat plants to grow well and develop plenty of side shoots. Each side shoot grows and produces a cluster of flowers at the top. Inside the flowers the seeds – or grain as we call it – form. To get a good crop, each of my original plants needs to produce about three side shoots.

Through the summer, the grain ripened: each seed filled up with starch which the plant made. It was a good summer, warm and sunny. But then something happened to spoil everything: there was a terrible thunder storm with very heavy rain. The rain flattened some of my wheat before it had matured. This upset me because it reduced the yield of grain, and lowered its quality. However, the storm was brief and I am lucky not to have lost more than I did. It just shows how dependent we farmers are on the weather, and how easily a single event can spoil our crops. My adviser has suggested that next year I should treat my crop with a chemical that will make the stems shorter and stiffer. This should reduce the chance of the weather spoiling my crop.

By the end of August my wheat had turned a golden brown and was ready for harvesting. My farm is small so I don't have a combine harvester of my own. I hire one. Its a wonderful machine, combining two actions in one: it cuts the wheat *and* separates the grain from the rest of the plant. I'll store the grain in my grain store until it's sold. As I said at the beginning, mine is a high-quality wheat. The grain will be milled into flour for bread-making.

As I look at all that grain in my grain store, I can't help thinking of the thousands of loaves that will be made from it. It's funny to think that my field of wheat will have turned sunshine into bread!

Questions

1 Can you think of one other thing, besides sunshine and nutrients, for which weeds might compete with wheat? In what weather conditions might this be a particular problem?

2 How are small weeds kept down by the wheat itself?

3 In what way does leaving weeds in a wheat field help with conservation?

4 In natural countryside such as a woodland, fertilisers are not added to the soil every year, and yet the plants thrive. Why, then, is it necessary for farmers to add fertilisers to their wheat fields?

5 Suggest reasons why less grain is produced by wheat which has been flattened by the rain.

6 Do you agree with the farmer that wheat turns sunshine into bread? Explain your answer.

Summary

1 **Germination** is the process by which a new plant starts growing from a seed.

2 To germinate successfully, seeds require moisture (water), warmth and oxygen.

3 Before a seed can germinate it must absorb water, which greatly increases its mass.

4 When a seed germinates the **root** grows out first, and then the **shoot** appears. The young plant is called a **seedling**.

5 At first the seedling is nourished from food stored inside the seed. Later the seedling develops green leaves which make food by photosynthesis.

6 For the seedling to grow properly, and for chlorophyll to develop in its leaves, light is needed.

7 Every spring the **buds** of a deciduous tree produce new leafy shoots.

8 A tree trunk increases in width by forming new layers of wood every year (**annual rings**).

9 Seeds and buds are **dormant** structures which enable the plant to survive unfavourable periods such as winter.

Explorations 2

H Is carbon dioxide needed for photosynthesis?

Your teacher will give you two potted geranium plants which have been kept in the dark for 48 hours, two polythene bags which are impervious to air, some pellets of soda lime which absorb carbon dioxide, and all the things you need for testing a leaf for starch.

Use the above to find out if carbon dioxide is needed for photosynthesis. You will need to start the experiment on one day and finish it about two days later.

Write down what you are going to do on each day. Show your plan to your teacher. When you have had it approved, carry out the experiment

Give an account of your results and conclusions.

I Setting up a bottle garden

Your teacher will give you a bell jar, a large glass plate, some Vaseline and a small selection of potted plants.

Using these things, find out if plants can survive in a sealed, air-tight container. This involves setting up a 'bottle garden'. Examine the plants at weekly intervals to see how they are getting on. Record any interesting observations.

1 Do you think the plants will survive? Explain your answer.

2 What would happen if you put some animals in the container?

J Growing plants

It's fun to watch plants grow, and even more fun if you can eat them afterwards!

Your teacher will give you a small plot of ground. First, prepare the soil so that it is suitable for plants to grow in. (You might like to find out more about soil, see page 145.)

Next, decide which plants you would like to grow in your plot. You may plant them as seeds, or as very young plants (seedlings). Your teacher will help you to decide what to grow.

Look after your plants as they develop. What should you give them to help them flourish? Make sure you give them everything they need.

Keep a notebook and record the progress of your plants.

Once your plants are established, write an account of your garden, how you kept it and what you have learned from it about the way plants grow.

Safety note

Use forceps when handling soda lime as it is corrosive.

K How does light affect a plant's rate of growth?

Does light speed up a plant's rate of growth, or slow it down? Investigate this question by testing the hypothesis: placing a plant in darkness slows down its rate of growth.

First choose the type of plant you wish to investigate, then plan exactly what you will do: decide how many plants to include, what measurements to make and what your control should be. When your plan has been approved by your teacher, carry out the investigation.

Write a full report of your investigation. Decide how best to present your results and conclusions. Finish your report with a brief discussion: are the results what you would expect, and do they fit in with the way plants behave in their natural environment?

Finally, do your results suggest further ideas which might be investigated?

L Which fertiliser is best?

Suppose you are asked by the magazine *Which?* to find out which of a number of garden fertilisers is best.

Plan an experiment to compare the efficiency of two (or more) different fertilisers provided by your teacher. First, decide how you will test each fertiliser so as to make the comparison *fair*. Pay particular attention to safety, outlining any precautions that should be taken. Don't forget to set up any necessary controls.

Write a report on your results.

M The effect of varying the concentration of fertiliser on plant growth

How much fertiliser should you give a plant to produce a maximum response? When you buy a fertiliser from a shop, the label tells you what concentration to use. Is it harmful to plants to use higher concentrations? Do you get a poorer response if you use less?

Devise an experiment to find the answers to these questions. Use a commercial fertiliser or 'plant food' such as Phostrogen or Liquinure. Decide what tests to carry out, and what plants to use. Make sure that any comparisons you make are fair and valid. Discuss your plan with your teacher before you start work.

If a farmer puts too much fertiliser on his or her fields, what are the consequences likely to be?

N The strength of plant stems

The stems of plants vary greatly in their strength and flexibility. Devise a way of measuring either the strength or the flexibility of plant stems. Discuss and get your method approved with your teacher. Use it to compare stems of different types of plant.

Can you relate the strength of each stem to the kind of life that the plant leads?

Chapter 11   The numbers of living things

Fig 11.1 Spectators at a football match.

How many people can you see in Fig 11.1? You will probably say that it is impossible to count them. Biologists often need to know the number of each kind of animal or plant living in a habitat. This is called the size of the **population**. If we cannot count every individual then we have to make an **estimate** of the population.

Experiment 11.1
How many organisms are there in an aquarium?

The aquarium which you set up in Chapter 1 should now contain large numbers of several species of organisms. In this experiment we shall estimate how many there are.

You will need a bench lamp, several shallow dishes, a hand net, a beaker, a wide-mouthed teat pipette and a hand lens.

1 Copy Table 11.1 into your notebook.

Table 11.1

Name of organism	Brief description	Population estimate

2 Examine your aquarium carefully. A bench lamp and beaker will help you to look at the bottom of the tank (see Fig 11.2) but do not disturb the mud.

Fig 11.2 Examining the bottom of an aquarium through a beaker lowered into the water.

3 Start with the plants. Identify them as far as you can, using the key in the Appendix. If you cannot find the name, just write a brief description in your table.

4 Carefully remove one individual of each kind of small animal with a wide mouthed pipette or small net and place it in a shallow dish containing a little water. If it is too small to see clearly, use a hand lens to examine it. The key in the Appendix may help you to name it.

5 When you have identified most of the animals and plants, estimate the number of each species in the whole aquarium tank. Write your estimate in the third column of the table. It does not matter if your estimate is very approximate; it will still indicate whether the organism is common or rare.

If you have a pond, stream or canal near your school you could select a small area and estimate the size of the population of a species of animal or plant found there using this method.

Before doing this, check your plans with your teacher to make sure that the area you have chosen is suitable and safe.

Taking samples

A more accurate way of estimating the number of living organisms in a habitat is to choose a small area and count the number of organisms in it. Then work out how many small areas would fit into the whole habitat. The small area is called a **sample**.

If you take as many samples as you can your estimate of the size of a population will be even more accurate. You must not choose your sample areas because they have a large number of individuals or because they are easy to count; the samples must be selected from all over the habitat, that is, *taken at random*.

Experiment 11.2
Estimating the number of duckweed plants in a pond

Duckweed is a plant which floats on the surface of ponds and canals. You may have some growing in your aquarium. Each plant consists of a single leaf with one or more roots growing out of it. Fig 11.3 shows the surface of a pond covered with duckweed.

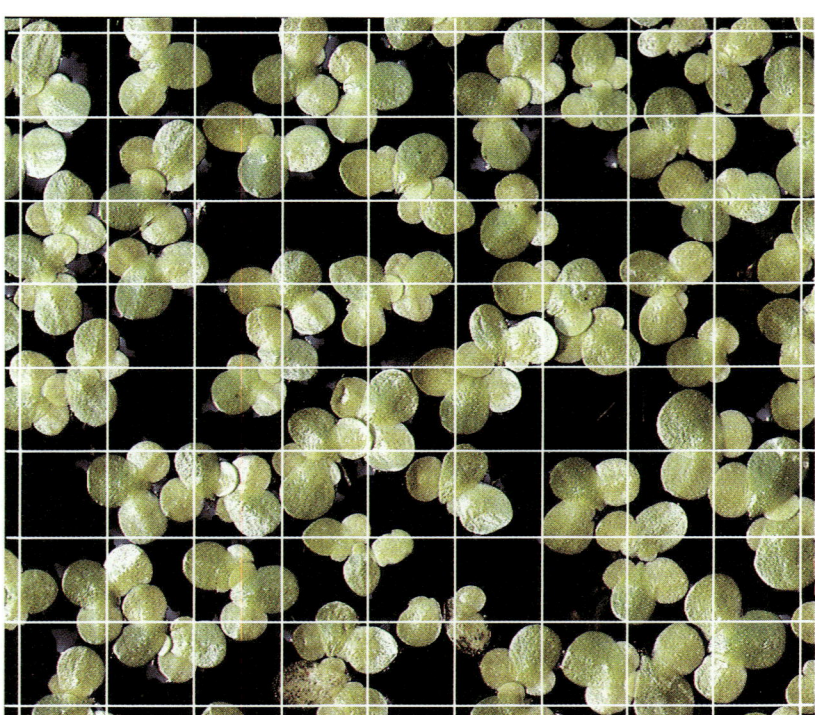

Fig 11.3 Duckweed on a pond.

1 The lines drawn on the photograph divide the surface of the pond into a grid. They are 1 cm apart. What is the area of one of the squares in the grid?

2 Draw the grid in your notebook.

3 Count all the leaves in any *one* of the squares. Leaves which are on the edge of a square should be included if they are mainly in that square (see Fig 11.4). Write the number of leaves in the square in your notebook.

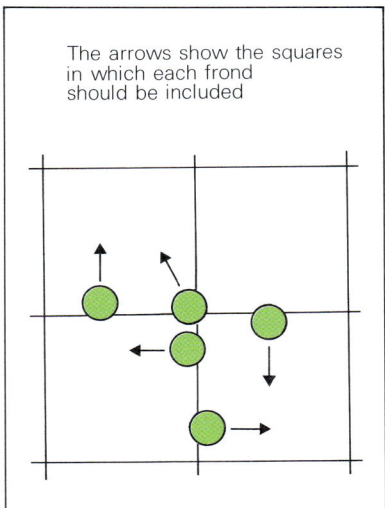

The arrows show the squares in which each frond should be included

Fig 11.4 Counting duckweed leaves.

Fig 11.5

4 Count the leaves in nine more squares chosen randomly.

5 Write down the number of leaves in each square in your notebook, and add them up to find the total number of leaves in ten squares.

6 Work out the average number of leaves in one square. From this calculate the total number of leaves in the part of the pond visible in Fig 11.3.

Questions for class discussion

1 Use the sample method to estimate the number of animals in each of the photographs in Fig 11.5. Write down the number in each sample area as well as the total population in each picture.

2 In Question 1, how many samples did you take to make your estimate of the number of animals in each photograph? Would it have been better to take
  a more, smaller samples or
  b fewer, larger samples? Explain your answer.

(a) A flock of geese.

(b) A herd of wildebeest.

(c) A colony of penguins.

(a) Place your quadrat frame flat on the ground as close to the tree as you can

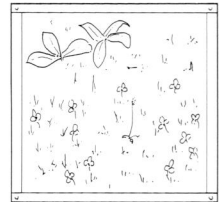

(b) Look carefully at the different kinds of plants inside the square and identify them. Then count the plants in the square. Write the number of each species in your table. This is sample 1

(c) Now use your metre rule to move the quadrat one metre away from your starting point. Count the plants here and write the number on the second line of your table (sample 2)

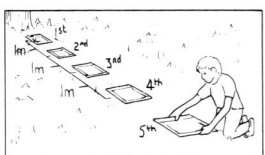

(d) Take about 8–10 samples altogether, keeping to a straight line as far as possible

Fig 11.6 Studying a lawn.

Homework assignments

1 A pair of golden eagles requires a nesting territory of at least 2500 hectares. If the whole of the Cairngorm Mountains (25 000 hectares) is suitable for golden eagles, what is the largest number of pairs which could nest there?

2 The soil beneath a typical square metre of grassland may contain a hundred earthworms. How many worms are you running over when you are playing hockey? (A hockey pitch is approximately 4000 m^2.)

3 James and Mary decided to estimate the number of sticklebacks in a pond. Each of them caught sticklebacks at opposite ends of the pond. After 20 minutes James had caught ten fish and Mary had caught twenty. They concluded that sticklebacks were twice as common in Mary's half of the pond.
  a Why is this an unfair method of comparing the population of the two ends of the pond?
  b Suggest some other explanations for their results.
  c Suggest how James and Mary could improve this method of estimating the number of sticklebacks in the pond.

4 You wish to find out how many bottles of the new drink 'Supa-Coola' should be taken on a school outing. You cannot ask all the pupils if they want one, so a sample must be asked. How would you choose your sample? From the results, how would you decide how many bottles to take?

Experiment 11.3
Studying the pattern of plants in a lawn

You will need a small, square frame called a **quadrat** enclosing a square of 25 cm side. A metre rule will also be required. Work in small groups of 3 or 4. All groups should study the same habitat.

1 Your teacher will tell you which plants are present in the lawn you are studying and how to recognise them.

2 Copy Table 11.2 into your notebook.

Table 11.2

Sample	Number of plant A	Number of plant B . . .
1		
2		
3		

3 With your notebook and pencil, quadrat frame and metre rule, take samples at the base of a tree, working gradually outwards, as shown in Fig 11.6.

4 When you return to the laboratory, make a bar chart of your results. Each member of your group should draw a graph for a different species of plant. Write 'sample number' along the horizontal axis and 'number of plants' up the side. Your graph might look something like Fig 11.7.

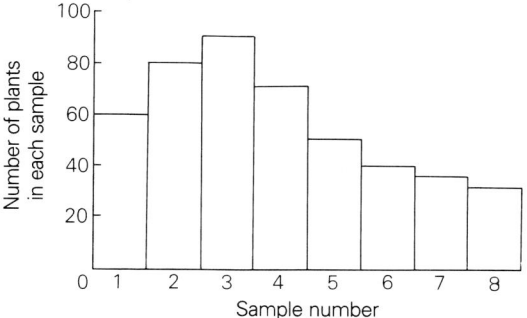

Fig 11.7 Graph to show the number of plants in different sample areas of a lawn.

5 Write a heading above your graph and compare your results with those of other groups.

Questions for class discussion

1 Which quadrat samples in Experiment 11.3 contained the highest number of each of the species examined? Can you suggest why?

2 Compare your results with those of other groups. How much do they differ? Would your answers to Question 1 have been different if all the groups had added their results together?

Estimating the percentages of different plants in a lawn?

At first sight, a lawn may appear to consist of nothing but grass. However when you looked at the lawn in Experiment 11.3 more closely you saw that there were other plants as well, for example, clover, daisy and dandelion. Moreover there were different kinds of grass.

Look carefully at Fig 11.8 overleaf. How many different species of plant can you see? Each species of plant prefers a different area. Clover is often found in hollows where the mower cannot cut it; chickweed is common on the higher parts of the lawn. We call this arrangement of species **uneven distribution**, and we can study it by estimating the percentages of the various species in different parts of the lawn. Fig 11.9 shows how this can be done.

Fig 11.8 A plant community in a lawn.

Find a habitat with more than one species of plant distributed unevenly

Place a quadrat over a part of the habitat

Identify the species of plant present in the square

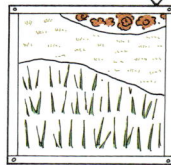

Imagine each species gathered together in one part of the square

Estimate the area occupied by each species and express it as a percentage of the square

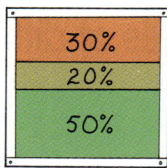

Repeat for several squares chosen at random and average the results

Fig 11.9 Using a quadrat to estimate the percentages of different plants in a lawn.

Questions for class discussion

A group of students investigate the occurrence of a certain type of weed on a piece of waste ground. One of them places a quadrat frame on the ground. Fig 11.10 shows the positions of the weeds inside the frame.

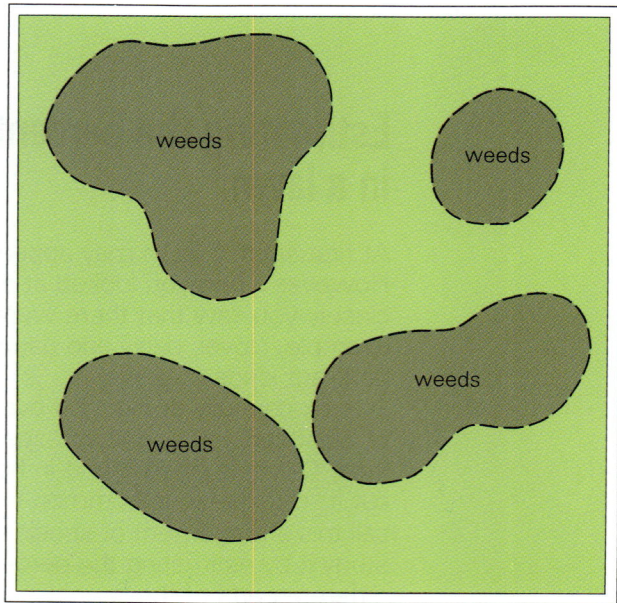

Fig 11.10 Diagram showing the position of weeds inside a quadrat frame.

1 What percentage of the area inside the frame is occupied by the weeds? How did you arrive at your answer?

2 Is your estimate a good one? How could you improve it?

3 When you use a quadrat frame to investigate the occurrence of plants on a piece of ground, you should put the frame down *randomly* and in as many different places as possible. Why?

4 In some experiments you need to put the quadrat frame in definite positions on the ground rather than randomly. Can you think of an experiment where this would be necessary?

Homework assignments

1 A group of students studied the distribution of grass and daisy plants round the base of a large pine tree in their school grounds. They also recorded the distribution of fallen pine needles. The results are shown in Table 11.3

Table 11.3

Metres from base of tree	1	2	3	4	5	6	7	8	9	10
% pine needles	85	60	25	12	10	3	3	2	1	0
% daisies	0	0	0	0	0	1	6	8	10	15
% grass	15	40	75	88	90	96	91	90	89	85

    a What is the most likely explanation for the gradual decrease in the percentage of pine needles as you go further from the base of the tree?

    b Describe an experiment which you could do to test your explanation.

    c Why do you think there are no daisies close to the trunk? What could you do to find out if you are right?

    d The percentage of grass increases up to six metres from the trunk and then begins to decrease. Why do you think this is?

    e What results would you expect to get if you placed a quadrat twenty metres from the base of the tree? Write down percentage figures for each plant at this distance and explain briefly why you chose them.

2 Earthworms can be brought to the surface of the soil by spraying the soil with water containing detergent from a watering can. Describe how you would use this method to estimate the number of earthworms in a large field.

3 A friend makes his own wine by adding yeast cells to fruit juice. He ferments the wine in 5 litre jars (1 litre = 1000 cm^3) and checks the state of the population by counting the number

of cells in a 0.1 cm³ sample every week. This week's count was 100 cells. Estimate how many yeast cells there are in the jar.

4 Gannets nest in colonies, usually on remote islands. Each pair of gannets defends a territory of roughly 1 m² round its nest. The largest colony in the world is situated on St Kilda, off the west coast of Scotland. It covers 10 hectares (1 hectare = 10 000 m²). Estimate how many pairs of gannets could nest there.

5 Sitka spruce trees are planted 5 m apart in rows with 10 m between the rows. Estimate how many young trees would be needed to plant a 10 000 m² wood.

Populations can grow

Do you ever do the weeding in your garden? If you do, you will know how quickly weeds can appear again after you have done the weeding. Most populations of animals and plants can grow very rapidly. Their numbers increase in two ways:

Immigration New organisms move into the habitat. Every winter the resident birds in Britain are joined by thousands of birds immigrating from countries with colder weather conditions.

Reproduction New organisms result from reproduction. Asexual reproduction (see Chapter 5) can produce particularly large numbers of offspring at a time.

The population game

Fig 11.11 is a program which can be used with a pocket calculator if it has a 'memory'. Discover how to enter figures in the memory; in some calculators, information can be stored in the memory by pressing the button marked 'Min', 'M+' or 'STO'. Find out how information can be recalled from the memory; the button may be marked 'MR' or 'RCL'. Use the program to find out how rapidly a population of rabbits can increase.

1 Copy Table 11.4 into your notebook.

2 To start the game we will assume that a pair of rabbits produces a litter of ten babies each time they breed (i.e. in each **generation**). Press the buttons on the calculator in the order indicated in Fig 11.11.

3 Each time you reach the 'generation completed' box, write down the number on the calculator display in your table. This gives the rabbit population at the end of each generation.

4 The rabbits breed every three months, so if you follow the instructions and go round the program eight times, you will find the population after eight generations, that is, after two years.

Table 11.4

Generation	Time of year	Population
1	Jan	
2	April	
3	July	
4	Oct	
5	Jan	
6	April	
7	July	
8	Oct	

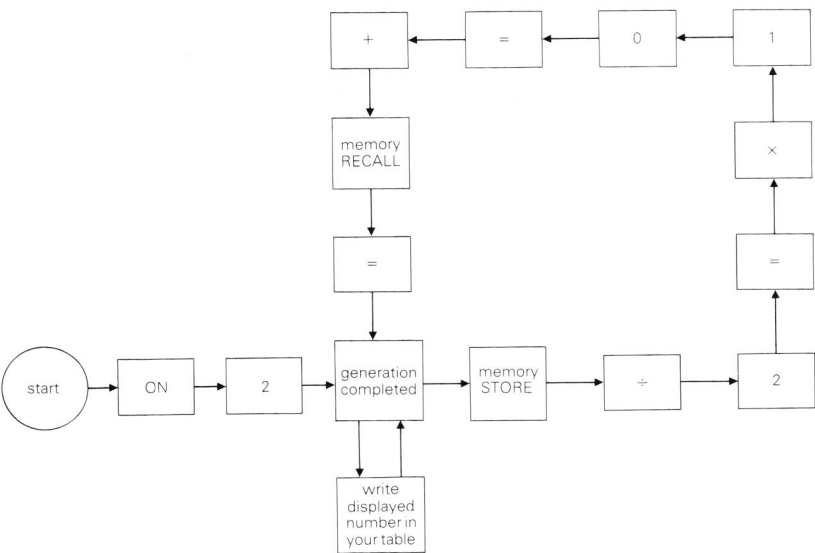

Fig 11.11 The population game.

Questions for class discussion

1 How many rabbits would the population contain after two years if each pair bred every three months and produced ten young in each generation?

2 In fact the population is unlikely to reach this figure even if the rabbits did breed every three months and did produce ten young in each generation. Suggest two reasons for this.

3 Suggest two reasons why the rabbits' breeding rate might fall below the figures suggested above.

How populations are kept steady

You may have been surprised to find that two rabbits can produce half a million descendants in two years. But plagues of rabbits are rare. Something must prevent the rabbit population growing in this way. Fig 11.12 shows one of the things which kills rabbits. The disease **myxomatosis** first appeared in Britain in 1953 and is now an important check on the number of rabbits. Other factors also help to keep rabbit populations steady, including **predation** and **competition**. Predation means being eaten by other animals (**predators**). The main predators of rabbits are foxes and birds of prey. Rabbits compete with each other and with other species for such things as food and burrowing sites.

Individuals that fail to compete successfully do not breed and will die. As result of disease, predation and competition, the rabbit population normally stays more or less steady despite their

Fig 11.12 Rabbit with myxomatosis.

high breeding rate. Most animals and plants maintain steady populations under natural conditions. However, one animal with a population which has been growing for several hundred years is the human animal.

Human population growth

The total number of human beings in the world (**human population**) was about 150 million in the year AD1. The changes since then are shown in Table 11.5.

1 Plot a graph showing the growth of world population. Put the years (0–2000 AD) along the horizontal axis and the population (0–6000 million) on the vertical axis.

2 Join the points with a smooth curve.

3 What would you expect the population to be in the year 2010? Explain how you estimated your answer.

4 *Homo sapiens* has existed for at least half a million years and yet it is only in the last few thousand years that there has been a rapid increase in human population. Why?

5 List as many things as you can which might slow down the rise in world population in the future.

Table 11.5

Year (AD)	Estimated world population (millions)
1	150
1500	400
1650	550
1750	750
1800	900
1900	1600
1950	2400
1975	4000
1995	5750

The causes and results of human population growth

The remarkable increase in the human population during the last 150 years has not affected all groups of human beings. A few tribes in less developed parts of the world still show the same steady populations as most other species of animals and plants. This suggests that in communities in the more developed countries some of the factors controlling human population no longer work. Here are two possible explanations:

1 Improved food supply reduces deaths from starvation during periods of drought, etc.

2 Improved medical care leads to fewer people dying of diseases.

Can you think of any other explanations?

As populations grow, the pressures on the environment increase. In developed countries, the demand for construction, energy and consumer goods can only be met at the cost of more pollution, more destruction of the natural environment and more exploitation of resources. Industrial processes may leave permanent scars on the landscape (Fig 11.13) or release harmful waste materials which damage the environment (Fig 11.14). In underdeveloped countries, living standards may fall and the risk of disease, famine and natural disasters increases.

One of the harmful effects of the increase in human population can be seen all round us. Buildings are constructed from raw materials such as sand, gravel and stone. The extraction of these building materials is a multimillion pound operation providing employment for thousands of people (Fig 11.15). But the excavation of sand and gravel and the quarrying of stone destroy large areas of

Fig 11.13 China clay deposits in Cornwall.

Fig 11.14 Industrial pollution.

Fig 11.15 Stanton Harcourt Pit.

Fig 11.16 The same pit after restoration.

countryside. Sand, gravel and stone cannot be replaced or renewed. The natural animal and plant communities removed when they are extracted are destroyed for ever.

However, once the sand and gravel has been extracted, the pits may be flooded and turned into lakes for water sports, fishing or nature conservation (Fig 11.16).

Homework assignments

1 A population of the duckweed *Lemna minor* was started with five fronds (see Experiment 11.2). The number of fronds were counted every three days. The results are shown in Table 11.6.

Table 11.6

Days from start of the experiment	Number of fronds	Days from start of the experiment	Number of fronds
0	5	24	49
3	7	27	65
6	9	30	85
9	12	33	100
12	16	36	120
15	21	39	125
18	28	42	121
21	37		

a Plot these results on a graph, putting time along the horizontal axis and number of fronds on the vertical axis. Draw a smooth curve as close to the points as you can.
b After the first two weeks the experimenters expected the final number of fronds to be more than 250. Why do you think they expected this? Suggest two reasons why the numbers of fronds did not increase as rapidly as they expected between two and six weeks.
c Choose one of the reasons you have suggested and say how you could carry out an investigation to test it.

2 How would you estimate the numbers of a small invertebrate living in a habitat such as a pond, small wood or stretch of seashore?

3 Explain the difference between the words *population* and *community* by using each word in a sentence describing a habitat you know.

4 In the autumn a maple tree in a garden had 60 small maple seedlings growing beneath it. In spring all the seedlings except one had disappeared. The one remaining seedling was twenty metres from the base of the tree, further than any of the other seedlings. Why do you think this one seedling survived, and what caused the others to disappear?

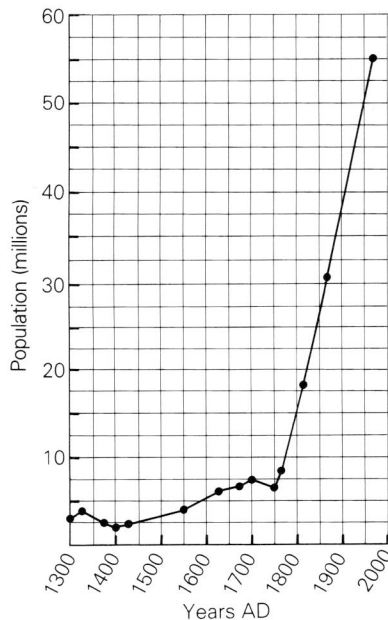

Fig 11.17 Graph to show the changes in population in Great Britain.

5 Look carefully at the graph in Fig 11.17, which shows the changes in the population of Great Britain since 1300.
  a What was the population in (i) 1550 and (ii) 1950?
  b The Black Death killed at least one third of the population of Britain. When do you think it occurred?
  c How long did it take for the population to return to the number which existed before Black Death?
  d During which 100-year period did the population increase by the greatest number?
  e The number of babies born per year in Great Britain has been falling recently, but the population is still rising. Can you suggest two reasons?

Background Reading

Man against the pests

It has been estimated that about one third of the world's food crops are destroyed by a wide selection of pests before they are harvested. More are spoiled by pests infesting stored food. The most destructive of these pests is, without a doubt, the locust.

Locusts breed in very large numbers when the conditions are right. A high rainfall is needed just when the locust eggs are hatching. If the rain continues, more and more eggs will be laid, and swarms of hoppers – the early stage in the locust life cycle – will be produced. When they mature, they fly off in search of more food, and thus spread over wide areas. Swarms can cover as much as 500 km^2. A locust eats its own weight (2–3 g) in food each day and a swarm covering 1 km^2 could contain 40 to 80 million locusts. This means hundreds of thousands of tonnes of vegetation are being devoured each day.

A huge area of the world, including 60 countries in North Africa and West Asia, have been threatened by the recent increase in locust numbers. This is a fifth of the Earth's land surface and contains a tenth of the world's population. To control the billions of locusts it is necessary to spray the swarms, preferably at the hopper stage, and destroy at least 90 % of the insects. But there are problems. One of the most common, cheap methods of control is spraying with DDT, and in some areas, previously untroublesome species are now multiplying as their natural enemies are wiped out by DDT. DDT *residues* are known to build up in animal tissues, and many birds and animals have declined in numbers because of this. Other forms of pest control need to be developed, such as the use of natural predators and safer chemicals. But a careful balance must be kept in the meantime between the destructive powers of pests and the side effects of control methods.

(Adapted from *Together for children*, published by Oxfam/Unicef.)

Questions

1 Write down the meaning of the word 'residues'.

2 Explain in your own words how 'untroublesome species' might multiply after DDT treatment. Why might this be harmful?

3 The use of 'natural predators' against pests is referred to as **biological control**. Using the information given in the passage, suggest two reasons why biological control of locusts might be better than chemical control.

4 Two populations are mentioned in this passage. What are they? How do they affect each other?

Summary

1 The number of each kind of animal or plant in a habitat is called the size of the **population**.

2 All the different kinds of organism living together in a habitat make up a **community**.

3 The way in which living organisms are arranged in a community is called their **distribution**.

4 The number of living organisms in a habitat can be **estimated** by taking **samples**.

5 The distribution of living organisms in a habitat can be studied by using small square frames called **quadrats**.

6 Populations can increase in number by **immigration** and **reproduction**.

7 Most natural populations of animals and plants are kept steady by a variety of checks such as **disease**, **predation** and **competition**.

8 Human populations have increased enormously in the last 200 years and have doubled in the last fifty years.

Chapter 12

The distribution of living things

The lawn which you studied in Chapter 11 contained several kinds of weeds among the grass. You probably found more weeds under the tree and more grass in other parts. It is unlikely that any of the weeds were spread evenly over the whole area of grass.

The animals and plants in most habitats are unevenly distributed. In this chapter you will discover some of the reasons for this uneven distribution.

Experiment 12.1
The distribution of small invertebrates

In this experiment you will make your own collection of small animals by setting **pitfall traps**. The trap, which can be made from any small containers (for example, two plastic yoghurt pots), is dug into the ground so that the top of the pots is level with the surface of the soil (see Fig 12.1). Small animals walking along the ground fall into the container and cannot escape.

1 Draw a habitat map (see Experiment 1.4 page 6) of the area you are going to use.

2 Try to set at least one trap in each different part of the habitat – under a hedge, in a flower border, under a tree and in a grassy area. Fig 12.1 shows how to set a pitfall trap.

3 Indicate the positions of your traps on the habitat map and copy Table 12.1 into your notebook.

4 Visit the traps as often as you can. Remove the inner pot and empty the contents into a large jar. Replace the trap carefully.

5 Identify the animals using the key in the Appendix, and fill in Table 12.1. Write down the number of each kind of animal caught in the trap in the last column, for example, woodlouse (3).

Table 12.1

Date	Time	Weather conditions	Trap position	Animals caught

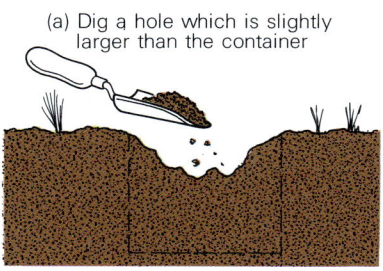

(a) Dig a hole which is slightly larger than the container

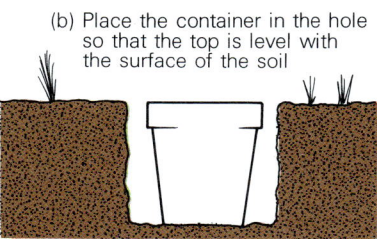

(b) Place the container in the hole so that the top is level with the surface of the soil

(c) Put a second container inside the first one. Fill in any gaps around the outer container.

(d) Place a few leaves and small sticks in the trap to shelter the animals, and cover the top with a piece of wood supported by small pebbles

Fig 12.1 Setting a pitfall trap.

6 Return the animals to the places where they were caught.

7 After several days, gather together all the results. Find the total number of each kind of animal caught in each trap.

Questions for class discussion

1 In the questions which follow, give actual numbers *and* an explanation.

   a Which trap caught most animals? Which caught the least?

   b Which species was most frequently caught?

   c Were more individuals caught in the traps during the daytime or overnight?

   d Which species was most common in the daytime and which one at night?

   e Was there any species which was only caught in one area or in one trap?

2 Do your results show that the animals are unevenly distributed? Select one species with a distribution that is clearly uneven and indicate the areas where it lives on your habitat map. Is there a connection between the distribution of this species and the distribution of plants?

3 Did you catch more or less animals in the traps during wet weather? Can you suggest why rainfall might affect the distribution of small animals?

Physical and biological factors

There are many different explanations for the uneven distribution of living organisms in a habitat. Consider the results of Experiment 12.1. Can you suggest reasons for the distribution of the species you caught in your pitfall traps?

In the last chapter you studied the ways in which populations are kept in check by **biological factors** such as disease, predation and competition. **Physical factors** such as light, water and temperature may explain why you caught more animals in some traps than in others.

Experiment 12.2
Choosing a place to live

If you were given ten minutes to collect as many woodlice as you could, where would you look? Why would you expect to find them there? What conditions do you think they prefer?

Your answer will probably include darkness as one of the things that woodlice prefer. One way to test this hypothesis is to use a **choice chamber**. There are several different kinds, but they all work in a similar way (see Fig 12.3).

To test the hypothesis that woodlice prefer dark places, follow the instructions given on the next page.

Fig 12.2 Woodlice under a log.

1 Collect 10–12 woodlice and place them in a dark, moist container for ten minutes.

2 Open the choice chamber, remove the perforated platform and place moist blotting paper or cotton wool at the bottom of the chamber.

3 Replace the perforated platform, making sure that it is tight and smooth all round.

4 Fix two small pieces of blue cobalt chloride paper to the inside of the lid of the choice chamber (cobalt chloride is blue when dry and pink when moist).

5 Replace the lid and after a few minutes check that the cobalt chloride paper has turned pink indicating that the atmosphere throughout the chamber is moist.

6 Take the lid off quickly and place about ten animals inside the chamber, spreading them evenly over the gauze. Replace the lid (see Fig 12.3).

Fig 12.3 A common type of choice chamber.

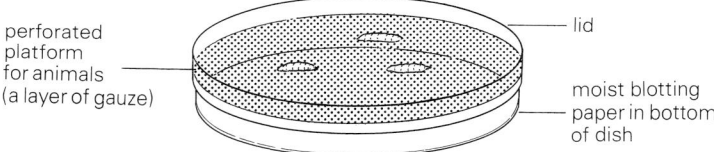

perforated
platform
for animals
(a layer of gauze)

lid

moist blotting
paper in bottom
of dish

7 Cover one half of the chamber with black material and leave the other half uncovered.

8 After two minutes, record the number of animals on the dark and light sides.

9 Spread the animals out again and then cover the other half of the chamber.

10 After two minutes, record the numbers again. Keep changing the light and dark sides every two minutes until it is clear which side the woodlice prefer.

11 Now cover the *whole* container and record the positions of the animals after two minutes by means of a simple sketch.

12 Finally uncover the whole container and record the positions after two minutes in the light. Watch the animals this time and notice how and where they move before settling down. Make sure you do not cast a shadow on the container and that the light is even.

Questions for class discussion

1 Why were the woodlice placed in a dark, moist container for ten minutes before the experiment (instruction 1)?

2 Why were the dark and light sides of the choice chamber interchanged every two minutes (instruction 10)?

3 Why was the whole container covered (instruction 11)? What is the name given to this part of the experiment?

4 Briefly describe your observations when the container was left uncovered, and suggest an explanation for the final distribution of the woodlice (instruction 12).

5 Explain why the habit of avoiding light is useful to woodlice.

6 In your experiment, one side of the choice chamber was light and the other side was dark. Can you suggest one other difference between the two sides which might have affected the behaviour of the woodlice?

7 List all the procedures which helped to make your experiment a fair test of the preferences of woodlice.

Homework assignments

1 Look carefully at the photograph in Fig 12.4. The plants are unevenly distributed.

Fig 12.4 An unmown meadow with a path through it.

    a Describe the experiments you would perform to record the distribution patterns of the plants.
    b Suggest an explanation for their distribution patterns.
    c Describe an experiment which you could do to test your explanation.

2 Design an experiment which would test the hypothesis that 'woodlice prefer damp places'. Remember to include suitable controls, to ensure that the test is a fair one.

3 Explain, with reasons, the main physical factors that affect the distribution of the following organisms:
  a woodlice in a garden
  b grass beneath a large tree
  c mushrooms in a field
  d locusts in the desert
  e human beings on the Earth's surface.

4 Refer back to Chapter 8 and list the things green plants need in order to survive and grow. Can you think of any parts of the natural environment where you would not expect to find any green plants growing?

Reaching new habitats

Fig 12.5 shows the island of Surtsey which lies off the south coast of Iceland. This island is remarkable because it has only existed since 1965 when a volcanic eruption on the sea bed produced a pile of rocks and lava which cooled to form Surtsey. Biologists visiting the island a few years later found that a number of living organisms – mostly plants and insects – had reached it and started to live there.

Fig 12.5 The island of Surtsey.

The arrival of an organism in a new habitat is the result of **dispersal**. When the organism has established itself, we say it has **colonised** the habitat. If an animal or plant is absent from a habitat it may be because it has not reached it, or because it has failed to colonise the habitat.

Question for class discussion

The island of Krakatoa in the East Indies erupted in 1883 leaving a lifeless surface, 40 kilometres away from the nearest island. Fifty years later, 47 species of vertebrates had colonised the island including thirty-six birds, five lizards, three bats, a rat, a crocodile and a python. How do you think each of these groups of vertebrates reached the island?

Experiment 12.3
Colonisers in your aquarium

If your aquarium has been kept outside the laboratory, it will probably now contain several species of animals and plants which were not included when you originally stocked it up. Compare your lists of species from Experiment 11.1 with Experiment 1.3 and write in your notebook the names of all new arrivals.

The amount of colonisation which has taken place in the aquarium can also be studied by examining the microscope slides which have been suspended in the water.

1 Wipe the *lower* surface of the slide clean using a paper tissue or towel and place it on the microscope stage.

2 Using low power, examine as much of the slide as you can, looking carefully at all the living organisms.

3 Count the number of different kinds of animals and plants on each slide, and write the numbers in your notebook.

4 If you have time draw and identify the species present.

5 Alternatively you could scrape the side of the tank and place the scrapings in a drop of tap water on a slide.

Questions for class discussion

1 How many new species of animals and plants have appeared in your aquarium? By what means might they have arrived there?

2 Two similar aquarium tanks were stocked with the same species of animals and plants. One was left outside while the other was kept in the laboratory under bench lights. A year later the two tanks were compared and the one which had been kept outside contained twice as many species as the other. Suggest *two* reasons for this difference.

Homework assignments

1 A student set up an aquarium in September and hung twelve microscope slides in the water. Each month a slide was removed and examined. At first the number of species increased steadily from month to month, but in spring and summer the number began to fall again. Suggest an explanation for:
   a the steady rise
   b the gradual fall in the number of species.

2 Having heated some soil to kill any organisms it might contain, a gardener placed the soil in a plant tub outside. After a year, the following plants were growing in it:
   seedlings of yew, holly, oak and sycamore, a patch of moss, some mould growing on the side of the tub where it was kept wet by water dripping from the roof above, and small plants of shepherd's purse, thistle and groundsel.
   Choose any four of these plants and explain how they might have reached the soil in the tub without any human help.

Becoming established in a habitat

What does an organism need in order to survive and multiply in a habitat? How many different things can you think of? List them in your notebook.

Even if all these requirements are available, the animals and plants may not colonise the habitat. There may be **competitors** which are already established and which eat the same food or use up the oxygen. There may also be **predators** which feed on the newcomers. Competitors and predators keep out colonisers unless they can reproduce very rapidly.

Soil as an environment

What is soil made of?

Look at Fig 12.6 overleaf. It shows a section cut through the soil to a depth of about 1 metre. The upper, dark section which is about 35 centimetres deep is called **topsoil**. Most of the plant roots are confined to the topsoil. The lower, lighter section is called the **subsoil** which rests on the rocks below. The subsoil contains few living organisms.

The topsoil consists of three major components:
1 Mineral matter – including soil particles and mineral nutrients (see page 93).
2 Organic matter – both living and dead organisms.
3 Water.

Fig 12.6 A section through the soil.

Soil particles are the basis of soil. They are produced by the action of wind, water and frost on rocks. Different kinds of soil have different sized soil particles.

A **clay soil** has a high proportion of small particles. These particles fit tightly together leaving little room for air. They have a large surface area which holds onto water very tightly. The soil is said to be 'heavy' and is difficult to dig. A **sandy soil** consists of larger particles with large air spaces between them. Water drains away quickly, making the soil 'light' but in dry weather it will suffer from drought. Another disadvantage of a sandy soil is that minerals are easily washed away by heavy rain.

Living organisms are very important in the soil. Micro-organisms such as bacteria and fungi help to break down plant and animals remains into a sticky black material called **humus** which gives many soils their blackish colour (see page 162).

Plant roots bind the soil together helping to hold onto water and mineral nutrients.

Animals such as earthworms break up the soil, speeding up the movement of air and water and adding organic material.

In the following experiments you can get some idea of the composition of your local soil.

Experiment 12.4
Separating soil particles

1 Bring a sample of soil into the laboratory: a cupful is all you will need.

2 Remove any large stones or pieces of debris and then tip the soil into a 250 ml measuring cylinder. It should be not more than half-full of soil.

3 Add water until the cylinder is about two-thirds-full.

4 Seal the top of the cylinder with a cork or your hand and shake it from end to end for three minutes. The soil and water should now be thoroughly mixed together.

5 Leave the cylinder until next lesson to allow the soil to settle.

6 Examine the contents carefully. How many layers can you see in the soil? The largest particles (sand) will be at the bottom and the smallest particles (clay) will be at the top. There is usually a clear boundary between the two. The remains of dead plant material may be floating on the surface of the water.

Questions for class discussion

1 Using the results of your experiment, how could you compare the amount of clay in the soil samples brought in by different members of your class?

2 The sand and clay particles usually differ in colour. Describe the colour of the different particles in your cylinder. Suggest reasons for the differences you have described.

3 Examine the soil particles under a microscope. Describe the differences between the appearance of the sand and clay particles.

Experiment 12.5
Measuring the amount of water and organic material in the soil

1 Weigh a small metal dish or crucible. Record its mass in your notebook.

2 Half fill the dish with soil from your soil sample. Weigh it and record the mass of the dish and soil in your notebook.

3 Subtract the mass of the dish (instruction 1) from the mass of the dish plus soil (instruction 2) to calculate the mass of the soil. Write this in your notebook.

4 Place the dish in an oven overnight at about 50 °C to dry.

5 Weigh the dish once again and record its mass now that all the water has been removed.

6 Subtract the mass of the dish plus dry soil (instruction 5) from the mass of the dish plus wet soil (instruction 2) to find how much water has been lost. Write this in your notebook.

7 Place the dish on a tripod and heat it for about 5 minutes with a Bunsen burner until it is red hot.
   Most of the organic matter will now be burnt off leaving only the mineral particles. Allow the dish to cool and then weigh it once more. Record the mass.

8 Subtract the mass of the dish plus mineral particles (instruction 7) from the mass of the dish plus dry soil (instruction 5) to find how much organic matter the soil contained.

Questions for class discussion

1 a What percentage of water does your soil sample contain? Show your calculation.
  b What percentage of organic matter does your soil sample contain?
  c Compare your results with those of other students in your class. Try to explain the differences by considering the time and place of collection of the different samples.

2 Relate the results obtained in Experiment 12.5 to the amount of clay in the soil (Experiment 12.4). Soils which contain more clay usually hold more water. Which type of soil has the most organic matter?

3 Describe the colour of the mineral particles left at the end of the experiment. Suggest why they look so different from the original soil.

Looking after the soil

A farmer or gardener has to look after his soil if his crops are to flourish. It may need digging or ploughing to allow air and water to penetrate. Clay soils may be helped by adding lime: sandy soils need binding with manure or compost. Even in temperate countries crops may need watering (**irrigation**). More commonly, excess water must be removed from the soil by good drainage, helped by ploughing or digging. The mineral content of the soil has to be maintained by adding plant or animal remains such as **manure** or **compost** or by direct application of artificial **fertilisers** containing such elements as nitrogen, phosphorous and potassium (see page 273). Lime will also provide calcium for crops.

Extreme environments

There are very few parts of the Earth which remain uncolonised by living organisms. Can you think of any?

Animals and plants may be specially suited or **adapted** to survive in places where other species would find it difficult to live (see page 1) Here are some examples.

Polar regions

The Arctic and Antarctic regions have average temperatures of 45 °C *below* freezing point (see Fig 12.7). Animals such as penguins and polar bears have thick coats of feathers or fur, short limbs and squat bodies to reduce their energy loss. This helps them to keep their temperatures constant. Other animals such as fish may contain 'antifreeze' to stop their blood freezing.

Fig 12.7 A polar region.

Desert regions

The Sahara desert (see Fig 12.8) has an average temperature of 35°C *above* freezing point and it rains, on average, once every three years. Most desert animals keep out of the sun during the day if they can, and excrete very little water. Many animals and plants store food and water; plants may survive as seeds for a very long time until the rain comes. They then flower and produce more seeds within a few days. Plants that live in deserts usually have thick outer surfaces and small leaves to reduce evaporation, and long roots for absorbing water from deep down in the soil.

Mountain tops

Few living things are found at the tops of high mountains because of the combination of low temperature, strong winds, lack of water

Fig 12.8 A desert region.

Fig 12.9 A mountain top habitat.

and lack of oxygen (see Fig 12.9). Few species are able to survive these all the year round. Most animals migrate to lower ground in winter. The plants are only a few centimetres high, thereby avoiding the wind and reducing water loss.

Experiment 12.6
Comparing water loss from plants

Plants lose water by evaporation from their leaves (see page 92). In this experiment we will compare the rate of water loss from the leaves of a plant which lives in a damp environment with that of a plant which lives in a dry environment.

Your teacher will give you four pieces of dry cobalt chloride paper. Remember that this is blue when dry but turns pink when moist.

1 With transparent sticky tape, fix the pieces of paper to the upper and lower surfaces of two well-watered pot plants, one of which is a desert species. Completely cover the pieces of paper with sticky tape.

2 Note the time and observe the colour of the paper at intervals. Record the time it takes for the first trace of pink to appear and for the paper to turn completely pink.

Questions for class discussion

1 How long does it take:
   a for the first trace of pink to appear on each piece of paper
   b for each piece of paper to turn completely pink?

2 Which side of the leaf loses water faster, the upper side or the lower side? Why does one side lose water faster than the other?

3 Which species of plant loses water faster? Explain the difference. Are there any differences in the appearance of the leaves of the two species which might help to explain your results? (Hint: refer back to page 92.)

4 If time allows, repeat this experiment on the leaves of a deciduous plant (for example, lilac) and an evergreen plant (for example, holly) from your own locality. Explain your results.

Homework assignments

1 a What is meant by the word habitat?
   b Name a habitat you have studied and describe its main characteristics.
   c Name the most common plant species in the habitat.
   d Suggest reasons why it grows there successfully.
   e How might this plant have arrived in the habitat?
   f How did it become established in the habitat?
   g Describe the way in which the plant survives the winter.

2 Living things do not normally inhabit totally dry places.
  a Give reasons why organisms need water.
  b Describe ways in which animals reduce their water loss.
  c Describe ways in which plants reduce their water loss.

3 A path runs through a grassy field. Five sample areas were chosen on the path, and five on each side of the path in the grassy field. Table 12.2 shows with a tick (✓) the species present in each sample area.

Table 12.2

Species	Grassy field					Path					Grassy field				
	1	2	3	4	5	1	2	3	4	5	1	2	3	4	5
grass type A	✓	✓	✓	✓	✓							✓	✓	✓	✓
grass type B		✓	✓	✓	✓	✓	✓	✓	✓	✓	✓	✓	✓	✓	✓
grass type C						✓	✓	✓	✓	✓					
daisy						✓	✓	✓	✓	✓		✓			
plantain						✓	✓	✓	✓	✓		✓			
rock rose		✓	✓	✓										✓	✓
hawkweed			✓		✓	✓		✓	✓	✓	✓				
ribwort	✓	✓		✓	✓		✓					✓		✓	✓
salad burnet	✓	✓	✓	✓		✓			✓		✓	✓		✓	✓

  a (i) Which species of plant is not found on the path?
      (ii) Suggest a reason why it is not found there.
  b (i) Which species is found only on the path?
      (ii) Suggest a reason why it grows there.
  c Which species grows most abundantly in both path and field?
  d Calculate the average number of species per sample area
      (i) in the grassy field
      (ii) on the path.
  e Which of the following grasses is more likely to have been grass type C? Explain your choice.
      Poa annua Height 10 cm; broad, blunt leaves.
      Brachypodium pinnatum Height 30 cm; narrow, stiff leaves.

4 What are the main differences in composition between a light and a heavy soil? List the advantages and disadvantages to a farmer of having a farm on light soil.

5 Some of the world's great natural forests such as the Amazonian rain forest in Brazil are being cut down to provide raw materials and food for the rapidly growing human population.
  a Explain briefly how this may affect the soil beneath the trees.
  b What are the arguments for and against the commercial development of areas such as the Amazonian rain forest?

Background Reading

The great coloniser

Of all organisms, the human race is the greatest coloniser. Other organisms can only live in places to which nature has adapted them. Humans, however, can live in even the most hostile environments. For example, Los Angeles in southern California, was once a hot, dry desert, populated only by organisms that could survive long periods of intense heat and severe drought. Today it is an ultra-modern city with 3.5 million inhabitants who enjoy one of the highest standards of living in the world.

Instead of being restricted to a narrow range of environments to which our bodies are adapted, we can create our own environment wherever we want to go. People can watch television in warmth and comfort in the Arctic, or relax in air-conditioned luxury on the Equator. By surrounding ourselves with a space capsule we can even leave our planet altogether and explore the universe. Perhaps one day there will be a luxury hotel on the moon!

All this is relatively recent, even by human standards, and most people would agree that it is a good thing – a triumph of technology over the elements. However, it has brought problems too. This is mainly because of numbers. The human population has grown enormously, particularly in the last two hundred years. To meet the needs of this ever increasing population, more and more land has had to be taken over for agriculture, industry and housing, and more and more energy has had to be obtained from our natural resources. In some places we have improved the environment, but all too often we have damaged or destroyed it. The human race is a great coloniser but also a great exploiter.

Questions

1 Give examples of areas on Earth where, in your opinion, humans will never be able to settle permanently. Give reasons for your suggestions.

2 Give examples from your own experience of cases where human activities have
   a spoiled a local environment
   b improved it.

3 What special problems face organisms that live in the desert and how do you think these problems are overcome?

4 How can 3.5 million people live comfortably in a desert? What is the cost to the environment?

5 Which natural environments in the world are most under threat at the present time and what do you think should be done to protect them?

Fig 12.10 The desert in California.

Fig 12.11 The city of Los Angeles.

Summary

1 Most animals and plants are **unevenly distributed** in a habitat.

2 Uneven distribution may result from variation in light, water and temperature.

3 Important factors which decide where animals and plants are found include **dispersal** (could it get there?) and **colonisation** (could it survive and multiply when it arrived?).

4 Successful colonisation depends on the habitat providing enough **food**, **oxygen** and **water**.

5 Colonisation may be prevented by **competitors** and **predators**.

Chapter 13 Feeding relationships

In a habitat, the plants and animals depend on each other and affect each other: we say that they **interact**. The reason why they interact is often because of the ways they feed.

Animals depend on plants

Green plants are able to make their own food by using sunlight. They are called **producers** because they produce all the materials they need by photosynthesis.

Animals are unable to use the energy of the Sun's radiation, so they have to eat plants, or other animals which may have eaten plants. They are called **consumers** because they consume other living organisms to obtain the materials they need.

Food passes from plants to animals in a chain, called a **food chain**. We can show it like this:

plants ⟶ animals
(producers)   (consumers)

The arrow in the food chain means 'eaten by'. For example

grass ⟶ cow ⟶ human

shows that cows eat grass and in turn are eaten by humans.

As you can see, food comes to us via food chains. Copy Table 13.1 into your notebook. Write all the food materials you have eaten today in the first column. Next write down beside each food the animal or plant from which the food was made. Then list any animals or plants which were consumed by the animal you ate.

Table 13.1

Food	obtained from	which ate
bread	wheat	
milk	cow	grass

Experiment 13.1
The inhabitants of a tree

A tree is a major producer; it provides food for a large number of consumers. It may also provide a good place for other producers to live. In this experiment you should choose a large tree and study the animals and plants living in, on and under it.

You will need a pooter for catching small animals (see Fig 13.1a–b), a pointed instrument for investigating cracks (see Fig 13.1c), a sheet or newspaper for collecting animals from leaves and branches (see Fig 13.1d), small containers for the animals and polythene bags for the plants.

When you have chosen your tree find out its name and then make five separate collections.

Fig 13.1 (a) A pooter. (b) Sucking up small animals with a pooter. (c) Probing a crack with a pointed instrument. (d) Collecting animals from leaves and branches.

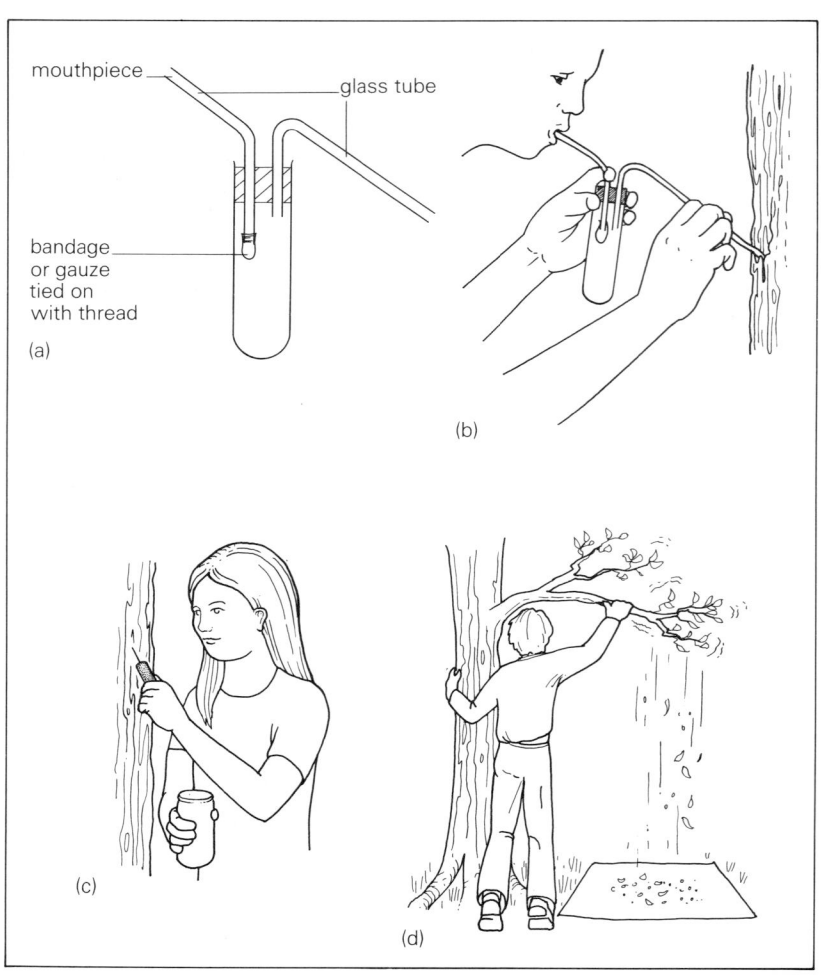

Collection 1: the base of the tree Here it begins to spread out to form the root system. Collect any animals you find, and identify the plants. Mosses often grow in the cracks at the base of trees.

Collection 2: the trunk Green powdery growth on the bark is a single-celled organism called *Pleurococcus*. If your school is in the country, lichens may grow on the trunk. They consist of two kinds of living organism growing together, a single-celled protoctist and a fungus (see page 166).

 **Safety note**

wash your hands thoroughly with soap and water after you have completed this investigation.

Collection 3: cracks, forks and hollows Look carefully but do not damage the bark. The animals living here are often very well camouflaged. If the forks and hollows contain water, you may find some aquatic animals there. Do not forget to include the plants: mosses, ferns and even flowering plants may be found in tree forks.

Collection 4: branches, twigs and leaves Examine the twigs and leaves carefully; you may find caterpillars, aphids (greenfly), leaves with marks, spots or tracks on them or galls (large solid lumps on leaves or twigs). Place a sheet under a low growing branch, or spread newspapers beneath it. Shake the branch hard for several minutes and collect any animals which fall on to the sheet.

Collection 5: the ground The dead leaves, twigs and fruits which cover the ground under the tree make up the **litter**. Fill a polythene bag with litter, noting any plants, fungi or small animals which you see.

Before you leave the tree, make a habitat map to show where your collections were made (see Fig 13.2). Back in the laboratory, identify the organisms in your collection using the key in the Appendix. List the plants and animals found in each part of the tree. Also note the date and the general weather conditions.

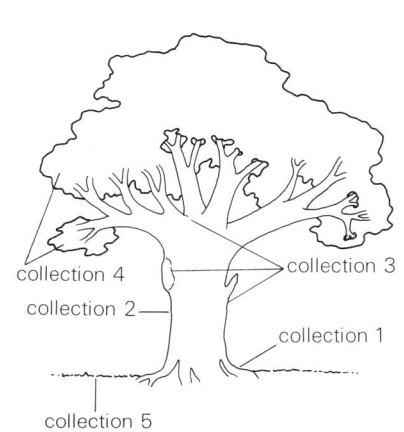

Fig 13.2 Habitat map of a tree.

Questions for class discussion

1 Did you see signs of any other animals in or on your tree? There may have been holes made by beetles or birds, droppings, pellets or nests of birds or bits of acorns left by squirrels. Add these animals to your list.

2 Which part of the tree had the largest number of consumers feeding on it? Suggest one reason for this observation.

3 Select one of the consumers from this part of the tree and describe how it obtains its food.

4 Select one of the producers living on the tree and describe how it obtains its food.

5 Explain why different trees contain different numbers and different kinds of animals and plants.

Carnivores, herbivores and omnivores

All animals are consumers, but different animals eat different things. Animals such as ladybirds and spiders are called **carnivores** because they mainly eat the flesh of other animals. Greenfly and woodlice feed on the tree itself and are called **herbivores** (plant eaters). Animals such as humans, which eat both flesh and plants,

Fig 13.3 (a) Classify these animals as carnivores or herbivores. ▲   (b) What are these animals eating? ▼

are called **omnivores**. Fig 13.3a shows six different animals with their food. Which are carnivores and which herbivores? Fig 13.3b shows two omnivores. What are they eating?

Now return to your list of animals from the tree (Experiment 13.1) and with help from your teacher, write 'carnivore', 'herbivore' or 'omnivore' beside each one.

You can now make three-link food chains for the tree community. Two examples are shown in Fig 13.4.

Fig 13.4 Oak tree food chains.

Can you write down any more? Remember that the arrow always points to the consumer, showing the direction in which the food passes through the food chain.

Food webs

The oak tree was providing food for several different consumers, so we can join food chains together (Fig 13.5).

Fig 13.5 Branched food chain.

Although ladybirds feed almost entirely on greenfly, spiders will eat a wide range of foods including greenfly as well as woodlice. Where animals feed in more than one food chain, we join the chains to make a **food web** (Fig 13.6).

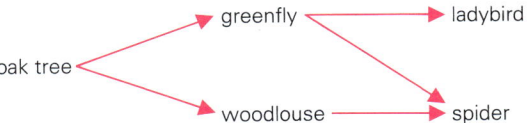

Fig 13.6 Simple food web.

The food web can be further extended if we introduce a larger carnivore such as a blue tit. This in turn may be eaten by yet another carnivore such as a hawk. The final carnivore in a food chain or web is known as the **top carnivore** (Fig 13.7).

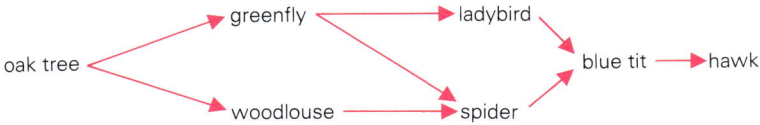

Fig 13.7 Food web with top carnivore.

Copy this food web into your notebook, adding one more herbivore (for example, a caterpillar), one carnivore (for example, song thrush) and one top carnivore (for example, owl).

Homework assignments

1 Why is a tree called a 'producer'? Write down the names of four more producers which all grow in the same habitat as a tree.

2 a Name an animal which feeds as a herbivore and state its normal food.

  b Name an animal which feeds as a carnivore and state its normal food.

3 What is a food chain? Why must it begin with a plant?

4 Write down the names of four producers and four consumers found in your aquarium. Join some of these producers and consumers together in a food chain.

5 In an area of woodland there are foxes, grass and rabbits.
  a Place these organisms in their correct order in a food chain.
  b Add the name of one more herbivore to make a branched food chain.
  c Make a food web by adding the name of a carnivore which feeds on both the herbivores.

Decomposers

When animals and plants die, they rot (decay). You may have wondered what is happening to the dead remains. An important group of living organisms, mainly small animals, fungi and bacteria, feed on the dead remains of other living things. Because they break the material down we call them **decomposers**.

A large deciduous tree may shed hundreds of kilograms of leaves, twigs, bark and other material each year. You collected some of this material (the *litter*) in Experiment 13.1 (page 157). Now you can find some of the animals which live in it by using a **Tullgren funnel**.

Experiment 13.2
Extracting the animals from leaf litter.

1 Cut out a piece of stiff paper to make a cone. The narrow end of the cone should be about 5 mm wide.

2 Pour a little water into a beaker and fit the narrow end of the cone into the beaker as shown in Fig 13.8.

3 Tip the litter carefully into the cone and place a bench lamp above it. The lamp must be at least 10 cm above the litter.

 **Safety note**

the lamp must be at least 10 cm above the litter to reduce the risk of the litter catching fire.

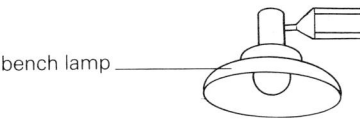

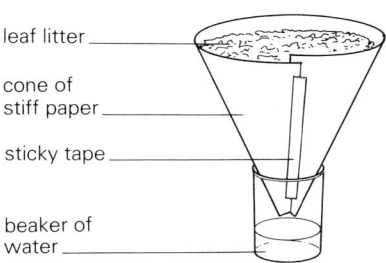

bench lamp

leaf litter

cone of
stiff paper

sticky tape

beaker of
water

Fig 13.8 A simple Tullgren funnel.

4 Switch on the lamp and leave the apparatus for 24 hours.

5 Carefully tip the contents of the beaker into a petri dish and examine under a lens or binocular microscope.

6 Use the drawings in the Appendix to identify the animals. Write down the names and number of each type of animal caught.

Questions for class discussion

1 The high temperature, light and dryness produced by the lamp cause the animals to move away and fall into the beaker. Why do small invertebrates mostly move away from these conditions?

2 Which producer provides food for the animals which you extracted with the Tullgren funnel?

3 Some of the animals you caught will be decomposers, but there may have been some carnivores as well. What is their food?

4 At what time of the year would you expect to find the largest number of animals in the leaf litter of deciduous trees? Explain your answer.

5 Table 13.2 shows some of the invertebrates found in 2 kg samples of leaf litter (dead leaves, twigs and soil under the trees) taken from three different habitats.

Table 13.2

	Woodlice	Mites	Spiders	Snails	Centipedes
beech wood	27	6	12	14	1
mixed scrub	68	19	10	57	6
pine wood	1	5	9	0	1

a Describe very carefully how you would obtain the leaf litter samples from the habitats.

b Suggest two reasons why pine wood leaf litter contains fewer invertebrates than the other habitats.

The food cycle

The animals which you extracted from leaf litter by using the Tullgren funnel play an important part in beginning the breakdown of dead animals and plants (see Fig 13.9).

If you examine rotting wood, fruit or dead animals or the waste products of animals such as 'cow-pats', you can often see signs of another important group of decomposers – moulds or fungi. The surface may be 'mouldy' and covered with fine threads. You may see spore-producing structures such as toadstools. These and other decomposers obtain energy and material for growth from the dead remains on which they feed. As a result, the dead remains are turned into sticky black **humus** (see page 146). The breakdown of humus is completed by bacteria. It has been estimated that the number of bacteria in a teaspoonful of soil is greater than the human population of the world.

The final step in the decomposition and decay of living organisms is the release of the chemical materials which they contain so that they can be used again by other living organisms. Carbon dioxide is returned to the atmosphere and mineral ions such as nitrate and sulphate, which are essential for plant growth (see Chapter 8), are released into the soil. If decomposers did not exist, the soil would quickly be covered with the dead remains of numerous animals and plants. Growing plants would not be able to obtain the essential chemicals they require, and animals would soon run short of food. The materials in living organisms thus find their way back into the soil ready to be used again (Fig 13.10).

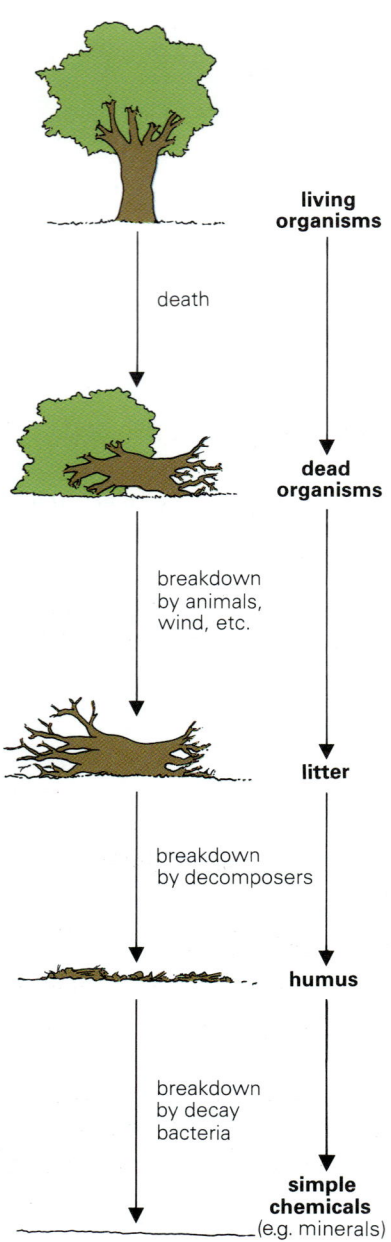

living organisms

↓ death

dead organisms

↓ breakdown by animals, wind, etc.

litter

↓ breakdown by decomposers

humus

↓ breakdown by decay bacteria

simple chemicals (e.g. minerals)

Fig 13.9 The stages in decay of a tree.

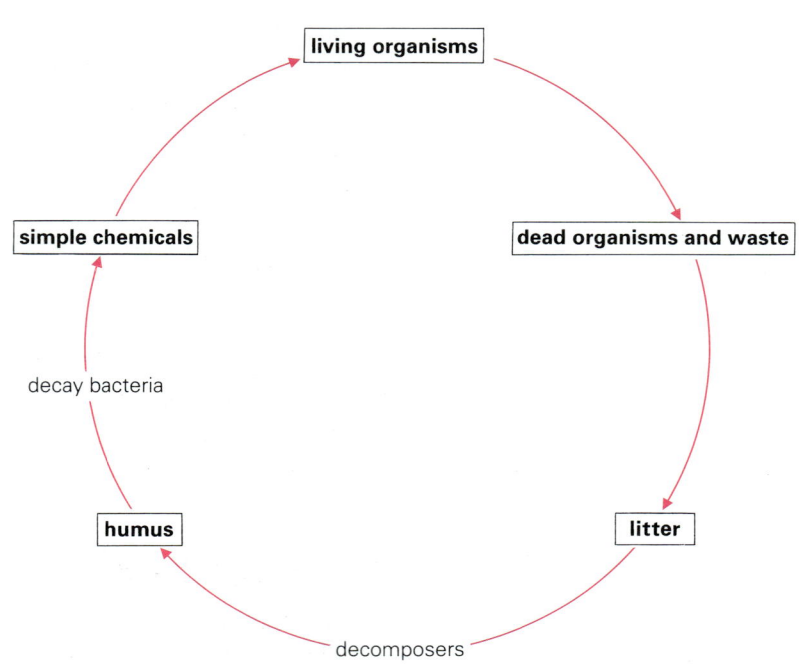

Fig 13.10 The food cycle.

Questions for class discussion

1 What is humus? Why do farmers spread manure on fields?

2 Peat consists of the incompletely decayed remains of plants and it is found in wet, acid soil such as that on moorland. Suggest possible reasons why complete decay does not take place in such areas.

Experiment 13.3
Decomposition and decay

Most human food is made from the dead remains of living things. Unless it is preserved in some way, it will decay.

1 Take a thick slice of white bread and dampen it with tap water. Do not make it too wet.

2 Place the bread inside a polythene bag and seal it tightly.

3 Label your bag and leave it in a warm place.

4 Examine the bread regularly *without opening the bag* and make a series of sketches to show the gradual growth of moulds on the surface.

Questions for class discussion

1 Plants are green, and make their own food by photosynthesis. Fungi are not green so they have to use ready made food. How is the bread fungus feeding?

2 How does the structure of the fungus help it to obtain food?

3 How many different kinds of fungus did you see on the bread?

4 Suggest two ways by which the fungi might have got into the polythene bag.

5 Describe the changes you would expect to see if the damp bread was left in a sealed container for a long time. What would be found in the container when it was eventually opened after several years? Would the mass of the contents of the bag be the same as the original mass of the piece of bread?

6 In what conditions could you keep bread for a week without it going mouldy? Explain why decay and decomposition is prevented by keeping bread in these conditions.

Homework assignments

1 Explain why decomposers are so important. What would be the result if they all disappeared?

2 a Name a decomposer that you have studied.
  b Describe one way in which it reproduces.
  c On what did you grow it in the laboratory?
  d Why are decomposers so important in natural communities?

3 The graph in Fig 13.11 shows the number of fungi in the soil at different depths from the surface.
  a Where is the greatest number of fungi found?
  b What are the fungi feeding on?
  c Why are there fewer fungi further down in the soil?

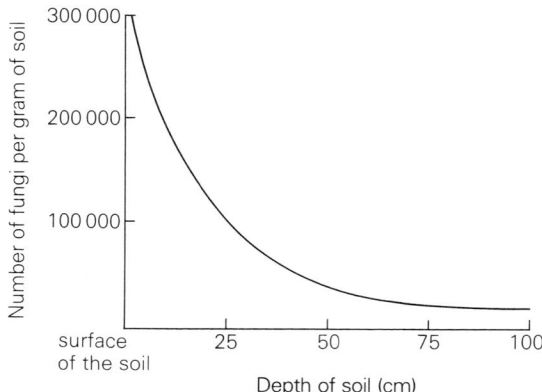

Fig 13.11 Fungi in soil.

4 a Describe how you could find how many small invertebrates there were in the leaf litter underneath the trees in a forest.
  b The graph in Fig 13.12 compares the numbers of mites and other arthropods in leaf litter throughout the year.
  Suggest one reason why the number of mites varies in the course of the year while other arthropods remain constant. Briefly describe how you might test your hypothesis.

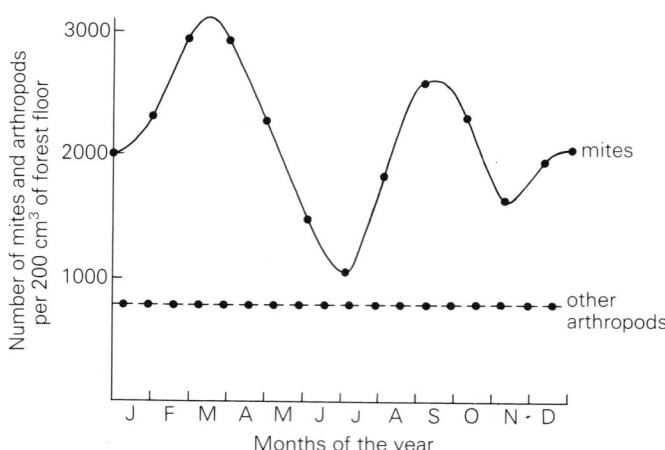

Fig 13.12 Mites and arthropods in leaf litter.

Maintaining the balance between animals and plants

Consider the simple food chain:

grass ——→ cow ——→ human

How many of each organism are needed for the chain to survive?

In a lifetime, a person might eat several cows and each cow would eat several million plants. As you go along the food chain, the number of organisms and the total mass of organisms (the **biomass**) usually decreases and their size usually increases. This can be shown diagrammatically by a **food pyramid** (Fig 13.13).

Fig. 13.13 Food pyramids. The one on the left is a pyramid of numbers, the one on the right is a pyramid of mass. The width of each bar represents the number, or mass, of the organisms in the community.

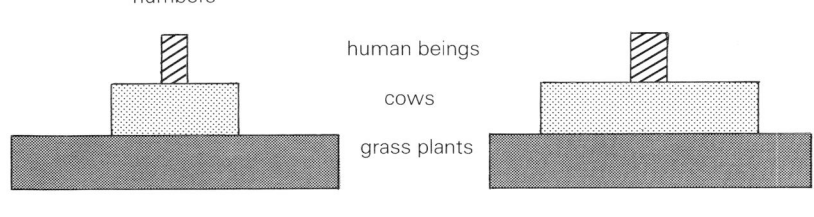

If one of the links in a food chain is removed, the whole chain will be affected. The disease myxomatosis (see Chapter 11) which almost eliminated rabbits in some parts of Britain in 1955, affected many other species. Can you suggest what happened to buzzards and hawthorn trees in the following food chain when myxomatosis killed the rabbits?

hawthorn seedlings ——→ rabbits ——→ buzzards

All the living organisms in a habitat form a community. Look at the stool in Fig 13.14. It will balance only if the legs are the right length. In the same way, the correct numbers of different kinds of animals, plants and decomposers, and the right kind of environment, are required for a **balanced community**.

Fig 13.14 A balanced community.

Parasites

Some species of living organisms do not live on their own; they need another species to live with – a sort of partnership. If the partnership is one sided, with only one of the organisms benefiting and the other being harmed by the association, it is called **parasitism**.

Parasites are animals or plants which live inside or on the outside of other organisms. The organism they live on is called the **host** and is the main source of their food. All parasites cause their hosts some sort of damage.

Many human diseases are caused by parasites. Viruses, which cause such diseases as the common cold, and bacteria live inside

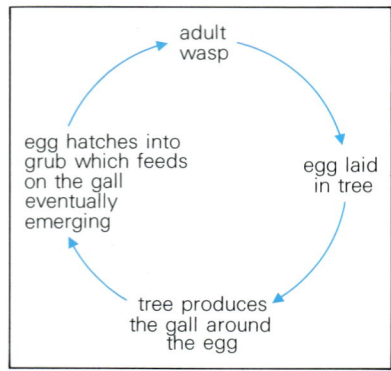

Fig 13.15 The life cycle of the gall wasp.

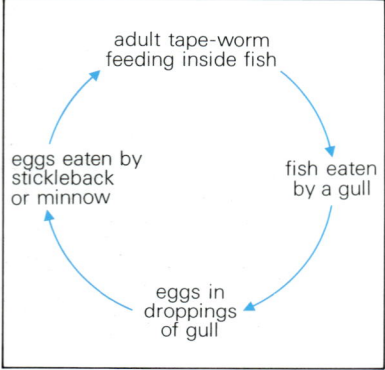

Fig 13.16 The life cycle of the fish tapeworm.

the human body. They can spread from person to person mainly through the air or by contact.

Experiment 13.4
Looking for parasites

Most living organisms have parasites which live on them. Here are two examples:

Plant galls

You may have noticed outgrowths on the twigs or leaves of the tree you have studied (Experiment 13.1). Some of these will be galls, caused by a parasitic wasp. Open them carefully with a sharp knife and look for a tiny grub inside. You may find that the grub has left the gall leaving only the tunnel through which it escaped. The life cycle of a gall wasp is shown in Fig 13.15.

Fish tapeworms

If you have a pond near your school, the small fish in it may contain tapeworms. These can sometimes be seen by opening the body cavity of a recently dead stickleback or minnow. The segmented white tapeworms inside can be as long as the host. The life cycle of these tapeworms is shown in Fig 13.16.

Mutualism

Sometimes two different organisms live together in a partnership from which *both* organisms benefit. This is called **mutualism**.

A lichen is made up of threads of fungus wrapped round cells of a protoctist. The protoctist contains coloured pigments for absorbing light to make food by photosynthesis. The threads of fungus absorb and store water and mineral ions. Neither the fungus nor the protoctist can survive on its own, but together in a lichen they can live in the most inhospitable places (Fig 13.17). You can find details of another example of mutualism on page 255.

Questions for class discussion

1 A tapeworm living in the intestine of its host is surrounded by food. What special problems does it have compared with an earthworm? How are they overcome?

2 Make a list of some important diseases, and the parasites which cause them.

3 It is sometimes very difficult to discover whether two organisms are living together as parasite and host or to the benefit of both organisms. Many kinds of bacteria live inside the human intestine making use of our food. Some may provide us with useful chemicals. How could a scientist show whether these bacteria are useful to us or parasitic upon us?

Fig 13.17 Lichens can grow where many other organisms cannot. This yellow lichen is growing on a bare rock.

Homework assignments

1 Match the descriptive terms in the first column with the most appropriate example in the second column. Write down the pairs in your notebook.

decomposer	oak tree
parasite	toadstool
carnivore	sheep
herbivore	tapeworm
producer	fox

2 a Why do most communities contain fewer carnivores than herbivores?

   b What would happen to the number of
     (i)   carnivores
     (ii) producers
   if all the herbivores in a community died suddenly?

3 a Write down the name of a habitat that you have studied.

   b From this habitat write down the name of one example each of:

a decay organism	a herbivore
an arthropod	a carnivore
an animal without a hard skeleton	a green plant

4 a Name the *three* most common kinds of plants found in a habitat you have studied.

b Give a clear description of this habitat.

c List *three* different ways in which the plants you mention are of benefit to animals in the habitat.

d If most of the plants had suddenly died out, say what you think would happen to the remaining animals, and why. Give examples.

e Give *two* possible reasons why the plants in such a habitat might suddenly start to die out.

5 What are the main differences between a decomposer organism and a parasite? Name one example of each and describe how they feed.

6 On a particular coral reef, sea slugs feed on sea anemones; sea anemones catch rockfish; copepods (small shrimp-like creatures) feed on plankton (small floating plants) and the copepods are eaten by rockfish.

a Which are the producers?

b Which are the top carnivores?

c The plankton feed like normal plants. How do they get their food?

d Write down the food chain for this coral reef.

7 If all the organisms in the food chain were collected and their total masses found, which would have the most mass? Explain your answer.

8 Write out the following sentences using the phrase which completes them most accurately.

a Humus is . . .
  found in fertile soil.
  essential for photosynthesis.
  a bone in the arm.
  destroyed by light.

b When left uncovered, food will decay because it . . .
  contains parasitic bacteria.
  reacts with the air.
  loses water vapour.
  is consumed by bacteria.

c A parasite is an organism which . . .
  feeds only on dead materials.
  only attacks plants.
  kills its prey and then feeds on it.
  feeds on living material.

d Lichens are . . .
  dead plants.
  decomposer organisms.
  an association between a protoctist and a fungus.
  plants which live as parasites on other plants.

9 a Describe the main features of a habitat you have studied.
b Of all the organisms found there, which do you consider to be the most interesting plant or animal? Give reasons for your choice.
c Draw a simple food web for this habitat, including not less than *eight* clearly named organisms.

10 In an experiment to investigate the food of the common earthworm, *Lumbricus terrestris*, 100 discs of the same size were cut from oak leaves, and another similar set from beech leaves. The discs were scattered at random on a grass plot which was surrounded by a wooden frame and covered by a lid of nylon mesh. Each month, from July to January, the frame was examined and some discs were found to have been eaten. The number of oak leaf discs and of beech leaf discs that remained were counted and the number of each was made up once more to 100. The results in Table 13.3 were obtained.
a Draw a graph to compare the consumption of beech and oak discs.
b Why was the number of leaf discs made up each month to 100?
c Suggest why more leaf discs of both kinds were eaten in September and October than in any other months.
d Suggest why so few discs were eaten in December and January.

Table 13.3

Month	Number of beech discs eaten	Number of oak discs eaten
July	33	8
August	5	2
September	8	30
October	10	25
November	5	15
December	0	0
January	1	3

Background Reading

Spaceship Earth

For millions of years we have known a world whose resources seemed limitless. However fast we cut down trees, nature unaided would replace them. However much sewage we dumped into the rivers, nature would purify them, just as she would purify the air however much smoke and fumes we put into it. Today we have reached the stage of realising that rivers can be polluted beyond repair, that seas can be overfished and that forests must be managed and fostered if they are not to vanish. In fact earth is a spaceship with strictly limited resources. These resources must, in the long run, be recycled, either by nature or by man.
(Adapted from *The Doomsday Book* by Gordon Rattray Taylor, published by Thames and Hudson.)

Questions
1 Explain in your own words why the author likens the Earth to a spaceship.

2 What is meant by the term 'recycling'? How does *natural* recycling take place in

a a forest

b a river or the sea

c the air?

3 Suggest *two* reasons why 'Spaceship Earth', which has existed for millions of years, now requires human assistance to survive.

4 Select one other 'limited resource', not mentioned in the passage, and explain what steps must be taken to preserve it for future generations.

Summary

1 In a habitat, the plants and the animals **interact**.

2 The animals (**consumers**) in a community depend on the plants (**producers**) to provide them with their ready made food.

3 Animals can be divided into meat eaters (**carnivores** or **predators**), plant eaters (**herbivores**) and those that eat animals *and* plants (**omnivores**).

4 **Food chains** and **food webs** show the path of food from one organism to another in a community.

5 The dead remains of living organisms and their waste products are broken down by **decomposers** which include animals, fungi, and decay bacteria.

6 Some living organisms live in partnerships. In **mutualism** both partners benefit; in **parasitism** the **host** is always harmed by the **parasite**.

Chapter 14   The human animal

As human beings we belong to the animal kingdom. Our scientific name is *Homo sapiens*, but we are usually referred to simply as humans. We perform the same basic life processes as other living things. Thus we breathe, feed, move and respond to changes in our environment, just as other organisms do.

What group of animals do we belong to?

Fig 14.1 The human with some other mammals.

We are mammals, one of the groups of backboned animals or vertebrates (see page 29). A human is shown with some other mammals in Fig 14.1.

Mammals possess two main features (see page 79): they have **hair**, and the young are fed on **milk** which is produced by the mother's **mammary glands**. This applies as much to humans as to other mammals.

Humans as mammals

Young mammals obtain milk by sucking their mother's nipples. Most mammals have many nipples. However, humans have only two.

The main function of a mammal's hair is to keep the body warm. Mammals are warm-blooded and it is important to prevent the body temperature falling. Humans have less hair than most other mammals, but they make up for this by wearing clothes.

We have many features in common with other mammals, but we also differ from them in a number of ways. For example, we walk on only one pair of legs, that is we are **bipedal**. Most mammals walk on all-fours, that is they are **quadrupedal**. Being bipedal means that we can use our arms and hands for other jobs, such as making things and writing.

Another way in which we differ from other mammals is in what our brain can do. All mammals have complicated brains, but humans have the most advanced brain of all. We use it to reason things out and solve problems. Moreover, we can communicate with each other by means of language. It is largely because of our brain, and our ability to communicate, that we can live in an advanced technological society.

One more way in which the human differs from other mammals is that the young are born at a stage when they are completely helpless, and it takes them a relatively long time to develop to maturity. During this time they learn from their parents and others how to fend for themselves. No other mammal goes through such an elaborate period of training and takes such a long time to reach adulthood.

Questions for class discussion

1 Make a list of the ways in which you are similar to, and different from, a mammal such as a dog. Why are humans and dogs both included in the mammal group?

2 Why do you think humans have fewer nipples than most other mammals?

3 What are the advantages of being bipedal? Can you think of any other mammals which are at least partly bipedal?

4 Look at Fig 14.1. Which of the mammals in this picture is most like the human? Give reasons for your choice. Why are they all regarded as mammals?

5 Someone has said that the human brain not only solves problems but also *creates* problems. What world-wide problems have been created by the human brain?

The parts of the body

The human body consists of three main parts: the **head**, **trunk** and **limbs** (Fig 14.2). The head is joined to the trunk by the **neck**. The trunk is divided into two parts, the **thorax** and the **abdomen**. The limbs are the arms and legs.

Fig 14.2 Me and my skeleton! The main parts of the human body.

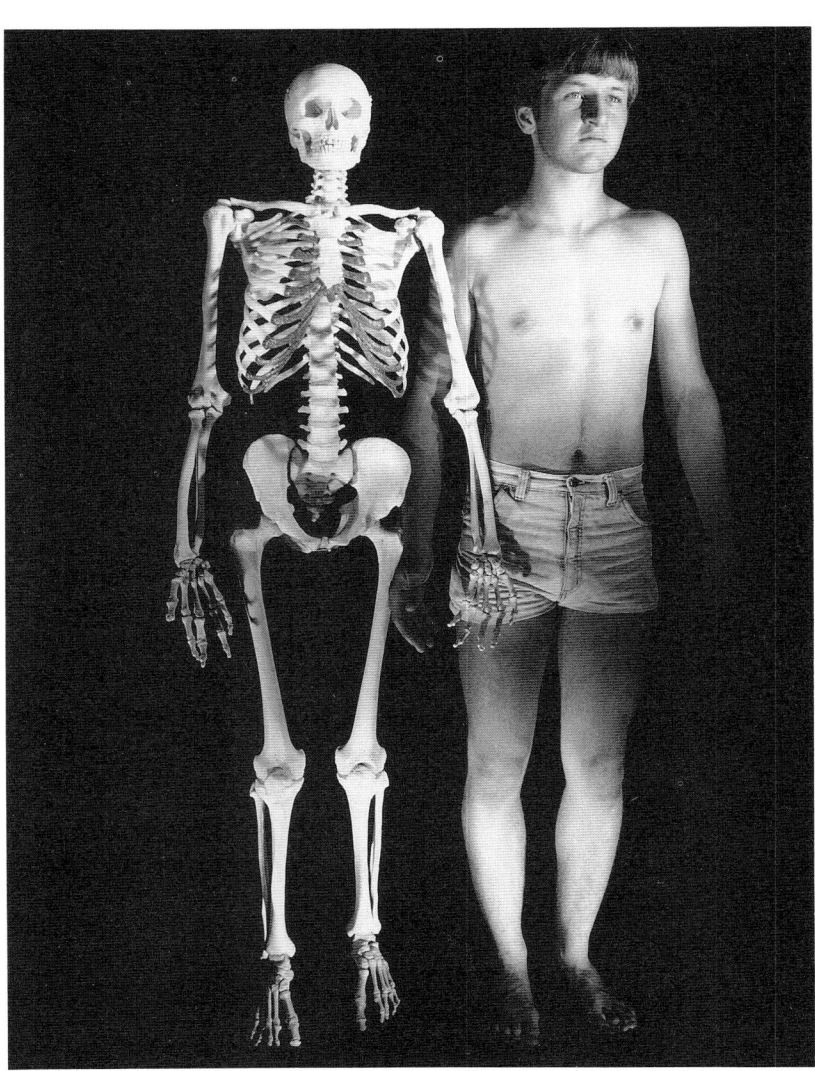

Organs

Inside the body there are all sorts of important structures. We call these **organs**. You have already met some of them in previous chapters. Each organ has one or more special jobs to do.

Fig 14.3 shows the main organs found in the human body. With each label there is a brief note on what the organ does.

Fig 14.3 Some of the more important organs of the human body, and their main functions.

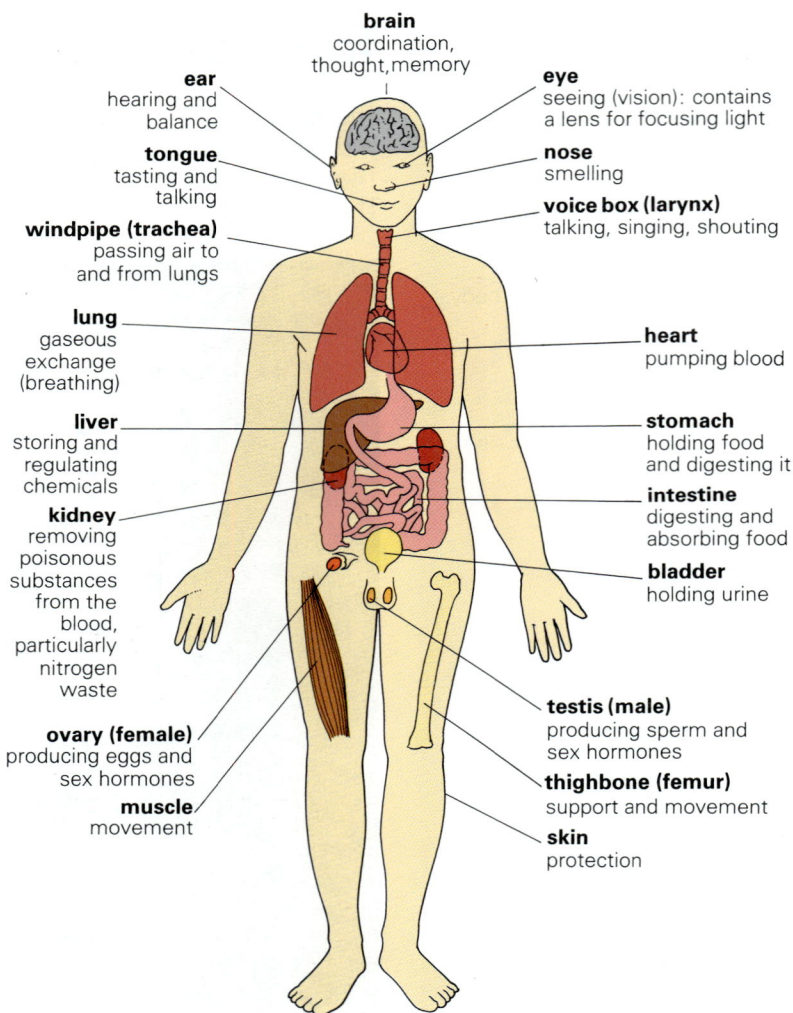

brain
coordination, thought, memory

ear
hearing and balance

eye
seeing (vision): contains a lens for focusing light

tongue
tasting and talking

nose
smelling

windpipe (trachea)
passing air to and from lungs

voice box (larynx)
talking, singing, shouting

lung
gaseous exchange (breathing)

heart
pumping blood

liver
storing and regulating chemicals

stomach
holding food and digesting it

kidney
removing poisonous substances from the blood, particularly nitrogen waste

intestine
digesting and absorbing food

bladder
holding urine

ovary (female)
producing eggs and sex hormones

testis (male)
producing sperm and sex hormones

muscle
movement

thighbone (femur)
support and movement

skin
protection

Questions for class discussion

These questions relate to Fig 14.3.

1 Certain organs are at, or close to, the surface of the body. Which ones are in such a position, and why?

2 One of the organs can be said to 'store information'. Which one?

3 Where does blood go after it has left the heart?

4 What gases are exchanged in the lungs?

5 Which organs are joined to one another, and why?

6 Which organs occur in pairs? Why is this useful?

7 An important function of the skin is 'protection'. What does the skin protect us from?

8 Are there any organs which are not shown in Fig 14.3?

9 One of the organs contains a lens. Which one?

10 Which organs occur in only one place, and which ones are dispersed throughout the body?

Organs are made of **tissues** (see page 46). We can relate the functions of each organ to the types of tissue which it contains. For example, the brain contains nerve tissue which enables it to send messages from one place to another. This is the basis of coordination, as we shall see in Chapter 17.

Systems

Different organs may be combined into a **system**. For example, the windpipe and lungs belong to the **breathing system**; and the stomach, intestine and liver all belong to the **digestive system**.

Each system in the body carries out a particular function or range of functions. The main systems in the human body are summarised in Table 14.1. Note that the liver belongs to two systems, the digestive and excretory systems. The part it plays in each of these is explained in the next chapter.

Table 14.1 Summary of the main systems in the human body.

Name of system	Main organs in the system	Main functions
digestive system	gut and liver	to digest and absorb food
breathing system	windpipe and lungs	to take in oxygen and get rid of carbon dioxide
circulatory system	heart, blood vessels	to carry oxygen and food round the body
excretory system	kidneys, bladder, liver	to get rid of poisonous waste substances
sensory system	eyes, ears, nose	to detect stimuli
nervous system	brain and spinal cord	to transmit messages from one part of the body to another
musculo-skeletal system	muscles and bones	to support and move the body
reproductive system	testes and ovaries	to produce offspring

Question for class discussion

Do you think a plant can be described as having organs and systems in the same way that an animal can? Try to make a table like Table 14.1 for a plant.

Homework assignments

1 Write down one feature of the human which is:
   a Common to all living things.
   b Common to all animals.
   c Found in all vertebrates but not in any other group.
   d Found in all mammals but not in any other group.
   e Different from any other mammal.

2 Each of the following statements applies to at least two different organs in the human body. Write down the names of all the organs to which each statement applies.
   a They get rid of unwanted substances from the body.
   b They store substances.
   c They enable us to walk about.
   d They produce gametes.
   e They tell us about our environment.

3 The pictures in Fig 14.4 are of five organs found in the human body. Give the name of each one, say whereabouts it occurs, and write down one function which it carries out.

Fig 14.4 Five organs found in the human body.

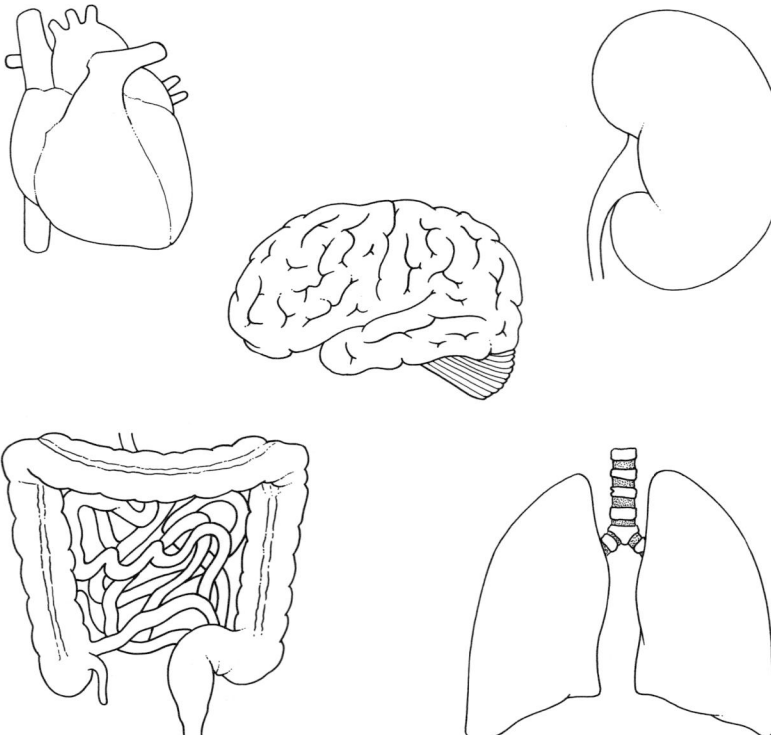

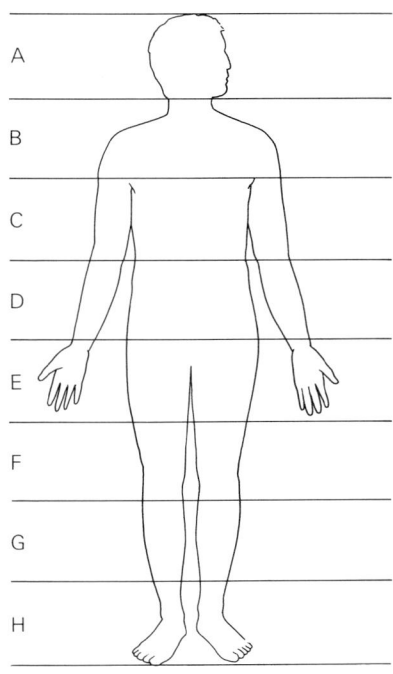

Fig 14.5

4 In Fig 14.5, the human body is divided into eight parts labelled A to H.
  a Which parts contain the thorax, and which ones contain the abdomen?
  b Name one organ which is found only in each of the parts labelled A to E.
  c In which part or parts would you find
    (i) the larynx
    (ii) the muscles
    (iii) the kidneys?

5 Some of our organs work together and their jobs are closely interlinked. Arrange the organs shown in Fig 14.3 into pairs according to how close they are in the jobs they do. In each case explain why you have linked them together.

6 The human is generally regarded as the most advanced of all mammals. Write down those features of the human species which, in your opinion, have made it so successful.

Background Reading

Tribes and super-tribes

Imagine a piece of land 30 km long and 30 km wide. Picture it wild, inhabited by animals small and large. Now visualise a compact group of sixty human beings camping in the middle of this territory. Try to see yourself sitting there, as a member of this tiny tribe, with the landscape spreading out round you farther than you can see. No one apart from your tribe uses this vast space. It is your exclusive home range, your tribal hunting ground. Every so often the men in your group set off in pursuit of prey. The women gather fruits and berries. The children play noisily round the camp site, imitating the hunting techniques of their fathers. If the tribe is successful and swells in size, a splinter group will set off to colonise a new territory. Little by little the species will spread.

Imagine a piece of land 30 km long and 30 km wide. Picture it civilised, inhabited by machines and buildings. Now visualise a compact group of six million human beings camping in the middle of this territory. See yourself sitting there, with the complexity of the huge city spreading out all round you, farther than you can see.

Now compare these two pictures. In the second scene there are a hundred thousand individuals for every one in the first scene. The space has remained the same. It has taken a mere few thousand years to convert scene one into scene two. The human animal appears to have adapted brilliantly to his extraordinary new condition. This civilising process has been accomplished entirely by learning and conditioning. Biologically the human is still the simple tribal animal depicted in scene one.

(Adapted from *The human zoo* by Desmond Morris, published by Jonathan Cape.)

Questions

1 What do you think the author means by 'learning and conditioning' in the second to last sentence?

2 Make a list of as many ways as you can think of in which humans show that biologically they are still simple tribal animals.

3 **a** What major advances have made it possible for a hundred thousand individuals to inhabit an area previously occupied by one individual?

   b What problems may result from so many people occupying such a small area?

Summary

1 Humans belong to the group of animals known as **mammals**.

2 In common with other mammals, humans are warm-blooded and have **hair** on their bodies. They have **mammary glands** with which to feed the young.

3 Humans differ from other mammals in being **bipedal**, in having the most advanced brain, and in giving birth to young that are helpless at first and take a long time to reach maturity.

4 The human body consists of three main parts: **head**, **trunk** and **limbs**.

5 The human body contains many important structures known as **organs**. Organs are made of **tissues**.

6 Different organs may be combined into a **system**.

Chapter 15 Nutrition and the human

How many meals do you have each day, and how much food do you eat? Estimate the approximate mass of food in grams which you eat in one day. Then calculate the mass of food which you would consume in, say, twenty years.

Diet

What sort of food do you eat at each meal? If you were to make a list, it would probably include things such as cornflakes, eggs, bread, meat and so on. All these make up our **diet**.

However, there is a more scientific way of describing our diet, and that is to list the different chemical substances that our food contains. They are these:

carbohydrates	vitamins
fats	salts
proteins	water

It is most important that our diet should include all these substances in sufficient amounts – and the same applies to other animals too. They are essential for good health and if one or more of them is lacking from our diet, we may become very ill. One of the problems in poorer countries is that many people do not get as much of these substances as they need.

Now let us see what the substances are needed for.

Carbohydrates

We get energy from carbohydrates. The two main carbohydrates are **sugar** and **starch**. Fig 15.1 shows a few examples of foods that contain sugar and starch.

Sugar dissolves in water; in other words it is soluble. In contrast, starch will not dissolve in water: it is insoluble.

You can usually tell if a particular food contains sugar because it tastes sweet. To find out if starch is present, a simple chemical test can be carried out. You used this test on an earlier occasion. Can you remember what the test was? (See p. 83).

Fig 15.1 These foods are rich in carbohydrate. They are called energy foods as they give us lots of energy.

Another important carbohydrate is **cellulose**. This is the chemical substance of which plant cell walls are made (see page 43). The cellulose in our diet is called **dietary fibre**. There is lots of fibre in wholemeal bread, bran cereals and fruits such as apples. Humans cannot digest fibre, and we get no energy from it. However, it is important in the diet because it helps to prevent constipation and keeps the gut healthy.

Experiment 15.1
To find out if starch is present in various foods

Try this test on a small piece of bread.

1 With a pipette place one or two drops of dilute iodine solution on the bread. If you get a blue-black colour, starch is present.

2 Now try this test on other foods which your teacher will give you. Make a list of the foods in your notebook, and in each case say whether or not starch was present.

Questions for class discussion

1 Foods containing starch come mainly from plants, whereas foods without starch come mainly from animals. Is this true of the foods you tested?

2 Why is it useful to know if a particular food contains starch?

Fats

We are all familiar with fatty foods: some examples are shown in Fig 15.2. Fat is important for two main reasons:

1 It gives us energy, particularly when the body runs short of carbohydrate. Fat is stored in the body mainly under the skin.

2 The fat under the skin serves as an insulator, keeping us warm in cold weather.

Animals such as whales and seals, which live in very cold water, have a particularly thick layer of fat: this is known as **blubber**.

Fig 15.2 Some fatty foods.

Experiment 15.2
To find out if there is any fat in a food

Try this with some butter or lard.

1 Rub the food on a piece of brown paper. If this leaves a transparent mark on the paper even when the paper dries, it means that fat is present.

2 Now try this test on other foods given to you by your teacher. Record the results in your notebook.

Questions for class discussion

1 Fat is sometimes described as an 'energy store'. Why is it useful for an animal to have an energy store in its body?

2 Two boys dive into an unheated swimming pool. One of the boys is fat, the other thin. Which boy is likely to get cold more quickly? Give reasons for your answer.

Proteins

Fig 15.3 shows some foods which are particularly rich in protein. We need proteins for two main reasons:

1 It forms the main structures in the body. For example, our muscles, skeleton and cells all contain protein. Protein is the basic material in every living cell.

2 It helps to regulate the chemical reactions that go on inside the body. The proteins that do this are **enzymes** (see page 48).

Proteins also provide energy, particularly if carbohydrate and fat are in short supply.

Fig 15.3 Some protein-containing foods.

Questions for class discussion

1 It is particularly important that pregnant mothers and growing children should get plenty of protein. Why?

2 Adults need protein to replace worn out or damaged cells. In fact a process of continual replacement of materials goes on in the body all the time.
  a Think of some ways in which cells may get damaged.
  b Why do you think cells wear out eventually?

Vitamins

Vitamins are special substances which are essential for good health. Most of them are needed only in very small amounts. Each one performs a particular function, and if any of them are missing from the diet, illness and even death may result.

The different vitamins are known by letters (A, B, C etc.). As an example let us take **vitamin C**. This vitamin helps our cells to stick together. If it is missing from the diet, the person gets a disease called **scurvy**. One of the signs of this disease is that the gums bleed around the teeth.

Vitamin C is abundant in citrus fruits such as oranges and lemons. It is also found in green vegetables. It is easily destroyed by prolonged heating.

In general, fresh fruit and vegetables are a good source of vitamins. One of the best animal foods for vitamins is liver.

Questions for class discussion

1 In Admiral Nelson's day, limes were included in ships' rations. Why do you think this was done?

2 A hundred years ago diseases caused by lack of vitamins were common in Britain. Nowadays such diseases are rare. What has brought about this change? Do you think there are any sections of society where vitamin diseases still occur?

3 It is unwise to overcook cabbage. Why?

Salts

For healthy life the body requires the salts of certain mineral elements such as calcium, phosphorus and iron. For example, calcium and phosphorus are needed to make bones hard. Iron helps our blood to carry oxygen round the body; this is because it is needed for the formation of **haemoglobin**, the red substance in the blood.

Fig 15.4 The bones of this child are bent as a result of a lack of calcium in the diet. This disease is called rickets.

Like vitamins, mineral salts are needed only in small amounts. However, if any are missing from the diet the person may become very ill. Fig 15.4 shows what happens if a baby does not get enough calcium: the bones are soft and may bend. Like vitamins, salts are particularly plentiful in fresh fruit, vegetables and liver.

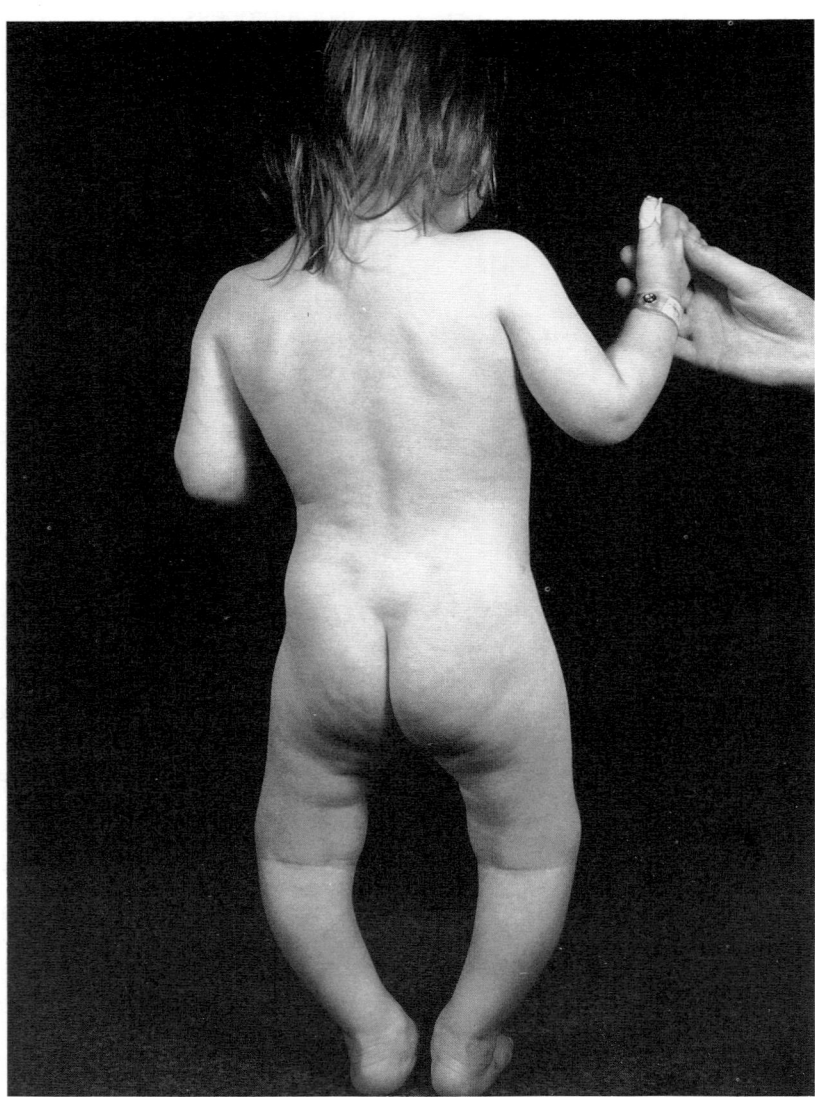

Questions for class discussion

1 The disease shown in Fig 15.4 is called rickets. It is caused by lack of calcium in the diet. The same disease can be caused by lack of a certain vitamin. Find out which vitamin is needed for hardening bones, and what sort of foods contain it.

2 Sometimes people who are tired and lack energy take iron tablets. In what way might this help them?

Water

Fig 15.5 Water is an extremely important part of all living things.

Water is an extremely important part of all living things. In fact the human body is about 70 per cent water. There are many reasons why water is so important. Here are two of them:

1 Many substances which occur in the body are dissolved in water. In solution these substances can come into contact with each other and react together.

2 Being a liquid, water can move easily around the body, carrying things with it. This is important in transporting materials in our blood system.

Question for class discussion

You have just read two reasons why water is important to living things. Make a list of as many other reasons as you can think of why water is important. Do not restrict your list to humans; include other organisms as well.

Experiment 15.3
To find out how much water an organism contains

You cannot do this experiment on a human. However, you can

try it on a lettuce. Make sure that the lettuce has received plenty of water beforehand.

1 Weigh the lettuce and write down its mass in grams.

2 Put the lettuce on a metal dish and place it in an oven at 100 °C for an hour.

3 Take the lettuce out of the oven and let it cool down. Then put it in a desiccator overnight.

4 Reweigh the lettuce. Calculate the percentage decrease in mass.

$$\text{Percentage decrease in mass} = \frac{\text{decrease in mass}}{\text{original mass}} \times 100$$

Questions for class discussion

1 What percentage of the lettuce is water? What assumptions have you made in arriving at your answer?

2 How could you estimate the amount of water in the plant more accurately?

A complete diet

Every day our bodies use a certain amount of carbohydrate and other food substances. How much of each substance the body uses will depend on many things. For example, an active person will use up a lot of carbohydrate, and a growing child will use up a lot of protein.

The amount of each substance used must be replaced in the person's food. A diet which achieves this is called a **complete diet**. A complete diet provides all the substances the body needs. If the various substances are present in the right proportions, we call it a **balanced diet**.

People who organise the feeding arrangements in schools and hospitals must make sure that a complete diet is provided. To do this they need to know how much of each essential substance occurs in different foods, and how much of each substance we need per day.

One of the main things which our food provides is energy. It is important to know how much energy can be obtained from different foods, that is their **energy value**. This can be found by estimating how much energy is given out when a sample of food of known mass is burned. The energy value of the food is often expressed in units called kilocalories, and the apparatus for determining it is called a **calorimeter**. However, in scientific circles kilocalories have been replaced by another unit; kilojoules.

Knowing the energy value of different foods, and how much energy people need, dieticians can make sure that the people in their care get enough energy foods each day. In devising diets, it has to be borne in mind that people's energy needs differ. For example, an 11 to 14 year-old boy or girl needs less energy each day than an adult, and a pregnant mother needs more energy each day than she did before she became pregnant.

Homework assignments

1 'An apple a day keeps the doctor away'. Explain the reasoning behind this well known saying.

2 You are a scientist working in a remote village in a developing country. The inhabitants are suffering from an unknown disease which you *think* might be caused by the lack of a certain vitamin in their diet.
  a What would you do to test your idea?
  b Assuming that your idea turns out to be right, what remedy would you recommend?

3 A scientist fed some mice on a diet consisting of water, salts, carbohydrates, fat and protein. After a while their hair became sparse.
  a What might have caused their hair to become sparse?
  b Describe an experiment which could be done to find out if your answer is correct.

4 Write a letter to the newspaper either supporting or condemning the use of animals in experiments of the kind outlined in Question 3. (In Britain it is illegal to perform experiments on animals such as mice without a special licence.)

Malnutrition

In many developing countries people do not get enough to eat: their diet is incomplete and they suffer from **malnutrition**. Approximately two thirds of the world's population is believed to be undernourished. In many cases the diet does not contain enough energy food to meet the person's needs. As a result the body's reserves are used up and the person becomes thin. In some cases the diet contains enough energy food but lacks certain vitamins or mineral elements, resulting in diseases such as scurvy and rickets.

Malnutrition is one of the world's most pressing problems. It is mainly a problem of developing countries, but occasionally it occurs even in countries like Britain. For example, people sometimes suffer from a nervous condition in which they refuse to eat, although they may be more than usually active. This is called **anorexia nervosa**. It is particularly common in teenage girls, and it may be brought on by worrying too much about being 'overweight'.

Diet and health

In developed countries such as Britain, people tend to eat too much. In particular we eat too much energy food such as sweets, cakes and butter. The body gets as much energy as it needs from the food, and stores the rest mainly in fat. As a result the body mass increases and the person becomes **obese (overweight)**.

There are many disadvantages in being obese. Obese people are more prone to certain diseases, and are likely to die younger, than people of normal body mass. For example, having too much fat in the body can lead to heart disease (see page 212).

Eating a lot of protein does not matter so much. Our bodies can get rid of protein that we do not need. Later we shall see how this happens.

Questions for class discussion

1 What are the disadvantages of being obese (overweight)? Make a list of as many disadvantages as you can think of. Can you think of any advantages?

2 Some people who are obese reduce their body mass by going on a high protein diet, that is a diet which contains a lot of protein but relatively little carbohydrate and fat. Why should this result in a loss in body mass? If a person goes on such a diet, what precautions should be taken?

3 Suggest two reasons why eating lots of fried chips over many years might be bad for health. How might a person reduce the possible harm without giving up chips?

What happens to the food we eat?

Much of our food is in an insoluble form. For the body to use it, the insoluble substances must be turned into soluble ones. This process is known as **digestion** and it occurs in the **gut**.

You can see what the gut looks like in Fig 15.6. The human gut is about eight or nine metres long altogether, so you can imagine how coiled up it must be inside the abdomen. Fig 15.7 shows the gut spread out so that you can see the different parts.

Digestion starts as soon as food is put in the mouth. Here starch is turned into a soluble substance. This conversion is brought about by **saliva** (spit).

Experiment 15.4
To find out what happens to starch in the mouth

1 Cut a cube of bread about 1 centimetre square and put it in your mouth.

Safety note

To avoid any possibility of infection, test only your own chewed bread.

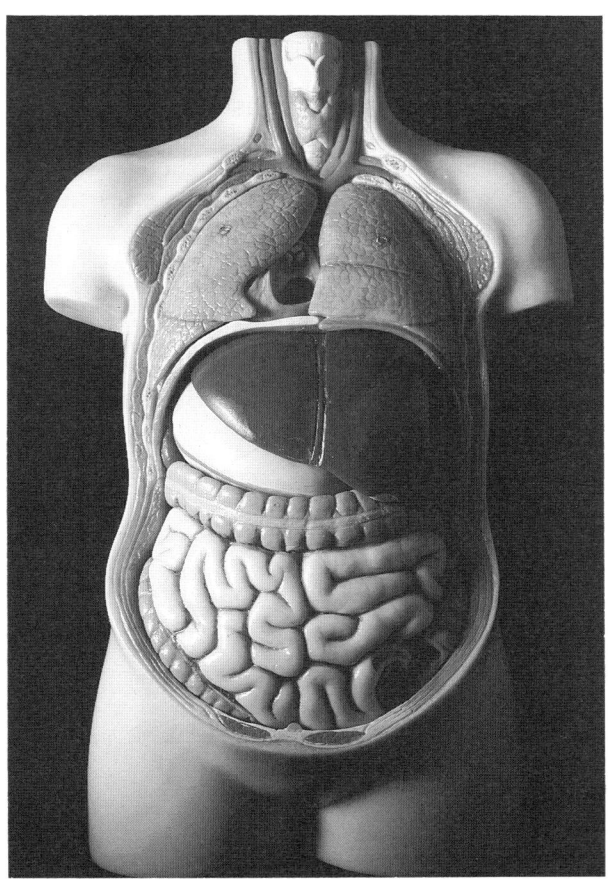

Fig 15.6 In this model the human gut is shown in its normal position inside the abdomen.

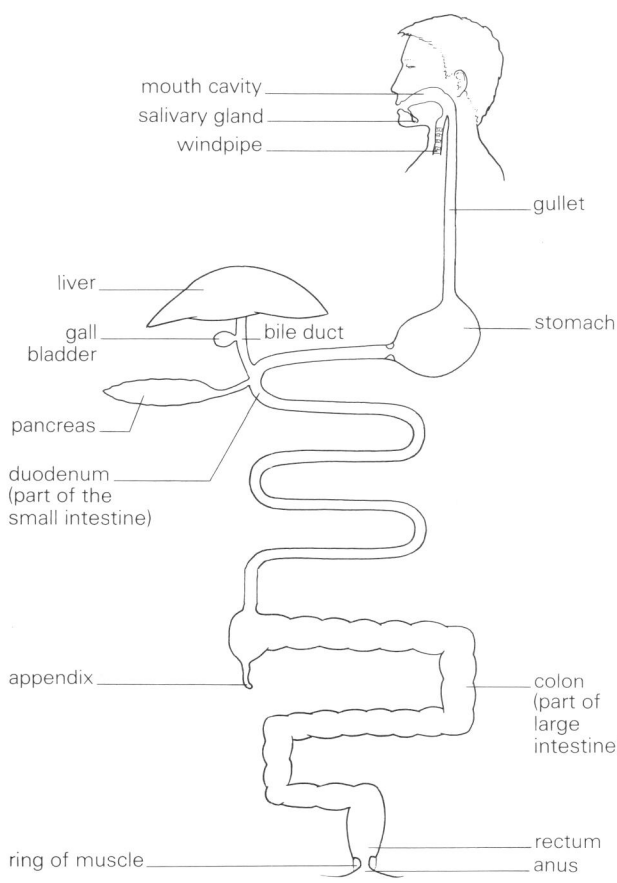

Fig 15.7 This diagram shows the human gut, spread out so that you can see its various parts.

2 Chew the bread without swallowing it.

3 After two minutes spit out a small amount of the food into a beaker, and add a drop of dilute iodine solution. Is a blue-black colour produced? If it is, starch must be present.

4 Continue to chew the rest of the food, without swallowing it. After a further two minutes test another sample of the food with iodine. Is any starch still present?

5 Test further samples at two-minute intervals until a blue-black colour is *not* given. When this stage is reached, we conclude that starch is no longer present in the food.

Questions for class discussion

1 You may have noticed that towards the end of the experiment the food tasted sweet. What is the sweet taste due to?

2 Write a simple word equation for the chemical change which has taken place in your mouth.

Digestive enzymes

What is it about saliva which enables it to digest starch? The answer is that it contains an **enzyme** (see page 48). The enzyme in saliva is able to turn insoluble starch into soluble sugar. Enzymes which help us to digest our food are called **digestive enzymes**.

Although digestion starts in the mouth, most of our food is digested in the stomach and intestine which contain many different digestive enzymes. They turn the food into a variety of soluble substances.

The enzymes are of three different types;

1 **Carbohydrases** act on carbohydrates like starch, turning them into soluble sugars.

2 **Proteases** act on proteins, turning them into soluble amino acids.

3 **Lipases** act on fats, turning them into soluble fatty acids.

Table 15.1 summarises the actions of these different enzymes in the human gut.

Table 15.1 Summary of the main digestive enzymes which our food meets as it passes along the gut.

Part of gut	Where the enzymes come from	Main enzymes present	What the enzymes do
mouth cavity	salivary glands	a carbohydrase called amylase	starts digestion of starch
stomach (acidic)	wall of stomach	a protease called pepsin	starts digestion of protein
small intestine (alkaline)	pancreas and wall of small intestine	a carbohydrase called maltase	finishes digestion of starch
		a protease called peptidase	finishes digestion of protein
		lipase	digests fat

Digestive enzymes flow into the gut from various **glands**. Saliva, for example, comes from **salivary glands** on either side of the mouth cavity beneath the tongue. The stomach enzymes come from glands in the wall of the stomach. And some of the enzymes in the intestine come from the **pancreas**, a large gland close to the first part of the intestine.

The contents of the stomach are acidic. This is because the wall of the stomach produces hydrochloric acid. Sometimes when you belch you can feel a burning sensation in your chest. This is caused by acid going up into the gullet. The acid in the stomach kills germs and also helps the protease enzyme (pepsin) to work. This particular enzyme works best in acid conditions.

In contrast, the contents of the small intestine are alkaline. This is because there is a lot of sodium hydrogencarbonate there. The enzymes in the small intestine work best in alkaline conditions.

Some of the enzymes which complete the digestion of our food are found inside the cells lining the small intestine.

Teeth

Teeth enable us to chew our food. Chewing breaks large lumps of food into smaller pieces, mixing it with saliva and helping the enzymes to act on it.

Fig 15.8 shows the structure of a tooth. The surface is made of very hard **enamel**. Beneath this is a less hard material called **dentine**, and in the centre there is a **pulp cavity** containing blood vessels and nerves.

Bacteria in the mouth can cause teeth to decay: the hard parts of the tooth become eroded away and the bacteria may eventually get into the pulp cavity, causing great pain. Of course the decayed parts can be drilled out by a dentist and the cavity filled. However, it is better to avoid the decay in the first place (see page 269).

A human gets two sets of teeth in his or her lifetime. The first set is usually complete by the age of three years. Between the ages of about six and twelve years the first set is gradually replaced by the second set. Any teeth lost after that will never be replaced – except by false ones.

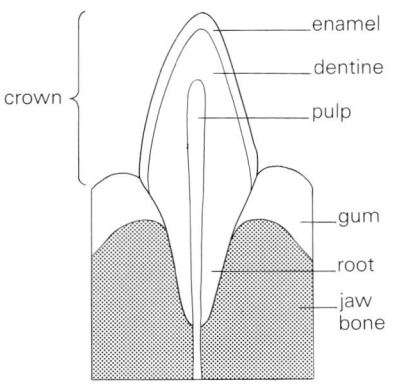

Fig 15.8 Section of a tooth showing its internal structure.

The liver

The liver produces a fluid called **bile**. Bile is stored in the **gall bladder**. During and after a meal, bile flows down a tube called the **bile duct** into the small intestine. Bile breaks fat into lots of little droplets. This process is called **emulsification**: it is similar to what happens when you pour washing-up liquid onto fat. Emulsification helps the action of the enzyme which digests fat. This is because it is easier for the enzyme to break down many small droplets of fat than a single large lump.

The liver does another important job too: it helps to get rid of unwanted protein, that is protein which we have eaten but is not needed. The nitrogen part of the protein is turned into a substance called **urea**. Urea would poison us if it stayed in the body. However, it passes in the bloodstream from the liver to the **kidneys** which get rid of it in the urine via the bladder.

What happens to indigestible food?

Some food substances, such as cellulose (fibre), cannot be digested because we do not have the necessary enzymes. This indigestible matter passes along the lower part of the intestine to the **rectum**. As it moves along, water is absorbed from it into the bloodstream. It is stored in the rectum as **faeces**. Periodically the faeces are

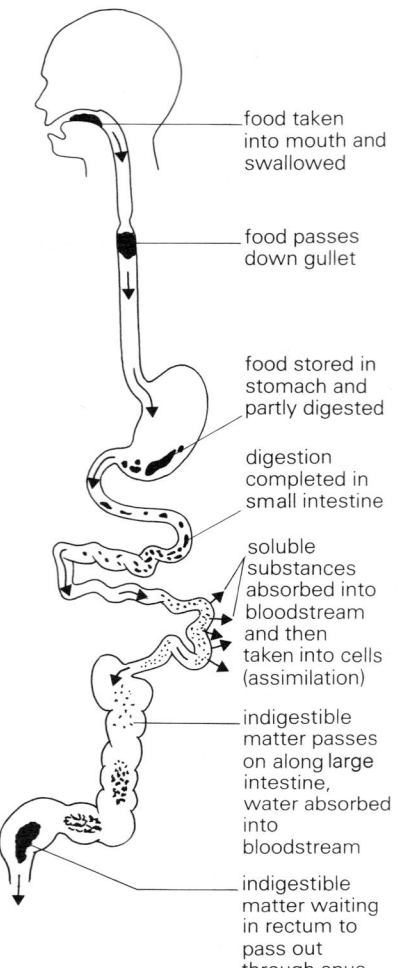

food taken into mouth and swallowed

food passes down gullet

food stored in stomach and partly digested

digestion completed in small intestine

soluble substances absorbed into bloodstream and then taken into cells (assimilation)

indigestible matter passes on along large intestine, water absorbed into bloodstream

indigestible matter waiting in rectum to pass out through anus

Fig 15.9 This diagram summarises what happens to our food after it has entered the mouth.

expelled from the rectum: this process is known as **egestion** or **defaecation**.

Movement of food along the gut

In order for all the processes just described to take place, food has to pass along the gut from the mouth to the **anus**. This is achieved by muscle tissue in the wall of the gut. The muscle contracts, forming a ring, which moves along the gut pushing the food before it. This process is called **peristalsis**. You can see it in Fig 15.9 where a ring of contraction is shown pushing food down the gullet.

The appendix

The appendix can be seen in Fig 15.7. It is a narrow bag leading from the intestine. It has no function in humans. However, in herbivorous mammals such as rabbits it contains micro-organisms which can digest cellulose. Some of the soluble sugar so formed is absorbed and used by the mammal, so these micro-organisms are helpful to the animal which harbours them.

In humans the appendix sometimes gets infected and has to be removed in an operation. Infection of the appendix is called **appendicitis**.

Absorption

In the small intestine, the soluble substances are absorbed into the bloodstream. They are then transported to all the cells of the body where they are used for releasing energy and carrying out other vital functions.

So you see that many hours after they have been eaten, the chemical substances in our food get into our cells. We call this **assimilation**.

Fig 15.9 summarises what happens to our food from the moment it enters the mouth to when it becomes assimmilated into our cells.

Questions for class discussion

1 The wall of the small intestine contains lots of blood vessels. Suggest two functions of these vessels.

2 The flow of blood to the intestine increases after a meal. Why do you think this is?

3 In humans, the cellulose contained in plant foods such as potatoes and cabbages cannot be digested in the gut. Why can it not be digested? What happens to it eventually? Why is it important?

4 Biological washing powders can remove food stains from table cloths. What do you think they contain which enables them to do this, and how do you think they work? When using a biological washing powder it is important not to have the water too hot. Why?

5 The association between a rabbit and the micro-organisms in its appendix is one in which both partners benefit. What does the rabbit gain, and what do the micro-organisms gain, from the association?

Homework assignments

1 Starch has to be digested before the body can make use of it.
  a What does the word 'digested' mean?
  b Why does the starch have to be digested?
  c What use does the body eventually make of the starch?

2 Two athletes, A and B, wanted to give themselves a source of extra energy just before a race. A had a drink of glucose (sugar), and B ate a slice of bread. Which one was the more sensible, and why?

3 When you have not eaten anything for several hours you feel hungry. Put forward two theories to explain how the feeling of hunger is brought on.

Background Reading

What makes fat people fat?

Dr Andrew Prentice, a scientist at the Medical Research Council, Dunn Clinical Nutritional Centre, Cambridge, discusses some of the reasons why people are fatter than they used to be.

Changes in lifestyle during the past 50 years are to blame for many of us becoming slightly fatter. In general, we have become extremely inactive by relying on cars instead of our feet and by using machines instead of our hands. A recent study of adults in Cambridge showed that many were using up only 40 per cent more energy in their normal life than they would have done had they stayed asleep all day. Perhaps the most pervasive influence is the 30 hours a week that the average Briton spends watching television.

A second major feature of modern affluence is the type of food we now eat. Modern diets (particularly junk foods) contain nearly 50 per cent of their energy as fat and little in the form of unrefined carbohydrates such as starch and dietary fibre. When studying fatness, it is not enough to think solely in terms of the total amount of energy consumed. Fat, carbohydrate, protein and alcohol must be considered individually as sources of fuel for the body.

When we do this, fat emerges as the real villain. It is quite difficult for the body to make fat from carbohydrate, and it avoids doing so if possible. However, it is extremely easy to transfer fat straight from the diet into the body's fat stores. An excellent illustration of this comes from studies on laboratory animals. Rats remain lean when fed an unlimited supply of their normal low-fat diet – but when switched to a 'cafeteria' diet, including chocolate-chip cookies, they soon become fat.

(Reproduced from 'The Body Report, Part 4, The digestive system', published in *The Observer Magazine*)

Questions

1 Give some examples of 'junk foods' and explain why they can make people fat.

2 To avoid getting fat, some people go in for jogging. How does jogging help to prevent fatness?

3 Suggest other reasons, apart from the ones discussed here, why some people are fatter than others.

Summary

1 A complete diet is made up of **carbohydrates** (sugar, starch and cellulose), **fats**, **proteins**, **vitamins**, **salts** and **water**.

2 Carbohydrates and fats are energy foods, proteins are for body building, vitamins and salts are for general health, and water performs a variety of functions.

3 The carbohydrate **cellulose** (fibre) cannot be digested by humans, but it helps to keep the gut healthy.

4 Dieticians need to know the **energy value** of different foods, and how much energy is needed by different people each day.

5 Many people in developing countries suffer from **malnutrition**. In developed countries many people are overweight.

6 Most food is insoluble. As it passes through the mouth cavity, stomach and intestine it is **digested** by **digestive enzymes.**

7 The soluble products of digestion are **absorbed** into the blood and taken to the cells.

8 **Teeth** play a part in digestion by breaking up the food. Bacteria in the mouth can cause tooth decay.

9 The liver emulsifies fat. It also helps to get rid of nitrogen waste from unwanted proteins.

Chapter 16   **Energy and respiration**

All living organisms need energy in order to continue their activities. Where does this energy come from?

In chemistry you will have learned that when a carbon compound such as candle wax or coal is burned, three things happen:

1 Oxygen is used up.

2 Water and carbon dioxide gas are formed.

3 Energy is transferred to the surroundings which become warm.

The same kind of thing happens inside our bodies. Food substances which we have eaten are **oxidised** and as a result energy is transferred, water is formed, and carbon dioxide gas is given off:

$$\underbrace{\text{food} + \text{oxygen}}_{\text{raw materials}} \longrightarrow \underbrace{\text{water} + \text{carbon dioxide} + \text{energy}}_{\text{products}}$$

We call this process **respiration**, and it is an important part of metabolism (see page 47).

Although the raw materials and products are the same as when carbon compounds are burned, respiration takes place much more gently and in a series of small steps. When sugar is burned in a test-tube there is a fizz and a crackle and the temperature shoots up. If this happened in our bodies we would die immediately.

Respiration is important because it gives us energy for running about and playing games. We also need it for growing and for repairing parts of the body which get worn out or damaged, and we need a certain amount of energy just for staying alive. Some of the energy, in fact most of it, helps to keep us warm.

Producing carbon dioxide

The main type of food from which we get energy is sugar, which is a carbohydrate. Carbohydrates contain carbon, hydrogen and oxygen. The carbon dioxide which is given off in respiration comes from the breakdown of the carbohydrates.

Fig 16.1 Breathing out through limewater.

Experiment 16.1
To find out if we breathe out carbon dioxide

1 Pour some limewater into a test-tube to a depth of about two centimetres. Limewater is a solution of calcium hydroxide and it turns milky in the presence of carbon dioxide.

2 Breathe out into the limewater through a disposable drinking straw or sterilised glass tube, as shown in Fig 16.1. Does the limewater turn milky? What do the results tell you about the air we breathe out?

Questions for class discussion

1 The limewater *might* have been turned milky not by carbon dioxide in the air you breathed out, but by carbon dioxide present in the air around you.

Describe an experiment which you could do to rule out this possibility. A number of different methods could be used: do not be afraid to put forward your ideas.

2 Why does carbon dioxide make limewater go milky? If you do not know the answer, see *Chemistry 11–14* page 104.

We have seen that human beings give out carbon dioxide. We shall now do an experiment to find out if other organisms do the same.

Experiment 16.2
To find out if germinating seeds give out carbon dioxide

You will need some seeds which are in the process of germinating. Peas will do.

1 Put some moist cotton wool at the bottom of a flask, and place about twelve germinating seeds on top of the cotton wool.

2 Set up the flask as shown in Fig 16.2. Make sure that all the joints are airtight.

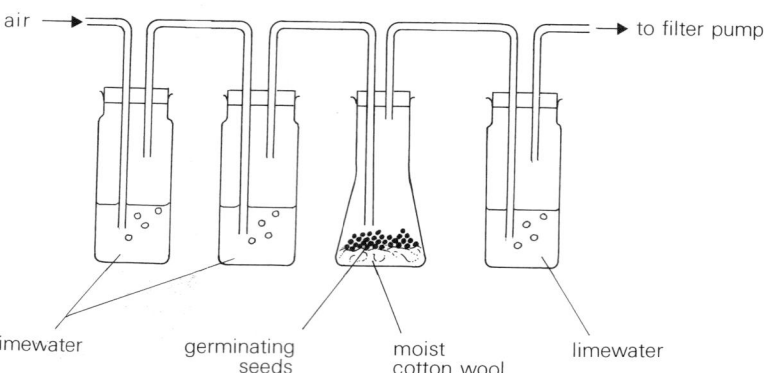

Fig 16.2 Apparatus for finding out if germinating seeds give out carbon dioxide.

3 Leave the apparatus for about ten minutes, then start the suction pump and gently draw air through. What happens to the limewater in the third bottle? Does it turn milky? If so, why?

Questions for class discussion

1 What is the point of passing the air through *two* bottles of limewater before it reaches the seeds? Is one not enough?

2 Why did you have to leave the apparatus for ten minutes before starting up the suction pump?

3 It is possible that the limewater in the third bottle might have turned milky because the cotton wool in the flask gave out carbon dioxide. Using the same apparatus, how could you rule out this possibility?

4 What experiment could you do to find out if the seeds have to be *alive* to give out carbon dioxide?

5 The results of this experiment suggest that plants, as well as animals, respire. What process in a germinating seed requires energy transfer?

6 The apparatus in Fig 16.2 can be used with other small organisms, for example woodlice, earthworms or snails. You can even use it with a mouse or gerbil, but for such animals you need to have a large jar instead of the flask, and you must start drawing air through the apparatus as soon as you have put the animals in the jar. Why do you think this is necessary?

This experiment should only be done under strict supervision by your teacher.

Homework assignments

1 Living things need energy in order to live.
  a What is the name given to the process which provides energy from food?
  b Give three ways in which this energy is used by living things.
  c What gas is:
   (i) used up
   (ii) given out in this process?

2 Which organs in your body do you think might need a particularly good supply of oxygen when you:
  a are running a race
  b are taking an examination
  c are eating a sandwich
  d have just had your lunch?

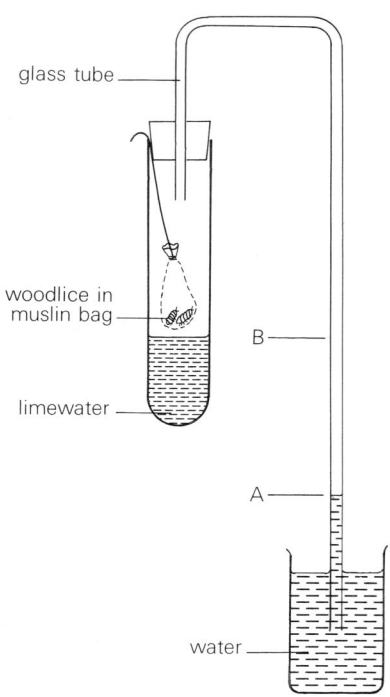

glass tube

woodlice in muslin bag

B

limewater

A

water

Fig 16.3 A simple respirometer.

3 In an attempt to find out about respiration, a student set up the experiment shown in Fig 16.3. The apparatus is called a respirometer. She found that at the start of the experiment the water level in the glass tube was at point A. Half an hour later it had risen to point B.

a Why was limewater placed in the test-tube with the woodlice?

b Why do you think the water rose in the glass tube?

c What further experiment should the girl do to be certain that the woodlice caused the rise in the water level?

d Another girl set up exactly the same experiment, but found that the water did not rise in the glass tube at all. Suggest reasons for this.

Respiration without oxygen

Suppose there is no oxygen present. Usually this means that respiration can no longer take place. However, in certain circumstances respiration can take place without oxygen. This is called **anaerobic respiration**. Respiration with oxygen is called **aerobic respiration**.

An organism which can respire anaerobically is yeast, a single-celled fungus. In the absence of oxygen it breaks down sugar into ethanol (alcohol) and carbon dioxide with the release of energy.

This reaction is important to humans because it is how wine, beer and other alcoholic drinks are produced. It is also involved in making bread (see page 258).

When we take a bout of exercise, such as a hundred metre sprint, our muscles cannot get oxygen quickly enough to provide all the energy they need. So the muscles respire anaerobically. In this case the product is not ethanol but a substance called **lactic acid.** If a lot of lactic acid builds up it can make your muscles ache.

Breathing

We have seen that we need oxygen to obtain energy from food. Carbon dioxide, on the other hand, is poisonous, and we must get rid of it as quickly as possible. Both these functions – taking in oxygen and getting rid of carbon dioxide – are achieved by **breathing**.

When we breathe in, air is drawn into our **lungs**. These are complicated sacks situated in the chest. When breathing in, the chest increases in size and air is drawn in. When breathing out, the chest decreases in size forcing air out.

How does the chest increase and decrease in size? The sides of the chest are formed by the **ribs**, and the bottom is spanned

Fig 16.4 The chest and lungs before and after breathing in.

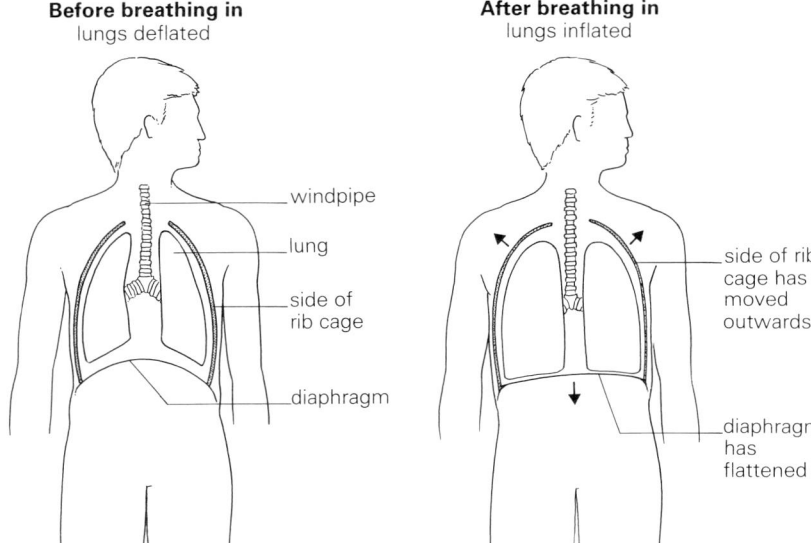

Before breathing in
lungs deflated

windpipe
lung
side of
rib cage
diaphragm

After breathing in
lungs inflated

side of rib
cage has
moved
outwards

diaphragm
has
flattened

by the **diaphragm**, a dome shaped sheet of muscle. When you breathe in, your ribs move outwards and your diaphragm flattens. As a result the chest gets larger (Fig 16.4). When you breathe out, the opposite happens: your ribs move inwards and your diaphragm bows upwards. The result is that the chest gets smaller.

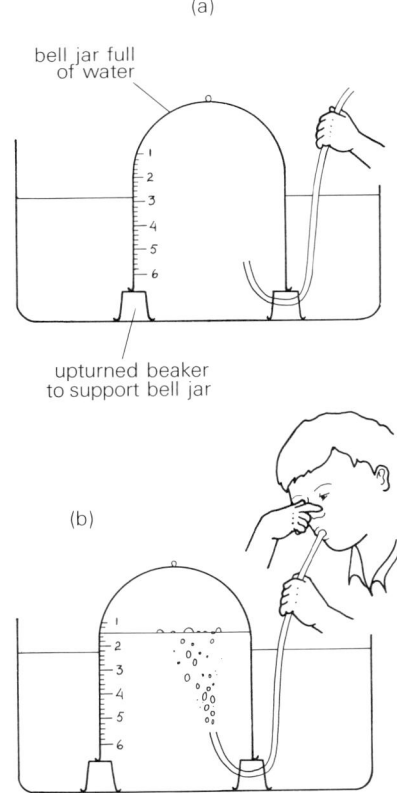

(a)

bell jar full
of water

upturned beaker
to support bell jar

(b)

Fig 16.5 Apparatus for finding how much air you can take into your lungs.

Experiment 16.3
To find out how much air you can take into your lungs

1 Fill a sink with water. Lay a bell jar on its side in the sink, so as to fill it with water. Then place the bell jar in an upright position on supports. Insert a sterilised bent tube under the rim as shown in Fig 16.5a.

2 Take as deep a breath as you can. Then put the end of the bent tube in your mouth and hold your nose. Now breathe out as much as you possibly can: this will displace some of the water from the bell jar as shown in Fig 16.5b. As soon as you have finished breathing out, take the tube out of your mouth.

3 From the scale on the side of the bell jar, read off the volume of air in litres which you have breathed out.

4 Try this experiment on different people in your class (and on your teacher) and compare the results. Wash and re-sterilise the tube after each person has used it.

Questions for class discussion

1 There is considerable variation in people's lung capacities. Can you suggest possible reasons for this? Do you think a person's lung capacity is related to his or her size?

2 In this experiment you have found out the *maximum* volume of air which you can take into your lungs. However, in normal breathing, you take in only a fraction of this amount.

Using the same apparatus, how could you find out what this 'normal' amount is? In what circumstances do we breathe more deeply and thereby take more air into our lungs?

The structure of the lungs

The lungs are not just simple sacks. They are made up of thousands of microscopic cavities called **air sacs**. Fig 16.6 shows the air sacs and the passages which lead to them. Now think of your own two lungs. To fit into your chest, the lungs cannot be very large, can they? However, each lung contains over 70 million air sacs. If all the air sacs were laid out as a single flat sheet, they would have the same area as a tennis court! So the lungs have a huge surface area and this ensures that we get enough oxygen when we breathe.

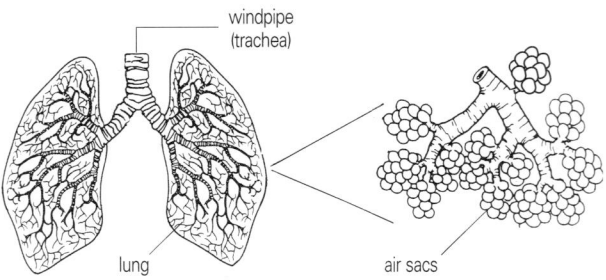

Fig 16.6 Structure of the human lung.

The windpipe and its branches are lined with **ciliated epithelium** which prevents germs and dust particles getting into the lungs (see page 47). Smoking stops the cilia beating for a while. This is why smoking irritates the air passages and makes people cough.

An air sac is shown in Fig 16.7. It has a very thin wall. Alongside the wall is a tiny blood vessel - a capillary. When you breathe in, oxygen passes from the air in the air sacs to the blood, and carbon dioxide passes from the blood into the air sacs. We call this process **gaseous exchange**. Gaseous exchange takes place by diffusion. Diffusion is explained in *Physics 11–14* Chapter 10.

The blood which arrives at the lungs has had oxygen removed from it in the tissues: it is **deoxygenated blood**. The blood which leaves the lungs has had oxygen added to it: it is **oxygenated blood**.

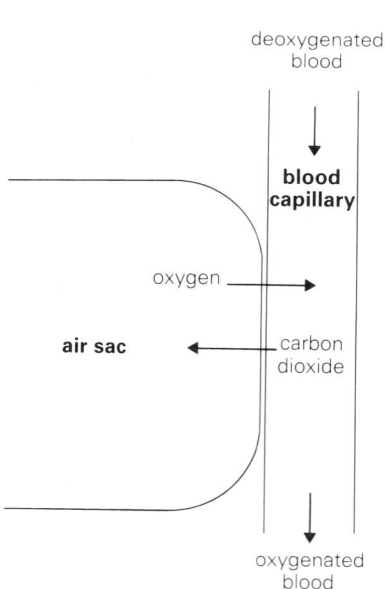

Fig 16.7 An air sac in the lung. The diagram shows gaseous exchange between the air in the air sac and the blood in the neighbouring capillary.

Questions for class discussion

1 Why is it better for a lung to consist of thousands of tiny air sacs rather than one large sack?

2 One effect of heavy smoking is to cause the walls between neighbouring air sacs to break down. What effect would you expect this to have on gaseous exchange and breathing?

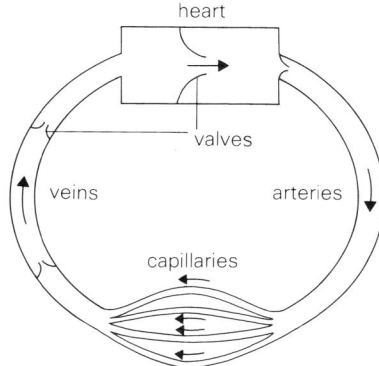

Fig 16.8 The main structures that make up the circulation. The arrows indicate the direction in which the blood flows.

Blood and the circulation

Think of the air we breathe in. Oxygen is taken out of this air and carried to all parts of our bodies. This job is performed by our **blood**.

Our blood is kept moving by the **heart** which pumps it through a series of tube-like **blood vessels** (Fig 16.8).

Vessels which carry blood from the heart to the various organs of the body are called **arteries**. The arteries split up into narrow **capillaries** which then join up again into **veins**. The veins take the blood back to the heart. The heart and the veins contain **valves** which keep the blood moving in one direction and stop it flowing backwards, just as the valves in a foot pump prevent air going backwards.

So the blood flows round and round the body. We call this **circulation** and the structures involved make up the **circulatory system.**

Experiment 16.4
Listening to the heart

You will need a **stethoscope**, the kind that doctors use for listening to the heart (Fig 16.9a).

1 Put the ear pieces in your ears and the end piece on your chest (Fig 16.9b). Listen! Can you hear regular thud-like sounds?

2 Try listening with the end piece in different positions. Where is the best place to put the stethoscope for the sounds to be loudest? What does this tell you about the position of the heart in the chest?

3 With a water-based felt pen draw a cross where you think the heart is, or mark the place with a safety pin fastened to your clothes. Compare the position with those of other pupils in your class.

4 Count the number of thuds in one minute. This will tell you the rate at which your heart is beating.

Questions for class discussion

1 There is quite a lot of variation between people in the rate at which the heart beats, but for a person at rest it is generally about seventy beats per minute.
Assuming this figure, how many times does the heart beat:
a in one year, **b** in sixty years?

2 If you listen extremely carefully, you will notice that each sound from the heart really consists of two thuds one after the other, the first being louder than the second. The thuds are caused by the closing of the valves inside the heart. Why do you think there are *two* thuds?

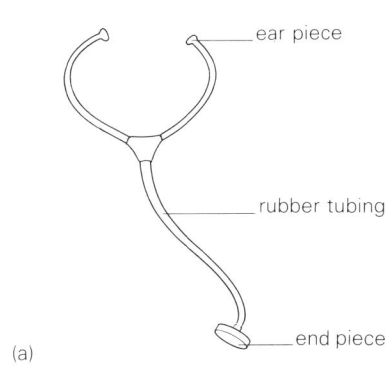

(a)

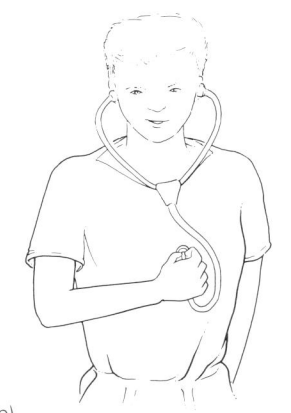

(b)

Fig 16.9 Using a stethoscope for listening to your heart.

The heart as a pump

Clench your fist repeatedly once a second for a minute. What does your hand feel like afterwards? Is it tired? Does it ache? Your heart pumps at about the same rate and with the same force, but it does not ache and it does not get tired. This is because the muscle in the wall of the heart has a very special property: it can contract repeatedly throughout life without tiring.

To contract in this way the heart muscle needs a good supply of oxygen. It gets this from arteries in its wall. They are called **coronary arteries**.

The structure of the heart

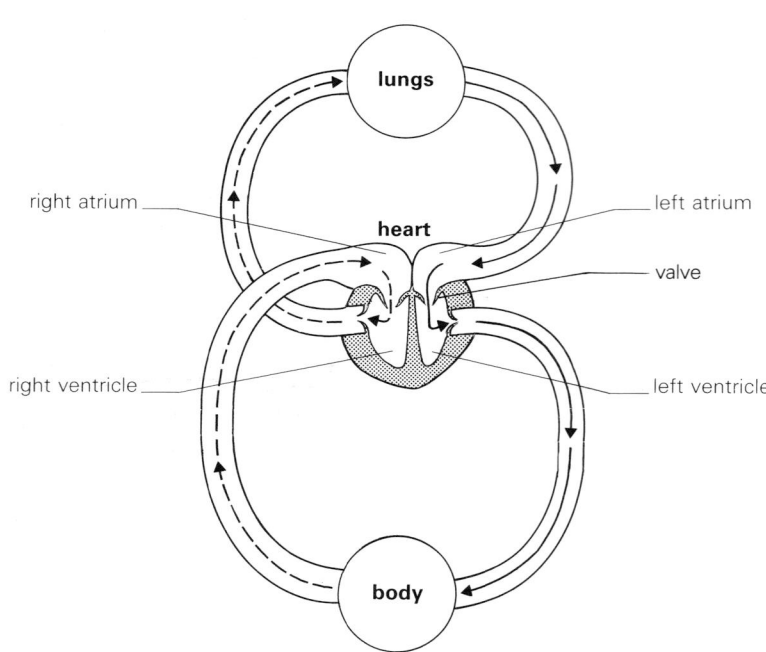

Fig 16.10 Simplified diagram of the heart and circulation. Diagrams of the anatomy are always viewed from the belly (ventral) side, so left and right are inverted, as shown here. The solid arrows represent oxygenated blood, the broken arrows deoxygenated blood.

The heart is much more complicated than the simple box in Fig 16.8. It is shown in more detail in Fig 16.10. It is divided down the middle into two halves. The right half receives deoxygenated blood from the various parts of the body, and pumps it to the lungs. Oxygenated blood then flows to the left half of the heart, which pumps it to the body. So blood flows from the heart to the lungs, then back to the heart, and then to the body.

Each half of the heart consists of two chambers, an **atrium** which receives the blood, and a **ventricle** which pumps it out. The wall of the ventricles is particularly thick and muscular. When the ventricle muscle contracts, blood is pumped out of the heart into the arteries.

There are **valves** between the atria and ventricles, and at the entrance to the arteries. The valves consist of flaps which open only in the direction in which the blood should flow. They therefore prevent blood flowing backwards.

Experiment 16.5
Looking at the heart

Your teacher will show you the heart of a pig or sheep which has been obtained from a butcher.

1 Identify the atria and ventricles. Notice that the wall of the ventricles is particularly thick. Why?

2 Observe the narrow blood vessels branching over the surface of the ventricles. These are the coronary vessels. What is their function?

3 Look at the two main arteries which are connected to the heart. One carries blood to the lungs, the other carries blood to the body. Your teacher will help you to tell one from the other. How does their arrangement differ from the simplified diagram in Fig 16.10?

4 The ventricles will be cut open so that you can look inside. Notice the valves between the atria and ventricles, and at the entrance of the arteries. Look carefully at these valves. What is their function? How do you think they work?

Questions for class discussion

1 Why do you think blood is sent back to the heart from the lungs before going on to the body? Why is it not sent straight to the body from the lungs?

2 The wall of the left ventricle is thicker and more muscular than the wall of the right ventricle. Suggest a reason for this.

3 Can you think of any human-made systems which involve valves that serve the same kind of purpose as those in the heart and circulatory system?

The arteries

Every time the heart beats approximately one cupful of blood is forced out into the arteries. This starts a wave of pressure which travels quickly along the arteries.

Certain arteries are situated close to the skin, and if you put your finger on one of them you can feel the pressure wave as it passes by.

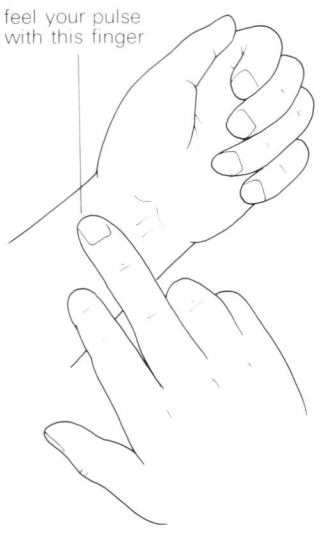

feel your pulse
with this finger

Fig 16.11 How to feel your pulse.

Experiment 16.6
Feeling your pulse

1 Gently place the middle finger of your right hand on the wrist of your left hand in the position shown in Fig 16.11. Can you feel a regular throb?

Move your finger around until you find the right place. At this point the artery serving the hand lies over a bone close to the skin.

2 Count the number of throbs in one minute. This should be the same as the number of heart sounds per minute.

Questions for class discussion

1 If a person loses a lot of blood, for example in an accident, the pulse may become very weak. Why do you think this is?

2 If a bandage was tied tightly round your arm, you would not be able to feel your pulse at all. Why do you think this is?

The capillaries

Once an artery has entered an organ, it splits up into a large number of narrow capillaries (Fig 16.12). As blood flows through the capillaries, it brings to the cells all the substances they need. These include oxygen from the lungs and dissolved food from the gut. At the same time the blood takes away any substances which the cells do not want, such as carbon dioxide.

How does oxygen pass from the blood to the cells? The answer is by **diffusion** (see page 200). Carbon dioxide passes from the cells to the blood in the same way.

Experiment 16.7
Looking at capillaries

1 With a pipette put a drop of clove oil or cedar wood oil on to the skin at the base of one of your finger nails as shown in Fig. 16.13. This will make the skin more transparent.

Fig 16.12 Photograph of human capillaries taken down a microscope. (Magnification × 200 approx.)

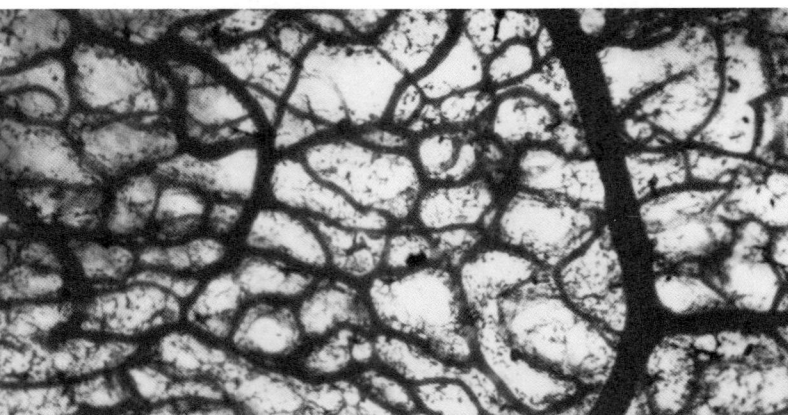

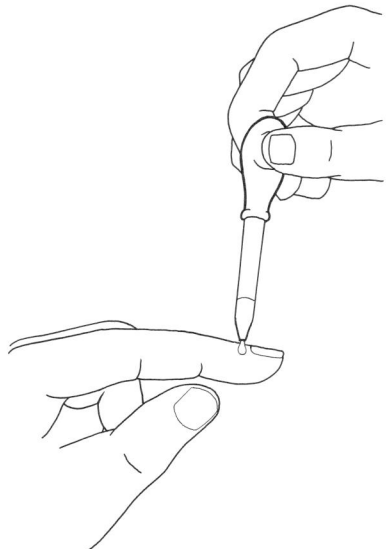

Fig 16.13 Putting a drop of clove oil or cedar wood oil on your skin will make the capillaries show up under the microscope.

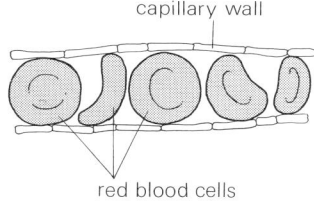

Fig 16.14 Red blood cells in a capillary.

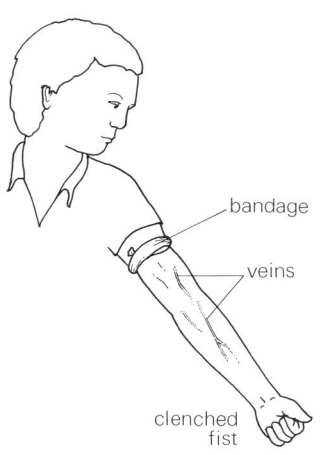

Fig 16.15 Making the veins show up in your arm.

2 Put your finger under a microscope (low power) with a strong light shining down on it from above. Can you see any capillaries? Squeeze your finger so as to force blood into it. Does this make the capillaries easier to see?

3 Your teacher may show you a film of blood flowing along capillaries. You will see disc-shaped objects passing along the capillaries. They are red blood cells, and it is they that carry the oxygen. The capillaries are just wide enough to let them through (Fig 16.14). We shall come back to the red blood cells shortly.

Questions for class discussion

1 Capillaries have extremely thin walls – much thinner than either the arteries or veins. Why do you think this is important?

2 If you were to lay out a person's capillaries end to end, they would extend right round the world two and a half times. Why do you think we need so many?

3 An important function of blood, apart from carrying oxygen and other substances, is to maintain an even temperature round the body. What process in our cells helps to keep us warm? Which organs are particularly important in this respect? Why should different parts of the body not be different temperatures?

The veins

After the blood has been through the capillaries, it is collected up into the veins which take it back to the heart.

Experiment 16.8
Looking at veins in your arm

Work in pairs. Get your partner to hang one arm downwards for a minute or so. Then wrap a bandage round the upper part of the arm just below the shoulder: do not make it so tight that it hurts! The bandage will make the veins near the surface in the lower part of the arm stand out clearly, and this is further helped if the fist is clenched (Fig 16.15). The arteries are deeper down so you will not be able to see them.

When the veins are visible, lightly ink in their course with a water-based felt pen.

Questions for class discussion

1 Why do you think tying the bandage round the arm helps to make the veins show up?

2 Some people have clearer veins in their arms than others. Why do you think this is?

Homework assignments

1 Draw an outline of the human body viewed from the front.
   a By means of an arrow and the letter H, indicate the position of the heart.
   b By means of an arrow and the letter X, indicate a place, a long way away from the heart, where you can feel that your heart is beating.

2 What do we call blood vessels which:
   a carry blood away from the heart
   b carry blood towards the heart
   c supply oxygen through their thin walls to our cells.

3 Assuming that a person's heart beats at a constant rate of seventy times per minute, how many beats does it undergo in the course of one year?

4 Approximately 150 cm³ of blood are expelled from the heart every time it beats. How many litres are expelled from the heart in:
   a one minute
   b one day
   c one year?

5 The human body contains approximately 5 litres of blood altogether and about 150 cm³ of blood are expelled from the heart at each beat.
   a What percentage of the total volume of blood in the circulation is pumped out of the heart every time it beats?
   b Assuming that the heart beats seventy times per minute, how long does it take for all the blood in the circulation to pass through the heart?

Changes during exercise

We know from everyday life that if we exert ourselves we breathe more quickly. In this way, we take more air into our lungs and thus supply our muscles with more oxygen. Does the same kind of speeding up occur in our circulation?

Experiment 16.9
The heart beat during exercise

1 Sit down for 2–3 minutes, and then count the number of your heart beats per minute (see page 204).

2 Now take some strenuous exercise. Your teacher will tell you what kind of exercise to take and how long to take it for. Then sit down again and count the number of your heart beats per minute.

By how much has your heart beat rate increased? There are several ways of expressing the answer to this question. Choose the way you consider to be the best.

Questions for class discussion

1 This experiment has shown that the heart beats much faster immediately after exercise. Why is it important that this should happen?

2 When the exercise begins, how do you think the heart 'knows' that it should beat faster? Think of as many theories as you can: you will not be asked to prove them.

Keeping cool

When you take exercise your muscles work faster and transfer more energy, making you hot. The body responds by cooling itself. One way of achieving this is by sweating.

Experiment 16.10
To show sweating

You will need a piece of dry cobalt chloride paper approximately 1 cm × 2 cm. The paper is blue when dry, but turns pink when moistened with water.

1 With tape, stick the paper to the skin on the back of your hand. Note the time, and observe the paper at intervals. Does any part of it turn pink? How long does it take for the first trace of pink to appear? Does the entire piece of paper turn pink eventually, and if so how long does it take? What substance must be present in sweat?

2 Repeat this experiment immediately after taking strenuous exercise. How long does it take for the paper to turn pink this time? Explain the difference.

Questions for class discussion

1 After taking strenuous exercise you often feel thirsty. Why do you think this is?

2 Why do you think sweating helps to cool the body? To help you answer this question try this simple experiment. Lick the back of one of your hands, and leave the other one dry. Gently wave both hands in the air. Which one feels cooler? What happens to the moisture on the back of the hand which you licked?

3 Coal miners are advised to eat plenty of salt. Why do you think this is done? (Hint: what does sweat taste of?)

Keeping warm

Sometimes we need to keep our bodies warm. When do we need to do this? Humans keep themselves warm mainly by wearing clothes. However, other mammals are kept warm by their hair. The hair reduces energy loss, in other words it helps to insulate the body. Fat under the skin also helps to insulate the body. In birds insulation is achieved by the feathers.

As a result of this insulation, much of the energy which is produced by respiration can be kept inside the body. For this reason, mammals and birds are described as **warm-blooded.** Warm-blooded animals can keep their body temperatures constant whatever the surrounding temperature. If it is cold, they retain the energy produced by respiration (metabolism) inside the body: if it is hot, they let some of the energy out.

Other animals, such as fishes and reptiles, are **cold-blooded**. They have no insulation devices, and their body temperatures are the same as the surrounding temperature.

The only way in which a cold-blooded animal can control its body temperature is by making sure that it is in a place where the surrounding temperature is agreeable.

When a person is exposed to the cold for a long time, the temperature-control mechanism may stop working. As a result the body temperature falls to that of the surroundings. This is called **hypothermia** and it can be fatal.

Questions for class discussion

1 Lizards are described as cold-blooded, but if you pick up a lizard it may feel warm. Explain.

2 What are the disadvantages of being cold-blooded, and what are the advantages of being warm-blooded?

3 In the Arctic and Antarctic there are many species of mammals and birds, but very few amphibians and reptiles. Suggest reasons for this.

4 Old people who have recovered from hypothermia say that they did not realise that their room was so cold, otherwise they would have turned the heating up. Why do you think they did not realise that the room was so cold? What might be done to help old people in this respect?

Homework assignments

1 In the following statement, which of the words in the brackets are *correct*? During exercise a person produces more (carbon dioxide/oxygen/carbohydrate/energy/sugar/sweat) than when resting.

2 A student dashes up three flights of stairs to collect a book. At the top he notices that his heart is beating very fast.

   a Put forward an explanation to account for the change in the rate of his heart beat.

   b List other changes in the functioning of his body which he might detect after this bout of exercise.

3 A girl rushed to catch the bus. When she got to her seat she felt very hot. What caused her to feel hot?

   Later in the day the girl competed in a 3-km cycle race, at the end of which she felt in need of a long drink. Explain why she felt thirsty.

4 A scientist measured the amounts of oxygen taken in by a human adult and by a locust at rest and when active. The results, expressed in cubic centimetres of oxygen consumed per gram of body mass per hour, are shown in Table 16.1.

   a Why do you think the figures for the human are higher than those for the locust?

   b Why does oxygen consumption increase during activity?

   c Suggest two changes which took place in the human's body while running which enabled more oxygen to be taken in.

Table 16.1

	Oxygen consumption (cm³ per g per h)
human at rest	60
human running	905
locust at rest	0.63
locust flying	15

What does blood consist of?

If you cut yourself, blood flows from the cut. If you were asked to describe the blood, you would probably say it was a fluid.

Now suppose you were to look at a small sample of the blood under the microscope. Fig 16.16 shows what you would see.

Fig 16.16 Photograph of blood taken down a microscope. (Magnification × 1500)

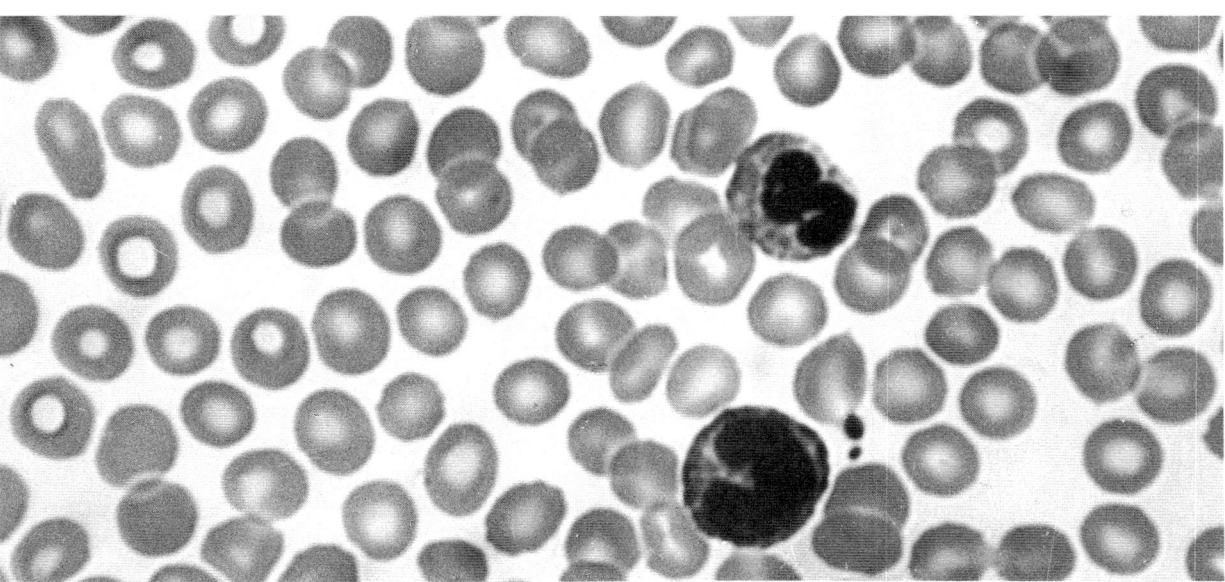

You can see straight away that it is not just a fluid. It is a fluid containing millions of cells. Most of the cells are **red blood cells**. They contain a red substance called **haemoglobin** (pronounced hee-mo-globin). This gives the blood its characteristic red colour. Haemoglobin is the part of the blood which carries oxygen.

Blood also contains other kinds of cell called **white blood cells.** They are fewer in number than the red blood cells, two are visible in Fig 16.15. The white blood cells destroy micro-organisms such as bacteria and viruses. Their job is therefore to defend us against disease. Certain types of white blood cell achieve this by producing substances called **antibodies**. The antibodies combine with **antigens** on the surface of the micro-organisms, and this causes the micro-organisms to be destroyed (see page 266).

The fluid part of the blood is called **plasma**. It contains all sorts of dissolved substances which are carried from one part of the body to another. These substances include soluble food substances such as glucose, and excretory substances such as urea (see Chapter 15).

Also present in blood are tiny cell fragments called **platelets**. They play a part in the way blood clots.

Clotting of blood

You will have noticed that if you cut yourself the blood soon hardens and you stop bleeding. The hardening of the blood is called **clotting**. Blood clots when tissues are damaged or when it comes into contact with an unfamiliar surface.

Some unfortunate people have blood which takes a very long time to clot. If they cut themselves, the cut goes on bleeding. This condition is called **haemophilia** (see page 66).

Blood transfusions

If a person loses a lot of blood in an accident, he or she may be given blood which has been obtained from another person, a **blood donor**. The blood is put into a vein in the arm through a narrow tube. This process is called a **transfusion**.

When blood from two different people is mixed, the red blood cells may stick together. If this were to occur in the circulation, the blood vessels would get blocked up and the person would die. Before carrying out a transfusion the doctors make sure that the two lots of blood will mix together satisfactorily. In practice this means that they should belong to the same **blood group**. People's blood is classified into groups according to whether or not the red blood cells stick together when they are mixed.

Questions for class discussion

1 Why is it an advantage for our blood to clot when we cut ourselves? Think of as many reasons as you can.

2 When the virus that causes measles gets into your body, your white blood cells respond by producing antibodies which specifically attack the measles virus. Using this information, suggest why people usually get measles only once.

3 When you are vaccinated against a disease, a small quantity of dead or inactivated micro-organisms (the vaccine) is put into your bloodstream. How does this protect you from the disease?

4 Haemophiliacs require blood transfusions more often than people with normal blood. When and why do you think a haemophiliac is likely to need a transfusion?

5 What precautions have to be taken when someone is given a blood transfusion?

Background Reading

Training and circulation

In this passage a former Olympic gold medallist discusses the importance of training in improving the circulation.

The athlete strengthens his heart by training – it is mostly muscle and responds in the same way, thereby becoming more efficient. This can be proved by taking someone's pulse rate before he starts a training programme, and continuing to measure it as training proceeds. Over a period of weeks it will be found that the rate of the heart beat, when the person is completely at rest, gradually decreases. This resting pulse (usually measured immediately after waking in the morning) will be seventy or eighty beats per minute for the average man or woman, but with training it may well drop to sixty or below. My own resting pulse, when really fit, has been as low as thirty-eight. This is because the heart, being stronger than before and capable of pumping more blood at each beat, does not have to work as hard to keep the body supplied with oxygen.

The other effect of training is to improve the circulation to the working muscles with the result that more capillary vessels develop in the muscles that are being used most. These capillaries are not in use when you are at rest, but in an emergency, when more oxygen is needed, they open up to allow more blood to flow. This means that you can 'switch on' to a higher rate of exercise when you really need to. Of course this would not be any good unless your heart had also strengthened so that it could deal with this extra effort.

(From *Naturally fit* by Bruce Tulloh, published by Arthur Barker Ltd.)

Questions

1 Why is a trained athlete's heart able to pump more blood at each beat?

2 Why is it best to take the resting pulse first thing in the morning?

3 What other organs, besides the heart, improve with training? Explain your answer.

4 What other changes might occur in your blood circulation as you get fitter?

The heart and health

All too often we hear of people who have had a heart attack. What happens in a heart attack? A block occurs inside one of the coronary arteries, and this prevents blood flowing along it. As a result, the part of the heart served by that particular artery no longer gets any oxygen, so it stops beating. If only a small part of the heart is involved, the person may recover. But if a large part is involved, the attack may cause sudden death.

The block is brought on by a substance called cholesterol being laid down in the walls of the artery. This makes the artery narrower and slows the flow of blood. This happens gradually over years, and it can give rise to severe pain. It is called heart disease. Eventually the artery walls become damaged and blood clots inside the artery, just as it does after you cut yourself. This blocks the artery completely – that is when the heart attack takes place.

What causes cholesterol to be laid down in the artery walls? The exact reason is not known, but two things are certain.

1 It is linked with eating too much animal fat such as butter and lard.

2 It can start at an early age when you are still in your teens.

How can we reduce the risk of getting heart disease? One way is not to eat too much animal fat. Thickly buttered bread, and chips fried in lard, are not good for us if eaten too often. It is better to use margarines of the kind illustrated in Fig 16.17. These margarines are made from vegetable oils and they contain relatively little of the substances that cause heart disease.

Regular exercise also helps to reduce the risk of heart disease. It uses up unwanted fat and helps to keep the blood flowing properly.

Scientists have shown that the chance of getting heart disease is increased by smoking. So another way of reducing the risk is not to smoke.

Heart disease is also linked with stress. Stress is caused when we worry about things we find difficult or feel we have no control over. Different people find different things stressful.

A person with severe heart disease may have the heart replaced with a healthy heart from someone who has been killed in, for

Fig. 16.17 One of a large number of margarines which many people use instead of butter.

example, a road accident. This is called a heart transplant. Before carrying out a transplant operation, the surgeons make sure that the tissues match each other as closely as possible. Otherwise the transplanted heart will be rejected by the same kind of processes which destroy germs when they get into the body.

Questions

1 Suppose you were asked to find out if there is a link between heart disease and eating too much animal fat. How would you set about your task?

2 Imagine you are a doctor. What advice would you give to someone who has had a mild heart attack?

3 To what extent is heart disease connected with people's lifestyle?

How the circulation of the blood was discovered

William Harvey was Court Physician to Charles I in the early part of the seventeenth century. At that time people thought that blood seeped from the heart to the various parts of the body, and then seeped back again in the same vessels – rather like the tide flowing in and out.

Harvey did not agree with this. He believed that the blood circulated round the body, flowing away from the heart in certain vessels (arteries) and back again in other vessels (veins).

Harvey did a simple but clever experiment to support his idea. (Some of the best experiments *are* simple!) The experiment is illustrated in Fig 16.18. Study it carefully. It shows that blood flows only in one direction in the arm vein – towards the heart. Valves occur at intervals along the course of the vein, and they prevent the blood flowing backwards.

In Fig 16.19 you can see Harvey demonstrating his experiment to Charles I and his son. You can try the experiment yourself, on a friend. However, tying a band round the arm can be dangerous if it is too tight, so do the experiment only when your teacher is present.

This was just one of many experiments which Harvey did on the blood system. They all supported his idea that the blood circulates round the body, pumped by the heart. However, Harvey never found how the blood gets from the arteries to the veins. This was discovered towards the end of the century by an Italian scientist, Marcello Malpighi.

Malpighi's approach was quite different from Harvey's. Instead of doing experiments of the kind that Harvey did, he used a microscope to examine the detailed structure of the body. In this way he discovered the capillaries and showed that they connect the arteries with the veins.

Scientists often come into conflict with religion. This was true of Harvey. He saw the human body as a machine, obeying the same laws that govern non-living things. This idea upset many

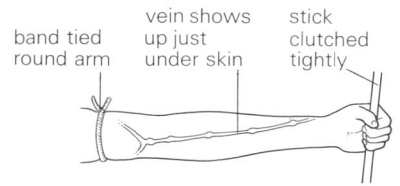

Swellings in the course of the vein mark the positions of the valves

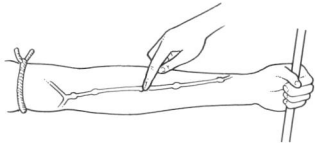

Block vein with right finger

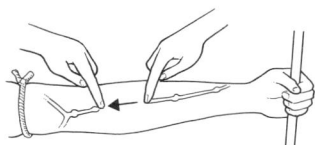

Then push blood to next swelling with left finger

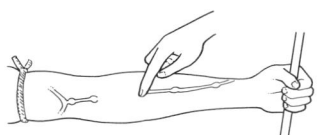

Take left finger away
Note that blood does not flow back . . .

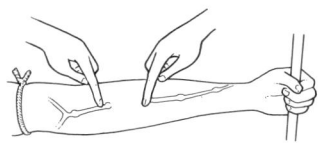

. . . even if you try pushing it with your finger

Fig. 16.18 Harvey's experiment on the circulation of the blood.

Fig 16.19 Harvey demonstrating his theory of the circulation of the blood to Charles I and his son.

people who believed that the human body was something special, created by God. The idea that the heart is nothing more than a pump was, to most people, a particularly horrid idea. It led to Harvey losing a lot of his patients to other doctors.

Questions

1 Does Harvey's experiment on the arm *prove* that the blood circulates round the body?

2 Suppose our blood did flow from the heart and back again in the same vessels. How do you think this would affect our lives?

3 How did Malpighi's approach differ from Harvey's? Do you think one was better than the other?

4 Why do you think Harvey failed to find the capillaries? (Hint: don't jump to conclusions, find out when the microscope was invented.)

5 Can you think of a present-day example of where science is in conflict with people's religious or moral beliefs?

Summary

1 **Respiration** is the process by which energy is transferred in living things.

2 The raw materials of respiration are normally food and oxygen, and the products are carbon dioxide and water.

3 In certain circumstances respiration may take place without oxygen. This is called **anaerobic respiration**.

4 We obtain oxygen and get rid of carbon dioxide by **breathing**. In this process air passes in and out of the lungs.

5 The lungs are made up of tiny **air sacs** where **gaseous** exchange takes place. The air sacs give the lungs a large surface area to help with gaseous exchange.

6 Oxygen is carried from the lungs to all parts of the body by the **circulatory system** which consists of the **heart** and **blood vessels**.

7 The heart pumps blood by repeated contractions of its muscular wall. The heart muscle gets its oxygen supply from **coronary vessels**.

8 The heart is divided into two halves. The right hand side receives deoxygenated blood from the body and sends it to the lungs; the left hand side receives oxygenated blood from the lungs and sends it to the body.

9 When we exert ourselves we breathe faster and more deeply and the heart rate increases.

10 In humans and other warm-blooded animals the body temperature is kept constant.

11 Blood contains two types of cells: **red blood cells** which carry oxygen, and **white blood cells** which defend the body against disease.

12 When a blood vessel is damaged, or blood comes into contact with an unfamiliar surface, it **clots**.

Chapter 17 **Responding to stimuli**

Fig 17.1 Ouch!

Suppose your friend puts a drawing pin on your chair and you sit on it. You would jump up quickly! (Fig 17.1). The pricking is called the **stimulus**, and your **response** is to jump up.

Responding to stimuli is important to all living things. It helps to protect them from harm and in some cases it may guide them towards food or help them to find a mate.

Experiment 17.1
Observing the response of blowfly maggots to light

This experiment should be performed in a darkened room.

1 Lay a sheet of rough brown paper, approximately 30 centimetres square, on a table, and place a lamp on one side as shown in Fig 17.2. The lamp should be switched off.

2 Put one maggot in the centre of the brown paper, and observe its behaviour.

3 Switch on the lamp and watch the maggot. Write down what it does.

4 Repeat the experiment six times. Describe the maggot's response each time.

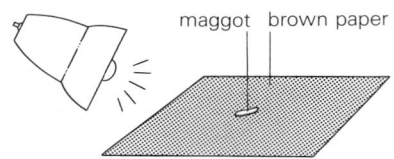

maggot   brown paper

Fig 17.2 How to investigate the response of a blowfly maggot to light.

Questions for class discussion

1 Why was it necessary to repeat the experiment six times? Do you think it should have been repeated more times than that?

2 It is possible that the stimulus to which the maggot responded was the high temperature of the lamp, rather than the light. How could you find out if this is true?

3 The eggs from which blowfly maggots develop are normally laid in dung or rotting material. Why is the behaviour which you observed in Experiment 17.1 useful to them?

4 Suggest other stimuli to which maggots might respond. In each case, devise an experiment to find out if they really do respond to the stimulus.

Homework assignments

1 The pictures in Fig 17.3 show five situations, each involving a stimulus and a response. Describe the stimulus and the response in each picture.

2 Given a corked test-tube, some black paper, a lamp and a tinful of maggots, describe fully how you would test the hypothesis that maggots prefer darkness to light.

3 It has been said that one species of toad finds its food by smell. Describe how you would set up and carry out an experiment to test the truth of this statement.

Fig 17.3 In each of these pictures, what is the stimulus and what is the response?

4 A scientist carries out an experiment on the behaviour of woodlice. Twelve woodlice are placed in a dry dish at one end of which there is a piece of damp bark from a tree. Every five minutes the scientist counts the number of woodlice that are in the open part of the dish and, by subtraction, works out how many are underneath the piece of bark. The results are shown in Table 17.1

Table 17.1

Time (minutes)	Number of woodlice in the open	Number of woodlice under the bark
0	12	0
5	10	2
10	7	5
15	5	7
20	3	9
25	4	8
30	0	12

a Plot these results on graph paper.
b How do you think the woodlice might find their way to the piece of bark?

Human responses

Think of the various things you do during the day. Which ones involve responding to a stimulus? Make a list of the various stimuli you receive, and in each case describe your response. Two examples are given in Table 17.2 to get you started.

Look carefully at your list. You will probably find that in some of your examples the response is quick and does not go on for long. This is the case, for instance, when you jump up after sitting on a pin. We shall now look at two other quick responses.

Table 17.2

Stimulus	Response
1 I receive a prick on my bottom from a drawing pin	I jump up and let out a cry
2 I hear the alarm clock go off	I get out of bed

Experiment 17.2
Some human responses

Work in pairs, one person acting as the subject.

Blinking
1 The subject should open his or her eyes and look straight ahead.

2 The experimenter should suddenly wave his or her hand in front of the subject's eyes. Describe what happens. Why is this response useful?

3 The experimenter should repeat the stimulus approximately once every three seconds. Does the subject blink each time?

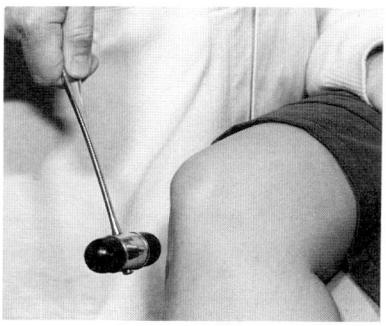

Fig 17.4 How to test a person's knee jerk.

The knee jerk

1 The subject should sit, with legs crossed, on a laboratory stool. The top leg should hang loosely.

2 The experimenter should locate the soft part of the knee, just below the hard knee cap. There is a tendon here. (Tendons are tough strands of tissue by which muscles are attached to the bones.)

3 The experimenter should now tap the knee tendon lightly with a medical hammer or the side of the hand.
What happens to the leg?
How do you think the response is brought about?

How are responses brought about?

For a response to occur three things are needed.

Receptors: these are structures which receive the stimulus.
Nerves: these are like cables and they conduct messages from one part of the body to another.
Muscles: these are attached to the **skeleton** and when they receive a message from a nerve they contract and make the body move.

Clearly our nerves are very important in bringing about responses. The human nervous system is shown in Fig 17.5. It includes two main parts: the **brain** and the **spinal cord**. The brain is enclosed within the skull in the head, and the spinal cord runs down the middle of the backbone (vertebral column). The brain and spinal cord are connected to our skin and muscles by nerves.

Now suppose you get into the starting position for a hundred metre sprint. At the sound of the pistol your ears are stimulated and a message is sent through your nervous system to certain muscles in your legs. The muscles then contract and you start running (see Fig 17.6 overleaf).

Responses are not always produced by muscles. For example, when a delicious smell comes from the kitchen, your mouth 'waters'. In this case the organ that responds is not a muscle but your salivary glands. The general term for any structure that responds is **effector**.

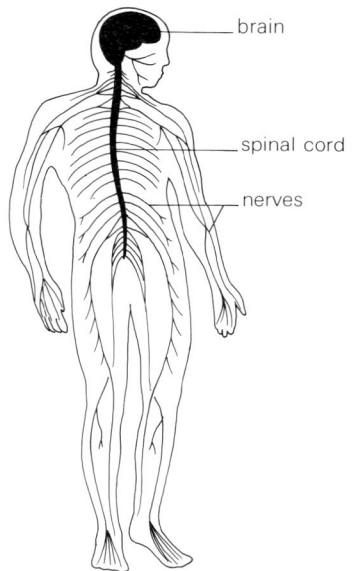

Fig 17.5 The main parts of the human nervous system.

brain

spinal cord

nerves

What part does the brain play?

Look at Fig 17.6 overleaf. Notice that the message travels from the ears to the muscles by way of the brain.

Our brain is like an immensely complicated telephone exchange with millions of connections. It makes sure that messages are sent to the right muscles so that the correct response is given. The word we use for this is **coordination**.

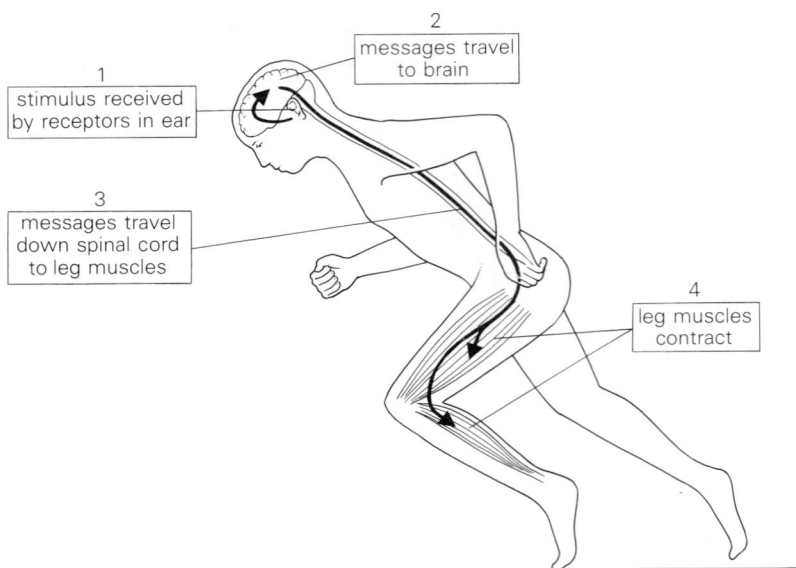

1
stimulus received
by receptors in ear

2
messages travel
to brain

3
messages travel
down spinal cord
to leg muscles

4
leg muscles
contract

Fig 17.6 The pathway through which messages travel in bringing about a response.

The brain is also responsible for thought, memory and intelligence. It is also responsible for our emotions, and the way we see the world, that is perception.

Questions for class discussion

1 Write down a *stimulus* and describe the *response* in each of the following situations. Try to think of a different stimulus in each case.
  a The end of a school lesson
  b Lunch time
  c Reading a book
  d A fire practice
  e A game of football.

2 What part does the brain play in bringing about the responses which you have given in your answers to the previous question?

The brain and drugs

The brain is readily affected by **drugs**. A drug is any substance which alters the way our bodies work. For example, certain drugs speed up the action of the brain and make you more alert. We call such drugs **stimulants**. An example of a mild stimulant is caffeine which occurs in coffee and certain other drinks.

Other drugs slow down the action of the brain, making you sleepy. These are called **sedatives**. An example is alcohol. Some people believe, wrongly, that alcohol is a stimulant. In fact it suppresses the brain and makes people careless and clumsy. This is why it is so dangerous to drink and drive.

Some drugs cause hallucinations: the person sees or hears things which do not exist. In other words, perception is altered. An example of this kind of drug is cannabis (marijuana), nicknamed 'pot'.

Of course people can be helped by certain drugs, the sort you can buy in a chemist shop or get from the doctor. When you take aspirin for a headache you are taking a drug, in this case a **painkiller**. However, if taken under the wrong circumstances drugs can be extremely dangerous. We shall return to this in Chapter 20.

The speed of nervous messages

Messages travel very rapidly through the nervous system, and this enables us to respond quickly to stimuli. You can get an idea of the speed by measuring how long it takes for you to respond to a stimulus. This is called your **reaction time**.

Experiment 17.3
Comparing people's reaction times

Work in pairs, one person acting as the experimenter, the other as the subject.

1 Experimenter: hold a ruler as shown in Fig 17.7 so that zero is level with the edge of a table top.

2 Subject: place your hand on the table so that you are ready to catch the ruler.

3 The experimenter should now let go of the ruler and the subject should catch it as soon as possible after it begins to fall.

4 Note the position along the ruler at which the subject catches it. Read off the distance to the nearest millimetre.

5 Repeat this test with the same subject twenty times, and record the distance each time.

6 Write down the shortest distance achieved by each member of the class.

Questions for class discussion

1 What was the shortest distance, and the longest distance, which was recorded in the class? (This is a good example of human variation: see pages 11–16.)

2 Did your reaction time get shorter with practice? If it did, how would you explain the improvement?

3 Trace the pathway through which messages travel in bringing about this response. Where are the receptors and muscles?

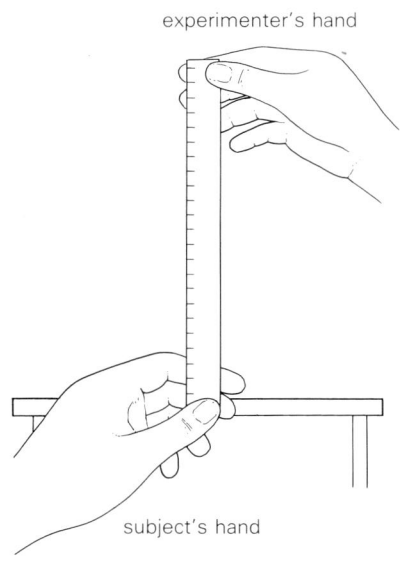

experimenter's hand

subject's hand

Fig 17.7 Measuring reaction times.

Receptors

In order to respond to stimuli, an animal has to have **receptors**. A receptor is a structure which can receive a stimulus and send a message in the nervous system.

The main receptors in the human body are shown in Fig 17.8. Most of them are complex **sense organs**, the eye and ear being two important examples. Each receptor is adapted to receive a certain kind of stimulus. Thus the eye receives light, and the ear receives sound waves.

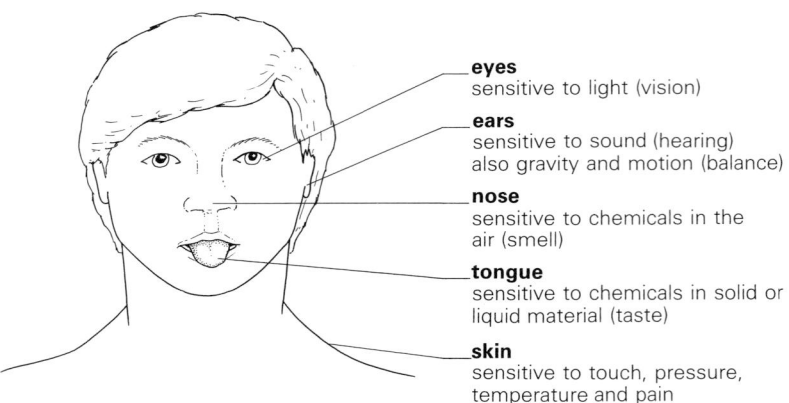

eyes
sensitive to light (vision)

ears
sensitive to sound (hearing)
also gravity and motion (balance)

nose
sensitive to chemicals in the air (smell)

tongue
sensitive to chemicals in solid or liquid material (taste)

skin
sensitive to touch, pressure, temperature and pain

Fig 17.8 The main receptors of the human.

Questions for class discussion

1 An animal's receptors are situated mainly in its head. Why is this an advantage?

2 What kind of receptors in the human body are *not* situated in the head?

The eye

Close your eyes for about a minute. While your eyes are closed, think what it must be like to be blind. Your eyes are very precious sense organs, so it is important to know about their structure and how they work.

The structure of the human eye is shown in Fig 17.9 and 17.10. It consists of a spherical **eyeball**. The back and sides of the eyeball are covered by a thick coat, the 'white' of the eye.

The eyeball is filled with a fluid which helps it to keep its shape. If the fluid were to leak out, the eyeball would go floppy.

The front of the eyeball is transparent. It is called the **cornea**. The cornea is covered by a thin, sensitive membrane called the **conjunctiva**. The conjunctiva is kept moist by a fluid which

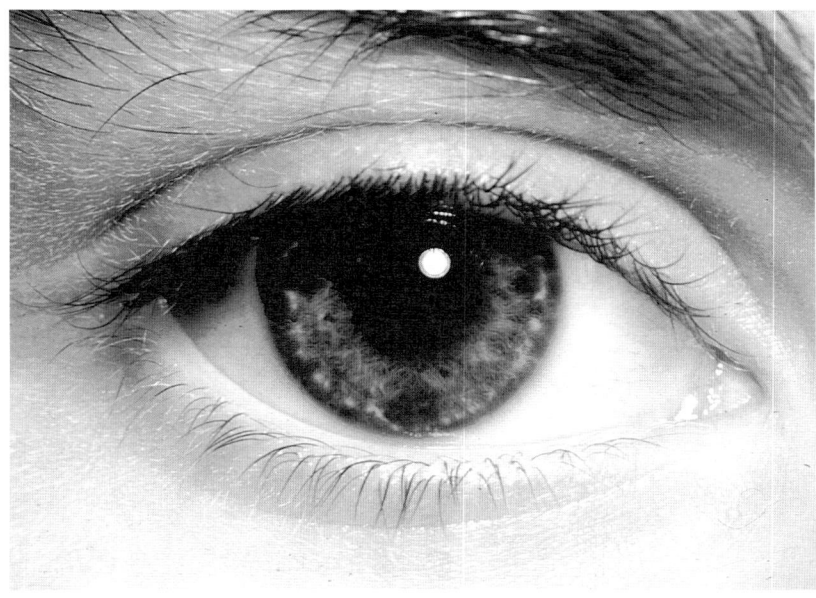

Fig 17.9 The human eye.

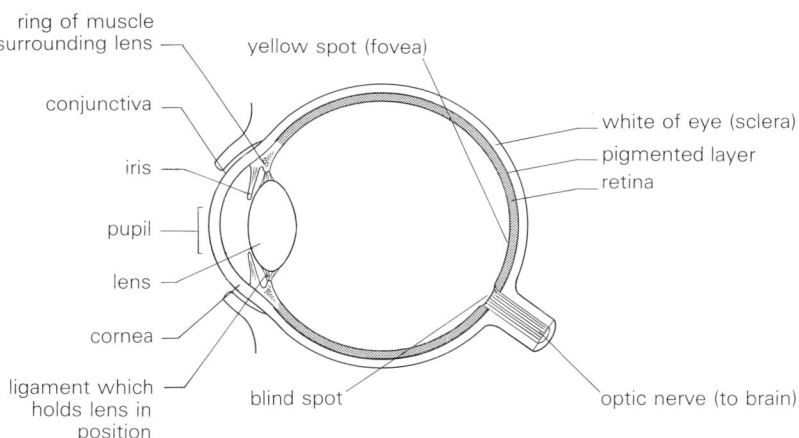

ring of muscle
surrounding lens

yellow spot (fovea)

conjunctiva

white of eye (sclera)

iris

pigmented layer

retina

pupil

lens

cornea

ligament which
holds lens in
position

blind spot

optic nerve (to brain)

Fig 17.10 Diagram of the human eye
sliced down the middle to show the
structures inside.

comes from a gland just under the eyelid; the same gland produces
tears when we cry. Blinking spreads the fluid over the surface of
the eye and helps to protect the eye from damage.

Behind the cornea is what looks like a black hole. This is the
pupil. The pupil is surrounded by a circular ring of tissue called
the **iris**. This is the coloured part of the eye. It contains muscles
which enable the pupil to get narrower or wider. In this way the
amount of light that enters the eye can be controlled.

Just behind the pupil is the **lens**. This is like a soft transparent
bag. The lens is held in position by fine strands (ligaments) which
run from its edge to a surrounding ring of muscle, called the
ciliary muscle. When the ring of muscle relaxes it springs
outwards, pulling the lens into a thin, flat shape. When the ring of
muscle contracts, the pull on the lens is released and it returns to
its rounder and fatter shape. It is important that the lens should
be able to change its shape like this. We shall see why in a
moment.

The inner surface of the eyeball is lined with a delicate layer of tissue called the **retina**. The retina contains millions of receptor cells. They are sensitive to light which has entered the eye through the pupil. Behind the retina is a layer of dark pigment. This absorbs the light after it has been through the retina and prevents it being reflected within the eye.

The part of the retina responsible for seeing things most clearly, and in colour, is the small area right in the middle. This is called the **yellow spot** or **fovea**. When you look straight at something, this is the part of the retina you are using.

The eye is connected to the brain by the **optic nerve**. The point where the optic nerve leaves the retina is called the **blind spot**. It is the only part of the back of the eye without receptor cells, hence its name.

How does the eye work?

Suppose you look at a dot on the wall on a piece of paper. Light rays from the dot travel towards your eye. The rays pass through the cornea which bends (refracts) them inwards. The rays then pass through the lens which bends them inwards even more. As a result, the rays are brought to a focus on the retina and an image is formed. This is shown in Fig 17.11.

Fig 17.11 How light rays from an object are brought to a focus on the retina.

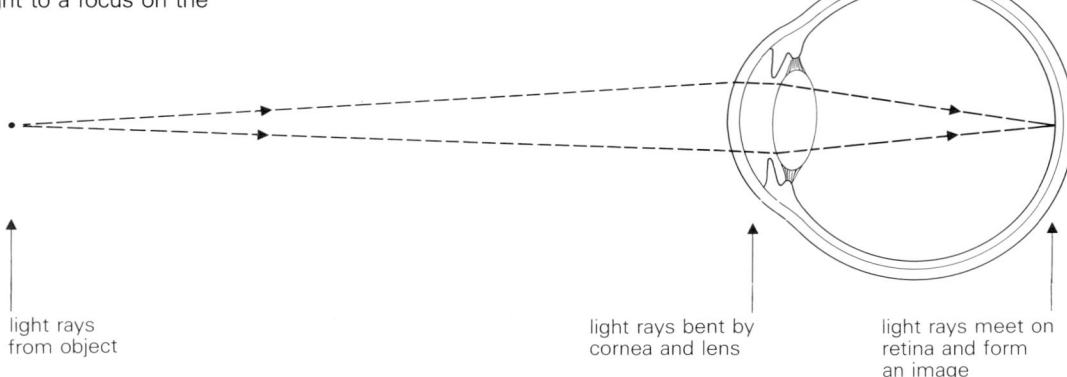

light rays
from object

light rays bent by
cornea and lens

light rays meet on
retina and form
an image

When the light rays strike the retina, the sensory cells are stimulated. As a result, messages are sent via the optic nerve to the brain. Only then do you actually see the dot.

Suppose you look at something a long way away and then close-to. To bring the near object into **focus** on the retina, the lens has to bend the light rays more than it did before. It does this by becoming fatter and more spherical (Fig 17.12).

Some people are unable to focus objects clearly. This can be put right by wearing **spectacles**.

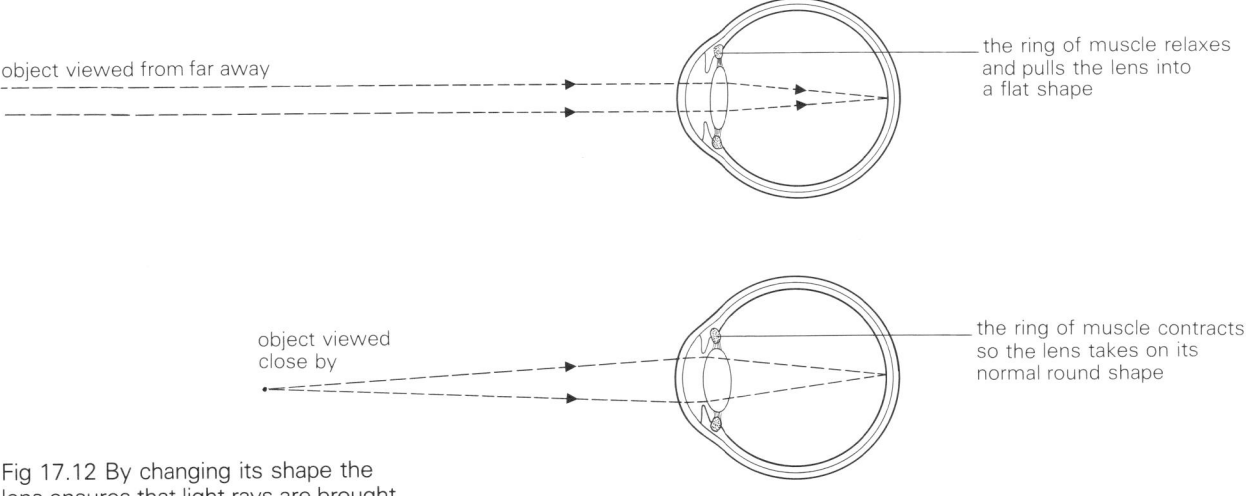

object viewed from far away

the ring of muscle relaxes
and pulls the lens into
a flat shape

object viewed
close by

the ring of muscle contracts
so the lens takes on its
normal round shape

Fig 17.12 By changing its shape the
lens ensures that light rays are brought
to a focus on the retina.

Experiment 17.4
Looking at your eyes

1 Look at your eyes in a mirror. Identify the parts of the eye
which are labelled in Fig 17.10.

2 Still looking in the mirror, point a torch towards your eyes.
Switch on the torch and watch your pupils. Describe how your
pupils change. How is the change brought about, and why is it
useful?

Questions for class discussion

1 The black pigment behind the retina prevents light being reflected
inside the eye. How might our eyesight be affected if light *was*
reflected inside the eye?

2 Why is it important for the fronts of the eyes to be kept moist?
What would happen if they became dry?

3 In elderly people the lens tends to go hard. What effect do you
think this has on their eyesight, and why?

4 What are the advantages of having two eyes rather than only
one?

The ear

Can you imagine what it must be like to be completely deaf? If
you cannot imagine it, try blocking your ears with cotton wool. It
will make you realise how important our ears are.

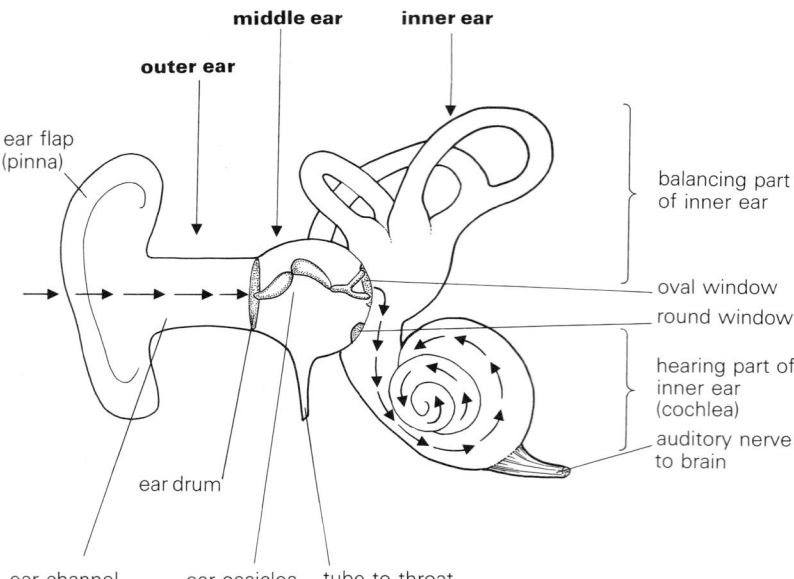

Fig 17.13 Diagram of the human ear. The outer and middle ear are full of air. The inner ear is full of fluid. The arrows show how sound waves which hit the ear drum are transmitted to the cochlea.

The human ear is shown in Fig 17.13. The outside part of the ear consists of a flap of skin, the **pinna**, with a hole just in front. The hole leads into a short tube called the **ear channel**. The skin lining the first part of the channel is hairy and produces wax. The hairs and wax help to prevent germs and dust getting in.

Stretched across the inner end of the ear channel is a membrane called the **ear drum**. On the other side of the ear drum is a chamber called the **middle ear**. This contains three little bones called the **ear ossicles**. On the other side of the middle ear is a small hole called the **oval window**. The three ear ossicles connect the ear drum with the oval window.

Below the oval window is another small hole covered by a membrane. This is called the **round window**.

On the inner side of the oval and round windows is the **inner ear**. This consists of a series of chambers and canals filled with fluid. It is made up of two parts: one part helps us to keep our balance, the other part enables us to hear. The hearing part consists of a coiled tube rather like a snail's shell. It is called the **cochlea**.

The cochlea contains millions of receptor cells. They are sensitive to movement of the fluid inside the inner ear. It is the movement of this fluid that enables us to hear things. The cochlea is connected to the brain by the **auditory nerve**.

How does the ear work?

Suppose your friend calls you from the other side of the room. The voice sets up vibrations or sound waves which quickly reach your ears. The pinna catches the sound waves and directs them into the ear channel.

The sound waves then pass along the ear channel to the ear drum. When they hit the ear drum they make it vibrate. This vibrates the ear ossicles, which in turn vibrate the oval window. Vibrations of the oval window then move the fluid in the cochlea. This stimulates the receptor cells which send off messages in the auditory nerve. The messages then pass via the auditory nerve to the brain. Only then do you actually hear what your friend has said.

Your ears can tell the difference between sounds of different loudness (intensity). Loud sounds cause larger movements of the ear membranes than quiet sounds. The louder a sound, the greater the amplitude with which the membranes vibrate.

You can also tell the difference between notes, in other words your ears can detect the pitch of the sound. This is because different notes are registered by different parts of the cochlea.

High notes cause faster vibrations of the ear membranes than low notes. In other words, the frequency of the vibrations is greater. The frequency is normally expressed as hertz (see *Physics 11–14*, page 264). The average human can hear frequencies between 20 and 20 000 hertz. Dogs can hear higher notes than this, and bats higher still (see page 232).

A sound has to be of a certain minimum loudness for it to be heard. This is called the **threshold of hearing**. If you have your ears tested, your threshold of hearing is measured for a series of different notes. In this way it can be found out if you are deaf.

Deafness

There are different kinds of deafness depending on which part of the ear is involved.

Sometimes the ear channel gets filled with wax, making it difficult to hear. However, this can easily be put right by the doctor syringing out the ears with warm water. My doctor used to say that he liked doing this because his patients always left feeling better than when they arrived.

A much more serious type of deafness occurs when the ear ossicles do not move properly. This can happen if extra bone tissue grows round one of the little bones in the middle ear chamber. The person's hearing may be improved by a **hearing aid** which amplifies the sound waves.

Deafness may also be caused by damage to the cochlea. This can happen if a person is continually subjected to a very loud sound of a particular pitch. The vibrations in the cochlea are so great that the receptor cells get damaged, making the person deaf to that particular note. For this reason, people who work with noisy machinery should alway wear ear muffs.

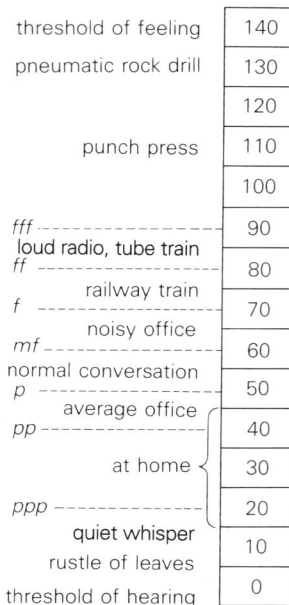

threshold of feeling	140
pneumatic rock drill	130
	120
punch press	110
	100
fff ------------	90
loud radio, tube train	
ff ------------	80
railway train	
f ------------	70
noisy office	
mf ------------	60
normal conversation	
p ------------	50
average office	
pp ------------	40
at home	30
ppp ------------	20
quiet whisper	
	10
rustle of leaves	
standard threshold of hearing	0

Fig 17.14 Scale giving the relative loudness (intensity) of different sounds. The letters on the left are the musical markings used by the conductor Leopold Stokowski: p, piano; f, forte.

Noise in the environment

Noise can be irritating, even harmful, without actually causing deafness. Heavy traffic at close quarters, an aeroplane taking off – even certain kinds of pop music – can hurt the ears and give you a headache. Excessive noise is a serious aspect of pollution (see page 278). For this reason it is important that the amount of noise in the environment should be controlled.

Questions for class discussion

1 What part do you think the brain plays in hearing?

2 The middle ear chamber is connected to the throat by a tube. Why do you think this is necessary?

3 What are the advantages of having two ears rather than only one?

4 Fig 17.14 shows the relative loudness of different sounds from 0 units to 140 units. You can actually *feel* a sound of 140 units. At what loudness do you think a sound should be regarded as pollution? Are there any other factors besides loudness which should be taken into account in reaching a decision?

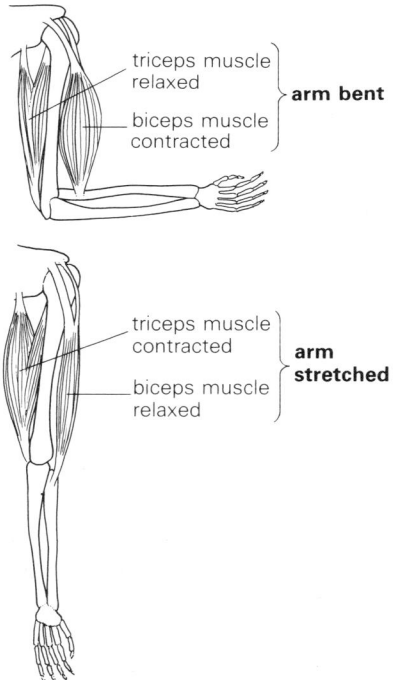

triceps muscle relaxed
biceps muscle contracted
arm bent

triceps muscle contracted
biceps muscle relaxed
arm stretched

Fig 17.15 The muscles and bones involved in bending and stretching your arm.

Muscles and the skeleton

An animal must be able to move if it is to respond to a stimulus. This is achieved by muscles. In the human, the muscles are attached to the skeleton. The skeleton is made up of **bones** which are connected to each other at **joints**. When our muscles contract, the bones move against each other at the joints.

As an example, consider the bending of your arms (Fig 17.15). The elbow joint is like a hinge, and the action of the muscles is rather like opening and closing a door. You can find out about the forces involved in movement from your physics book (*Physics 11–14*, Chapter 6).

Look at Fig 17.15 carefully. Notice that there are two muscles, the **biceps** and the **triceps**. When they contract they produce opposite effects: the biceps bends the arm, and the triceps stretches it. When one of the two muscles contracts, the other relaxes.

The arm has to be bent and stretched by two separate muscles because muscles can only pull, they cannot push. The same applies to movement of other parts of the body such as the legs.

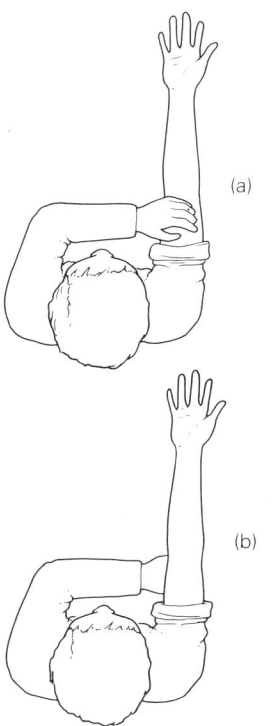

Fig 17.16 Feeling your arm muscles in action.

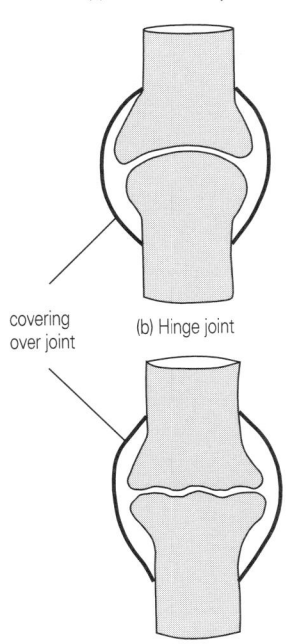

(a) Ball and socket joint

covering over joint

(b) Hinge joint

Fig 17.17 Two kinds of joint found in the human skeleton.

Experiment 17.5
Feeling muscles in action

If you put your hand on the surface of the body where a muscle is contracting, it feels hard and a bulge develops.

1 Roll up your sleeve, and stretch out your right arm in front of you.

2 Place your left hand on the upper side of your right arm (Fig 17.16a).

3 Slowly bend your arm. Can you feel a bulge? This is your **biceps muscle**.

4 Straighten your arm, and continue to feel the biceps with your left hand.

5 Get someone to place a heavy object such as a book on your right hand. What does the biceps do? Explain your observation.

6 Keeping your right arm straight, press downwards on a table. What does the biceps do now? Explain your observation.

7 Now place your left hand on the lower side of your arm (Fig 17.16b). Can you feel a bulge? This is your **triceps muscle**.

8 Repeat steps **5** and **6** with your hand on the triceps. What does the triceps do at each step? Explain your observations.

Questions for class discussion

1 What happens to the length of a muscle when it contracts? Why does it bulge and go hard?

2 What can you say about the functions of the biceps and triceps muscles?

3 What other muscles in the human body work on the same principle as the biceps and triceps muscles?

Experiment 17.6
Investigating joints

1 Move your upper arm at the shoulder. Note the freedom of movement at the shoulder joint. You can move your upper arm in any plane, i.e. backwards and forwards, from side to side, or you can rotate it. What makes this possible is the structure of the shoulder joint. It is a **ball and socket joint** (Fig 17.17a).

2 Now move your lower arm at the elbow. In this case you have less freedom of movement. You can move your lower arm in only one plane, i.e. backwards and forwards. This is due to the structure of the elbow joint, which is a **hinge joint** (Fig 17.17b).

3 Move your upper leg at the hip, and your lower leg at the knee. In each case, describe how much freedom of movement there is at the joint. What kind of joint (ball and socket or hinge) do you have in the hip and the knee?

4 Your teacher will give you some joints from the butcher. Test their action and see how much freedom of movement they give. Relate your findings to the structure of the joint.

Questions for class discussion

Our joints must have two important properties.

1 They must allow the bones to move against each other with minimum friction, so the ends of the bones must be well lubricated.

2 They must cushion the impact of one bone against the other when, for example, we jump up and down.

Looking at the butcher's joints, can you find any evidence of how these properties are achieved?

Homework assignments

1 What structure, or structures, in the human body:
   a transmit messages from one place to another
   b are stimulated by light rays
   c store information in the form of memory
   d can get shorter?

2 An athlete gets into the starting position for a hundred metre sprint. At the sound of the pistol the athlete begins to run. Describe the route through which messages travel in the athlete's body to bring about the response.

3 Suppose someone throws a ball to you and you catch it.
   a Write down the stimulus which you receive before you start responding.
   b What receptor or receptors receive the stimuli?
   c Describe your response.
   d What muscles, bones and joints are involved in the response?
   e What organ of the body coordinates the response?

Plant responses

Do the plants in your garden respond to stimuli? At first sight you might say no: after all, if you prod a geranium it does not move away. However, plants *do* respond to stimuli. They do so by growing in a particular direction. One of the most important stimuli to which plants respond is light.

equal growth on all sides of shoot

more growth on the left

Fig 17.18 How a shoot bends towards the light.

Fig 17.19 A plant bending towards the light.

Experiment 17.7
Observing the response of a seedling to light

1 Lay a sheet of blotting paper on the bottom of two dishes.

2 Moisten the blotting paper with water.

3 In each dish sprinkle some seeds of mustard or cress, then cover the dish.

4 After the seeds have germinated, put one dish in a window where it will be brightly lit from only one side, and put the other dish in a place where it will be lit equally from all sides.

5 Observe the seedlings at intervals during the next week.

6 After a week, make a sketch of one seedling from each dish to show the difference. In each sketch, show the position of the light source.

Questions for class discussion

1 What conclusion can you draw about the way shoots respond to light?

2 Why is this response useful to the plant?

3 What other stimuli might a shoot respond to? In each case devise an experiment to find out if your suggestion is correct.

4 What kind of stimuli do you think a *root* might respond to? In each case devise an experiment to test your suggestion.

How does a shoot bend towards light?

The answer to this question is that the shoot grows more quickly on the darker side than on the lighter side. The result is that it bends towards the light (Fig 17.18).

Can you think of any experiments which could be done to show that this is true?

Homework assignments

1 You put a potted plant on a windowsill. After ten days you notice that it has bent over as shown in Fig 17.19.
  a Suggest two stimuli which might have caused the plant to bend like this.
  b Describe an experiment which you could carry out to find which of your suggestions is correct.
  c How could you straighten the plant?

2 The grass in the shade of my beech tree grows faster than the unshaded grass beyond the tree. How would you explain this?

Hormones

Look again at Fig 17.18. What might cause the shoot to grow more quickly on the left hand side? Scientists believe that a chemical substance is produced inside the tip of the shoot. This substance makes the shoot grow. The light causes the substance to move to the left hand side of the shoot, resulting in faster growth on that side.

The chemical substance produced in the tip of the shoot is a **hormone**. A hormone is a substance which is produced in one part of an organism and has an effect in another part. Several different hormones are found in plants. They affect growth and other processes such as flowering and the formation of fruit. Artificial forms of these hormones are used in agriculture and horticulture to increase the growth and productivity of crop plants.

Hormones also occur in animals. For example, in humans a hormone called **insulin** helps to control the amount of sugar in the blood. Have you ever had that sinking feeling in your stomach? That is associated with a hormone called **adrenalin** which prepares the body for emergencies. Sexual development is controlled by **sex hormones**. These will be mentioned in the next chapter.

In humans and other animals hormones are produced by **glands** and shed into the bloodstream. They then circulate round the body and bring about changes in parts of the body which may be a long way from where they were produced.

Questions for class discussion

1 What would be the effect of cutting the tip off a shoot? Explain your answer. Why might a gardener do this in the garden?

2 What sort of emergencies do you think adrenalin prepares us for? What changes do you think it brings about in the body?

3 Nerves and hormones both provide ways by which one part of the body can bring about a response in another part. What are the main ways in which a response produced by a nerve differs from a response produced by a hormone?

Background Reading

Bat and whale 'hearing'

The champions of hearing, by any standard, are the bats. Bat sounds long went undetected by man because they are pitched two or three octaves above what we can hear. But to a number of bats flying around on a calm, still summer evening – and to the unfortunate moths that can hear them and must try to avoid them – the evening is anything but calm. It is a madhouse of constant shrieking. Each bat sends out a series of screams in short pulses, each lasting a hundredth of a second.

What is important to the bat is not its sound but its echo.

Bouncing off obstacles like trees, walls and flying insects, the echoes of its cries keep the bat informed of things in its way and food on the wing. This echo-location device, which acts much like the sonar employed in submarines, has evolved in different ways. Some bats send out a wide, scattered beam, others a narrow one that can be changed in its direction and thus used as a scanning device. We know that echo-location involves the bats' ears, mouths and, in some species, noses, because if any of these are blocked, the bats fly 'blind'. But how the bats' ears and brains process the information they receive from the echoes is still a mystery – their hearing equipment must be complex.

Whales use a similar 'sonar' system in the water. We know that at least some whales can transmit ultrasonic sounds as high-pitched as those of bats. But we still do not understand how they produce these sounds, since they have no vocal cords. We also know that whales use echo-location as bats do for avoiding obstacles and for finding prey, and that they have their own vocal 'language'.

(From *Animal behaviour* by Niko Tinbergen, published by Time-Life International.)

Questions

1 In the process by which a bat avoids an obstacle, what is the stimulus and what is the response?

2 Why did bat sounds go undetected by humans for a long time?

3 In the vocal language of whales and dolphins what kinds of things might the animals be saying to each other?

Summary

1 Human beings and other living things respond to **stimuli**.

2 A response is brought about by a **message** which passes rapidly from a **receptor** to an **effector** by way of **nerves**.

3 Two of our most important receptors are the **eye** and the **ear**.

4 The **brain** serves as a coordinator. It ensures that the right responses are given and it also enables us to think and remember things.

5 The brain is readily affected by drugs which, if taken in the wrong circumstances, can be very dangerous.

6 Movement is brought about by the contraction of **muscles** which are attached to the **skeleton**.

7 The **bones** of the skeleton move against each other at well-lubricated **joints**.

8 Plants respond by growing towards, or away from, a stimulus. For example, shoots grow towards light.

9 Plant responses are brought about by **hormones**. Hormones also occur in animals where they play an important part in controlling internal processes.

Explorations 3

O Finding out what earthworms eat

Make a wormery. To do this, fill a large jar or tank with good garden soil and put at least six earthworms on the surface. The worms will soon burrow down into the soil. (What do you think makes them do this?)

At night, when the weather is mild and damp, earthworms come up to the surface of the soil and pull leaves and other objects into their burrows. They may then eat these things.

Use your wormery to find out what objects earthworms will pull into their burrows.

1 If a worm pulls something into its burrow, does this prove that the earthworm will eat it? How could you make sure that it does?

2 Earthworms are good for the soil, in fact they have been described as the gardener's best friend. Does pulling things into their burrows help the soil, and if so how?

P Finding the effect of cooking on the starch in a potato

When you cook a potato, what effect, if any, does the cooking have on the starch in the potato?

Plan experiments to answer this question. Test the possibility that heating might change the starch into another chemical substance. Also test the idea that heating might alter the structure and appearance of the starch grains.

Discuss your plan with your teacher, then carry out the experiments. Write a full report of your results and conclusions.

Q How does exercise affect your rate of breathing?

The job of your breathing system is to bring oxygen into the body. When your tissues need extra energy, you would expect more oxygen to be brought into the body. The purpose of this exploration is to test the hypothesis: the harder your muscles work, the faster is your rate of breathing.

It is best to work in pairs, one of you acting as the subject, the other as the experimenter. Plan the investigation carefully. Decide exactly what the subject should do, and what measurements should be made. Get your plan approved by your teacher before you start work.

Write a full report of the investigation, presenting your results in the most suitable way. What can you say about the relationship between the work done by the muscles and the rate of breathing?

R What affects the human pulse rate?

This investigation must be done in pairs. First, practise taking each other's pulse. Then take your partner's pulse when he or she is engaged in different kinds of activity.

Plot your results as a graph. What conclusion would you draw from your investigation?

1 In what circumstances does the pulse rate
   a increase
   b decrease?

2 Do you think the pulse rate would be a useful thing to measure in a 'lie detector'? What other changes in the human body might be useful in a 'lie detector'?

S How do snails behave?

Your teacher will give you a snail. Its scientific name is *Helix*. Find out as much about its behaviour as you can. Here are some questions for you to try to answer.

1 How does it move?

2 Is it sensitive to light?

3 What sort of stimuli cause it to pull back into its shell?

4 Where does it like to be within its natural habitat?

Plan your investigations carefully and check them with your teacher before you start work. Always be careful not to harm your snail in any way.

T Gaining a skill

Devise a simple, standardised test by which you can find out how quickly different people gain a particular skill. Your teacher will help you to choose a suitable skill: it may be one involving memory (such as learning a poem by heart) or manual dexterity (such as drawing an object accurately).

After devising a suitable test, try it on all members of your class. Score the results and present them in a suitable way. What conclusions do you draw?

Chapter 18

Human reproduction and development

Human beings can produce offspring only by means of sexual reproduction. This requires two partners, a male and a female. Both produce sex cells or **gametes** (see Chapter 6). The female's gametes are **eggs**, and the male's are **sperms**.

The female's reproductive organs

The reproductive organs of the human female are shown in Fig 18.1.

The eggs are produced by the **ovaries**. There are two ovaries, one on each side of the body. A tube, called the **oviduct** (or **Fallopian tube**), leads from each ovary. The oviducts open into a chamber called the **uterus** (or 'womb'). The uterus has a soft inner lining surrounded by a thick muscular wall. It is here that the baby develops.

From the uterus, a tube called the **vagina** leads to the outside. Close to the vagina is another much narrower tube called the **urethra** which comes from the bladder.

Just in front of the opening of the urethra is a small organ called the **clitoris**. It is equivalent to the penis in the male.

Fig 18.1 The reproductive organs of the human female. Notice that the vagina and bladder have separate openings to the outside. The urethra carries urine.

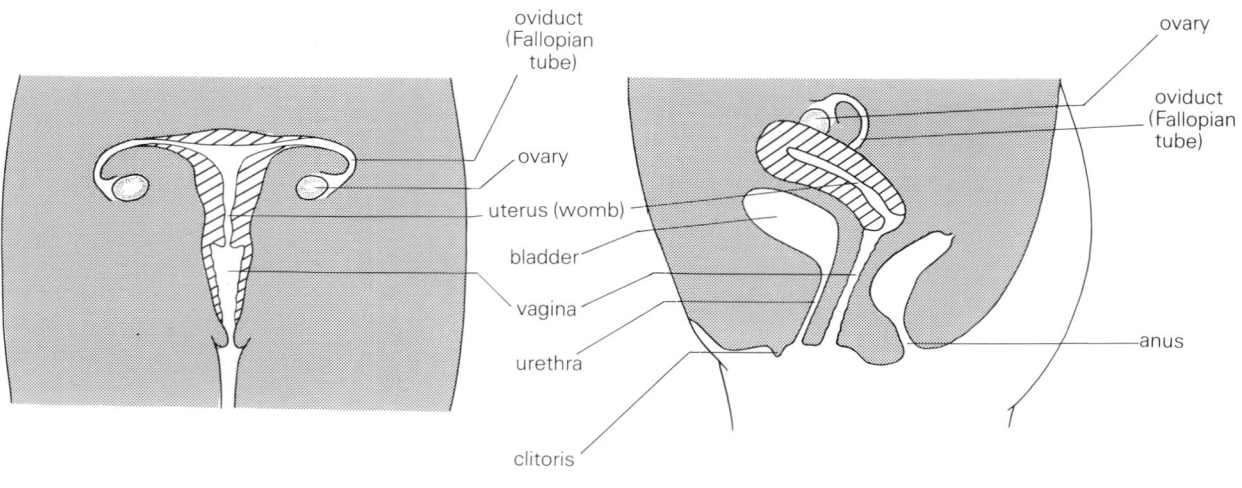

oviduct (Fallopian tube)

ovary

ovary

uterus (womb)

oviduct (Fallopian tube)

bladder

vagina

urethra

anus

clitoris

front view
(bladder and urethra not shown)

side view

The male's reproductive organs

The reproductive organs of the human male are shown in
Fig 18.2.

The sperms are produced by the **testes**. There are two testes
and they lie side by side in a bag called the **scrotal sac**. The
testes are thus located outside the main body cavity. Here the
temperature is slightly lower than the general body temperature;
sperms develop best at this lower temperature.

From each testis, a tube called the **sperm duct** leads towards
the lower part of the abdomen. The two sperm ducts join the
urethra which runs down the centre of the **penis**. The head of
the penis is very sensitive and is protected by the sheath-like
foreskin.

The foreskin may be removed early on in life by an operation
called **circumcision**. This may be done because the foreskin is
too tight. In some cultures it is done for religious reasons.

Fig 18.2 The reproductive organs of
the human male. Notice that the
urethra is connected to the bladder
as well as to the sperm ducts; it
carries urine as well as sperms, but
never at the same time.

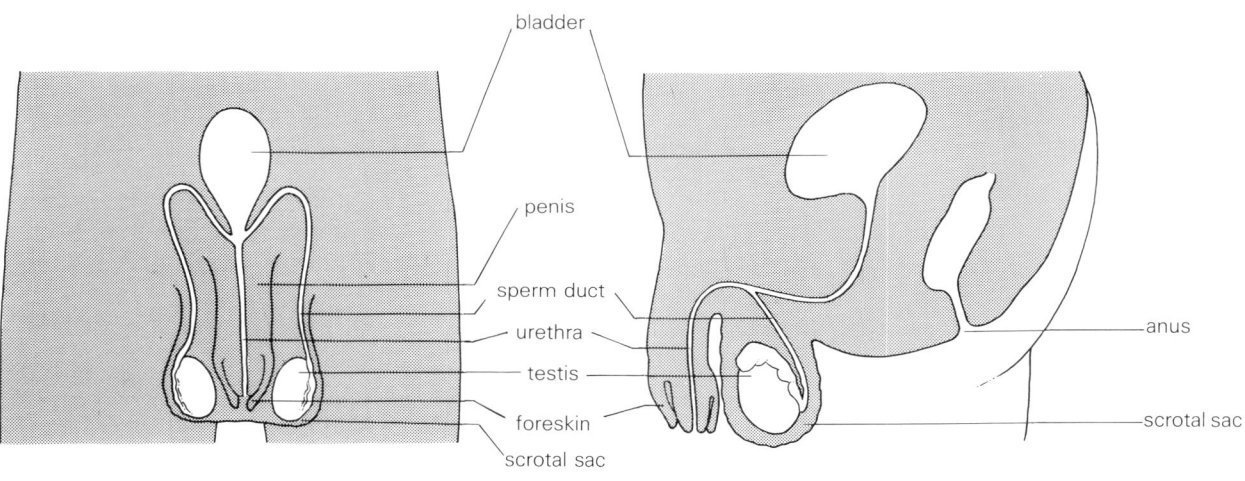

frontal view   side view

Puberty

The ovaries and testes do not start releasing eggs and sperms
until the person is about twelve or thirteen years old. The time
when this happens is called **puberty**. Puberty is brought on by
sex hormones (see page 232). These hormones are produced by
the ovaries and testes and pass round the body in the bloodstream.

Various other changes take place at puberty. In boys the penis
grows larger, the voice breaks, and hair starts growing on the
body. In girls the breasts develop, and approximately every 28
days a small amount of bleeding occurs from the womb. This is
described as a 'period'; its proper scientific name is **menstruation**
which comes from the Latin word 'menstrualis' meaning 'monthly'.

Menstruation is the first of a whole series of changes which take place in the female's body during the course of about a month. These changes make up the **menstrual cycle** which we shall come back to in a moment.

In boys, fluid containing sperms may be released from the penis early on in puberty. The fluid builds up in the tubes leading from the testes and it has to be released. This may occur at night, during sleep, and is called a 'wet dream'. Not everyone experiences this, but it is quite normal and nothing to worry about.

Women generally stop producing eggs about the age of 50. This is known as the **menopause** or the 'change of life'. Men can go on producing sperms all their lives.

The menstrual cycle

This is what happens in the menstrual cycle. First menstruation occurs: it goes on for about five days and during that time the inner lining of the uterus is cast off and a small amount of blood passes out of the vaginal opening. Then the lining of the uterus thickens and lots of blood vessels develop in it. At the same time, an egg develops in one of the ovaries. About fourteen days after menstruation began, the egg is released from the ovary. The egg enters the upper end of the oviduct. If it is not fertilised within a day or two, it dies. The lining of the uterus continues to thicken and it gets richer in blood vessels. Fourteen days later it is shed and menstruation occurs again.

So menstruation and the release of the egg alternate, with an interval of about fourteen days between each.

The thickening of the uterus lining provides a soft base for the embryo to sink into if fertilisation occurs. However, if fertilisation does not occur, the lining is not needed and so it is cast off: that is what causes menstruation.

For a day or so before menstruation begins, one may feel depressed and 'off colour'. This can be annoying, especially if one has a hockey match that day. However, it is quite natural. The monthly period and the feelings which go with it are part of every woman's life, and men should show understanding towards women in this respect.

Adolescence

The time between the beginning of puberty and adulthood is called **adolescence**. It lasts until the age of about 18 years when growth ceases. During these years profound changes take place in the body, many of them brought on by hormones (see page 232). Some of the changes are accompanied by side-effects such as spots on the skin. Feelings change too, and there may be times when one feels frustrated and resentful, even angry.

These changes are all part of growing up, and most young people cope with them very well. However, some people have difficulties. If you have difficulties it is better to talk them over with someone you trust than to bottle them up. Parents and teachers are usually ready to help.

Intercourse and fertilisation

In order to fertilise an egg, the sperms must be placed inside the female's body. This is achieved by **sexual intercourse** (Fig 18.3).

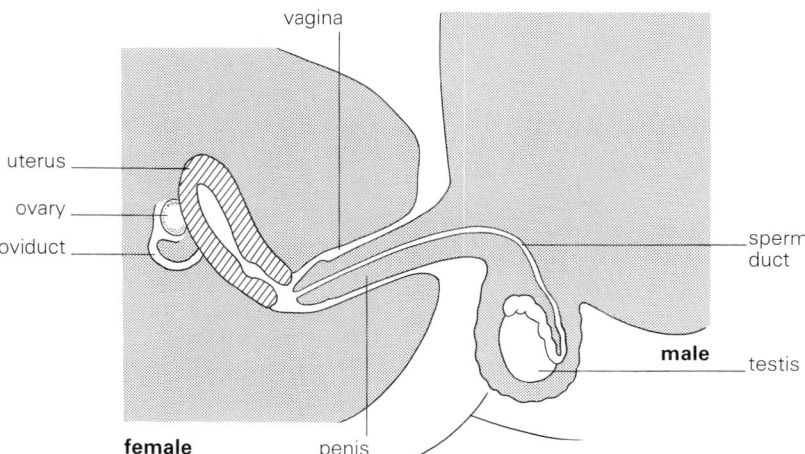

Fig 18.3 In the act of intercourse, sperms are introduced by the male into the vagina of the female.

First the penis has to become hard. This is called an **erection**. The male puts his erect penis into the vagina of the female and moves it rhythmically in and out. This stimulates the sensitive penis and after a short while about a teaspoonful of whitish fluid shoots out of the opening of the penis. This process is called **ejaculation**. The fluid is called **semen** and it contains millions of sperms.

At the same time as he ejaculates the male gets a pleasant feeling. This is called an **orgasm** and it occurs as a result of the rubbing of the penis. The rubbing of the clitoris may produce a similar feeling in the female.

The sperms swim through the fluid lining the uterus and into the oviducts. If an egg is present in an oviduct, one of the sperms may fertilise it: the head of the sperm penetrates the egg and its nucleus combines with the egg nucleus (see Chapter 6).

The fertilised egg now divides into a ball of cells which moves down the oviduct to the uterus. Once in the uterus, it sinks into its soft inner lining. The ball of cells is an **embryo**, and the female is now **pregnant**. She will have no more periods, and her ovaries will produce no more eggs, until after her baby has been born.

Development of the embryo

The embryo grows and develops, and it becomes surrounded by a bag of watery fluid. The bag is called the **amniotic sac**, and the fluid inside it is called **amniotic fluid**. It helps to protect the developing embryo from damage.

By the end of the third month the embryo is approximately 10 cm long, and it looks like a miniature human being. It is called a **fetus**.

The fetus is nourished by a structure called the **placenta**. This is shaped like a plate and is attached to the lining of the uterus. The placenta is connected to the fetus by the **umbilical cord** which contains blood vessels from the fetus.

Inside the placenta, blood from the fetus flows very close to the mother's blood (Fig 18.5). As the fetus' blood flows past the mother's blood, it picks up oxygen and food substances and it gets rid of carbon dioxide and nitrogen waste. The fetus also gains certain antibodies from the mother, and these help to protect it from disease during early life (see page 210).

The fetus' and mother's blood flow very close to each other in the placenta, but they do not mix. People differ in their blood groups (see page 210). If a mother and her fetus belong to different blood groups, the blood vessels might get blocked if the two bloods mixed. Another reason why the two bloodstreams must not mix is that the mother's blood pressure is much higher than that of the fetus.

The time between fertilisation and birth is known as the **gestation period**. In the human this is approximately nine months. During this time the fetus grows considerably and the uterus expands to make room for it.

It is important that the mother should eat enough of the right kinds of food while she is pregnant, and that she should not take into her body anything that might harm her baby. Smoking and alcohol can be harmful to the developing baby. So can germs which get across the placenta. The germs that cause German measles are particularly dangerous: for this reason teenage girls are immunised against this disease (see page 266).

Birth

When the baby is ready to be born the amniotic sac bursts and the amniotic fluid passes out through the vagina. Then the muscles in the wall of the uterus contract powerfully and the baby is pushed through the vagina, usually head first.

After the baby has emerged, the placenta comes away from the lining of the uterus and passes out through the vagina: this is called the **afterbirth**.

As soon as the baby has been born it starts to breathe. The umbilical cord, of no further use, is cut and the scar becomes the baby's **navel** or 'belly-button'.

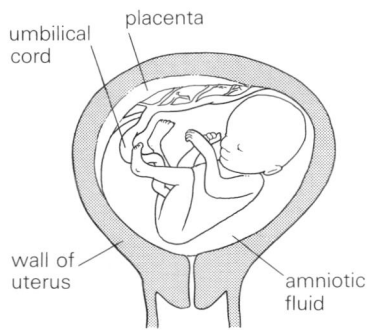

Fig 18.4 A human fetus in the uterus about 3 months after the egg was fertilised.

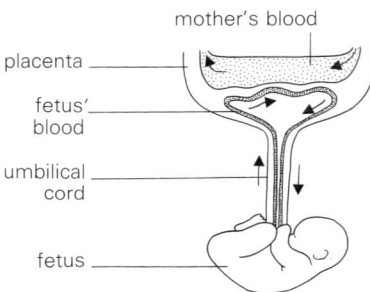

Fig 18.5 Simplified diagram of the placenta. The arrows show the flow of blood.

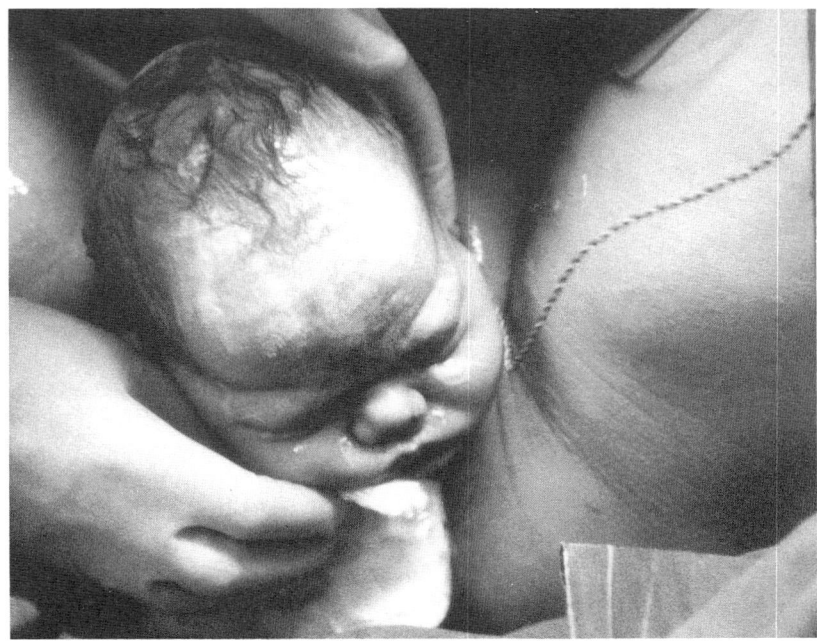

Fig 18.6 A baby is born.

Growth and development

During the first few months of its life the baby can get all the food it needs by sucking the nipples on the mother's breasts (Fig 18.7). The breasts contain **mammary glands** which produce

Fig 18.7 A mother breast-feeding her baby.

milk. This is a complete food and contains all the substances necessary for the baby's healthy growth. Alternatively, the baby may be fed on milk from a bottle with a teat.

Breast feeding has certain advantages over bottle feeding. For example, mother's milk contains antibodies which help to protect the baby from diseases until it starts making its own antibodies. Breast feeding also gives the baby close contact with the mother.

After a few months the baby can be given some solid or semi-solid food. When the change-over from milk to solid food is complete, the baby is said to be **weaned**.

The child grows rapidly for the first few years, then more slowly. Growth speeds up again during **adolescence** – approximately between the ages of twelve and eighteen years. It then slows down and stops by the age of about twenty years. The different parts of the body do not all grow at the same rate: for example, during the first four years or so, the head grows much more quickly than the rest of the body.

It is important that the growing child should have an adequate diet and lead a healthy life (see Chapters 15 and 19). It is the parents' responsibility to make sure of this. It is a good idea to give the baby plenty of fresh air. However, a young baby must not be allowed to get cold. This is because the mechanisms for keeping the body temperature constant have not yet developed fully.

Questions for class discussion

1 Chapter 15 deals with the various substances which must be included in our diet. During pregnancy the mother has to eat extra amounts of these substances. Why?

2 Why is mother's milk said to be a 'complete food'?

3 The fetus has a gut and a pair of lungs. However, neither are working. Explain the reason for this. When do they start working?

4 An important feature of human development is the care of the young by the parents. Make a list of all the ways in which human parents care for their offspring.

5 The semen of a human male may contain as many as 500 million sperms, and yet only one is needed to fertilise an egg. If only one is needed why are so many produced?

Homework assignments

1 Answer these questions about the human female.
   a Name the structures which produce eggs.
   b Whereabouts does fertilisation normally occur?
   c Which structure receives the male's penis during intercourse?
   d What structure houses the developing embryo?
   e Name the structure which nourishes the developing fetus.

2 Answer these questions about the human male.
  a Name the structures which produce sperms.
  b Where are the structures located, and why?
  c What passes down the urethra, and when?

3 a Why can humans produce babies only after both partners have reached puberty?
  b Why can a couple have no more children after the woman reaches the age of about 50?

4 a What is the period between fertilisation and birth called, and how long does it last?
  b Describe how the developing embryo is protected.
  c Materials are exchanged across the placenta between the mother's blood and the fetus' blood.
    (i) Name two needs of the fetus that are met in this way.
    (ii) Name two waste substances that leave the fetus in this way.
  d One function of the placenta is to keep the mother's blood separate from that of the embryo. Why is this necessary?
  e In most births, which part of the baby emerges from the mother's body first?

5 Find out, either from books or by asking people who know, when (approximately) each of the following events occurs during human development. Qualify your answers where necessary.
  a A baby starts eating semi-solid food.
  b The first tooth breaks through.
  c The colour of the eyes changes.
  d The child starts crawling.
  e The child starts walking.
  f The child says 'mum'.
  g The child says 'dad'.
  h The first set of teeth is complete.
  i The second set of teeth is complete.
  j A girl can become pregnant.

6 The graph in Fig 18.8 compares the growth of three different parts of the body from birth to the age of twenty years.
  a If the legs were 84 cm long at the age of twenty years, approximately how long were they at five, ten and fifteen years?
  b Why does the head grow so quickly in the early years?
  c Why does the growth of the reproductive organs speed up at the age of twelve years?

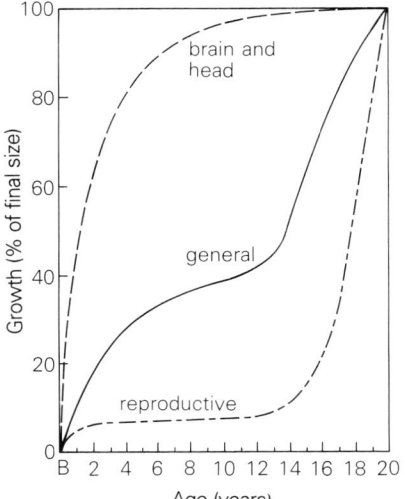

Fig 18.8 Graph to show the rates of growth of different parts of the human body as a percentage of final size.

A boy or a girl?

What decides whether a baby will be a boy or a girl? It depends on certain chromosomes which the baby gets from its parents. (Chromosomes are explained on page 64.)

The cells in the human body each contain twenty-three pairs of chromosomes. This set of chromosomes includes a pair of **sex chromosomes** which make the person male or female. There are two types of sex chromosome: a large one called the **X chromosome**, and a smaller one called the **Y chromosome.**

Females have two X chromosomes in their cells, so we can describe the female as XX. In contrast, males have an X and a Y chromosome, so we can describe the male as XY.

Now let us think what happens when these sex chromosomes are passed on from the parents to the children. Fig 18.9 shows what happens. First notice the sex chromosomes in the parents: the father is XY and the mother is XX. Next, notice that the eggs and sperms carry only one sex chromosome. The egg always contains an X chromosome – it must. But a sperm may contain an X or a Y chromosome. In practice approximately half the sperms are X, and half are Y.

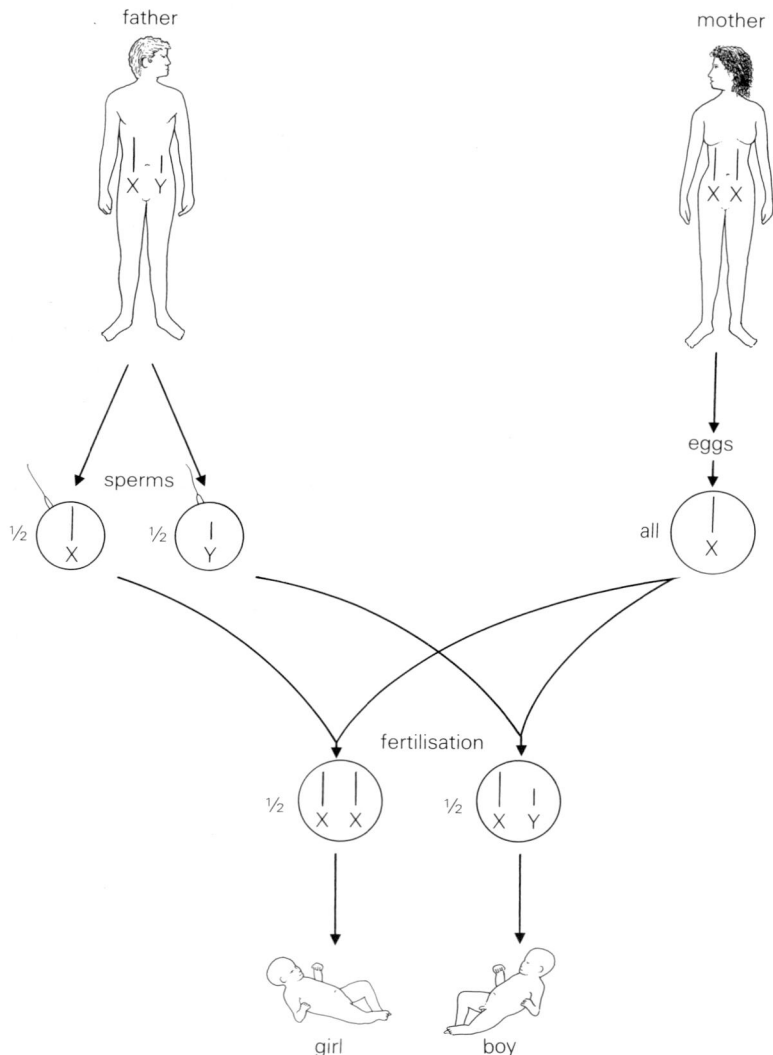

Fig 18.9 Will it be a boy or a girl? It all depends on the sex chromosomes.

When reproduction takes place, it is pure chance whether the egg is fertilised by an X sperm or a Y sperm. So there is an equal chance of the baby being XX (a girl) or XY (a boy).

Test-tube babies

We hear a lot about test-tube babies nowadays. What are they?

A test-tube baby is one which has developed from an egg that was fertilised outside the mother's body. A surgeon takes an egg from one of the mother's ovaries. The egg is then fertilised in a dish or test-tube, and allowed to develop into a small embryo. The embryo is then placed in the mother's uterus where it continues to develop in the usual way.

What is the point of this procedure? Some couples find it difficult to have children; for some reason or other the woman fails to become pregnant. Test-tube babies provide a way of helping some of these couples to have children.

Family planning

There may be times when some couples wish not to have children. For example, they may already have as many children as they can support. Such couples may want to prevent pregnancy. This is called **family planning** or **birth control**. Generally it involves using some method of **contraception**.

The most natural method of contraception is for the woman to avoid having intercourse at times when she is likely to become pregnant. This is when an egg is present in one of her oviducts, ready to be fertilised. How does she know when this is? The answer is that it is very difficult to know exactly, but it should be roughly midway between one menstrual period and the next. If you are not sure why this is, read again the section on the menstrual cycle on page 238. This is not a very reliable method of contraception unless carried out under expert guidance.

More reliable methods of contraception involve an artificial device called a **contraceptive**. There are several kinds of contraceptive and they work in different ways. For instance, some form a barrier, stopping sperms from reaching the egg; an example is the condom, a rubber sheath which fits over the penis. Another kind of contraceptive involves the use of chemical substances; an example is the 'pill' which the woman takes orally (by mouth) — it prevents eggs being produced by the ovaries.

Some methods of contraception are more efficient than others. Some carry health risks, and not all of them are approved of by the various religious groups. Deciding which one to use is a very personal matter, and many considerations have to be taken into account. Family planning clinics are available where couples can seek expert advice.

Abortion

An abortion is the death of the fetus, and its loss from the uterus, before birth is due to take place. Sometimes a woman has an abortion naturally: we call it a **miscarriage**. But there are also occasions when an abortion may be carried out by a doctor. This is when the health of the mother may be at risk if she continues with the pregnancy, or when the baby is likely to be severely handicapped.

Having an abortion is one of the most distressing things that can happen to a woman. Many moral issues are also involved. It is something that people should think about very carefully.

Questions for class discussion

1 What are the main risks in fertilising a human egg outside the body? How might the risks be overcome?

2 Some people feel that every woman should have the right to be given an abortion if she wants one. Others feel that abortion should never be carried out in any circumstances. What do you think?

Sexually transmitted diseases

Certain diseases can be passed from one person to another by sexual intercourse. They are called **sexually transmitted diseases**.

An example of a sexually transmitted disease is syphilis. It is caused by a bacterium. The disease takes a long time to develop fully. If untreated, people eventually die of it. However, like other bacterial diseases, it can be cured by antibiotics.

Another important sexually transmitted disease is AIDS. AIDS stands for Acquired Immune Deficiency Syndrome. 'Immune deficiency' means that your immune system does not work properly. Your immune system is extremely important: it consists of many different kinds of cells which together help to defend the body against disease. 'Syndrome' means a set of illnesses associated with a particular disease.

AIDS is caused by a virus. The virus attacks certain cells in the immune system. As a result the person gets various diseases which normally he or she would be protected against. AIDS can take a long time to develop fully – many years in some cases. Most people who get AIDS die as a result of it eventually.

AIDS can only be caught by sexual intercourse or very close sexual contact, or by an infected person's blood getting into another person's body. Drug addicts who share the same needle to inject themselves with a drug are at particular risk. You cannot catch AIDS by touching a person who has AIDS, or by drinking from a cup which has been used by a person with AIDS.

At present there is no known cure for AIDS and people cannot be vaccinated against it. Once you have got the virus, there is no way of getting rid of it.

Sex and personal relationships

Animals mate whenever they have the chance and are in the right mood. With humans it is different. We have to control our feelings for all sorts of personal and social reasons.

For humans sexual intercourse is the greatest expression of love which one person can show for another. Ideally it should be part of a permanent partnership, such as happens in a successful marriage.

Of course the ideal does not always happen. Some people start having sexual intercourse in their early teens, possibly with many different partners. However, in Britain sexual intercourse is illegal below the age of sixteen years, and there are good reasons for this. Having frequent sexual intercourse during adolescence, while the body is still growing, can damage health; and if you have many different partners you run the risk of catching sexually transmitted diseases such as AIDS.

One of the most important things that distinguishes us from other animals is that we can predict the outcome of our actions. Applied to sexual relationships, this means that partners should respect each other's feelings, and neither should do anything which is likely to harm the other.

Background Reading

Bringing up children

A Health Visitor describes some important aspects of how children develop.

A baby's first experiences come from its mother. If the mother is calm and relaxed, the baby will probably be so too. In the first few weeks the baby will sleep most of the day and night, waking at regular intervals to be fed. As time goes by the baby will need less sleep and will be able to go for longer between feeds. The baby has to learn that there is a difference between night and day and that the night time is for sleeping – otherwise the parents may get many sleepless nights!

The baby is fed on milk only until it is about four months old when it can be introduced to small amounts of solid food. At about eight or nine months it can begin to eat normal family food.

Fig 18.10 Baby sitting and playing with toys.

Fig 18.11 Toddler learning to walk.

At about six weeks the baby will begin to respond to its parents by smiling at them. Gradually it becomes more aware of its surroundings. It will reach out for toys and, by about three months, it can hold a rattle briefly. By about six months the baby will probably be rolling over, playing with its feet and moving about the floor, but not yet crawling. By eight months it can sit unaided and crawl. At this stage it can hold things firmly and transfer them from one hand to the other. It can babble and say 'mama' and 'dada'. Now is the time for the parents to lock any cupboards near the floor, because the baby will soon be into them!

Most babies are walking after about a year. Toddlers between one and three years begin to explore the world around them. They become little people in their own right and begin to test their parents to see how far they can go. They need to know the limits. Parents should try to understand that much of their children's behaviour arises from the urge to explore, and they should be consistent in handling this urge. Children may have temper tantrums when they cannot get their own way. Tantrums are caused by frustration and not being able to communicate with others.

The basis of communication is, of course, speech. Speech begins to develop at about eighteen months and by two years most children will be joining some words together into sentences. By three years they should be able to speak clearly and get others to understand their needs. Parents should talk a lot to their children at this stage and encourage them to use a varied vocabulary.

By the age of three, most children are ready to go out and play with other children. Children thrive on imaginative play, and this is the aim of play groups which children often attend at this stage. By this time a child is well enough developed physically and emotionally to be parted from the parents for short periods and to come under the control of other adults.

By four years children are usually able to dress themselves and do up their buttons. They will be able to use a pencil and draw and colour simple shapes such as a person. They will be able to jump and climb and, by the time they reach their fifth birthday, they should be ready to go to infant school.

A balanced diet with three meals a day is essential if the child is to develop properly. Children should be encouraged to eat healthy foods such as wholewheat cereal and bread, milk, yoghurt, cheese, eggs, meat and plenty of fruit and vegetables. They should not be given too many sweet foods and drinks for these are bad for the teeth. It is important that children going to school should start the day with a good breakfast for this can affect their concentration and performance later on.

Parents can do much to encourage the development of their children. Love and security play a very important part. So do play and stimulation. The mother and father should talk to the baby right from birth, giving it lots of things to play with and look at. Research has shown that children brought up in a stimulating environment are more likely to do well later.

(by Mary Roberts, Bath and West NHS Trust)

Questions

1 Suppose you are a Health Visitor advising a young couple on how to bring up their first child. Give them a list of 'dos' and 'dont's'.

2 Grandmother to four-year old grandson: "Stop running that toy car over the table, you're making grooves in it."
Child's parent to grandmother: "Oh leave him alone, he's investigating the properties of wood".
Who's right?

3 In this passage it says that a good breakfast can affect a person's concentration and performance later on. How could a scientist find out if this is really true?

Summary

1 The main reproductive organs of the male are the **testes, sperm ducts** and **penis**.

2 The main reproductive organs of the female are the **ovaries, oviducts, uterus** and **vagina**.

3 When **puberty** is reached the testes start releasing **sperms** and the ovaries start releasing **eggs**. Usually one egg is released every 28 days, midway between one period and the next. This continues until the age of about 50 (the menopause).

4 During **sexual intercourse** sperms from the male are put into the vagina of the female. If an egg is present in one of the oviducts it may be fertilised by a sperm.

5 In the uterus, the **embryo** develops into a **fetus** which is nourished by way of the **placenta** and protected by the **amniotic fluid**.

6 Birth takes place approximately nine months after the egg was fertilised.

7 The child grows and develops through adolescence into an adult, reaching full size at the age of about 20 years.

8 **Test-tube babies** provide a way of helping childless couples to have children.

9 **Family planning (birth control)** is used by couples who wish to prevent pregnancy.

10 **Sexually transmitted diseases** can be passed from one person to another by sexual intercourse. An example is acquired immune deficiency syndrome (AIDS).

Chapter 19

Micro-organisms and people

Living organisms which are too small to be seen clearly without a microscope are grouped together and called micro-organisms or microbes. It has been estimated that the mass of micro-organisms in the world is greater than the total mass of all other animal life. They are found in every type of habitat from the depths of soil and sea to the limits of the atmosphere many kilometres above the Earth's surface.

There are many different kinds of micro-organism but most can be classified into four groups: **protoctists, bacteria, fungi** and **viruses**.

Protoctists

Although most protoctists consist of a single cell the largest are composed of many cells and may be several metres long, for example seaweeds. The largest single-celled protoctists, such as the pond-dwelling *Amoeba* (Fig 19.1), are just visible to the naked eye but most are truly microscopic. Some protoctists are parasitic and cause disease. An estimated 400 million people live in places where malaria occurs. Malaria is caused by the protoctist *Plasmodium* which is spread by the *Anopheles* mosquito (Fig 19.2). About $2\frac{1}{2}$ million deaths each year are caused by malaria.

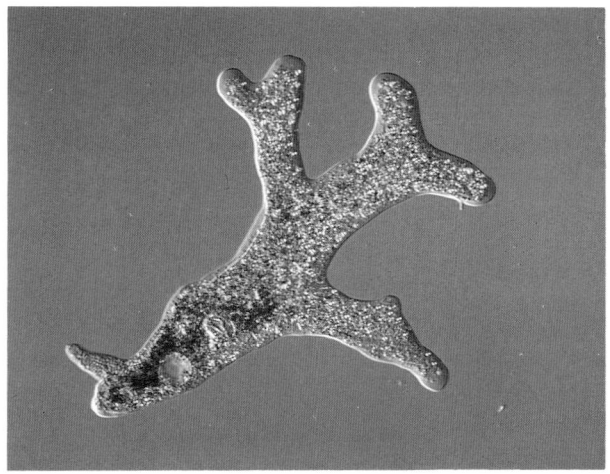

Fig 19.1 *Amoeba*.

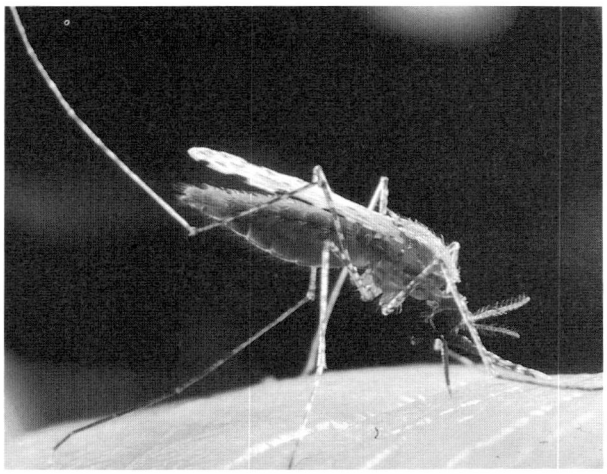

Fig 19.2 *Anopheles* mosquito on a human finger.

Bacteria

Most bacteria are about one-thousandth of a millimetre long and are just visible with a light microscope. The more powerful electron microscope shows them better (Fig 19.3). They are single cells but the cells are simpler than those of animals and plants.

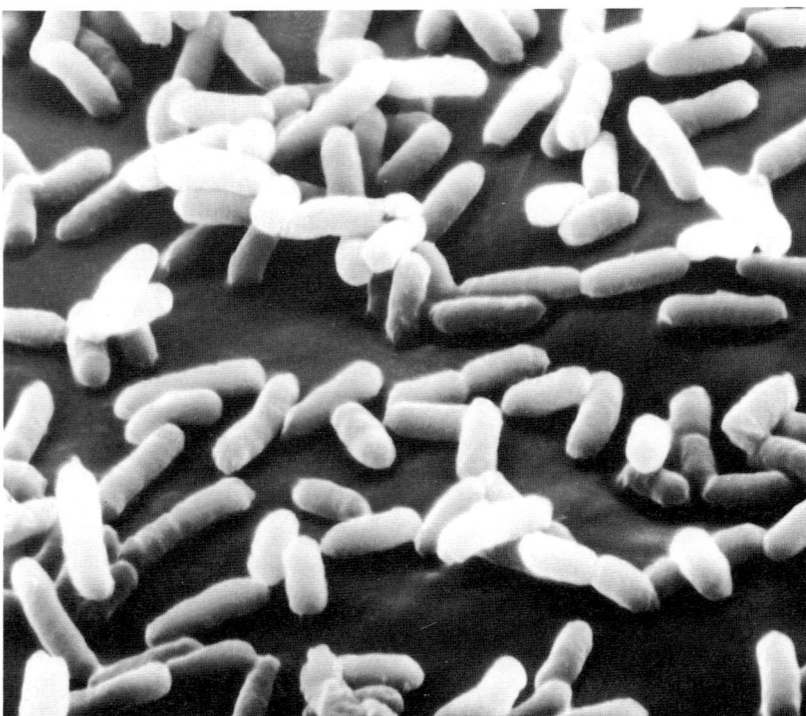

Fig 19.3 *Escherichia coli*, a type o bacteria found in the human gut.

Bacteria differ from each other in shape, size and in the conditions which they require to live and multiply. In good conditions, some bacteria can divide every eleven minutes. In poor conditions they form spores which can withstand high and low temperatures or a temporary lack of food and water. Although many bacteria are parasitic and cause disease (see Chapter 20), many others are free-living and play an important part in natural processes.

Viruses

Viruses are much smaller than bacteria, too small to be seen with a light microscope. They are on the borderline between living and non-living things. Under the electron microscope some of them can be seen to have complex shapes (Fig 19.4). All viruses require living cells in which to reproduce. Human diseases caused by viruses include influenza ('flu), smallpox and the common cold. The disease AIDS has been shown to be caused by a virus (see page 246).

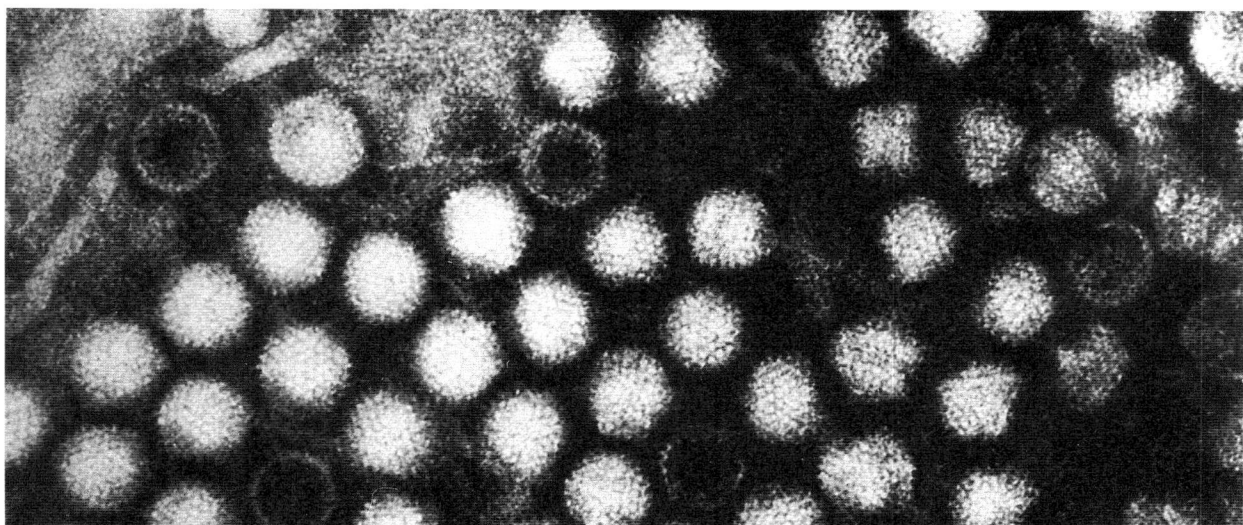

Fig 19.4 An electron micrograph of the virus which causes hepatitis.

Fungi

The moulds which you grew on a slice of bread in Experiment 13.3 are examples of fungi. Not all fungi are microscopic (Fig 19.5), but some of the most important groups of fungi are too small to be seen without a microscope, for example, the yeasts. All fungi are either parasites or feed on dead matter. They do not have chlorophyll and cannot photosynthesise. They usually reproduce by budding or spore production (see Chapter 5).

One of the commonest human diseases caused by a fungus is ringworm (Fig 19.6). This is an infection of the outer layer of the

Fig 19.5 *Amanita muscaria, a poisonous fungus.*

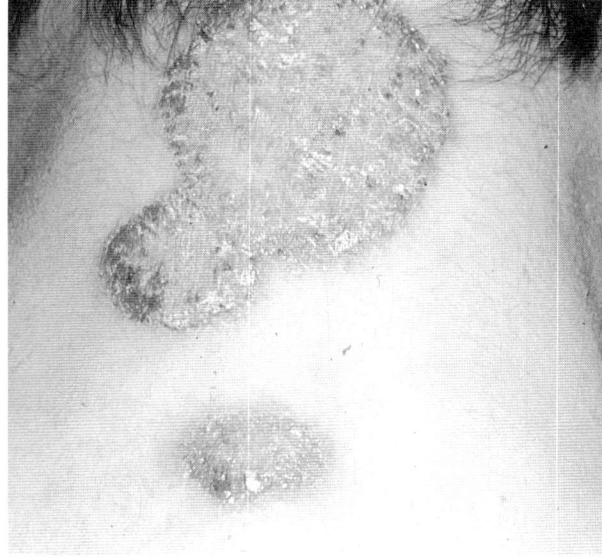

Fig 19.6 Raw, itching patches caused by ringworm.

skin which forms raw, itching patches. When it attacks the skin between the toes it is called 'athlete's foot'. It is spread by spores and controlled by various powders and ointments. Infection is less likely to occur if the feet are kept dry, cool and clean.

Plants can also be infected by fungi and the results can be very serious for human food production. The disease 'potato blight', caused by a fungus which enters the leaves of the potato plant, resulted in famine in Ireland in the 19th century.

Experiment 19.1
Growing micro-organisms in the laboratory

Individual micro-organisms are too small to be seen without a microscope. However if provided with ample food, warmth and a good supply of oxygen, they will divide rapidly to produce a **colony** which is clearly visible to the naked eye. They are usually grown in special dishes called **petri dishes** which allow air to pass freely in and out but exclude foreign organisms and their spores. They are provided with a jelly-like material called **agar** containing food extracts. All the equipment used for growing micro-organisms has to be heated to a high temperature to make sure that it is free from any contamination (**sterile**). You will be given two sterile petri dishes in this experiment.

1 Label one of the two dishes 'Control' and secure the lid (see Fig 19.7).

Fig 19.7

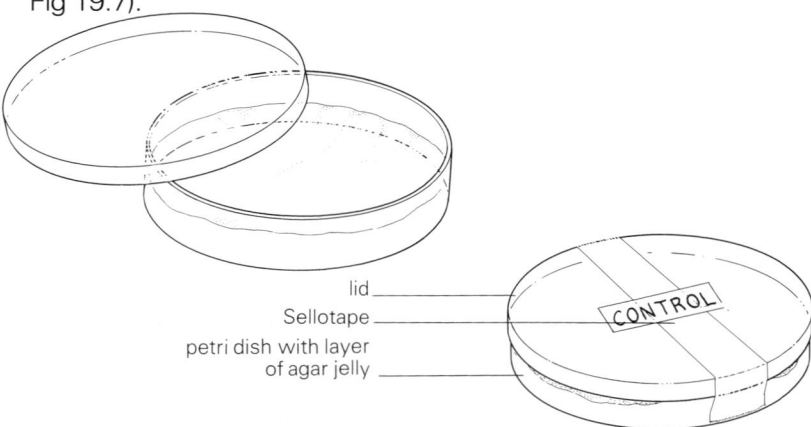

lid
Sellotape
petri dish with layer
of agar jelly

CONTROL

2 The surface of the jelly in the other dish is to be exposed to micro-organisms from *one* of the following sources: atmospheric air, soil, tap or pond water (only one or two small drops). You may be able to suggest more alternatives to your teacher so that the class can obtain results from different sources.

3 Secure the lid of the second dish with Sellotape and label it with your name, the date and the origin of the micro-organisms.

4 Both dishes should be placed upside-down in an oven or incubator set at 25–30 °C. (The lower temperature encourages fungal growth; the higher temperature favours bacterial growth.)

Safety note

Under no circumstances should any of the dishes be opened.

5 If possible, look at the dishes every day and record the growth of colonies of micro-organisms.

Bacterial colonies usually appear shiny whereas colonies of fungus are usually 'fluffy' or powdery. If you assume that each visible colony originated from a single organism or spore, you can estimate the number of bacteria and fungi which reached the surface of the jelly.

6 When you have finished with the dishes, give them unopened to your teacher who will dispose of them hygienically. Every precaution must be taken to avoid contamination with disease-causing organisms from the dishes.

Then wash your hands in soapy water.

Questions for class discussion

1 Why were the two dishes sterilised before the experiment? How was the sterilisation done?

2 What was the purpose of the control plate? Did any colonies of micro-organisms grow on it?

3 Why is it so important not to open the dishes after they have been incubated?

4 Record the class results in the form of a table. What do the results tell you about the distribution of bacteria and fungi?

5 Different methods have to be used in order to grow viruses in the laboratory. Look back to page 252 and then suggest why viruses cannot be grown on agar jelly in petri dishes.

Micro-organisms and the circulation of mineral elements

Mineral elements are essential for the healthy growth of plants and animals (see pages 93 and 183). For example, all living things contain the element nitrogen which is an important part of protein molecules. How do living things obtain this element for the manufacture of protein? Since the atmosphere is approximately 80 per cent nitrogen gas, there is no shortage of the element, but very few living organisms are able to make proteins from nitrogen gas because the element nitrogen is so unreactive.

However, certain micro-organisms contain the enzymes required to convert atmospheric nitrogen into compounds containing nitrogen. This process is called **nitrogen fixation**. Some of the most important nitrogen-fixers are bacteria which live in the roots

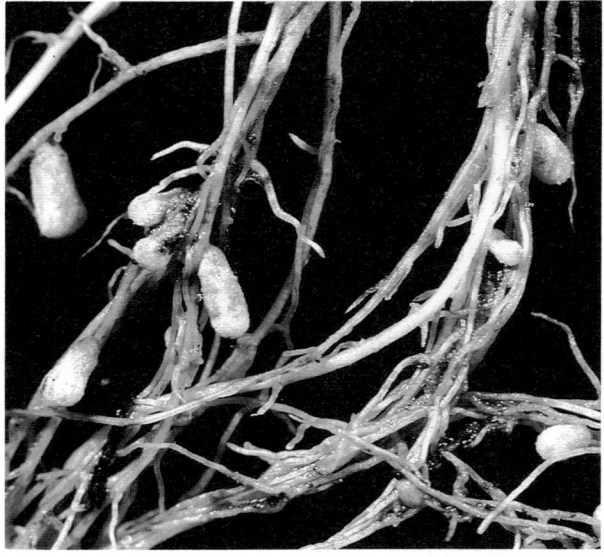

Fig 19.8 Nodules on white clover roots.

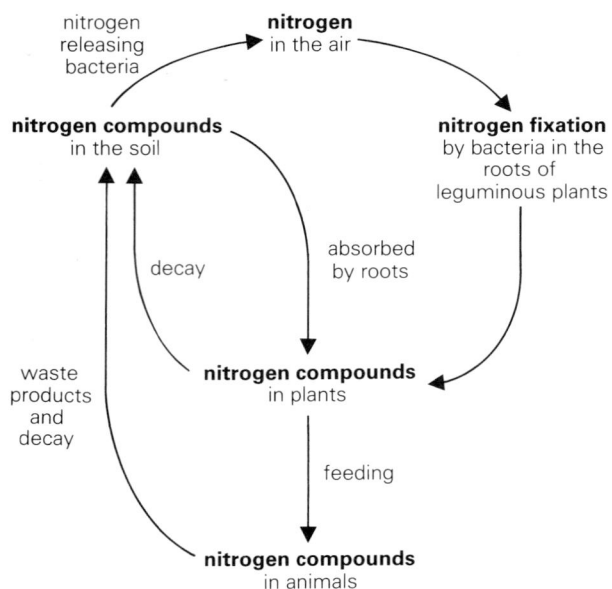

Fig 19.9 The nitrogen cycle.

of a group of plants called **legumes**. This group includes peas, beans and clover which are particularly useful to farmers because they can improve the nitrogen content of the soil. Fig 19.8 shows the roots of a clover plant and you can see the small lumps or nodules in which the bacteria live. This association of bacteria and leguminous plant is an example of mutualism (see page 166). The bacteria receive carbohydrates from their host which they use to provide energy to fix nitrogen. The nitrogen is then used by the bacteria to make proteins for the bacteria and the host plant.

Other micro-organisms play an important part in the circulation of nitrogen-containing compounds. Since much of the nitrogen eventually returns to the atmosphere, the movement is called the **nitrogen cycle**. It is shown in diagrammatic form in Fig 19.9. Similar cycles exist involving other essential elements such as carbon (Fig 8.20) and sulphur. In each case, micro-organisms play a very important part.

Micro-organisms and the disposal of sewage

The important part played by micro-organisms in the decay and decomposition of dead plants and animals has already been described in Chapter 13. Farmers and gardeners make use of this when they prepare a compost heap or spread manure on their fields. The activity of the micro-organisms is shown by the gradual disappearance of the compost and manure and also by the warmth generated inside the compost heap.

On a much larger scale, micro-organisms can be used to break down human waste products. One of the simplest forms of sewage disposal is the earth closet — a container of soil. The micro-organisms in the soil help to break down the chemical compounds in urine and faeces so that the contents of the closet can be safely emptied into a pit.

Water-borne sewage systems are commonly found in most developed countries. The sewage is usually carried in pipes to an effluent treatment works where solid matter is separated to form a sludge. The sludge is broken down by micro-organisms to give methane gas which may be used as a source of energy for the works. The liquid part of the sewage is thoroughly aerated to encourage the growth of bacteria. The bacteria produce 'activated sludge' which may be dried and sold as fertiliser. Finally the remaining liquid is allowed to trickle over filter beds where micro-organisms break down most of the organic chemicals leaving the water pure enough to run into a river or the sea.

Putting micro-organisms to use: the production of food and drink

Micro-organisms have been used for thousands of years to make food and drink for human consumption. The production of wine, beer, bread and cheese is made possible because the micro-organisms produce enzymes (see page 48). One of the most important micro-organisms is yeast. Yeasts are single-celled fungi and they are widespread in nature. Wild yeasts are found on the surface of fruits. For at least 60 000 years, humans have used yeast to convert sugar to alcohol, a process called **fermentation**. Since oxygen is not required, fermentation is a type of **anaerobic respiration** (see page 198).

Commercial yeast is grown on a large scale. The yeast cells are washed and purified, then pressed together to remove some of the water.

Wine is usually made from fermented grapes although many other materials can be used. The fruit is crushed and the juice, which contains naturally occurring yeasts and sugar, is left to ferment in a warm place.

Beer is brewed from barley seeds. The barley grain is first allowed to germinate so that the starch in the seeds is turned into sugar. The sugar is washed out, yeast is added, and fermentation takes place for about a week. The bitter flavour of beer is provided by the addition of hop flowers.

Wine and beer can be turned into **vinegar** by the action of bacteria.

Yoghurt and **cheese** are produced from milk by the action of bacteria. Yoghurt is made from whole milk and its sour taste comes from the lactic acid produced by the bacteria. Cheese is made by separating milk, curdled by bacteria, into solid curds (precipitated milk proteins) and liquid whey. The curds are turned into ripe cheese by the action of bacteria and, in some cases, fungi.

Experiment 19.2
Using yeast to ferment sugar

1 Take two test-tubes and pour sugar solution into them until they are about half full.

2 Add a pinch of dry yeast to one tube and shake it very thoroughly for a few minutes so that the yeast is dispersed throughout the solution.

3 Attach a balloon to each tube and label them. Place both tubes in a warm water bath at about 20 °C.

4 After a few hours note the appearance of the balloons. Remove the balloons and smell the contents of the tubes.

5 With a pipette, put a drop of the solution from each tube onto a microscope slide. Cover it with a coverslip. Describe what you see in as much detail as you can.

Experiment 19.3
Bread making

Yeast also plays an important part in the making of most kinds of bread as you will see in this experiment.

1 Place the yeast, sugar and flour provided in a bowl and mix very thoroughly. Make a second mixture without adding any yeast.

2 Add a little warm water and make each of the mixtures into a ball. If the ball is sticky, add more flour; if the ball is dry and cracked, add more water.

3 Knead the dough for several minutes.

4 Place the balls of dough in a dish in an incubator or oven at about 30 °C for 30 minutes.

5 Note any changes in the appearance of the dough balls.

Safety note

Because your bread has not been produced under hygenic conditions you must not taste or eat it.

Questions for class discussion

1 In Experiment 19.2 what name is given to the test-tube to which no yeast was added?

2 Why was this second tube particularly important in Experiment 19.2?

3 How could Experiment 19.2 be modified to demonstrate that:
   a the gas produced in fermentation is carbon dioxide
   b energy is released during fermentation.

4 Suggest two reasons why the dough you made in Experiment 19.3 should be thoroughly kneaded before being placed in the oven.

5 What changes took place in Experiment 19.3 when the dough was first placed in the oven or incubator? How can these changes be explained?

6 How and why does the 'bread' you made in Experiment 19.3 differ from commercially produced bread?

Putting micro-organisms to use: the production of chemicals and drugs

Micro-organisms are today being used by scientists to make an increasing variety of chemicals. These include an important group of drugs called **antibiotics**. The first antibiotic was discovered by Sir Alexander Fleming in 1928. He noticed that bacteria seemed unable to grow close to a small colony of a fungus which happened to have infected one of his experimental petri dishes. He eventually extracted a small quantity of the substance produced by the fungus and called it **penicillin**. However, it was not until 1941 that penicillin was produced commercially on a large scale for use in the treatment of bacterial diseases. There are now many different kinds of antibiotics produced by fungi and bacteria.

Many other chemicals are manufactured with the aid of micro-organisms. They include vitamins, citric acid (for soft drinks) and a wide variety of enzymes. 'Biological' washing powders, for example, contain enzymes extracted from bacteria which help to break down the dirt and stains in the clothes. The use of micro-organisms and the enzymes which they produce has been the subject of a great deal of research in the last decade or so, and is an important part of the new industry which is sometimes referred to as **biotechnology**. The potential benefits include more food for Third World countries and new cures for disease.

Questions for class discussion or homework

1 Fig 19.10 overleaf is a photograph of a petri dish containing the bacterium *Bacillus subtilis* growing on an agar jelly. The small discs which you can see on the surface of the jelly were placed there immediately after a suspension of the bacterium was spread evenly over the whole plate. Each disc contains a different antibiotic. The dish was then incubated for 36 hours at 30 °C.

    a Explain why the dish was incubated after the bacteria were introduced.

    b Describe the distribution of the bacteria after incubation.

    c What can you deduce about the effect of the different antibiotics on this strain of *Bacillus subtilis*?

    d How could a doctor use this technique to decide how to treat an unknown human bacterial infection?

Fig 19.10 Photograph of a petri dish containing *Bacillus subtilis* growing on an agar jelly with discs of antibiotics.

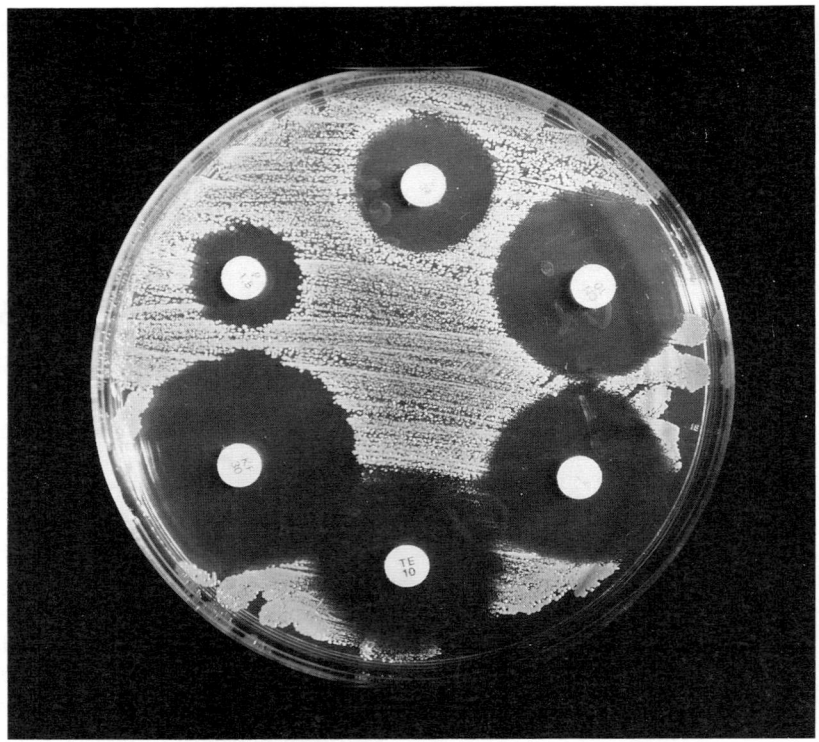

2 A popular brand of 'biological' washing powder gives the following advice on the packet:

'Detergent X gives best cleaning results when used in the hand wash or for soaking. Never soak silk or wool garments. People with sensitive or damaged skin should avoid prolonged contact with the washing solution.'

a What is added to a washing powder to make it 'biological'?

b Some of the most difficult stains to remove from fabrics are proteins (e.g. blood). Refer back to Chapter 15 to name the active ingredient of 'biological' washing powder which helps it to remove protein stains.

c Suggest a reason why prolonged soaking in a 'biological' washing powder might damage delicate fabrics or even human skin.

d What do you think would be the ideal temperature for a hand wash or for soaking clothes in a 'biological' washing powder? Explain the reasons for your choice.

Homework assignments

1 List the main differences between bacteria and viruses.

2 Describe the part played by micro-organisms in the circulation of chemicals in nature.

3 Yeast has been used by humans for thousands of years. Describe briefly *three* different ways in which yeast is used today.

Background Reading

The future of biotechnology?

The biotechnology revolution could transform medicine, health and food production as greatly as the microchip has affected communications. The potential benefits include more efficient animal production, cheaper products, cures for disease and more food for Third World countries. The merchant bankers, Rothschild, have already promised more than £1 million for the development of large-scale methods of producing cattle embryos. This is regarded as an important step towards food self-sufficiency in developing countries since it provides a method of upgrading cattle by introducing high-grade embryos into low grade stock.

Adapted from an article by John Young in *The Times*.

Questions
1 Name one disease which can be cured using a chemical substance produced by micro-organisms. What is the name of the substance?

2 Suggest two reasons why large-scale production of cattle embryos might provide more food for Third World countries.

3 **a** Explain what is meant by the term 'food self-sufficiency'.
   b What are the disadvantages of sending food surpluses from rich countries to developing countries?

The discovery, isolation and manufacture of the first antibiotic – penicillin

Penicillin was discovered by a Scottish surgeon and bacteriologist Alexander Fleming while he was working at St Mary's Hospital in London. It was September 1928 and Fleming was using a type of bacterium called *Staphylococcus*. He was growing a number of different strains of *Staphylococcus*. He would from time to time lift the lids of his culture plates to check on how they were getting on. One day he noticed that one of them had developed a green mould (see Fig 19.11 overleaf). His first reaction was annoyance and he put the dish to one side to be sterilised in antiseptic later on. Then something caught his eye in the plate with the green mould. All round the mould, the bacterial colonies were small or absent. Everywhere else in the dish they were flourishing. The mould was producing something that was preventing the growth of the bacterial colonies. We now know that the something was penicillin, a drug that was to revolutionise medicine. But Fleming did not know that and it required many months of hard and careful work to find out.

It is often said that Fleming discovered penicillin by accident. The arrival of the mould certainly was an accident but it needed the right person to notice it and realise its importance. Fleming was that person.

Fig 19.11 Alexander Fleming's original culture plate. The large white area on the left is the mould. The smaller white areas are bacterial colonies. Notice the almost complete absence of bacterial colonies near the mould.

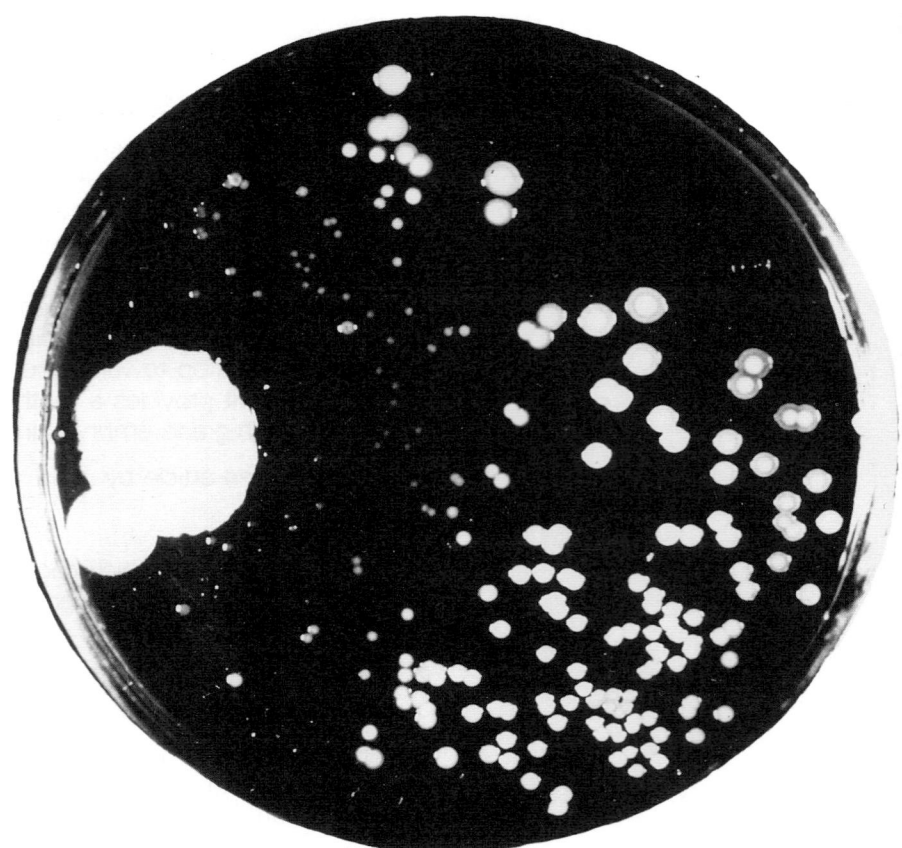

A number of things had to happen before penicillin could be made in useful amounts. Penicillin is an unstable substance. It very quickly goes off and so a chemist was required to prepare penicillin in a stable form. A young German chemist called Ernst Chain took on this task. Secondly, the pencillin had to be tested on animals and, later, on humans. This was undertaken by a young Australian pathologist, Howard Florey. The results of Florey's and Chain's experiments in Oxford were published in August 1940. Fleming was delighted and immediately set up a factory at St Mary's Hospital where vaccines were produced for the Forces. Later it was decided that production should be carried out in America. The people who had the necessary skills were the brewers and this is why some firms that started out making beer and lager became, and still are, drug houses. Fleming and Florey were both knighted in June 1944 and all three men shared the Nobel Prize for Medicine in 1945.

Penicillin is now only one of a great many drugs extracted from fungi and called **antibiotics**. Millions of human lives must have been saved by good team work and a stroke of good fortune!

(Adapted from W. Howard Hughes *Alexander Fleming and penicillin,* first published in 1974 by Priory Press.)

Questions

1 Great discoveries are sometimes the result of the efforts of a single man or woman. The discovery and development of penicillin was mainly due to a team of three men.
   a Name the three men.
   b What was the profession of each man?
   c State briefly what each man contributed to the work on penicillin.

2 Imagine that you are Alexander Fleming and you have just noticed the unusual culture plate (Fig 19.11). What would be your next scientific experiment in order to find out what had happened?

3 Suggest a reason why it was decided to switch large-scale commercial production of penicillin to the USA in 1944.

4 What skills would the brewing industry possess which might help them to manufacture a drug such as penicillin on a large scale?

Summary

1 The main groups of micro-organisms are **protoctists, bacteria, viruses** and **fungi**.

2 Bacteria and fungi can be grown in the laboratory on **agar** jelly and in **petri dishes**.

3 Micro-organisms play an important part in the circulation of elements in nature.

4 We use micro-organisms in the preparation of food and drink and, increasingly, in the production of chemicals and drugs.

Chapter 20

People and their environment

'Where do you live?' and 'What is your environment?'. These were two of the questions asked in the first chapter of this book. In this last chapter we return to these questions and consider the ways in which humans are affected by their environment and attempt to control it. Fig 20.1 summarises four important aspects of our environment. We will look at each of these aspects in the rest of this chapter.

Fig 20.1 Humans and the environment.

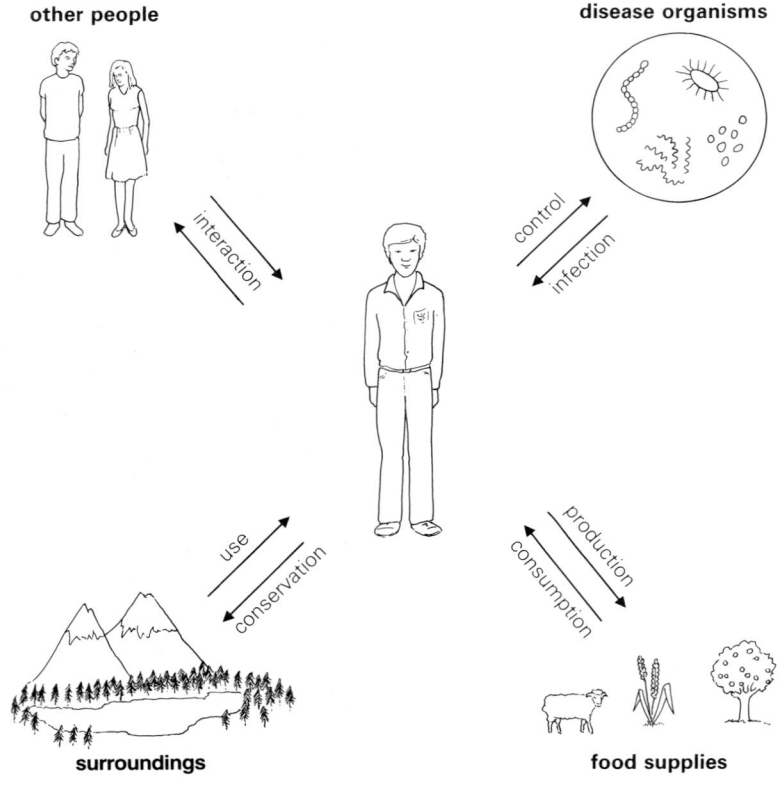

Health

It is said that over three quarters of the illness in the world could be prevented or cured by the following: better nutrition, a clean water supply, sanitation, immunisation and health education. In the last hundred years improvements of this kind have reduced deaths from infectious diseases in Britain from 30 per cent of all deaths to less than 1 per cent. The average life expectancy is now almost 75 years; in the world's poorest countries it is still only about 45 years.

Better nutrition

One-third of the world's population does not have enough to eat, and another third has a diet which consists of the wrong kinds of food. Carbohydrates, fats, proteins, dietary fibre, vitamins and minerals must be present in adequate amounts, especially in the diet of growing children (see Chapter 15). When crops fail because of drought or pests, and the shortage of food cannot be made good by emergency supplies, people suffer and die. The child in Fig 20.2 has a protein deficiency disease caused by insufficient protein in her diet. The addition of soya or groundnuts to a diet of maize would have prevented this disease.

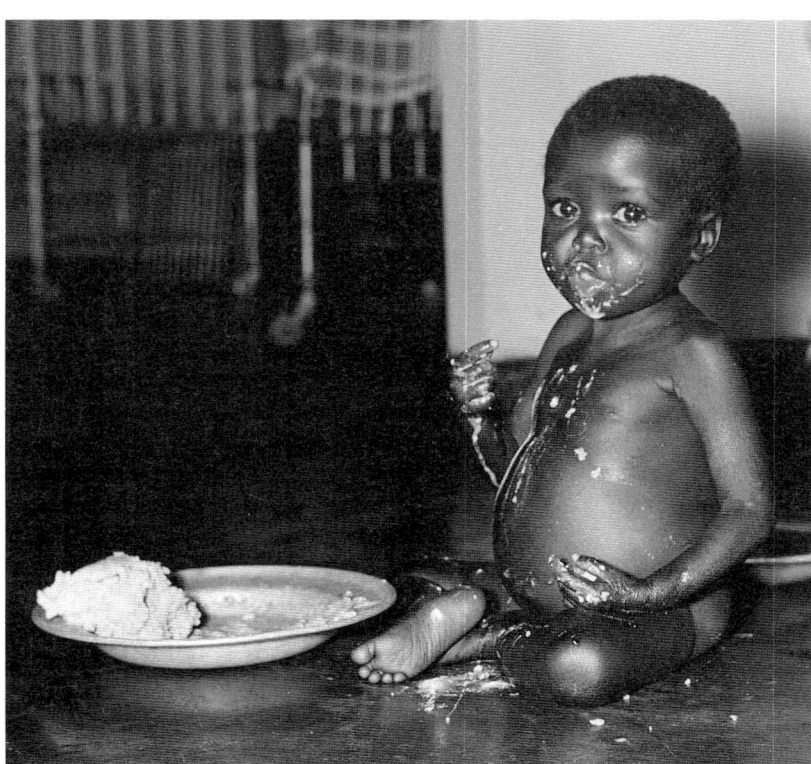

Fig 20.2 This child is suffering from a protein deficiency disease. In hospital she has been given a high protein diet.

In the richer countries the problem is often that people eat too much food of the wrong kind. If we eat more than our bodies can use we get fat. Doctors have found that people who over eat are more likely to suffer from diseases of the heart and arteries than other people (see Chapter 16).

Clean water and sanitation

Nearly half the world's people do not have a supply of clean drinking water. Basic sanitation is available to less than a quarter of those living in the world's poorer countries. Many of the worst diseases of the Developing World are associated with infected water supplies. Typhoid and cholera for example are caused by water-borne bacteria. The proper disposal of human excreta provides the best protection against these and other diseases.

Many countries in the world have insufficient water to provide for the needs of the people and of industry. Even in Britain, which has a relatively high average annual rainfall, the conservation of water is essential. Water is collected from rivers and reservoirs and distributed throughout the country. Used water is purified in effluent treatment works (see page 257) to make it fit for further use. London's water supply comes mainly from the River Thames which has already supplied Oxford and other towns further upstream. In spite of careful water management, Britain suffers from drought conditions in some years and water restrictions have to be introduced to conserve supplies.

Immunisation

When a disease-causing organism enters the human body it may cause the body to react in a number of different ways. We are all familiar with the first response to a skin infection: the skin becomes inflamed – swollen, red and perhaps painful.

Disease organisms contain chemicals which we call **antigens**. When the human body detects an antigen in the blood, the white blood cells (see page 210) produce chemicals called **antibodies** which react with the antigens making them harmless. The body is then protected against that antigen in the future; it has become **immune**.

Some antibodies are passed from mother to baby through the placenta. This gives the infant temporary protection against diseases for the first few months of its life. Since the antibodies are not made inside the babies' body, this is called **passive immunity**. Whenever the human body comes into contact with antigens, it produces its own antibodies. This provides long-term protection against disease. It is called **active immunity** and explains why there are many infectious diseases which we normally only catch once in our lifetime.

Active immunity can also be produced artificially by giving a **vaccine**. A vaccine may consist of a small dose of living micro-organisms which have been made harmless in some way (e.g. polio, tuberculosis, German measles and measles). Alternatively, dead micro-organisms may be used (e.g. typhoid, influenza, whooping cough), or even the harmful chemicals (**toxins**) produced by micro-organisms themselves (e.g. diphtheria and tetanus). The vaccines in routine use in Britain today are shown in Table 20.1.

Table 20.1 A typical programme of immunisation

Age	Immunisation
4–6 months	diphtheria-tetanus-whooping cough and polio
6–8 months	as above – second dose
12–16 months	as above – third dose
16–24 months	live measles and, perhaps, German measles
5 years	diphtheria-tetanus-whooping cough booster
10–13 years	B.C.G. (live tuberculosis vaccine)
15–19 years	diphtheria-tetanus plus polio booster doses

Perhaps the greatest success of immunisation has been the elimination of smallpox after a campaign by the World Health Organisation introduced in 1967. However, in the world's poorer countries scarcely 10 per cent of children are immunised against any of these major infectious diseases.

Health education

The aim of health education is to persuade people to live healthier lives. As we grow older we gradually take over responsibility for our own health and well-being from our parents.

The human body is like a very complicated machine. It needs to be maintained and protected all the time. A balanced and healthy diet (see page 186) and regular exercise (see page 211) are essential to our well-being. Sleep provides an opportunity for the body to recover from the day's activities. Cutting down on sleep can cause irritability and may increase the risk of disease. Throughout our lives, our bodies are exposed to many different chemicals, some of which are harmful. Some, such as radioactive radon gas released from the rocks under our feet, occur naturally in the environment. Others, such as lead compounds in vehicle exhaust fumes, are made by humans. But there are other harmful chemicals which we can choose to avoid.

Some of your friends may have begun to smoke; perhaps your parents smoke. Most adults would agree that, if they had known how harmful cigarettes were, they would not have started smoking. For example, it has been shown without any doubt that smoking is a major cause of diseases of the breathing system such as bronchitis (infection of the air tubes), emphysema (breakdown of the air sacs) and lung cancer. Over a third of all cancer deaths are now considered to be the direct result of smoking. Cigarette smoke contains many substances such as nicotine, tar and carbon monoxide all of which are known to have harmful effects on the human body. Doctors believe that smoking can increase the risk of heart attacks and even affect the health of unborn babies. The majority of doctors who used to smoke have now given it up. One of the best ways of protecting your health is to decide not to start smoking.

Nicotine, which is present in cigarette smoke is just one of the chemical substances (or drugs) which can be taken into the

"Five a day don't cost much"   "That's nearly £200 a year up in smoke"

Smoking. Who needs it?

Fig 20.3 Is smoking worth it?

human body (see page 220). You may know that children have died after sniffing glue. The solvent which is used to make glue is a particularly dangerous drug which can cause sudden heart failure. Of course many drugs are used by doctors to prevent or control disease. Others help to reduce pain. Drugs, such as alcohol, influence our behaviour and personality.

Drugs become a problem if our bodies start to depend on them. As we become **addicted** to a drug we need more and more of it to produce the same effect. Some drugs are more addictive than others and the use of these drugs may be banned by law. Other drugs can only be supplied and used under the direction of a doctor. But alcohol, which is readily available in the form of alcoholic drinks, is the drug which is most frequently misused. Used sensibly, alcohol is one of the pleasures of adult life; abused, it can destroy human happiness. Addiction to alcohol (**alcoholism**) is a very serious problem and is very difficult to cure.

Washing the skin regularly helps to reduce the risk of infection. Dirty skin also attracts external parasites such as fleas and lice. If you have a pet, it is important to check its health regularly; fleas and worms are sometimes spread to humans from other animals such as dogs. The head louse is particularly common in schools today. The female lays up to 300 eggs in her one month of life. The eggs, called 'nits', are cemented to the base of the hairs. They cannot be brushed out but must be treated with a special shampoo and combed out when they are dead.

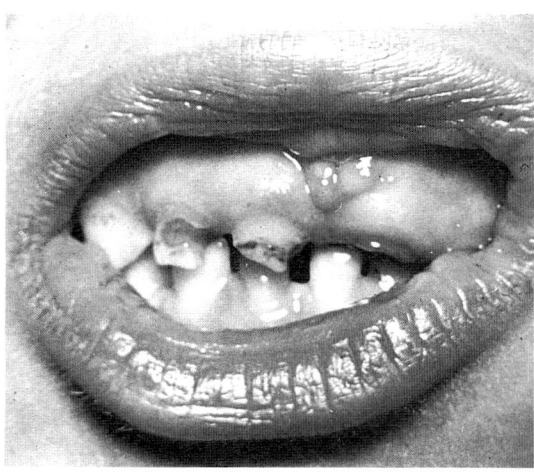

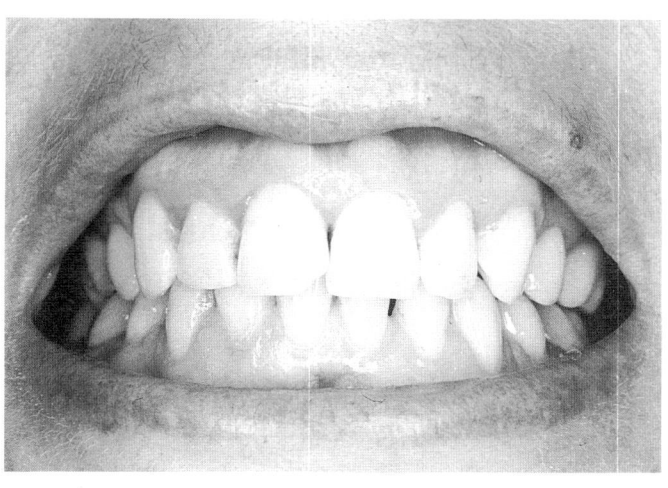

Fig 20.4 (a) Set of bad teeth.   (b) Set of good teeth.

Very few adults today have perfect **teeth and gums** (see page 191). By the age of five, one in every four children in Britain has already had at least one tooth extracted, and two-thirds of all eight-year olds have had extractions (Fig 20.4). The cause of most dental decay is **plaque**, a mixture of food remains and bacteria which coats the teeth. These bacteria break down sugary food remains releasing acid which attacks the teeth and gums.

There are four main ways of reducing tooth decay and gum disease:

1 Reduce the number of sticky, sugary foods and sweet drinks that you have.

2 Brush your teeth and gums regularly, between as well as on the surface of the teeth. Change your toothbrush as soon as the bristles become soft and bent. Use dental floss to remove food from between your teeth.

3 The presence of fluoride in the diet has been shown to reduce dental decay. Use a fluoride toothpaste or take fluoride tablets if your drinking water has no added fluoride.

4 Visit the dentist regularly to have your teeth and gums checked.

Experiment 20.1
How well do you clean your teeth?

Your teeth are normally covered with a layer of plaque. To show the presence of plaque we can use the red dye erythrosin.

1 Rub a little Vaseline on your lips to prevent them being stained by the dye.

2 Suck a disclosing tablet (containing erythrosin).

3 Wash out your mouth with water.

4 Examine your teeth with a mirror and make a drawing in your notebook showing the areas of plaque (stained red).

5 Now brush your teeth thoroughly.

6 Suck a second disclosing tablet.

7 Make a second drawing to compare the areas of plaque after brushing.

Questions for class discussion

1 Which parts of your teeth were stained red? Which method of brushing is most likely to remove plaque from these areas: side to side, up and down or a circular movement?

2 The amount of stain will vary considerably from person to person. Suggest explanations for this.

3 If toothpaste is tested with a suitable indicator, it can be shown that it is alkaline. How does this help to reduce decay?

4 Carry out a dental survey in your class. Beside each name note the following information.
  a Number of visits to the dentist in a year.
  b Number of times the teeth are cleaned each day.
  c Brand of toothpaste used. Does it contain fluoride?
  d Number of sweets eaten each day.
  e Number of teeth.
  f Number of extracted teeth.
  g Number of teeth with fillings.

  What conclusions can you draw from the results?

5 There is strong evidence to suggest that cigarette smoking causes lung cancer. Some of the evidence has been obtained from a study of British doctors. The death rate from lung cancer among doctors who smoke is 1.26 per thousand: that is over 30 times greater than the death rate for non-smokers. The results of giving up smoking are shown in the graph in Fig 20.5. Describe in your own words what the graph shows about:
  a the results of giving up smoking
  b the connection between smoking and lung cancer.

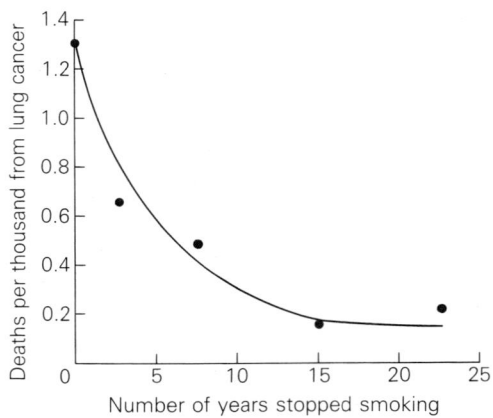

Fig 20.5 The effect on the death rate of doctors of giving up smoking.

Homework assignments

1 Prepare a short talk on one of the following:
 Preventing tooth decay
 The dangers of smoking
 Immunisation.

2 Design a poster to help prevent the spread of the head louse in schools.

3 Name a human disease which is caused by each of the following organisms, and describe briefly (i) how it spreads (ii) how it can be controlled.
 a a virus
 b a bacterium
 c a fungus.

Food supplies

In the 20-year period between 1980 and the year 2000, the world's population is expected to increase from 4400 million to over 6000 million. In some countries the rate of increase will be far greater than this and there are worries about how the world will cope with the numbers of people in future. By the mid-1980s, over 450 million people were going short of food. Yet the quantity and quality of food produced in the richer countries of the world has improved rapidly in the last thirty years. The main factors responsible for this improvement are the following.

New kinds of crops

Plant and animal breeders are constantly trying to select the best characteristics – yield, quality and disease resistance – to provide farmers with new and improved varieties (see page 66). When a valuable characteristic is found, it can be preserved by keeping seeds or sperms in stores called 'gene banks' and making them available to scientists all over the world.

Improved land use

Only about one quarter of the Earth's surface is land and less than one-tenth of the land is suitable for growing crops (see Fig 20.6). It is therefore essential to make the best possible use of the available area. This can only be achieved by careful soil management. Crop plants depend largely on the thin layer of topsoil for staying upright and obtaining the water and nutrients they require. This topsoil can easily be removed (**eroded**) by heavy rain or strong winds, especially if surface vegetation such

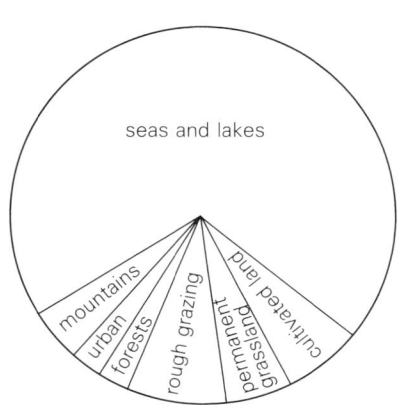

Fig 20.6 The division of the Earth's surface.

Fig 20.7 Soil erosion resulting from loss of plant cover in Zambia.

Fig 20.8 Irrigating farming land in Saudi Arabia.

as hedges and trees has been removed (see Fig 20.7). Plants hold the soil together and reduce the speed of the wind at the surface. So they help to prevent erosion. In deserts and semi-deserts, effective **irrigation** is essential if crops are to be grown (see Fig 20.8).

Better control of pests

New and improved methods of pest control are being introduced all the time. Great care has to be taken to ensure that new chemicals do not harm organisms other than the pests.
There is also a risk that the pests may develop resistance to the chemicals being used. These disadvantages can be avoided if a means of biological control can be discovered and used (see page 137).

Improving the soil

Plants cannot grow unless they are provided with an adequate supply of nutrients (see page 93). These would normally be provided by the death and decay of existing plants (see page 256). Growing and harvesting crops results in the removal of large amounts of mineral nutrients from the land. These must be replaced if continuous high yields of the same crops are required. At one time, this problem could only be overcome by spreading manure or compost on fields, or by changing the crop each year (**crop rotation**). This allowed the missing nutrients to be replaced by natural means. Most modern farms use large quantities of **fertilisers** to provide essential elements such as nitrogen, phosphorus and potassium. Excessive use of fertilisers can lead to pollution. Heavy rain washes the excess minerals out of the soil and into rivers and lakes where they cause a rapid growth of microscopic plants and harm the delicate balance of life in the water (see Exploration W on page 284).

Few crops grow well in an acid soil so farmers are careful to prevent this happening. If they find that the soil on their farms is acidic, they treat it with lime.

Experiment 20.2
Testing the acidity of the soil

1 Try to choose an area of ground which has not been cultivated recently. Remove any surface vegetation and take a small sample of soil.

2 Break up larger lumps of soil and remove any stones before placing the sample in a test-tube. The tube should be not more than half full of soil.

3 Fill up the tube with distilled water.

4 Seal the tube with a clean cork (not your finger) and shake hard for two minutes or more.

5 Filter the muddy water and add a few drops of full-range or soil indicator to the filtrate.

6 Match the colour of the liquid with the colour chart provided and work out the acidity of the soil. The figure you obtain, which is called a pH value, will probably be between 4 (very acid) and 8 (alkaline). Most soils, however, are close to 7 (neutral). See *Chemistry 11–14*, Chapter 6.

Questions for class discussion

1 Why should the soil sample be taken from an area which has not been recently cultivated?

2 Why was distilled water added to the soil rather than tap water?

3 Why should you not use your finger to seal the tube?

4 Compare the result you obtained with those of the other members of your group. Are soils in your area mainly acidic, mainly alkaline, or roughly neutral?

5 How do farmers or gardeners treat their local soils before planting crops or flowers?

6 Find out as much as you can about the *types* of soil found locally. What crops grow well in your locality?

Preventing food decay

All fresh food contains living organisms such as bacteria. If it is kept warm, these bacteria will multiply and make the food decay. They may also produce poisons (**toxins**). To prevent fresh food from going bad the bacteria must be killed or inactivated by some kind of **preservation**. The main methods of food preservation are

high temperature, e.g. cooking;
addition of chemicals, e.g. salting, smoking and pickling;
freezing;
irradiation.

It is important to realise that freezing food does not kill the bacteria; it only prevents them feeding and multiplying. Food which has been frozen should not be refrozen after being thawed; the bacteria may have increased to a dangerous level.

Special methods are used for the preservation of certain foods. UHT (**U**ltra **H**igh **T**emperature) milk, for example is obtained by heating it to 140 °C for a few seconds which will enable it to be kept for a long time without going sour. Most milk is **pasteurised** by heating it briefly to a lower temperature. This treatment kills or inactivates most bacteria so that the milk will keep for a few days.

Experiment 20.3
Testing the keeping qualities of milk

If raw milk is available, the effects of pasteurisation and sterilisation can be compared with untreated milk. However, it is increasingly difficult to obtain raw milk and therefore this experiment compares the keeping qualities of pasteurised and sterilised milk.

1 Pour pasteurised milk straight from the bottle into 4 screw-topped tubes labelled A to D and put the tops on immediately.

2 Place tubes A and B in a water bath of boiling water for five minutes. Loosen the caps first to prevent the tubes breaking.

3 Tubes A and C should then be placed in a refrigerator for a week. Tubes B and D should be left at room temperature.

4 After about a week, open the bottles and smell each one. Sourness can usually be detected by smell but can be confirmed by boiling gently in a water bath, since sour milk will curdle on heating.

5 Record your results in the form of a table.

Questions for class discussion

1 From the results of your experiment what can you deduce about the factors influencing the keeping of milk?

2 The process of pasteurisation is named after Louis Pasteur, a French scientist. What can you discover about the life and work of Pasteur? Apart from milk, name one other food which is preserved by pasteurisation.

Homework assignments

1 **a** Why does food decay?
  b List the methods available to preserve food.

2 The bacterium *Salmonella* is a common cause of food poisoning. *Salmonella* is regularly found in uncooked meat and eggs. If the food is not thoroughly cooked, or bacteria are transferred from the raw food to cooked food, then those who consume the food will be at risk. List the precautions which should be taken to avoid food poisoning from *Salmonella*.

Pollution

Look at the view through the window of the room in which you are sitting. What do you see? What effect have humans had on this view?

Many different things affect your environment; for example the lie of the land, the weather and the type of soil. But by far the most important factors are humans themselves. Almost every view we see is influenced by our own activities. In particular, when humans release substances or create disturbances in the environment, they may cause **pollution**. Overleaf is an example

Fig 20.9 The effect of air pollution on vegetation.

Fig 20.10 Bird death caused by oil pollution of the coast.

of atmospheric pollution and its effect (Fig 20.9). The effect of oil pollution in the sea is shown in Fig 20.10.

Some waste products eventually decay or decompose: they are said to be **biodegradable**. Other waste products cannot be broken down in the natural environment and are said to be **non-biodegradable**. Here is an example of the dangers of pollution by a nonbiodegradable chemical substance.

The insecticide DDT was first introduced in 1945 and was an immediate success in controlling the head louse in American soldiers in Italy. It was largely responsible for eliminating the malaria-carrying mosquito from Sri Lanka.

The discoverer of DDT was given a Nobel prize, one of the highest scientific awards. For the next twenty years DDT was widely used on crops, animals and even on humans. However DDT can be harmful as well as helpful. Suspicions were first aroused by the gradual disappearance or reduction of certain species of birds. After the spraying of a Californian lake against midges, no grebes (a fish-eating bird) hatched out. The peregrine falcon was almost eliminated as a breeding bird in Britain. Scientists gathered information which suggested that DDT might somehow be responsible, and DDT was banned or restricted in many countries. The bird populations recovered – but malaria returned to Sri Lanka! The explanations for the harmful effects of DDT are clearer now. It seems that three factors are involved:

1 DDT does not break down to simpler chemical substances very easily. In spite of the ban on its use, organisms now contain traces of DDT or its derivatives.

2 DDT is passed from one organism to another in a food chain, and becomes more concentrated at each level. In an estuary, for example, the concentration in the water is only 0.000 05 parts in every million parts of water (ppm). This rises to 21 ppm in the top carnivores.

water → producers → herbivores → carnivores → top carnivores
0.000 05 ppm   0.04 ppm   0.3 ppm   3.7 ppm   21.0 ppm

3 The high concentration of DDT sometimes killed the animals but often it affected them in other ways. In the case of the peregrine falcon, DDT interfered with the formation of the egg shell so that the eggs frequently broke when they were incubated.

So pollution may have most unexpected consequences for natural communities. We cannot hope to eliminate pollution of our environment but we can reduce it to a minimum and constantly check its effects on living organisms.

Questions for class discussion

1 If the rivers and lakes in your area are polluted, what has caused the pollution? What steps could be taken to reduce or eliminate the pollution?

2 Pollution of the environment does not always involve a chemical substance. Noise pollution can be just as harmful to our health and well-being as chemical pollution. What are the main sources and effects of noise pollution?

3 What harmful effects could air pollution have on animals and plants? List as many effects as you can.

Experiment 20.4
Testing your own environment for pollution

The following simple tests can be used for air, water and sound pollution. If you can compare places near cities or towns with places in the country, you will get some idea of the effects of pollution on your environment.
Air pollution
1 Remove a needle from an evergreen tree such as a pine. Pull it through a damp folded filter paper. Does it leave a mark on the paper?

2 Examine tree trunks, roofs and gravestones. How many different kinds of lichens can you find? Fig 20.11 shows some species you may find and the levels of pollution which they indicate.

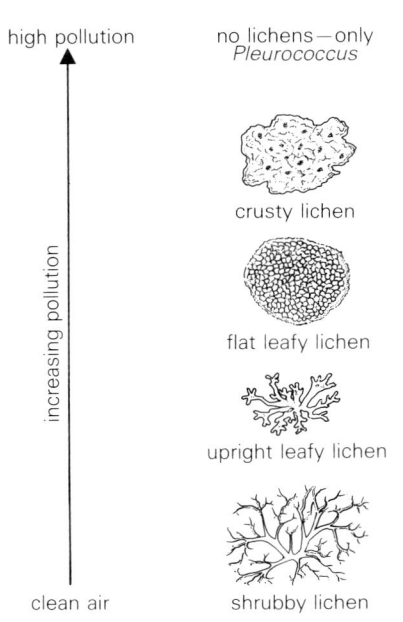

high pollution

no lichens—only
Pleurococcus

crusty lichen

flat leafy lichen

upright leafy lichen

shrubby lichen

increasing pollution

clean air

Fig 20.11 Lichens and air pollution.

Water pollution

1 Take a clean glass container and fill it with water from a pond or stream near your school. Avoid floating vegetation and stirred-up mud. Leave it to stand for a few minutes, then see how clear it is. Is it coloured? Does it smell?

2 Use a universal indicator paper to test the acidity of the water sample. If you find that the value is below 5 the water is unduly acid and is quite likely to be polluted.

3 Use a reagent strip to measure the nitrate concentration in the water. A high value may indicate pollution with fertilisers or sewage effluent.

4 Use a pond net to collect animals from beneath stones or mud. The variety and number of animals present can indicate the amount of pollution (see Fig 20.12).

Sound pollution

1 Use a noise meter to measure the intensity of sound in your environment at different times of day.

2 Devise your own tests to measure the effects of different noise levels on your powers of concentration.

Safety note

Wash your hands thoroughly with soap and water after experiments with pond or stream water.

Fig 20.12 Some indicators of pollution in fresh water.

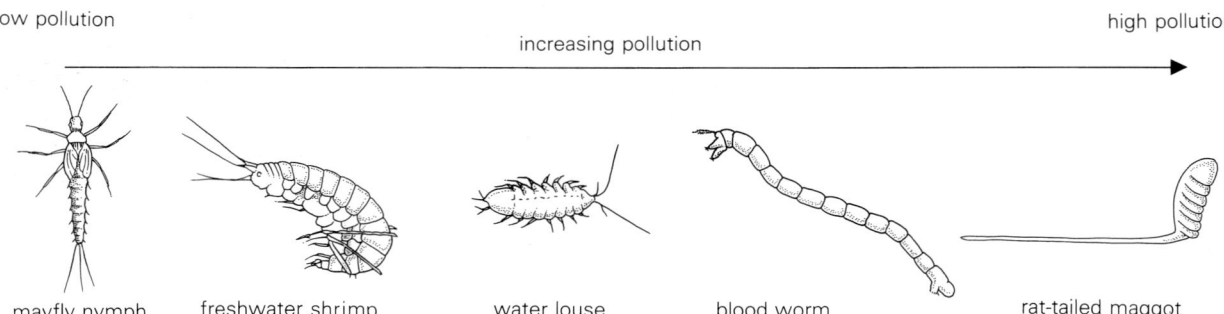

low pollution   high pollution

increasing pollution

mayfly nymph   freshwater shrimp   water louse   blood worm   rat-tailed maggot

Conservation

We know from the study of fossils (page 32) that animals and plants have appeared (**evolved**) and disappeared (become **extinct**) regularly through the history of life on Earth. One hundred million years ago there were thousands of different species of reptiles, including the dinosaurs, none of which exist today. Scientists believe that a change in the environment caused the dinosaurs to become extinct.

More recently the increasing human pressure on wildlife has led to the extinction of more and more species. The last dodo, a large flightless bird, was killed on the island of Mauritius in 1681. The aim of **conservation** is to try to save individual species, and the natural habitats in which they live.

The Hawaian goose or néné (Fig 20.13a) is a remarkable and successful example of a species saved from extinction. In 1950 the total population in Hawaii was believed to be under fifty and

Fig 20.13

(a) The Hawaiian goose or néné

(b) The osprey.

falling rapidly, but three birds were brought to England to the Wildfowl Trust Centre at Slimbridge in Gloucestershire. After a successful breeding programme, large numbers of geese were returned to the wild in Hawaii and the bird is no longer in immediate danger.

The osprey (Fig 20.13b) was a common bird in Scotland well into the last century. It was persecuted by landowners and egg and skin collectors until it was eliminated from Britain. The last pair probably nested in about 1916. However, from 1955 to 1958 a pair of ospreys returned to Scotland and attempted to nest at Loch Garten in Invernesshire. The Royal Society for the Protection of Birds established a local nature reserve and three young were reared in 1959. After a number of years of successful breeding at Loch Garten, ospreys are now nesting at about twenty different places in Scotland.

These and many other successes in conservation are the result of the work of large organisations such as the Nature Conservancy Council, Wildfowl Trust, World Wildlife Fund and Royal Society for the Protection of Birds. If you want further information, ask your teacher to give you their addresses so that you can write to them. You can play your part by careful observation and recording of animal and plant species. Remember to follow the Country Code and avoid damaging the environment. The six main rules of the Code are:

1 Do not drop litter.
2 Guard against fire.
3 Fasten all gates.
4 Keep to the paths.
5 Avoid damaging fences, hedges and walls.
6 Protect all wildlife – take notes, photographs or drawings rather than specimens and never interfere with any bird's nest.

Make sure that the world which your children inherit is a more attractive place to live in than the present one.

Fig 20.14 A notice encouraging people to protect the countryside.

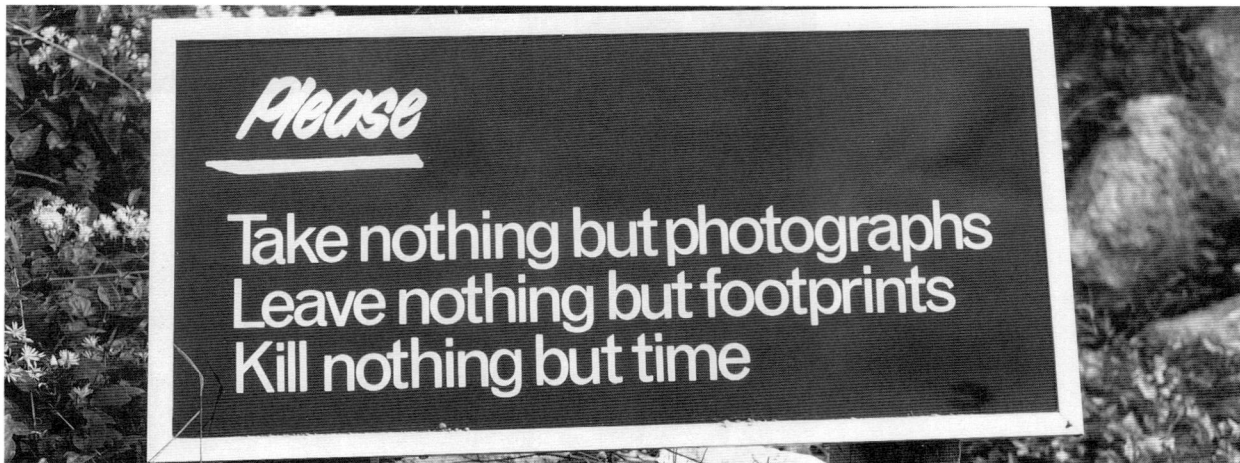

Homework assignments

1 Explain what is meant by:
   a pollution
   b conservation.

2 What evidence would you look for if asked to say whether or not a pond was free from pollution?

3 Human activities can drastically change natural habitats. Give three examples of such activities and their results.

4 Describe three ways in which fresh food can be preserved and explain why each method prevents decay.

5 Choose an animal which you have studied during your biology course and describe the main danger which threatens it in the wild.

6 We are at the end of many food chains. What special dangers does this involve for us?

Living with other people

We live in a world which is rapidly changing. Some of the changes are beneficial, others are harmful. Many of the changes can make it more difficult for people to live together. Here are a few examples:

Looking after the elderly

The number of people in the world over the age of 65 is expected to increase by over 50 per cent in the next 20 years. In the richer countries of the world, the proportion of elderly is rising rapidly as birth rates fall and people live to an older age. This raises important questions about where they will live, how they will be cared for, and who will be paying for their support. Traditionally, old people have been cared for by the family; they have enjoyed the respect of their children and grandchildren. Increasingly now they live in residential homes or 'sheltered' housing schemes and may have little contact with their families or friends. Young people can help by considering the special needs of the elderly and looking for ways to assist them whenever possible.

The family

Most children grow up among people of all ages. They learn how to respond to other people – to look after younger members of the family, to care for elderly grandparents and to make friends with others of their own age. Then, when they are old enough, they can provide a stable and loving environment in which to bring up their own children.

The sick, the handicapped and the dying

People with temporary or permanent disabilities frequently experience loneliness. They may have to be confined to hospitals, hospices or special schools, and their mobility may be restricted. There are many voluntary organisations dealing with sick and handicapped people which would welcome your help. Most hospitals need volunteers to talk to patients, to escort individuals or groups on outings, to help with children's playgroups and to participate in hospital broadcasting schemes.

Background Reading

Acid rain

The Clean Air Acts of 1956 and 1966 did much to clean up the atmosphere in the UK. However their main effects were to reduce fall-out of solids like ash, grit, etc, and the emission of corrosive, poisonous, yet invisible gases was largely unaffected. It is these gases that are now giving rise to *acid rain*.

Excessive environmental acidity is to be found in the soil, in lakes and rivers, as well as in the atmosphere, and acid rain is now blamed by many experts for the death or damage of many forest trees, polluted rivers, lifeless lakes, polluted soils, crop losses and the structural decay of buildings – especially in Scandinavia.

The unnaturally high levels of acid building up in the environment are due largely to emissions of smoke and fumes from factory chimneys, power stations and motor vehicle exhausts, heavily laden with such acid compounds as sulphur dioxide (SO_2) and the oxides of nitrogen (NO_X). When these acids are washed out of the atmosphere by rain, they reach the earth's surface in the form of dilute sulphuric or nitric acid ('acid rain').

Since atmospheric acid can be carried many hundred of miles by the wind, its environmental damage may be inflicted on countries far beyond the industrial areas that are the source of the pollutants. Like many other environmental problems, acid rain is now a matter for increasing global concern.

The UK is believed to be one of the main sources of the acid rain that is increasingly causing environmental damage in Scandinavia and other parts of northern Europe. The main producers of sulphur dioxide in the UK are the coal- and oil-fired power stations operated by electricity generating companies. Other sources have tended to decline, largely because of the reduction in coal consumption by domestic and industrial users. In 1986 the government announced that £600 million was to be spent on fitting special equipment at some of the largest power stations to reduce sulphur dioxide emission.

(From the *Conservation Trust Newsletter*, number 41.)

Questions

1 Here are five statements about acid rain.
   a Acid levels in the environment are increasing.
   b The increase in acid levels in the environment are the result of the emission of smoke and fumes.
   c Most of the increase in acid levels are the result of coal- and oil-fired power stations.
   d The increase in acid levels causes environmental damage.
   e Environmental damage in Scandinavia is caused by power stations in the UK.
   Read the passage carefully. Which of these statements is
   (i) supported by the passage
   (ii) suggested by the passage or
   (iii) not supported by the passage.

2 Choose *one* of the statements and describe in outline how you would carry out an experiment to test whether or not it is true.

3 If all five statements could be shown to be true, what do you think should be done to combat the problems of acid rain? Can you think of any problems which your proposals might cause?

Environment award

A miner who planted a wildflower meadow in an area of intensive farming is the first winner of a £3000 environment award.

Mr Roger Brunt, aged 42, turned a former rubbish tip into a stretch of old-fashioned countryside and paid for it by working 12-hour shifts at the coal face in Bevercotes Pit in Nottinghamshire.

His lone effort to return cowslips, butterflies and partridges to land near his home in the village of Walesby that was without hedges, chemically sprayed and devoid of wildlife, brought him the award. Chairman of the judges, Professor Jim Lovelock, FRS said last night 'It is up to each one of us to make an effort to save the environment and this is a great example of what one individual can do'.

Mr Brunt intends to spend the money fencing off his conservation area to stop cattle straying on it, create a pond for ducks and other wildlife and then put a bench in for the old folks who come down the lane so they can enjoy it too.

(Adapted from *The Times*, 14 March 1989.)

Questions

1 What is 'an area of intensive farming'?

2 Why is it difficult for cowslips, butterflies and partridges to survive in areas of intensive farming?

3 What would *you* do to improve your local environment if you won a £3000 award?

4 Can you suggest any problems which Mr Brunt's proposals to fence the land, create a pond and provide a bench might cause?

Summary

1 Our health and well-being is affected by our environment.

2 Better nutrition, purer water supplies, improved sanitation, a higher rate of immunisation and better health education could all help to reduce disease and suffering in the world.

3 It is estimated that one-third of the world's population is malnourished or short of food. Increased food production and better distribution of food are necessary if we are to keep pace with the increasing number of people in the world.

4 Our countryside is constantly under threat from destruction and pollution. A programme of conservation is essential if wild habitats and the living organisms which flourish in them are to be conserved.

5 Your relationships with other people affect you as well as them. By helping others you will gain in confidence as well as finding new friends.

Explorations 4

U Do biological washing powders work?

Your teacher will give you two washing powders. One is a biological powder which claims to have an enzyme action. The other is a non-biological powder with no enzyme action.

Plan an experiment to compare how good the two washing powders are at removing biological stains from a piece of cloth. Make sure that any tests you carry out are scientifically valid, and that your comparison is fair.

What precautions should a person take when using a biological washing powder?

V Finding out if litter is biodegradable or not

Litter may be biodegradable or non-biodegradable (see page 276). Select a part of your neighbourhood and carry out a survey of the litter there. Classify it into biodegradable and non-biodegradable. In some cases you will be able to see at once which category the litter belongs to. But in other cases you may have to carry out a test. Devise the test yourself. Discuss your plan with your teacher before you start work.

Litter is a major problem in society. Why has it become such a problem, and what should be done about it?

W Fertilisers and the environment

There is some debate about the use of fertilisers in agriculture and horticulture. Fertilisers help plants to grow by giving them nutrients (see page 273). However, the large-scale use of fertilisers can damage the environment and may be a health threat to humans.

With other members of your class, find out as much as you can about the fertiliser problem. Read books, articles and newspaper reports. You may also carry out your own investigations: plan them carefully first, and discuss your plans with your teacher before you start. Try to find answers to these questions.

1 How do fertilisers affect natural habitats such as ponds, lakes and rivers?

2 Can the chemical substances in fertilisers get into the human body, and if so how?

Safety note

Some of the litter may be dirty, even toxic. Be sure to take all necessary safety precautions.

3 If fertiliser chemicals get into our bodies what harm may they do?

4 Are more fertilisers used by farmers and market gardeners than is necessary?

5 What would have to be done to prevent fertilisers damaging the environment?

This exploration will help you to develop your own views about fertilisers. Write a short summary of your views, supporting them with information which you yourself have obtained.

X Hearing and how it is affected by noise

You will need a quiet room and a signal generator which produces sounds of different frequencies (pitch) and intensities (volume).

With the help of your teacher, use the signal generator to find:
a the highest *frequency* (i.e. highest note) that a person can hear
b the lowest *intensity* (i.e. quietest sound) that a person can hear.

Now plan an experiment, using the signal generator, to investigate the effect of environmental noise on **a** and **b**. One of the problems will be to standardise the environmental noise, and this is something you will have to think about carefully. Discuss your plan with your teacher before you start work.

What conclusions may be drawn from your results? When do you think environmental noise should be regarded as a pollutant?

Think of other useful information which might be obtained about hearing and noise pollution, using the signal generator. If circumstances permit, and your teacher approves, plan and carry out your own investigations.

Y The effect of human activity on the environment

We hear a lot about *global* pollution – things like the greenhouse effect, destruction of the ozone layer, and so on. But what about our own local environment? How do human activities affect that?

Choose one recent development in your area which has affected, or is affecting, the environment from a biological point of view. It might be a housing development or a new factory. Find out as much as you can about the effect of the development on the environment both now and in the future.

Investigate the advantages and disadvantages of the proposed change. Write up your investigations in the form of a balance sheet and draw your own conclusions as to whether the development should be allowed to proceed.

Z Thinking about the future

Select and describe a local area which, in your opinion, could be improved. Describe briefly the improvements which you would like to see introduced and the advantages (and any disadvantages) which might result.

Which plants and animals (including humans) would benefit: which would not? What contribution would your improvements make to reducing global pollution? Could you get your improvements carried out?

Appendix   Keys to living organisms

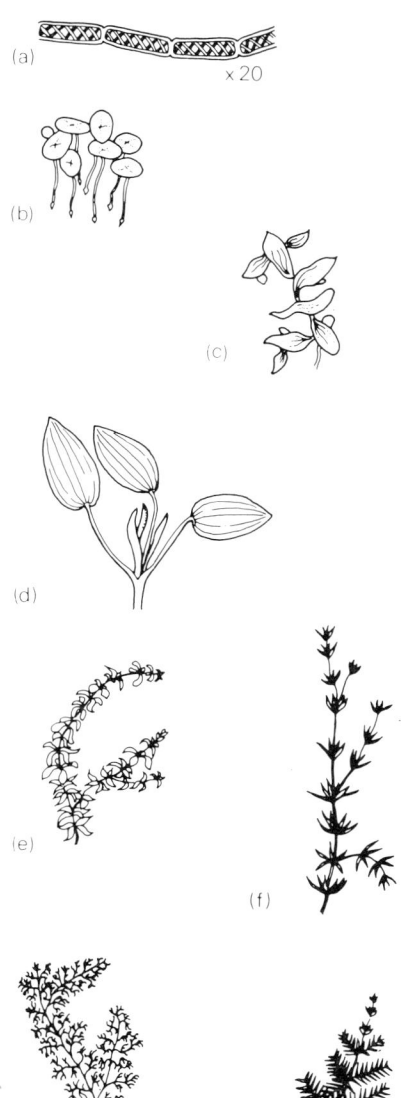

Key to plants and micro-organisms in aquarium tanks

Microscopic organisms		**1**
Others		**2**

1 Long strands or filaments — filamentous algae like *Spirogyra* (a)

Single green cells — unicellular green protoctists e.g. plankton

Moving, colourless organisms — non-green protoctists e.g. *Paramecium*

2 Free floating near or at the surface — **3**

Submerged and often rooted in mud — **4**

3 Flat on both sides, rounded leaves about 3 mm across floating on the surface — common duckweed (b)

Just below the surface, branched plant, pointed leaves — ivy-leaved duckweed (c)

4 Large broad leaves — common pondweed (d)

Small leaves, or fronds (leaf-like parts) — **5**

5 Overlapping leaves or fronds — Canadian pondweed

Leaves or fronds not overlapping — **6**

6 Whorls with unforked branches — stonewort (f)

Other whorls — **7**

7 Whorls with continuously forked branches and dense fronds at the top — hornwort (g)

Whorls with little branches on larger branches — water milfoil (h)

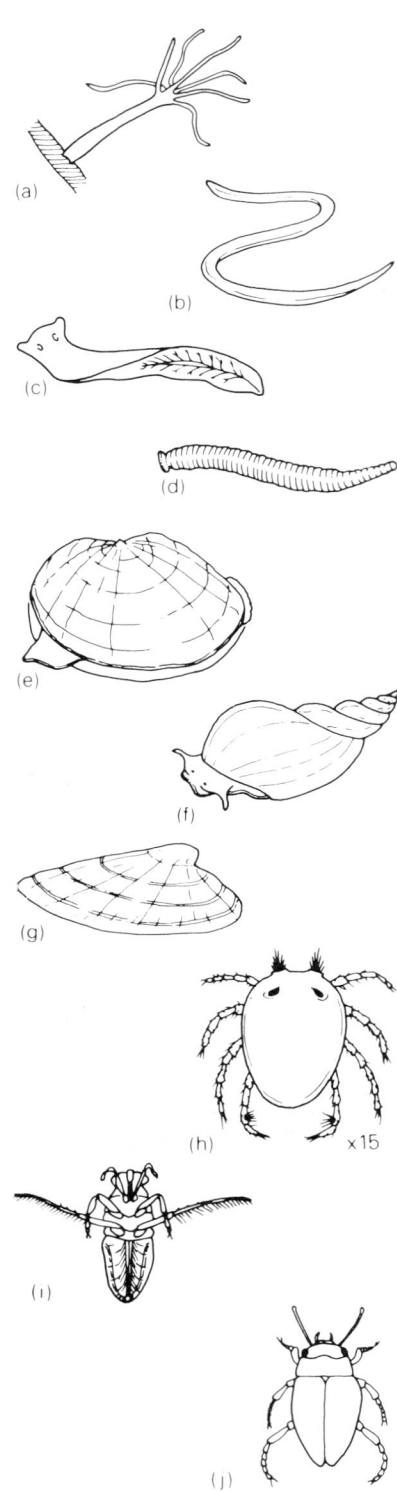

(a)
(b)
(c)
(d)
(e)
(f)
(g)
(h) ×15
(i)
(j)

Key to animals in aquarium tanks

Soft bodied, no hard covering or shell	**1**
Shell or other hard outer covering	**5**

1 Waving tentacles on the end of a tube-shaped body, about 10 mm long — *Hydra* (a)

No tentacles, worm-like body, long and flat or round — **2**

2 Body not divided into sections or segments — **3**

Body segmented — **4**

3 Body round and thread-like, free swimming — roundworm (b)

Body flat, pointed tail, mouth underneath, up to 26 mm long — flatworm (c)

4 Red in colour, no suckers, tail often waving out of the end of a tube sticking up in the mud, up to 85 mm long — *Tubifex*

Suckers at either end — leech (d)

5 Hard external shell of some sort into which animal can withdraw. No limbs — **6**

Animal with jointed limbs — **8**

6 Double shell up to 40 mm long — fresh water mussel (e)

Single shell — **7**

7 Shell a spiral — pond snail (f)

Shell not a spiral — freshwater limpet (g)

8 Four pairs of legs 1 to 3 mm long — water mites (h)

Other number of legs — **9**

9 Three pairs of legs — **10**

More than four pairs of legs — **16**

10 Wings or wing covers present — adult insects **11**

No wings — insect larvae **12**

11 Swims on back, third pair of legs fringed with hairs, sucking mouth parts — water boatman (i)

Hard wing cover, biting mouth parts — water beetle (j)

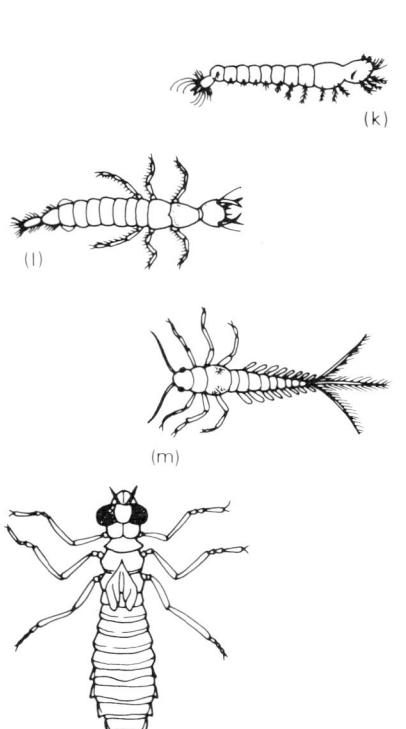

(k)

(l)

(m)

(n)

(o)

12	Mainly just under the surface with breathing tube	mosquito larva (k)
	Deeper in the water or on the bottom, no breathing tube	**13**
13	Larva in protective tube	caddis fly
	Not in tube	**14**
14	Two tail prongs	beetle larva (l)
	Three tail prongs	**15**
15	Long prongs	mayfly nymph (m)
	Short flattened prongs	dragonfly nymph (n)
16	Body more than 5 mm long	**17**
	Body less than 5 mm long	**18**
17	Body like a woodlouse, non-swimming	water louse (o)
	Swims on one side, body flattened from side to side	freshwater shrimp (p)
18	Pear-shaped body, single median eye	Copepods (q)
	Squat shaped	water fleas (r)

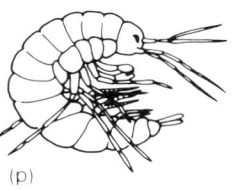

(p)

(q)   x 50

(r)   x 50

Key to animals on trees, in litter and in pitfall traps

Animals with no internal skeleton or bones	**1**
Internal skeleton	birds or mammals
1	Body not divided into sections called segments	**2**
	Body divided into segments	**4**
2	Worm-like body, no shell or tentacles, less than 1 mm long	nematode worm (a)
	Muscular foot, head bearing tentacles	**3**
3	Shell present	snail (b)
	No shell	slug

(a)

(b)

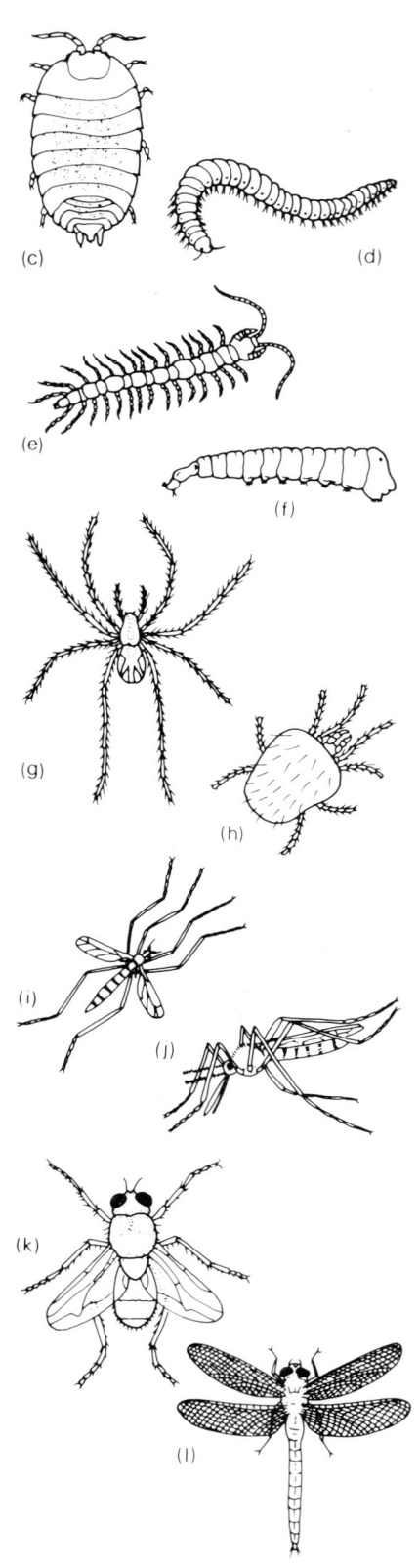

(c)   (d)

(e)

(f)

(g)

(h)

(i)

(j)

(k)

(l)

4 More than four pairs of legs   **5**
Four pairs of legs or less or
none   **7**

5 More than twenty segments   **6**
Less than twenty segments   woodlouse (c)

6 Two pairs of legs per
segment   millipede (d)
One pair of legs per segment   centipede (e)

7 No legs, less than 15
segments   insect larvae (f)
No legs, more than 15
segments   **26**
Legs present   **8**

8 Four pairs of legs   **9**
Three pairs of legs   **10**

9 Body clearly divided into two
parts   spiders (g)
Body not clearly divided   mites (h)

10 Wings present, sometimes
hardened   **11**
No wings   **22**

11 One pair of wings   **12**
Two pairs of wings   **14**

12 Body about 2.5 cm long,
antennae and legs   crane fly (i)
Body about 1 cm long or less   **13**

13 Slender body, long legs,
piercing mouth parts   gnat or mosquito (j)
Squat hairy body, short
antennae   other two-winged fly (k)

14 Both pairs of wings
membranous   **15**
Forewings hardened or
partially hardened   **19**

15 Long thin body, biting mouth
parts, complicated network
of veins on the wings   dragonfly (l) or lacewing
Squat body and veins not
complicated network   **16**

16 No distinct waist, sucking
mouth parts tucked under
head   greenfly
Distinct waist   **17**

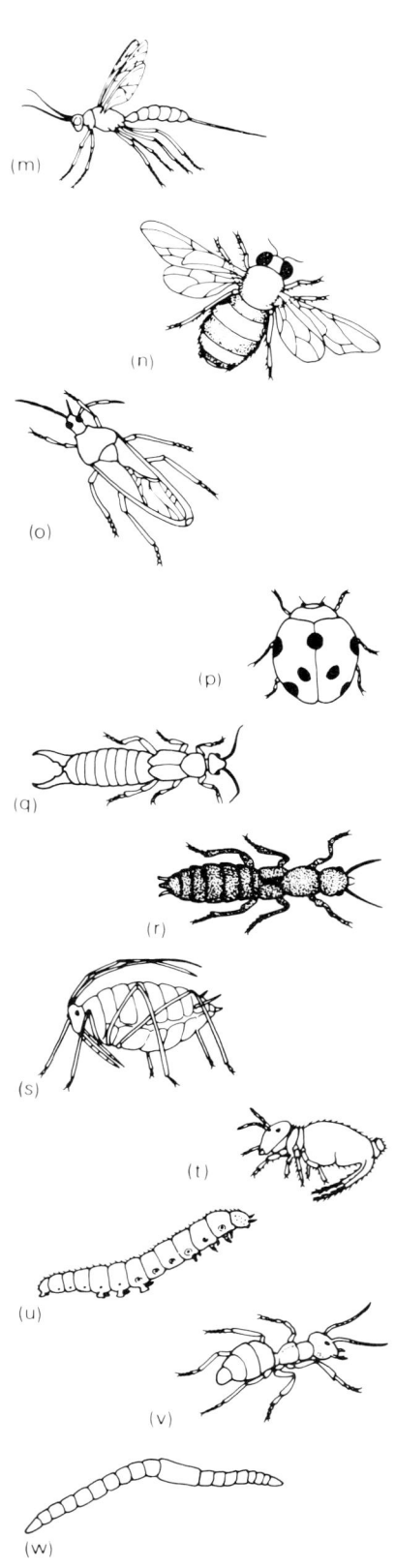

(m)

(n)

(o)

(p)

(q)

(r)

(s)

(t)

(u)

(v)

(w)

17 Large wings covered with scales, long antennae   butterfly or moth
Small wings   **18**

18 Very narrow waist, long abdomen, with egg-laying tube   ichneumon fly (m)
Hairy body, short abdomen, often striped   bee or wasp (n)

19 Forewing cover partially hardened, mouth parts for piercing or sucking   plant bug (o)
Forewing cover all hard, biting mouth parts   **20**

20 Forewing covers most of abdomen   ladybird or other beetle (p)
Narrow body, dark colour very short wing covers   **21**

21 Pincers at end of abdomen   earwig (q)
No pincers, tail often curled back   coach horse beetle (r)

22 Under 6 mm long   **23**
Over 6 mm long   **25**

23 Body oval-shaped, with no definite waist, up to 4 mm long   wingless greenfly (s)
Body not oval-shaped   **24**

24 Abdomen 6 segments or less, jumps by spring under abdomen, 1 mm long   springtail (t)
More than 6 segments in abdomen, no springs   other groups of small insects

25 Long, rather soft-bodied organisms   insect larvae (u)
Definite waist   ant (v)

26 Small (2 cm long)   whiteworms
Large (up to 15 cm long)   earthworm (w)

Index